Lordship
in France,
1500–1789

PETER LANG
New York • Washington, D.C./Baltimore • Bern
Frankfurt am Main • Berlin • Brussels • Vienna • Oxford

JAMES LOWTH GOLDSMITH

Lordship *in* France, 1500–1789

PETER LANG
New York • Washington, D.C./Baltimore • Bern
Frankfurt am Main • Berlin • Brussels • Vienna • Oxford

Library of Congress Cataloging-in-Publication Data

Goldsmith, James Lowth.
Lordship in France, 1500–1789 / James Lowth Goldsmith.
p. cm.
Includes bibliographical references and index.
1. Land tenure—France—History. 2. Feudalism—
France—History. I. Title.
HD644.G652   333.3'22'09440903—dc22   2005010683
ISBN 0-8204-7869-5

Bibliographic information published by **Die Deutsche Bibliothek**.
Die Deutsche Bibliothek lists this publication in the "Deutsche
Nationalbibliografie"; detailed bibliographic data is available
on the Internet at http://dnb.ddb.de/.

Cover design by Lisa Barfield

The paper in this book meets the guidelines for permanence and durability
of the Committee on Production Guidelines for Book Longevity
of the Council of Library Resources.

© 2005 Peter Lang Publishing, Inc., New York
275 Seventh Avenue, 28th Floor, New York, NY 10001
www.peterlangusa.com

Printed in Germany

To Marcella and Rob
my companions in retirement

TABLE OF CONTENTS

PREFACE

The history of French lordship under the old regime is far less contentious than the history of lordship during the Middle Ages. Since it is impossible either to prove or disprove conclusively any interpretation of the scarce and ambiguous medieval documentation available for French lordship prior to 1200, old and new interpretations linger on in historical debates. For the old regime however, the documentation is so abundant and unambiguous, that historians have readily abandoned old interpretations as new studies have refined and even refuted the views advanced by early scholars in the field.

Thanks to the steady accumulation of monographic studies during the last forty years, it is now perfectly clear that the rapid inflation of the sixteenth century did not produce a crisis of lordship. Likewise, the new managerial techniques supposedly brought to the administration of lordship by a conquering bourgeoisie in the sixteenth and seventeenth century were not new at all, but a continuation of old practices long used by medieval nobles and the church. Similarly, the sinister seigneurial or feudal reaction of the last few decades of the old regime, the dramatic upgrading of the land registers or *terriers* of lordship allegedly carried out by a threatened nobility determined to make a political come-back, was neither as new nor as significant as was once thought. Rather, the renewal of the *terriers* was a permanent feature of lordship in every province of France during the entire time span of the old regime. Finally, seigneurial justice, denigrated and vilified by generations of historians, turns out to have been an indispensable and heavily used component of the judicial apparatus of the old regime, staffed by well-trained legal professionals who functioned as public servants of the monarchy.

The picture that emerges from the mass of monographic studies now available on early modern lordship is that of an institution which was stable and rock solid generation after generation. Indeed, lordship was so deeply rooted in the legal and cultural traditions of the old regime that there were only two possible ways it could have been uprooted. A dynamic king could have introduced procedures to phase out lordship as part of a wider program to modernize the political, social, and administrative systems of the old regime. Failing that, a comprehensive revolution would have to do the job.

ACKNOWLEDGMENTS

I would like to express my gratitude once again to Paul B. Bell, Dean of the College of Arts and Sciences, to T. H. Lee Williams, Vice President for Research and Dean of the Graduate College, and to Robert L. Griswold, Chair of the Department of History, all of the University of Oklahoma, for the financial support that made the publication of this book possible.

I would also like to thank Phyllis Korper, Acquisitions Editor of Peter Lang Publishing USA, for enthusiastically agreeing to publish this second and last volume of my study on French lordship. Likewise, I would like to thank Maria Amoroso, Production Coordinator at Peter Lang, for her expeditious handling of the manuscript.

As has been the case throughout my professional career, I am deeply grateful for the support and guidance of my old friend and colleague H. Wayne Morgan, George Lynn Cross Professor Emeritus and former Chair of the Department of History at the University of Oklahoma.

CHAPTER ONE

Lordship Under the Old Regime

Lordship Under the Old Regime

Lordship was an ancient and deeply rooted component of the institutional, social and economic structures of old regime France. The king was the foremost lord of the realm. The Catholic church held *seigneuries* and collected tithes in every province and nearly every village in France. Nobles, the second estate of the kingdom, were above all else lords. The prestige of the nobility and the noble hierarchy itself was linked directly to the hierarchy of lordships. From top to bottom this hierarchy ran from ducal-peerages, to marquisats, counties, viscounties, baronies, castellanies, on down to simple lordships with justice, and fiefs without.

Nobility and lordship were not synonymous. Consequently, the history of the old regime nobility was distinct from the history of lordship.[1] At any given time between 1500 and 1789, roughly half of those claiming nobility did not own lordships.[2] They were nobles, but not *seigneurs*. Between 1500 and 1661, the number of nobles increased by 40% to 70% depending on the region of France.[3] Most of this increase came from the hiving off of collateral branches from old noble lineages in a period characterized by both rapid economic and demographic growth. In a setting of prosperity and rapidly rising agricultural prices, collateral branches of existing noble families could maintain a noble lifestyle.

Some of the increase also came from the proliferation of royal offices which conferred nobility, some too from grants of patents of nobility. Likewise, at least part of the increase in the number of nobles originated from upward social mobility and social osmosis. Wealthy men bought fiefs, married noble heiresses and took on the lifestyle of the nobility. This process of social osmosis, long the principal avenue for the renewal of the nobility, became less common from the late fifteenth century as the monarchy began to scrutinize more carefully claims of nobility. The royal ordinance of Orléans in 1570 officially ended at least in theory the acquisition of noble status by the acquisition of a noble fief. Under Louis XIV, this avenue closed completely.[4]

In the eighteenth century, the number of nobles fell by perhaps 40%.[5] All of the avenues of access to the nobility functioned less well in the eighteenth century than earlier. Social osmosis was blocked by a vigilant royal administration. Few new royal offices that conferred nobility were created, fewer still purchased. The number of patents of nobility dwindled and established families died out in the male line.

Also the sense of what constituted an appropriate noble lifestyle at every level of the hierarchy of lordships skewed upwards with the economic boom of the eighteenth century and the rising standards of living among the social elites. The total number of nobles fell in the eighteenth century and naturally the largest attrition occurred at the base. In addition, there was a polarization of wealth within the ranks of the surviving families that tended to shrink the middle ranks. The accumulation of more and more lordships and fiefs in the hands of individual lords at the top end of the noble hierarchy, a trend that was in evidence throughout the entire early modern era, continued in the eighteenth century. At the same time, the group of *seigneurs de village*, resident nobles of modest means, shrank. And, as always, the largest single group of nobles were the noble proletarians who claimed elite status but who did not own lordships.[6]

Noble families came and went, but lordship was timeless. Lordships changed hands incessantly within in the middle and upper ranks of the nobility. Ambitious and wealthy families gathered up separate *seigneuries,* expanded domain-farms, acquired larger blocks of forest and petitioned the king to elevate these noble estates to higher titled lordships.[7] Less fortunate families sold off bits and pieces of lordships or entire *seigneuries*. Although the arrival of a new lord often meant renewed vigor in seigneurial administration, in most fundamentals the individual lordships of 1789 were very similar to, often nearly identical with, the lordships of 1500.

At the beginning of the sixteenth century, French lordship was already nearly a thousand years old. Lordship was timeless, but not immutable. At every step of the way from its origins in the late Roman Empire until its demise in 1789–1793, the political, social and economic environment shaped lordship. Technically, the lordships in 1500 were often identical to what they had been under Saint-Louis IX in 1250, but socially and politically much had changed.

Under Saint-Louis, lords in France from princes of the realm down to village *seigneurs*, exercised the same sovereign governing authority over their lands as the king did over his domain.[8] In 1250, lordship was still the institutional expression of the sovereign authority of a governing aristocracy which took on concrete form in fiscal institutions, justice, police authority, military power, and general administration. From the fourteenth century, the governing authority of the intermediate and lower reaches of the hierarchy of lords faded in favor of the king and the great princes. Next the great princes disappeared and by the beginning of the sixteenth century, only one lord exercised the full sovereign authority of governance, the king of France.[9]

Although dukes and counts pullulated under the old regime, the dukes and counts of the early modern era were in no way comparable to medieval princes. They and all of the lesser lords of the old regime no longer possessed independent, sovereign powers of governance.[10] Lordship survived as a fiscal institution, as an apparatus of justice, as a vehicle for police activities and even as an organ of local governance, but the authority of the lords and their lordships functioned at the sufferance of the king. In the eyes of the king and his jurists, all lords derived their authority from the king.

Once the kings had arrogated to themselves the fullness of sovereign authority, there was no need to press on further to destroy lordship. Although lordship as a political institution was dead by 1500, as a fiscal, judicial, and administrative apparatus it was still very much alive. The *seigneuries* were patrimonial possessions, but they were incorporated into the apparatus of state and functioned as public institutions.[11] Lordships survived under the old regime because they performed essential tasks for the state and for society.[12] Even at its peak as an administrative apparatus in the eighteenth century, the absolute monarchy was institutionally underdeveloped. The *seigneurial* law courts were indispensable for the administration of justice at the local level. *Seigneurial agents still provided valuable assistance in local governance and in police affairs.*

Lordship had an absolutely unassailable foundation in customary law.[13] The codifications of the customary laws began in earnest in the fifteenth century and continued on until the end of the sixteenth century. Although the jurists who were trained in Roman Law were often hostile to many aspects of the customary laws of lordship, they were charged with the redaction of the existing laws, not with the creation of new law. The judges of the *Parlements* organized the law codes into general customs, regional, and local customs. Individual lordships retained their own customs provided that they were duly documented. In every instance, the legal standard for retention of a custom was the same: irrefutable written proof or immemorial custom confirmed by judicial inquiry.[14]

All of the jurists of the old regime and indeed of the Revolution, from Charles Du Moulin in the sixteenth century to Merlin de Douai in the *Comité des droits féodaux* of the National Constituent Assembly in 1789–1790, drew on the Roman Law notions of contract and double domain in their definitions of lordship. In their minds, every aspect of the *seigneurie* derived either from a grant of land in the form of a contract or from usurped public authority.[15] As long as the old regime lasted, however, all of the law courts from the *Conseil du roi* and *Parlements* down to the local seigneurial tribunal put aside the legal theories and simply enforced the customary laws.

Lordship was also an indispensable prestige property for nobles. The preeminence of a noble derived directly from the honor and prestige of his *terre et seigneurie*. Nobles bore the name of their lordship which was usually distinct from their family name. The rank of a noble depended on the rank of his lordship. Even the princes of the blood, whose exact position in the noble hierarchy depended on genealogy within the royal family, went by the name of their titled lordships or appanages.

Nobles cherished the honorific rights of lordship because they displayed social preeminence to the entire world.[16] Lords alone had the right to hunt. Lords installed their armorial bearings in the parish church, buried their dead in the church or under its floor, received communion, holy water and incense before all others, and were entitled to be named personally in public prayers. The lurid colors of noble dress set the lords apart from lesser mortals who dressed in muted shades of brown or black.

Expenditures for the acquisition of lordships, their embellishment, and their elevation within the noble hierarchy of fiefs were out of all proportion to what these prestige properties returned on investment. In strictly economic terms, an old regime lordship rarely made sense as a really sound investment. For the nobility as a whole at the end of the old regime, *droits seigneuriaux* brought in between 10% and 40% of revenues.[17] In eighteenth century Bordelais for example, strictly seigneurial assets, the various *droits seigneuriaux*, rarely returned more than 2–3% while prime vineyards easily yielded 8–10% per year.[18] The same disparity in returns between seigneurial dues and good agricultural land or forests, *biens fonds*, existed in virtually every province regardless of the level of economic development or the fertility of the soil. Everywhere too, the administrative costs of lordships far exceeded the administrative costs of domain-farms and forest.

The old regime had a society composed of social groups or corporations organized in a hierarchy of prestige and function, not a society of economic classes.[19] The social values were aristocratic and shot through with a sense of proper place and deference for rank. Between 1500 and 1700 few thought to question either the social system or its values. It was not until well into the eighteenth century that reflective observers of the old regime began to question its social structure or its values.

The growing sense of living in the midst of antiquated institutions, outmoded social corporations, and equally outmoded social values was the belated product of the accumulated force of multiplicity of changes, some great and some small, in the French economy, in the political climate produced by absolutism, by the Enlightenment, etc. In such a changing climate, lordship as well as a whole array of other old regime institutions and practices seemed out of date, even oppressive, and ridiculous. But, centuries of legal custom and jurisprudence upheld lordship as a legitimate form of property that simply could not be discarded like used clothing.

From the middle of the eighteenth century, reformers in the royal administration urged both Louis XV and then Louis XVI to modernize the institutions of

France from top to bottom. Lordship was only one item on a very long reform agenda. France needed fundamental change. In retrospect, it is clear that there were only two paths forward. Either the king could seize the initiative or, failing that, a profound political, social and legal revolution would push through the reforms.[20]

The Internal Structures of Lordship

The Fiscal Institutions

The fiscal institutions of lordship in place in France at the end of the Middle Ages survived with relatively minor changes until the Revolution. The principal differences between the manner in which lordship functioned as a fiscal system under the old regime and how it had operated in the Middle Ages were not the result of technical changes. Rather, they were the consequence of the significant transformation of the political system in which lordship operated.

By 1500, lords had lost sovereign fiscal authority.[21] At its peak in the Middle Ages, the fiscal apparatus of lordship functioned as the technical expression of the sovereign power of an aristocracy which exercised governing authority jointly with the kings. Kings, aristocrats, and high church officials levied a multiplicity of taxes on their subjects. They were not bound by established tradition. They created new taxes and occasionally recast entirely the fiscal institutions of their lordships. Under the old regime, however, the sovereign power of the king blocked the taxing authority of the lords. The royal courts upheld the established practices of the customary laws. Lords could collect traditional levies, but they were not free to establish new direct and indirect taxes.

The jurists spun out their legal theories about lordship and its fiscal expression.[22] As a rule, the customary law codes and the seigneurial documents simply recorded practice without legal analysis or commentary. The jurists of the old regime repeated and elaborated on the Roman law ideas which legal theorists had already developed in the late Middle Ages. They distinguished between levies which were tantamount to land rentals and those which smacked of sovereign governing authority. Similarly, they employed the notion of double domain to distinguish between the property rights of lords and the rights of use of the tenants.

For the jurists, the relationship between lord and tenant was not that of ruler and subject, but a contractual, tenurial arrangement of landlord and tenant that flowed from a grant of land. The jurists were uncomfortable with seigneurial dues that could not be construed as payments for a grant of land and normally grouped them under the rubric of justice. Since justice was a royal prerogative in the minds of the jurists, lords exercised justice and collected revenues that flowed from judicial authority only at the sufferance of the monarch. In 1789–1790, the men of the Constituent Assembly employed these same ideas when they separated seigneurial dues into two categories: those that were legitimate property rights and those which flowed from usurped sovereign authority.[23]

Legal theories aside, the decisive force which blocked the expansion of the fiscal grasp of lordship under the old regime was the sovereign authority of the kings. Although royal edicts issued under Charles VII and Louis XI in the fifteenth century asserted the exclusive taxing power of the kings, the great princes of the late Middle Ages ignored these royal claims and operated fiscal systems that closely resembled the royal *tailles* and *aides*. The mortal power struggle over sovereign authority in France ended in the last third of the fifteenth century with the triumph of the kings when a series of fortuitous deaths removed the great princes from the scene.[24]

By the early sixteenth century, virtually the entire top echelon of princes had disappeared. What was left was the king and the middle and lower reaches of the aristocracy. Although the kings created new duchies and counties, the dukes and counts of the early modern period were in no way comparable to the great princely dukes and counts of the Middle Ages who had exercised the fullness of sovereign authority. Rather, they were wealthy aristocrats rewarded with sonorous, but largely empty titles.

Under the old regime, the kings and the royal courts prevented the lords from simply modernizing the fiscal institutions in their lordships in keeping with economic and demographic changes. The kings tolerated no competition in the area of new, comprehensive taxes. The kings and the royal courts were particularly concerned about direct and indirect taxes on the inhabitants of a lordship that were not clearly linked to grants of land in tenure. Lords could collect existing direct levies, both long established annual seigneurial *tailles* and the periodic *tailles aux quatre cas* due on clearly specified occasions such as the marriage of a daughter or the payment of ransom. But, they could not raise the rates, increase the frequency of collection, or expand the area in which they collected *tailles*. Likewise, they could demand labor services, *corvées*, based on clear custom, but they could not demand unlimited labor services.

In some instances, lords certainly did alter *tailles*, but these changes were always the result of contractual arrangements between them and their tenants and did not amount to new or increased taxes as understood by the royal agents. In Bourgogne in 1612, the inhabitants of Vernois and their lord agreed to eliminate all existing dues in favor of a single annual *taille*.[25] Proportional renders also expanded in Bourgogne through negotiations to eliminate debts to lords.[26]

Similarly, lords could collect existing market taxes or tolls on roads and rivers, but the kings and courts prevented them from creating new ones and from altering the old rates. In the eighteenth century, royal ministers and intendants eliminated as many of the old tolls and market fees as they could in order to promote economic growth. In Aquitaine, over 206 out of 361 tolls disappeared between 1730 and 1789. Royal officials summoned lords to produce their titles in court, abolished outright unsubstantiated levies, and pressured those with legitimate property rights to agree to relinquish them for compensation.[27]

Evidence from Alsace and Lorraine suggests that the French kings were right in assuming that if lords had been given a free hand they would have modernized the fiscal institutions of their lordships and in the process would have competed with the taxing authority of the centralized monarchy. Alsace became a province of France only during the reign of Louis XIV. Unlike France, Alsace prior to annexation never had a powerful prince who limited the fiscal authority of the lords. From the late Middle Ages, both aristocratic and ecclesiastical lords largely ignored the minor seigneurial dues attached to land tenure, but repeatedly expanded and upgraded the taxes that fell on all of the inhabitants of their lordships. In other words, Alsatian lords developed modern systems of direct seigneurial taxation. The highest court in the Holy Roman Empire, the *Reichskammergericht*, upheld the right of Alsatian lords to impose new and comprehensive taxes on their subjects.[28] After annexation, French royal edicts instructed the sovereign court in Alsace, the *Conseil souverain*, and the intendants to uphold the practices of Alsatian customary law.[29]

The foundation of the modernized fiscal system of lordship in Alsace consisted of arbitrary *tailles* and arbitrary *corvées*.[30] Lords were free to alter at will the annual sums they demanded in *tailles* and the number of labor services, *corvées, Frondienste*. Normally lords demanded payment in lieu of *corvées*, rather than the full labor services themselves. In the seventeenth and eighteenth century, most Alsatian lordships derived the bulk of their seigneurial incomes from the *tailles* and *corvées*. A similar seigneurial fiscal system existed in many of the lordships in Lorraine and in the region of Montbéliard in Franche-Comté which was under the seigneurial authority of the Duke of Württemberg.[31]

Elsewhere in France, the fiscal systems of lordship in France were not completely immobile. There was always room for some modification, provided that the changes derived from a contractual arrangement between lords and tenants and were not the result of the arbitrary actions of the *seigneurs*. When tenures fell in, lords could transfer the holdings to new tenants with upgraded annual dues. Normally, they added new levies in cash or kind, *rentes foncières seigneuriales*, to the old dues, *cens*.[32] Lords and their agents often placed tenures up for bid. The last and highest bidder got the land at the rate offered. Since these modifications of the terms of land tenure took the form of contractual relationships, the kings and royal courts did not intervene. The difficulty with this sort of upgrading of annual renders and dues was that the changes occurred one tenure at a time. Unless a lordship was completely depopulated and then resettled, piecemeal upgrading could stretch over generations, even centuries.

The skyrocketing inflation of the sixteenth century and the more modest increases in prices in the eighteenth century undoubtedly emptied market fees, tolls, and fixed cash dues on tenures of much of their value. In parts of Haute-Normandie and the Hurepoix district south of Paris, *cens* were specified in cash at the close of the Middle Ages and in these areas inflation robbed the annual payments of much of their value by the end of the sixteenth century.[33] The collapse of the purchasing power of the *livre tournois* in the sixteenth century was not necessarily disastrous, provided that lords took care to upgrade the old cash *cens* one tenure at a time with additional payments in cash or kind. This was very meticulous and slow work, found more commonly in smaller *seigneuries* with resident lords than in title lordships that belonged to absentee *grands seigneurs*. Hence, in Haut-Poitou, the *gentilshommes compagnards* responded creatively to the economic challenges of the sixteenth century while the counts and dukes of Bretagne did not.[34]

However, the impact of the early modern inflation on seigneurial budgets should not be exaggerated. In most areas of France, the annual renders attached to land tenures at the close of the Middle Ages and in the early modern era were specified either as a fixed payment in kind or as a proportional levy, *champart, tasque, agrière, agrier*, and not just as a simple cash *cens*. For every region in France with only cash *cens* there were at least a half-dozen of equal size with renders in kind. Parts of Haute-Normandie had only cash *cens*, but all of Bas-Normandie and even a fair share of Haute-Normandie had renders in kind.[35] Similarly, while the poor soil regions of Hurepoix and Bière south of Paris had cash *cens*, the *plaine de France* north of Paris, the richest grain growing region in the realm, had *champarts* of 1/8 collected with exactitude right down to the Revolution.[36] Indeed, there were special seigneurial registers called *champartreaux* used for the collection of the *champart* near Paris.[37]

Proportional renders called *champarts* were the rule in Picardie and in Champagne where they were called *tierces* or *terrages*.[38] Lords in Champagne won cases in the royal courts in the 1780s which upheld their right to demand payment of *terrages* on potatoes.[39] *Terrages* or fixed payments in kind were widespread in Bourgogne and in Franche-Comté.[40] For newly cleared lands in Poitou in the sixteenth and seventeenth century, lords established either fixed renders in grain or *terrages* of 1/7 or 1/9.[41] The norm in all of central France was fixed renders in kind.[42] Languedoc and Provence had proportional renders, *tasques*, and increasingly fixed payments in kind that were more convenient for both lords and tenants.[43] Agenais in Aquitaine had renders in fixed quantities of grain.[44] In Bordelais, the *agrières* retreated in the early modern centuries, but lords demanded and got very hefty commutation payments for changing these proportional renders into either fixed payments in cash or fixed payments in kind.[45]

Even market taxes collected at rates set in the Middle Ages produced valuable revenues because of the enormous increase in the volume of transactions which occurred with the economic growth of the early modern centuries. In the 1760s and 1770s, lords, villages and towns collected seigneurial fees in cash and in grain in no less than 75 grain markets in Champagne.[46] More spectacularly, the Prince of Condé collected 100,000 *livres* a year at the end of the old regime from tolls and taxes on merchandise passing through Rouen.[47]

There were also many seigneurial levies whose value increased with inflation rather than decreased under the old regime. In addition to the proportional renders and the fixed *cens* in kind paid principally in grain, there was the tithe. The tithe was the single most productive feudal levy in the realm. At the end of the old regime, the total net revenue of the Catholic ecclesiastical lordships was between 150–180,000 million *livres* a year, a sum equal to about 80% of the revenue from all of the royal direct taxes, the *taille, capitation,* and *vingtième.* The tithe alone brought in about two-thirds of the total ecclesiastical net revenus.[48] The value of the tithes rose steadily with the price increases of the sixteenth and the eighteenth century as too did protests and litigation against this hated tax.

Entrance fees to tenures, *droits d'entrée,* and fees for transfers of urban and rural real estate, *lods et ventes,* also kept pace with rising prices. Although not unknown in the Middle Ages, entrance fees for tenures became standard practice only under the old regime. Once again, the kings and the royal courts did not intervene in what amounted to a contractual agreement. From the sixteenth century, lords routinely demand high entrance fees, *droits d'entrée,* for new tenures and for re-issued old tenures. They charged whatever the market would bear.

In 1728, the *seigneur* of Sourbs in Languedoc installed a new tenant in a parcel of land in his lordship for the customary *usages* attached to this tenure, 1 *quarte* of oats and 1 *quarte* of wheat, but demanded a hefty entrance fee of 300 *livres.*[49] Likewise, the baron of Tournefeuille in Languedoc installed a new tenant in a patch of vineyard near Toulouse in 1774 for an annual *cens* of 6 *deniers,* but collected a *droit d'entrée* of 2,100 *livres.*[50] Lords in Bordelais led by the magistrates of the *Parlement* of Bordeaux charged extortionate entrance fees in the eighteenth century.[51] Revenues from *droits d'entrée,* were often among the most important sources of seigneurial revenues in the early modern period. However, continuous fees to tenure were by their nature episodic in incidence, *droits casuels*, and revenues from them fluctuated constantly with the market for urban and rural real estate and with the vigilance of the lords and their agents.

The seigneurial transfer fees for real estate were also very lucrative. The most common rate in France for the *lods et ventes* was 1/12. In the sixteenth and seventeenth century, buyers and sellers of urban and rural real estate often attempted to avoid payment of this burdensome fee. In the notarized documents, they feigned ignorance and claimed that they did not identify the lord who had authority over the property. Similarly, buyers and sellers dissimulated sales through complex legal arrangements that involved exchanges, perpetual annuities and the like. Keeping track of transfers of real property in lordships was a daunting task. Even the regular upgrading of comprehensive land registers, *terriers*, was not enough to keep pace with changes in ownership. To encourage compliance, lords routinely offered rebates on the rates of the *lods et ventes*.[52]

In 1703, Louis XIV established a new indirect tax on all notarized documents, the *centième denier*, and a network of royal bureaus, the *Contrôles des Actes*, to register documents and collect the fees. The *Contrôle des actes* was a godsend for lords.[53] In the eighteenth century, seigneurial agents regularly reviewed the registers of the *Contrôle des actes* to identify properties that had recently change hands. In Bas-Maine, lords even paid royal *contrôleurs* to report any property transfers in their *seigneuries* and to carry out retrospective reviews of the registers.[54] Revenues from the *lods et ventes* increased dramatically. With the rapidly rising real estate prices of the last few decades of the old regime, the *lods et ventes* gushed out money into the coffers of lords.

At the end of the seventeenth and the beginning of the eighteenth century, the average annual revenues from *lods et ventes* for the archbishopric of Paris, the principal lord of the city, stood at 60,000 *livres*. In 1784–1786, the average for the archbishopric was 350,000 *livres* a year and in 1787 revenues from *lods et ventes* rose to 475,000 *livres*. Similarly in the 1780s at Paris, the abbatial *mense* of Saint-Germain-des-Prés collected an average of 180,000 *livres* a year from *lods et ventes*, while the king received 100,000 *livres* from the transfer fees on properties in the royal domain.[55]

Even lesser lordships frequently drew more revenue from *lods et ventes* in the eighteenth century than from the annual *cens* and renders. In the small *seigneurie* of Hautrives in Bas-Maine, special registers for the *droits casuels* and annual comprehensive income records for the years 1755 to 1792 show that *cens* brought in an average of 300 *livres* a year while *lods et ventes* produced 1000 *livres*.[56] In the tiny Breton town of Vitré, *lods et ventes* produced far from negligible revenues for the barony of Vitré in the eighteenth century.[57] Likewise, in one of the many lordships in Languedoc that belonged to the *Comtesse* of Montpeyroux the average annual value of renders and *cens* in the two decades from 1760 to 1780 was only 300 *livres,* while revenues from *lods et ventes* stood at 1,460 *livres*.[58]

Banal machines, most notably the grain mills, were also highly valuable seigneurial assets whose revenues increased as prices of grain rose.[59] Banal grain mills in Normandie produced very solid revenues year after year, and lords frequently built new ones to keep pace with demand.[60] Near Toulouse in the 1750s, many grain mills brought in 1000 *livres* a year and over 2000 *livres* in the 1770s near Montpellier.[61] In Provence, banal mills often yielded a third or more of the income from seigneurial dues in the lordships which belonged to the magistrates of the *Parlement* of Aix.[62] In Bas-Quercy, the Pechpeyrou, lords at Moissac, owned a very important grain mill. In the eighteenth century, Moissac was the capital of grain milling for flour shipped via Bordeaux to the West Indies. As commerce expanded, the Pechpeyrou increased the number of millstones from the original 4 mentioned in documents from the twelfth century to 20 at the end of the old regime. In the late 1780s, the banal mill at Moissac was leased for 50,000 *livres* a year. Pechpeyrou fled France as an *émigré* during the Revolution and in the Year II, a consortium of 20 investors bought the grain mill at a public auction for *biens nationaux* for 700,000 *livres.*[63]

Since the banal mills offered essential services to the agricultural economy at modest rates, they were rarely the subject of controversy for users. In Bas-Maine, the inhabitants of the lordships were collectively responsible for defraying the cost of replacing worn-out millstones. When millstones were replaced, seigneurial officials carried out an individualized assessment for the tenants of the village/*fresche* and apportioned the replacement tax by holdings.[64]

The fiscal and jurisdictional network of lordship encompassed virtually the entire land mass of France. Far from shrinking, the lands subject to *droits seigneuriaux* expanded in the early modern era. Lords established new tenures from unoccupied lands and they attacked in court claims that lands within the territory of their lordships were exempt from seigneurial dues. During the Wars of Religion, nobles at the *Etats généraux* of Blois in 1577 petitioned the king for a declaration that all lands in France were either fiefs or tenures, *censives*. The king turned down the request because the monarchy had long claimed that any lands free of feudal and seigneurial authority, allods, came under the authority of the king. In the Code Michau of 1629, Louis XIII formalized this claim and asserted that any allods that were not under the jurisdiction of individual lords came under the direct seigneurial and feudal authority of the king, *la (seigneurie) directe universelle*. Louis XIV repeated this claim in 1692.[65]

As was so often the case in the legal history of the old regime monarchy, the motivation for the assault on allods was fiscal. Richelieu and Louis XIII were desperate for revenues and were wringing money from every possible source. In this instance, the target was the royal domain. All owners of allods had to have their titles verified in court. Where titles were deficient, lands became either fiefs or tenures. These legal classifications opened the door to a search for additional revenues. Fiefs often owed transfer fees when they changed hands, and all were subject to the very burdensome tax of *franc fief* if they belonged to non-nobles. Likewise, tenures were subject to transfer fees, *lods et ventes*, and entrance fees, *droits d'entrée*.

From 1629, royal and seigneurial agents all over France redoubled their efforts in the war against allods.[66] Allods were not very numerous either at the end of the Middle Ages or during the old regime. Although rights to arrears of *cens* expired with time limits recognized in the various customary law codes, normally the legal status of lands was imprescriptible provided that the lords had good titles. As a rule, allods were either properties freed from seigneurial fiscal burdens by contract or properties that had become *de facto* allods because of decayed seigneurial administration.

In Limousin, Louis de Grantughan, *seigneur* of Croisiac, freed a tenure that belonged to Léonard de La Viale from the annual renders of half a chicken, 6 *deniers* and 7 *cartons* of wheat in a transaction dated 1511. The price for the transformation of this tenure into an allod was 6 *livres tournois*.[67] In 1693, Louis XIV, desperate to find money to pay for the War of the League of Augsburg, transformed all of the properties into allods in the small town of Buzet-sur-Tarn in Haut-Languedoc in exchange for ready cash. The contract specified that henceforth the properties were allods free from "*cens, lods, ventes et autres droits seigneuriaux,*" but that they remained under the jurisdiction of the king who was the direct lord.[68] In this same year, 1693, the municipal government of Agen bribed the king to confirm the allodial status of lands in the town for a payment of 7000 *livres*. Since the old regime monarchy always acted in bad faith in fiscal matters, the 1693 agreement did not end the affair. Royal agents soon resumed the harassment of the owners of allods, and in 1746 the *Conseil du roi* issued a judgment that repudiated the very principle of allodial status of lands for Agen, Condom, Marmande, Mézin and other towns in the Agenais.[69]

Buyers and sellers of urban and rural real estate often alleged in notarized documents that they could not identify the lord with jurisdiction over the property in question. More often than not, these declarations were simply ruses to avoid the payment of the burdensome seigneurial transfer fees, *lods et ventes*. Feigned ignorance seems to have been the explanation for the extraordinarily high incidence of putative allods in the relatively fertile valley of the Allier in Basse-Auvergne, a region called the Limagne. An astounding 30% of properties mentioned in the eighteenth century notarial records claimed to be allods, whereas in Haute-Auvergne allods were statistically insignificant.[70] At Bordeaux, only 300 notarized documents out of several thousand in the eighteenth century indicated that properties were allodial.[71]

Anyone with a good title could maintain the allodial status of his property in court. Nevertheless, many owners of allods eventually caved in under the relentless pressure of litigation. Neither the royal agents nor the administrators of lordships would accept defeat in court. Generation after generation, they called owners back to court to produce their titles. Many owners of allods found that the fiscal burdens of lordship were much less than the costs of the litigation to defend the allodial status of their properties.[72]

How important were seigneurial revenues in total noble budgets? For France as a whole, the normal range was from a low of 10% to a high of 33%–40% [73] These calculations leave aside income from tithes and any emoluments of office and consider only the relative importance of seigneurial revenues and domain lands in the total income of lordships. There were significant regional variations.

In Gascogne, lords collected substantially less than 10% of their revenues from *droits seigneuriaux*.[74] In Haute-Normandie, the Ile-de-France and Bordelais, the figure was around 10%,[75] but 19% for 48 lordships in Haut-Languedoc near Toulouse in the 1750s,[76] 30% in Bas-Languedoc near Montpellier,[77] 40% also in the lordships of the magistrates of the *Parlement* of Aix-en-Provence.[78] In Haute-Auvergne and in Limousin, the average was about 33%, and in Rouergue an astounding 70%.[79] The explanations for these regional variations are easy enough to identify historically, but they do not lend themselves to any simple formula. Rather, they reflected the totality of the historical context, political, legal, geographic, economic and social, in which lordship functioned in the various provinces and in sub-regions of these provinces in France.

How heavy were the seigneurial dues and the tithes? The seigneurial renders took 5–13% of the gross agricultural product and the most common rates for the tithe in France were 1/12 or 1/13 or around 8%. Added together, the seigneurial land taxes, *redevances foncières seigneuriales*, and the tithe, *dîme*, took about 15–30% of the taxable net agricultural revenues of farm land in France calculated from figures listed in the royal tax rolls of the *vingtièmes* in the second half of the eighteenth century.[80] However, there certainly were areas of France where lower rates for both seigneurial dues and tithes meant that the total burden of the feudal dues was substantially less. In parts of Haute-Normandie, the seigneurial *cens* and renders amounted to only 1–3% of the gross agricultural product.[81] By contrast, in Haute-Auvergne, the *droits seigneuriaux* absorbed 11% of the taxable net product of farm lands and the tithe took another 13% for a total of 24%.[82]

The figures for the weight of the seigneurial dues and the tithe by themselves tell only part of the story. In particular, they cannot be seen as clear proof that the economic burdens of lordship were crushing the French peasantry on the eve of the Revolution. In the late eighteenth century at least 40% of the population and in some places well over 50% were landless and hence paid no seigneurial land renders or *cens*. That the peasantry and the landless classes in France at the time of the Revolution hated the lords and their seigneurial dues is beyond question. They rose in violence against the tithe, the *droits seigneuriaux*, burned castles, and destroyed the symbols of seigneurial domination. However, this hatred flowed from a multiplicity of economic, social, and psychological causes and was not simply the result of the actual economic weight of the various dues.

Moreover, something like 65% of the farm land in France belonged to nobles, bourgeois and ecclesiastical institutions.[83] Probably half of this farm land was legally subject to *droits seigneuriaux*. Much of it was formerly peasant tenurial holdings that had been absorbed into expanding upperclass and ecclesiastical farms since the close of the Middle Ages. Lords who acquired *censive* land from within their own lordships for their domain-farms naturally did not collect *droits seigneuriaux* from themselves. Occasionally lords made arrangements with each other to free *censive* lands in their domain-farms from *droits* owed to other lords. But for the most part, the legal status of lands did not change just became it passed from the hands of impoverished peasants to upperclass land engrossers.

What all of this meant was that in the eighteenth century nobles, bourgeois and ecclesiastical institutions paid the bulk of the *droits seigneuriaux* and the tithes, not peasant proprietors. For upperclass owners, the feudal dues were just part of the operational costs of farming the land. In practice, it was the men who leased the upperclass domain-farms who normally paid the *droits seigneuriaux* and the tithe for the accounts of their landlords. For them too, the feudal dues were just a minor part of the operational costs of modern farming and not infrequently a source of additional profits. Often, the tenants and sharecroppers of the upperclass farms held lucrative leases for the collection of both the *droits seigneuriaux* and the tithes.[84]

The fiscal systems of lordship certainly did not wither away in the early modern era. Lordship as a fiscal system was as robust in 1789 as it had ever been. Moreover, this vitality was not the product of a seigneurial or feudal "reaction" in the last few decades of the old regime that suddenly resurrected a decrepit institution. Rather, strict management was a permanent feature of an ancient institution which had weathered every storm for well over a thousand years. Between the end of the Middle Ages and the Revolution, lords all over France routinely upgraded their *terriers*.[85] Also, between each refurbishing of the entire land register, lords demanded, received and carefully stored individual declarations of tenure occasioned by changes in tenants through inheritance, sale, or exchange of property.

The kings themselves provided highly visible example and leadership in the strict management of lordship. The king was the single most important lord of the realm. While sixteenth century kings may not have adhered to the very highest standards in managing the royal domain, the kings of the seventeenth and eighteenth century squeezed money from every available source. In the last two centuries of the old regime, there were repeated waves of renewed vigor in the administration of the royal domain that coincided with the great wars and with budgetary shortages. Richelieu and Colbert in the seventeenth century and Turgot, Necker and Loménie de Brienne in the eighteenth century, each in his own time, pressured royal officials to increase revenues from the royal domain.[86] In every province of the realm, the magistrates of the *Chambres des comptes*, the tax collectors of the local *Bureaux des finances,* the intendants and their subdelegates led the way in periodically upgrading the seigneurial records of the royal domain.

Not only was strict management the rule century after century, but also the legal procedures for the upgrading of the *terriers* offer a stunning example of multi-secular institutional continuity in French lordship. Under judicial authority, seigneurial officials called all property owners in the lordship to make a formal declaration of their holdings and of the seigneurial dues assessed on these properties. The legal procedures used for the renewal of the *terriers* during the reign of Louis XVI, were essentially the same as those used under Saint-Louis IX in the middle of the thirteenth century, under Charlemagne around 800 and indeed under the late Roman fiscal agents of the fourth and fifth centuries who designed these procedures for the periodic update of their tax rolls, the ancient polyptychs.[87]

Equally stunning examples of multi-secular institutional stability can also be found in the specific customs which governed the types of annual renders assessed on farm land in the different provinces. When lords in Champagne founded new villages in the sixteenth and seventeenth century, they used the charter of Beaumont-en-Argonne, first issued by the Archbishop of Reims in 1182, which employed a proportional render, or the even older royal charter of Lorris, first issued by Louis VII in early twelfth century, which used a fixed levy per unit of farm land.[88] Similarly, early modern lords in Lorraine used variants of either the charter of Beaumont or the charter of Lorris for villages newly freed from serfdom.[89]

Throughout central France where dispersed settlement was the rule, not only did the units of tenure in place at the close of the Middle Ages survive, but new tenures created in the sixteenth and seventeenth century replicated the old. In Bourbonnais and Nivernais, the tenures were called *bordelages*, while in Auvergne they were known as *affars* or *tènements*.[90] In Languedoc, the widespread incidence of the proportional *tasque* simply perpetuated local fiscal traditions that dated from the eleventh and twelfth centuries. New villages founded in the eighteenth century in Provence had charters that were virtually identical to the *actes d'habitation* used in the late fifteenth century to repopulate the province.[91] In Bas-Maine, large tenures called *fresches*, established at the end of the Middle Ages, survived as fiscal units with collective responsibility for renders and seigneurial taxes even though they had become hamlets and even villages.[92] Finally, the peculiar Norman fiscal units of tenure, the *vavassories*, *sergenteries*, *villenages*, and *bordages*, established by the Norman dukes in the late eleventh century were still in use at the end of the old regime.[93]

Domains

French nobles derived the majority, often the overwhelming majority, of their revenues from their domain lands rather than from seigneurial dues. If we leave aside the tithes, which admittedly were the single most important asset of the church, then the ecclesiastical lords also derived far more income from domain lands than from *droits seigneuriaux*.[94] These domain lands consisted of farmland, forests and uncultivated waste lands. The forests belonged to the king, the high aristocracy and to some of the most prestigious ecclesiastical lordships. For most lords, however, domain lands meant farmland.

At the end of the old regime, ecclesiastical institutions and nobles together owned about 40% of the farmland in France.[95] Roughly two-thirds of this 40% belonged to nobles, and the remaining third to the clergy. The properties of the nobles and clergy, who together formed barely 2% of the population, often accounted for half or more of the farmland in the most desirable agricultural regions of France, while in the remote and infertile areas their share faded away to 15% or less. In the Ile-de-France, the holdings of the privileged classes frequently exceeded 60%, even 70% or more in parts of Haute-Normandie,[96] 50% in parts of Champagne,[97] reached 40% along the northern border of the realm, fell to 25% in the less desirable parts of west of the kingdom, and dipped further to barely 20% in the remote and relatively unattractive central provinces. In the Midi, the privileged classes owned even less land, roughly 15% in the unattractive regions, but held 50% in the areas most affected by commercial development such as the region of Lauragais near Toulouse or in the best wine producing territory of Bordelais.[98] Even where peasant property still predominated, as in Maine, the estates of individual nobles often accounted for thousands of ha.[99]

The broad regional patterns of landownership for the privileged classes, strong in the north and much weaker almost everywhere else, were already well-established at the end of the Middle Ages. In the middle of sixteenth century in the Hurepoix south of Paris, an area which was far from being the most attractive in the Ile-de-France, ecclesiastical institutions, nobles and bourgeois already owned 60% of the farmland and 51% of the lands held on seigneurial tenure.[100]

Between 1500 and 1789, the privileged classes increased their share of farmland both through clearings and through the accumulation of lands previously held by peasants. Once again, the nobles outpaced the clergy in the expansion of their domains, but may well have fallen behind bourgeois in the competition for peasant properties. In the commercially desirable farming districts in the Ile-de-France, in parts of Haute-Normandie, in the best viticultural districts near Bordeaux, near Toulouse and along the Canal du Midi peasant ownership of farmland virtually disappeared.[101]

For the entire early modern period, 1500 to 1789, peasants lost 30% of the lands which they held at the close of the Middle Ages in economically desirable areas, and around 10% elsewhere.[102] The great majority of the land transfers from peasants to clergy, nobles and bourgeois occurred between roughly 1560 and 1660, or at the outer limits between 1500 to 1700. Quite remarkably, the same chronology of expropriation of peasant land holdings occurred in every region of France regardless of whether the area was economic advanced and dynamic, or relatively backward. Peasants lost land in the sixteenth and seventeenth centuries in the expansive economy of the Ile-de-France, in Bordelais, and in the far less dynamic Bourgogne, Auvergne, Bretagne, or Languedoc.[103] In the eighteenth century, land transfers from peasants to the upperclasses continued but at a considerably slower pace.

Two sets of forces, one positive and the other negative, accounted for the expansion of upperclass farms and the partial expropriation of the peasantry. Everywhere, the positive force behind the expansion of the upperclass farms was the growth in demand for agricultural products, both for human consumption and for industrial purposes. The growth in demand in the early modern centuries flowed from population increase, urbanization and the rapid growth of the non-farming or at best part-time farming classes, and not least from the rising wealth and standards of living at the top end of the social spectrum. Population increase and economic growth exploded in the sixteenth century, slowed in the seven-teenth, then took off once again in the eighteenth century. The relative scale of the expansion of upperclass farms differed from region to region according to the intensity of economic and demographic growth, but the chronology, and also the mechanisms of land accumulation were everywhere the same.

The negative force which undermined peasant land ownership was impoverishment. Peasants lost land through the mechanisms of indebtedness to upperclass creditors and occasionally to more financially secure individuals within the peasantry itself. The customary laws in France gave peasants very strong rights to the lands which they held on perpetual seigneurial tenure. They could not simply be expelled by the arbitrary actions of their lords. What the customary laws did not and could not give peasants was the economic security and the financial resources to hold on to their properties.[104] However one might judge the results of the partial expropriation of the French peasantry under the old regime, the process of land transfers occurred through perfectly legal transactions.

Whether acquired through inheritance or expanded through expropriation and clearing, the domain lands of the clergy and nobility consisted of fields pulled together into working farms, *corps de ferme*, which had arable land, hayfields, pastures and occasionally fish ponds. These domain-farms produced grain and livestock in proportions that varied with the economic geography of the realm. Lords also owned vineyards that were usually fairly compact. Finally they owned parcels of lands scattered about.

Lords worked their lands in one of three ways.[105] Some lords managed their lands directly with a salaried staff that consisted of a foremen and a core of key agricultural workers, supplemented with part-time, seasonal labor. Other lords leased their farms to financially secure tenant farmers, *fermiers*, who assumed the full economic burden of working the domain-farms and who paid a fixed annual rent in cash and/or commodities. Finally, many lords handed their properties over to sharecroppers, *métayers*, for a stated fraction of the agricultural commodities produced on the farm.

Direct management of lands, *faire valoir direct*, with a salaried staff of some sort was certainly very widespread in the lower reaches of the nobility in every province.[106] Direct management was also the preferred method of farming, at least in the eighteenth century, for resident lords of middling stature such as the magistrates of the *Parlements* of Toulouse.[107] These lords took great pleasure in visiting their lands and in supervising their operation. After the construction of the Canal du Midi in Languedoc in the late seventeenth century, direct management with a *maître-valet* replaced sharecropping as the grain trade became more and more profitable.[108] Lords in the *Parlement* of Bordeaux, men who as a whole were far richer than their colleagues at Toulouse or Dijon, also used hired stewards to manage their vineyards.[109]

In the most economically advanced regions of France north of the Loire, lords typically relied on tenant farmers to work their domain-farms.[110] The economic stature of the tenant farmers in the *plaine de France* north of Paris rose steadily between 1500 and 1789.[111] At the end of the Middle Ages, the tenant farmers still relied in part on the financial support of the lords to work domain-farms that were relatively small, 30 ha for a single lease-holder. By the late sixteenth and early seventeenth century, tenant-farmers were leasing farms of 66–76 ha, and from 1670–1730 farms of 135 ha, often pieced together by taking on leases from several different owners..

In eastern and central France, lords used sharecroppers or tenant farmers who often paid their rent in fixed quantities of agricultural commodities.[112] In much of western France and most of the Midi, sharecropping was the preferred method of management for seigneurial domain-farms.[113] What distinguished sharecropping contracts from fixed cash or fixed commodity leases was the on-going financial involvement of the lords in the farming of their lands. Sharecroppers were far less financially secure than tenant-farmers. The division of the crops between lords and sharecroppers varied depending on the financial contributions of the two parties. Reliance on sharecroppers was only one aspect of the fundamental economic contrast between the large-scale, economically advanced farming of northern France, *grande culture*, and small-scale, economically less developed farming of the Midi, *petite culture*.

Forests and Common Lands

The economic and demographic growth of France under the old regime led inexorably to conflicts over forests, common lands, and open pasture. Indeed, with the possible exception of the tithe, nothing caused more tension between lords and their subjects during the old regime than disagreements over the status and the use of the forests and common lands.[114]

These conflicts were certainly not new. Similar disputes driven by similar demographic and economic forces had appeared in France from the thirteenth century. In response, lords all over France, led by the kings and the great princes, held formal judicial inquiries about traditional rights of use in forests and commons and imposed regulations for their use in the future.[115] The judicial inquiries and the regulations that flowed from them were called *réformations*. The famous *réformation* of the royal forests in Normandie carried out by Hector of Chartres in the late fourteenth century was a model of its kind.[116] The later *réformations* of the early modern centuries were simply more precise versions of the inquiries and regulations of the late Middle Ages.

The traditional rights of both lords and the inhabitants of their lordships arose and hardened into established practice at a time when population was light and unappropriated lands abounded. In the Middle Ages, lords carved new villages, individual tenures, and fiefs from the unoccupied lands. Normally, all the landholders in the lordship also enjoyed rights of use in the remainder of the unoccupied lands for pasture, firewood, lumber, and often for temporary cultivation. Likewise, lords took parts of the unoccupied lands for their domain-farms, used other parts as forests, and gave vast stretches to monasteries and other churches. It was perfectly clear that lords had the right to dispose of these unoccupied lands as they saw fit; equally clear also, that the inhabitants of individual tenures, villages, towns, fiefs, monasteries, etc. had rights of use.[117] As long as there was a superabundance of unappropriated land, there was no need for further regulation of rights.

From the early sixteenth century, rapid population increase and economic growth led to ever greater demands on the forests for firewood, lumber, charcoal, and pasture.[118] Prior to the sixteenth century, lords typically derived most of their forest revenues from fees collected for grazing animals, especially for swine sent by the thousands to feast on acorns and nuts.[119] While there is no doubt that the traditional household uses of the forest increased with population growth, the real change in the sixteenth century was the massive expansion of commercial and industrial uses of wood. Demand for firewood and for lumber for construction in the major towns exploded as did demand for charcoal for industrial purposes. Similarly, the market for lumber suitable for the royal navy increased.[120] For many lords, the forests suddenly became one of their most important, often the single most important, landed asset which they possessed. To cash in on the profits promised by the burgeoning commercial and industrial demand for wood, it was essential to regulate the traditional household uses of the forests and to introduce more systematic forest administration. Regular rotations for cutting and regrowth as well as special sections of the forest reserved for old growth with far longer cutting cycles could only be established and maintained by strictly regulating household uses of the forest.

In the sixteenth century, the kings once again spearheaded the movement to regulate rights of use in the forests, just as they had in the Middle Ages. The task of regulation fell to the officials of a special branch of the royal bureaucracy ootablished in the fourteenth century, the masters of waters and forests, *maîtres des eaux et forêts*, and their tribunal called the Marble Table, *le table du marbre*. Eventually there were eight major *maîtrises* and eight *tables de marbre* at Paris, Rouen. Toulouse, Bordeaux, Aix, Dijon, Rennes and Grenoble. Decisions of the Marble Tables could be appealed to the regional *parlements* and even to the *Conseil du roi*.[121]

In the sixteenth century, the masters of the waters and forests carried out innumerable judicial inquiries and issued many regulations, *réformations,* in the royal and the ecclesiastical forests.[122] Often individual lords called in the masters to add the weight of royal authority to the regulation of their forests. For example, the Duke of Nevers called in the royal masters and the Table of Marble to preside over a *réformation* of the forests in the duchy in 1580–82.[123] Similarly, Coligny in the 1560s as well as the Dukes of Rohan in the 1580s and again in the early seventeenth century called in royal officials to preside over the regulation of their forests in Bretagne.[124] Similar regulations of forests occurred in Alsace and in Lorraine.[125] Since each forest had its own traditions and its own users with established rights, regulation proceeded one forest at a time.[126] The regulation of use was a perfectly legitimate exercise of police authority within a lordship, regardless of whether the lord was the king of France, a duke, or a simple *seigneur*.

The judges in the seigneurial and royal courts, all of whom were trained in Roman Law, were certainly well aware of the imprecision and deficiencies of the customary laws on forests and common lands. Although the judges and legal commentators on the customary laws undoubtedly employed the Roman Law concepts of property, eminent domain, usufruct, and servitude when thinking about the legal issues that involved the forests and commons, they shrank from imposing what were in essence totally alien legal definitions on the customary laws. The foundation of the customary laws was established practice, *saisine*, recorded and defended as such without any abstract analysis as to the nature of this practice.[127] The judges were charged with upholding the customary laws, not with reforming them. As a rule, the *parlements* were very conservative in their judgments and strove to defend both the rights of lords and the rights of users throughout the entire early modern era.[128]

Sixteenth and seventeenth century lords often opted for a regulation of use in the forests that took the form of sectioning off a portion of the forest, typically one third, for the use of the inhabitants.[129] The rest of the forest, often two thirds, was reserved for the lord. The terminology for this sectioning off of the forests was both abundant and imprecise. The terms *cantonnement, triage, tiercement,* even *régulation* and *réformation* were used interchangeably. The sectioning off of the forest occurred in the spirit of the customary laws of *saisine* without any reference to property rights. Normally, the terms *cantonnement, triage* and *tiercement* were not used in the royal forests at the insistence of the royal accountancy courts, *Chambres des comptes*. As the guardians of the royal domain, the accountancy courts were hostile to any term that might imply a legal diminution or alienation of crown properties. However, the masters achieved the desired result with minute regulations of use.[130]

In general, the *réformations, triages,* and *cantonnements* carried out in the royal, ecclesiastical and seigneurial forests between 1500 and 1660 strengthened the position of the lords.[131] The kings and the masters of the waters and forests were particularly concerned with the needs of the royal navy for old growth lumber in all of the forests of the realm, not just those on the royal domain. The masters were zealous in their work and often the *parlements* intervened to protect the traditional rights of users. Villages and towns on balance lost control of forests through regulation and through sales to lords and bourgeois creditors that arose from communal indebtedness. Recurrent famines, massive increases in royal taxes, the costs of billeting soldiers and unwise borrowing undermined communal finances between 1560 and 1660. To raise money, villages and towns sold their assets, often part or all of their forests.

By the second half of the seventeenth century and often much earlier, the king, the ecclesiastical institutions and the noble lords controlled most of the forests of commercial value.[132] Records from the 1540s show that in the western part of the Ile-de-France, royal and seigneurial forests accounted for 80% of the total wooded area, ecclesistical forests were rare, and communal forests were virtually non-existent. In northeastern France, and area that included Champagne, Bourgogne, and Lorraine, royal forests were rare, while ecclesiastical and secondarily seigneurial forests accounted for 75% of the total. In Normandie, royal and ecclesiastical forests were more extensive than seigneurial woodland, while seigneurial holdings represented almost all of the forests and unappropriated *landes* in Maine, Anjou, Vendômois, and Bretagne.[133]

Although villagers and inhabitants of towns enjoyed rights of use in the forests everywhere in France, communal forests were important only in the inaccessible reaches of the Pyrénées, the Massif Central, the Alps, as well as in the more remote regions of the provinces in northeastern France, Bourgogne, Franch-Comté, eastern Champagne, Alsace and Lorraine.[134] Normally, the communities used their forests mainly for the household needs of their inhabitants and derived modest revenues from them that helped defray the costs of maintaining communal properties.

The small village of Saint-Denis, a royal *bastide* founded in Bas-Languedoc in 1293, had a small communal forest. The consuls administered this forest largely unsupervised until the late 1660s. Thereafter, royal agents from the *maîtrise des eaux et forêts* at Castelnaudary supervised the consuls. In the eighteenth century, part of the forest was set aside for old growth, while the rest was divided into 20 sections for regular cutting and use. Revenue from this forest financed the amortization of communal debts and paid for the construction and repair of the church, the bridges, walls, and mills.[135] In a few instances, revenues from communal forests were very significant. The town of Hagenau in Alsace owned a huge forest of 15,000 ha jointly with the king who took over the rights of the Hapburgs. At the end of the old regime, the communal forest of Haguenau brought in an average of 200,000 *livres* a year from lumbering, half of which went to the municipal government.[136]

Louis XIV and Colbert brought tighter administration of the forests with the ordinances of 1667 and 1669. Although the monarchy was as solicitous as ever about the need to protect the old growth stands of trees for use by the royal navy, the forest legislation was also part of a larger corpus of laws and administrative actions designed to strengthen the financial position of the communities. By the 1660s village and town finances were in perilous condition, in large part because of the massive increase in royal taxes in the first half of the seventeenth century. Louis XIV and Colbert viewed the forests and common lands of all sorts as financial assets, potential sources of revenue that the communities could use to meet their fiscal obligations to the state. Henceforth, the intendants and their sub-delegates exercised a tight control over communal finances.[137]

As was so often the case with seemingly sweeping royal ordinances, application fell far short of intent. The 1667 ordinance called into question the legality of sales of communal lands since the early seventeenth century, but this legislation had little real impact since communities would have to indemnify purchasers in order to regain control of alienated forests and commons. Communities rarely had the means to do this. Also the monarchy undermined its own laws by confirming questionable transfers of forests and commons since 1555 by allowing the new owners to pay a special fee, essentially a bribe, to the crown.[138]

In general, it was well into the eighteenth century before the ordinances of the 1660s began to be applied with any rigor. Tight administration appeared in royal, ecclesiastical and noble forests precisely in those areas of northern France where the economic benefits of rigorous control promised really significant returns. Elsewhere, in much of central France, parts of the west, and in much of the Midi, slackness rather than rigor was the rule.[139] In some provinces, most notably Bretagne, royal officials made hardly any headway at all. In Bretagne, the officials of the *maîtrise* were outmaneuvered by the actions of men from noble judges in the *Parlement* down to simple peasants who were determined to usurp what was left of the royal forests.[140]

The 1669 ordinance defined precisely the meaning of *triage* and established clear guidelines for its application. According to the 1669 ordinance, a lord could demand a third, *triage*, of forests and commons only if users paid no fees to the lord for their rights of use. In this case, the lord was presumed to have granted rights of property to the community. Consequently the lord and the community were co-proprietors and co-users. Since no one could be forced to remain in a joint property arrangement, the lord could demand division. When division occurred, the lord received a third. The 1669 ordinance clearly broke new ground in that it attributed property rights clearly to communities over common lands in cases where no fees or renders were paid for their use.[141]

Although designed to throw roadblocks in the way of rapacious lords who were anxious to take control of valuable forests and commons, in practice this royal legislation did no more than limit the amount of land which lords took from judicially supervised divisions. In the eighteenth century, lords continued to expand their control over forests and common lands, normally through *cantonnement* rather than *triage*.[142] The 1669 ordinance defined very precisely the circumstances in which lords could demand *triage*. After 1669, lords rarely demanded *triage*, rather they opted for the sectioning off of use, *cantonnement*. Lords could demand *cantonnement* in all circumstances, whether there were fees paid for use by inhabitants or not. The lords stood on very firm legal ground since there was a mountain of documentation and jurisprudence from the period 1500 to 1669 which pertained to regulation of use or *réformations*. These early *cantonnements* normally gave lords two-thirds provided that one-third was sufficient for communal use.

At most, the 1669 ordinance tended to limit the amount of forest or common land effectively assigned to lords to a smaller share. After 1669, lords typically received 1/3, often called confusingly a *triage,* regardless of whether the procedure was technically a *triage* or a simply a *cantonnement.*[143] Similarly after 1669, lords received 1/3 of the proceeds of any sales of lumber cut on communal forests.[144] *Triages* and *cantonnements* continued right down to the Revolution. On the eve of the Revolution, the Count of Montmorency pushed ahead with a *cantonnement* of one of his forests in Normandie with the support of the royal courts despite the opposition of the local users.[145]

In Bourgogne, a living museum of archaic seigneurial institutions, nearly a third of the communities were still subject of mortmain in the eighteenth century. To free themselves from this remnant of serfdom, many impecunious communities bought their freedom by surrendering large sections of their forests or their common lands to their lords. In 1746, twenty families in the village of Clomot received a charter that freed them from mortmain by surrendering two thirds of their common lands to their lord, Pierre-Louis de Villiers-la-Faye. In 1782, Nicolas de Brûlart, first president of the *Parlement* of Dijon, freed the inhabitants of the village of Chamesson for one half of the village's forest, 112 ha.[146]

For the early modern period as a whole, the chronology of transfers of control over forests from peasants to lords was essentially the same as the chronology for transfers of farmland. Lords expanded their holdings of forests and commons mainly between 1500 and 1650, while they continued to make gains but at slower pace between 1650 and 1789.[147] At the end of the old regime, the forests in France covered roughly 4,807,752 ha. Of this, about 16%, 754,996 ha, belonged to the king and the holders of royal apanages. 20%, some 961,078 ha, belonged to ecclesiastical institutions. The largest share, 41%, about 1,968,600 ha, belonged to lords and individual commoners. The final 21%, roughly 1,123,088 ha, belonged to village and town communities. The 41% that belonged to private individuals was overwhelmingly in the hands of the *seigneurs*.[148]

Often, it was princes of the realm, members of the most eminent feudal families, and the most prestigious robe nobles who owned the most valuable seigneurial forests. In southeastern Champagne (Haute-Marne) at the end of the old regime, ecclesiastical institutions and high nobles owned nearly 50% of the forests, about 90,000 ha: the Duke of Penthièvre had 11,935 ha, the Duke of Orléans held 14,200 ha, the Count of Artois, 3500 ha, while the Broglie, Choiseuil, and Montmorency families also had significant holdings.[149]

For lords, forests were of far greater financial value than scruffy common lands. For lords lucky enough to own them, forests typically brought in far more revenues than domain-farms and seigneurial dues. In Normandie, revenues from forests accounted for 20% of seigneurial revenues in the late seventeenth century and 40% on average in the last decades of the old regime.[150] In 1781, the Duke of Penthièvre received 842,644 *livres* from the duchy of Rambouillet. 91% of this, 768,834 *livres*, came from the sale of lumber in 11,000 ha of forests. About 9%, 73, 810 *livres*, came from 2000 ha of domain-farms, and less than 1% from *droits seigneuriaux* collected from tenures that covered 10,000 ha. Two years later in 1783, the Duke of Penthièvre reluctantly sold Rambouillet, the center of his family for decades, to an insistent Louis XVI for 16,000,000 *livres*.[151]

In the much smaller *seigneurie* of Fleury-en-Bière, located near Fontaine-bleau, the d'Argouges, robe nobles from Normandie, derived annual revenues of about 6500 *livres* from the leases of their domain-farms in the 1760s and 3200 *livres* from a 250 ha stand of trees, but a major cutting of old growth in 1767–1769 brought in 71,681 *livres*.[152] At the end of the old regime, 54% of the annual income of the barony of Neubourg in Normandie, 33,000 *livres* out of

61,000 *livres*, came from the forests. Fees for pasturing animals brought in 600–800 *livres* and most of the rest came from the sale of lumber.[153]

As for the unappropriated common lands, they had largely disappeared in much of northern France by the end of the Middle Ages. They survived mainly in the lightly populated and economically backward areas of France that had soils with less than optimum fertility for arable agriculture. In areas where unappropriated commons with little commercial value existed in abundance, in parts of Auvergne and Limousin, in the interior or Bretagne, and in many parts of the Midi such as Bas-Languedoc, the western Pyrénées, Bordelais and Gascogne, traditional rights of household use as well as the establishment of new tenures and clandestine clearings continued throughout the early modern centuries without much tension.[154] In Béarn, common lands accounted for two thirds of the territory of the province.[155] Where they existed, the administration of common lands was often the central issue handled by the village governments.[156]

Elsewhere, conflicts between lords and communities over common lands were very frequent, especially in those parts of France where the unappropriated lands seemed to hold out solutions to mounting demographic and economic pressures. From the middle of the eighteenth century, disputes over commons and open pasture swelled to unprecedented levels, in part because of the rapid increase in landless or nearly landless peasants, in part too because the monarchy embraced the reform ideas of the physiocrats.[157] The physiocrats, who were anxious to promote increased agricultural production of grains, viewed the traditional rights of use in commons and open pasture as archaic impediments to growth. With the zeal of ideologues, they attacked the ancient uses and promoted agrarian individualism by advocating enclosure and division of the commons.

With a flurry of edits and letters patent for specific provinces issued in the 1760s, 1770s and 1780s, the monarchy urged the division of the common lands. At the same time, the monarchy embraced a startling new view of how the commons should be divided. For centuries, rights of use in the commons were tied to landownership in agricultural zone, the *finage*, of a village or town. By the second half of the eighteenth century, France was teeming with landless poor and the idea gained currency among royal administrators that one way of handling this problem was to give all residents, not just property owners, part of the commons.

By promoting equal division of commons among all residents, the monarchy violated the traditional rights of property owners and stirred up trouble among the inhabitants of the communities. At the same time, lords had rights too. Since any division of the commons as well as any sale of common lands would normally lead to a *triage* of 1/3 for the lord, the hapless royal efforts at reform provoked on outpouring of ill feelings directed against the royal administration, against the larger property owners, and against the lords.[158]

The old regime ended with a ground swell of disputes over the ancient rights of land use exacerbated by the inherent contradictions of royal policy. Many of these conflicts, especially those dealing with open pasture and enclosure, were not specifically related to lordship, but lords were major property owners who often had vast estates closed to the landless poor. Consequently, what can only be described as a class struggle over economic resources undoubtedly poisoned the air and worsened already tense relations between lords and the inhabitants of their lordships.

Serfdom

Under the old regime, a cluster of seigneurial practices, most notably mortmain, restrictions on marriage outside the lordship, mandatory residence, unregulated direct seigneurial taxes (*tailles*), and unregulated labor services (*corvées*) were commonly considered servile by both legal experts and ordinary inhabitants of the realm. The legal foundation of these seigneurial practices, as indeed of lordship in its entirety, was customary law. Between roughly 1500 and 1750, the entire range of law courts from the seigneurial tribunals of first instance to the highest royal appellate courts, the *parlements* and the *Conseil du roi*, upheld these and all other customary practices of lordship that were supported by legally sufficient title.

While the records of individual lordships and often the customary law codes themselves simply recorded established practice without any analysis as to the nature of these practices, jurists in their commentaries on the law attempted to analyze the customs with the aid of concepts drawn from Roman Law.[159] They commonly divided servile practices into those that were real and those that were personal. Real servile practices flowed from holding land in the lordship while personal servile burdens originated from subjection to the authority of the lord associated with inferior legal status. The efforts by the jurists to make sense of the servile practices by applying the logic of Roman Law were doomed to failure from the outset. No amount of subtle, logic-chopping ratiocination could reduce the recalcitrant practices of the customary law to a logically coherent system. Likewise, the notions of real and personal servitude are singularly unhelpful as tools to understand the history of the servile customs.

A full discussion of medieval serfdom would be out of place here.[160] A brief outline will suffice. In the Middle Ages, unregulated *tailles* and *corvées* were fairly common parts of the fiscal systems of lordship in many regions of France and were not originally seen as servile. From the twelfth century, formal charters and less formal seigneurial customs placed clear limits on both of these seigneurial taxes. By the end of the Middle Ages, unregulated *tailles* and *corvées* were unusual and because they were unusual they came to be seen as servile.

From the late fifteenth century, the *parlements* were normally quite hostile to unregulated or arbitrary seigneurial *tailles* which they viewed as contrary to the royal ordinance of Charles VII issued in 1439 which prohibited them. In the redactions of the customary laws in the late fifteenth and sixteenth century, the *parlements* made every effort to limit *tailles* and *corvées*. Some *tailles* and *corvées à volonté* survived because they were supported by firm title. However, the *parlements* through their jurisprudence subjected even these arbitrary seigneurial taxes to very tight regulation to prevent them from posing any threat to the sovereign fiscal authority of the king.[161]

Mortmain, restrictions on out-marriage, and mandatory residence arose in one of three ways in the Middle Ages. The oldest servile restrictions were associated in the late Roman and early medieval centuries with a caste of hereditary fiscal agents installed permanently to staff the lordships. These were exceedingly rare by the end of the thirteenth century and virtually non-existent by the early modern era.

The servile customs that lingered into the old regime had two origins. Either powerful lords imposed these restrictions on wide territories as a political act in the eleventh through the thirteenth century to control a territory against other rival lords or they incorporated these restrictions in new villages and individual tenures from the outset as a political or less commonly as an economic control. The politically inspired controls often encompassed entire provinces and were typically superimposed on towns and rural areas alike which frequently had a pre-existing network of fiscal obligations to the lords. These territorially widespread, politically inspired controls faded quickly from the middle of the thirteenth century as the princes gained firmer authority over their lands.

The economically inspired controls were far less widespread geographically and were typically found in economically unattractive regions that had difficulty in attracting and holding settlers. Because they were incorporated into the fabric of land tenure itself, the economically inspired controls tended to linger longer than the politically inspired controls. The Breton *quévaise*, a restrictive tenure that was impartible, subject to mortmain, transferrable in the direct line of succession to the youngest child, not the oldest, was an example of this sort of economically inspired servile control.[162] The *quévaise* appeared in particularly unappealing lands in the northern part of Bretagne given to the Cistercians and Hospitalers to settle in the twelfth century. Although the *quévaise* survived until the Revolution, it was already in an advanced state of decrepitude in the fifteenth century. Slack administration had allowed the *quévaise* tenures to become largely indistinguishable from common hereditary tenures, called *féages* in Bretagne and *censives* elsewhere in France.

Although tiny pockets of land with servile customs appeared here and there, in parts of Bordelais for example,[163] the largest concentrations of territory with servile customs under the old regime appeared in a semi-circle of economically backward and relatively unattractive lands that ran clockwise east of Paris and the Ile-de-France. This semi-circle of residual serfdom ran from Hainaut on the northern frontier of the realm, through eastern and southeastern Champagne, Lorraine, Bourgogne and Franche-Comté, then westwards through Nivernais, Bourbonnais, Marche and Berry.[164] Even in these areas, the servile controls were far from universal. They were most heavily concentrated in Bourgogne, France-Comté, and Nivernais where approximately one third of the villages had servile customs.

Champagne was under the jurisdiction of the *Parlement* of Paris and heavily influenced from the time of its annexation to the crown in 1285 by the customary law of Paris. From the thirteenth century, servile customs had no foundation in the customary law of the *vicomté et prévôté* of Paris. In Champagne, lingering servile practices disappeared very quickly at the end of the fifteenth and the first half of the sixteenth century.[165] The costs of administration exceeded the revenues from escheated lands subject to *mainmorte*, and often lax enforcement preceded formal enfranchisement.

Nearly half of the villages freed from mortmain in the region of Bar-sur-Seine in Champagne, 26 out of 57, received manumission between 1477 and the early sixteenth century. Normally there was a fee for freedom that took either the form of an increase in the annual hearth tax or an increase in the annual *taille*. Often enfranchisement was part of a comprehensive recasting of the fiscal structure of lordship in the villages that employed the charter of Beaumont. Mortmain was not introduced into newly cleared lands or on monastic *granges* converted into tenures. In the *bailliage* of Chaumont-en-Bassigny also in Champagne, a last wave of enfranchisement in the sixteenth century largely eliminated mortmain.[166]

Although rare after the sixteenth century, servile controls did not entirely disappear from early modern Champagne. In the eighteenth century, a number of lords turned the archaic restrictions to account. At Givry-en-Argonne, the 1229 charter required all property owners to reside. Any inhabitant of the lordship who left had to sell or otherwise dispose of his land to a resident of the lordship within fifteen days. No outsiders were allowed to own property in the community. Failure to conform to the law entailed loss of property, *déchéance*, to the lord. In the 1770s, the Marquis de Baillet was involved in a lawsuit with the inhabitants over this custom. In a 1777 transaction, the Marquis abandoned his rights in return for 22 *arpents* of communal forest.[167]

In Lorraine, servile customs survived in highest concentration in a band of land north and south of Nancy in what later became the *départements* of Meurthe-et-Moselle and Vosges.[168] Mortmain, mandatory residence, called *forfuyance*, and *droit de suite* typically went hand-in-hand. Some lordships even had unregulated *tailles* and *corvées*.[169] Serfdom was particularly widespread in the ducal domain. In 1711, Duke Léopold, inspired by fiscal rather than humanitarian motives, issued an edict in which he offered to abolish all servile customs on the lands of the ducal domain in return for an annual replacement tax. The subjects protested that the tax was more burdensome than the regulations of mortmain and pursuit which rarely came into play. The Duke withdrew the edit, but reissued it again in 1719 with a lower replacement tax. His subjects still refused to accept the offer. Later in 1719, Duke Léopold issued a third edict which simply abolished the right of pursuit without compensation. The rest of the servile burdens, most notably mortmain, remained in place in the ducal domain. Léopold encourage other lords in Lorraine to follow his example, but few did.[170]

Bourgogne and Franche-Comté were perhaps the strongest bastions of servile customs in the realm. Lightly populated and economically underdeveloped both in the Middle Ages and throughout the early modern centuries, these two provinces had quite remote hinterlands where servile customs survived undiminished. While mortmain, mandatory residence, and *droit de suite* had already disappeared from the river valleys and the more accessible regions, they survived in mountainous western part of Bourgogne and in the Jura mountain range in eastern Franche-Comté. Roughly a third of Bourgogne and nearly half of Franche-Comté still had servile controls in 1789. The magistrates of the *Parlements* of Dijon and Besançon were not only among the most influential lords of these provinces but were second to none in defending every archaic seigneurial custom. The servile traditions produced the petty profits often associated with generally backward economic zones.

In the Middle Ages, *mainmorte* had served to defend territory and to maintain in place a tax paying population that contributed substantially to the revenues of the duchy and county of Bourgogne in the form of annual seigneurial *tailles*.[171] These servile seigneurial *tailles* were older than and completely distinct from the more recent subventions or *tailles* voted periodically by the Estates of these two provinces in the late Middle Ages. Ducal officials mobilized an impressive administrative system to collected these and all other seigneurial dues in the fourteenth and fifteenth century.

After the death of Charles the Bold of Bourgogne in 1477, the duchy of Bourgogne was annexed to the French crown while Franche-Comté passed into the hands of the Hapsburgs where it remained from 1493 to 1678. The kings of France and Spain had their own more modern fiscal systems and the old seigneurial *tailles* on the crown lands dwindled in importance and were blocked by royal officials elsewhere.

After 1500, there was something of a reversal of the relative fiscal importance of the servile customs in Bourgogne and Franche-Comté. What had been the means became the end. Prior to 1500, mortmain had served to secure the fiscal base; after 1500, mortmain became a significant source of revenue itself.[172] Once the seigneurial *tailles* were abolished, commuted, or otherwise hemmed in by royal officials, the profits of escheated estates subject to mortmain and heavy new payments to secure release from mortmain replaced the seigneurial *tailles* as sources of revenue. This reversal of fortunes for seigneurial *tailles* and *mainmorte* occurred in ecclesiastical, aristocratic, and even in royal lordships pawned to *engagistes*.

Enfranchisement from *mainmorte* was certainly not an everyday occurrence in Bourgogne. There were not even a hundred cases of enfranchisement for entire village communities in the seventeenth and eighteenth century: 39 well-documented cases in the seventeenth century and 28 in the eighteenth. Lords always demanded a heavy price: a doubling of the annual seigneurial *taille*, a lump sum payments with or without a smaller annual tax, an increased in a proportional or fixed render, often called a tithe (*dîme*), payable in grain, legumes, oil seeds, etc.,or additional *corvées* Lords also granted freedom from mortmain in return for the surrender of substantial sections of communal forests.[173]

Franche-Comté passed back and forth between the kings of France and the Habsbourgs before coming to rest in France in 1678. These vicissitudes in the political fate of the province had no perceptible impact on the history of servile customs. The priory of Mouthe, a dependancy of the Abbey of Saint-Cloud in Franche-Comté, passed into the hands of the Jesuits in 1582. The Jesuits established the *Collège de l'Arc* at Dole and retained possession of the priory until the order was dissolved in France in 1765. The priory then passed under direct royal management. *Mainmorte* functioned with full rigor at Mouthe between 1582 and 1789. The 1296 foundation charter for the priory, confirmed by the abbey in 1322 and 1488, and repeated in the first Jesuit *terrier* in 1587, provided an unassailable foundation for mortmain.[174]

All residents in the nine communities which constituted the priory's *seigneurie* were subject to *mainmorte*. Residence and ownership of land for a year and a day made everyone *mainmortable*. Tenants could not mortgage land in mortmain without explicit approval of the lord. Unapproved liens dissolved with the death of the contracting party and at most could be collected from chattel and free holdings in the event of escheat to the lord. To inherit, heirs had to reside and had to maintain joint financial management at the time of death. Residence was mandatory for all property owners. Unless formally freed, the *droit de suite* remained in force and the lord could claim ownership of all the property of a dead *mainmortable*, servile, free, and chattels, wherever this might be. The Jesuits also strictly enforced *formariage*. They demanded fees for the approval of out marriage and maintained special records for *formariage*. These registers were useful in tracking down estates located outside the lordship that might be subject to the *droit de suite*.

The Jesuits enforced the *droit de suite* with an iron hand, but they had to have the cooperation of outside authorities to press their claims successfully. In 1675, they tried to seize an estate of an unfreed serf in Fribourg, but the municipal government refused to honor the claim. In France, the Jesuits were so successful in enforcing the *droit de suite* that between 1684 and 1716, when there were less than 200 households in the entire lordship, no less than 106 individuals made a formal disavowal of holdings to free the rest of their estates from the threat of eventual seizure. In the same time period, not a single estate in the priory's lordship was freed from mortmain.

This punctilious, pettifogging enforcement of archaic seigneurial customs was economically counterproductive, but symptomatic of a type of small-minded seigneurial administration. The lands of the priory of Mouthe were surrounded by lordships where mortmain had been abolished. The vexatious enforcement of mortmain discouraged new settlers and drove out old ones. The population of Mouthe peaked in 1635 at 243 households, fell to 157 in 1666, and was still only 173 in 1696. Population grew a little in the eighteenth century but never recovered to the level of 1635. The Jesuits persisted in their morbid enforcement of ovory jot and tittle of the servile laws and reaped petty profits for their labor. In all likelihood they would have derived far greater revenues from a prosperous and populous lordship without mortmain that encouraged new settlement and economic growth.

The rigorous enforcement of mortmain by the Jesuits at Mouthe was typical of the ecclesiastical and the aristocratic lords of Franche-Comté. Exactly the same sort of administration occurred in the Abbey of Luxeuil.[175] In 1789, mortmain affected between one third and one half of the villages in Franche-Comté, 400,000 out of 700,000 inhabitants in the province.[176] Servile customs were well protected by the Customary Law redacted in 1459. Many of the villages with mortmain were established through clearings in the Jura mountains between the thirteenth and fifteenth century. In addition to mortmain and impartible inheritance, these planned villages often had a distinctive geometric lay out.[177]

The counts and greater aristocratic lords freed the larger towns in Franche-Comté first, then the rural communities at the end of the Middle Ages and in the sixteenth century. in 1582, Philip II of Spain carried out a partial emancipation of the villages in the royal domain; the dukes of Montbéliard issued individual manumissions between 1431 and 1584.[178] By contrast, the ecclesiastical and the lesser aristocratic lords not only maintained mortmain, but reinforced it from the fifteenth century right down to the Revolution. Even the devastation of the wars of the late sixteenth century and the Thirty Years' War tended to reinforce rather than weaken mortmain on the lesser lordships.[179] Likewise, the relatively generous administrative practices of the fifteenth and sixteenth century in the county of Montbéliard faded. In the late seventeenth and eighteenth century, only a minority of villages in Montbéliard still had mortmain. However, the legal professionals of the regency of the dukes of Württemberg enforced the servile customs with the nitpicking spirit that was characteristic of the seigneurial administrators of the last century of the old regime.[180]

In Nivernais, the politically inspired controls of *mainmorte* and *formariage*, superimposed on the ancient *mansi* and *censives* faded in the late Middle Ages, while these same controls along with impartible inheritance survived in the *bordelage* tenures in planned villages.[181] With population recovery in the sixteenth century and with further clearings, the territory with the restrictive *bordelage* tenures expanded rapidly and soon accounted for most of the territory in the province.[182] Mortmain tenures with arbitrary *tailles* located in long-settled areas were also transformed and retroceded as *bordelages*.[183]

The *bordelage* tenures in Nivernais appealed to both lords and peasants. Nivernais was a remote and relatively unappealing poor-soil region. Lords wanted to hold in place a resident peasantry. The province had an abundance of uncultivated land and the impartible *bordelage* tenure with mortmain encourage further clearings rather than land fragmentation as population rose. Peasants normally did not find either mortmain or impartibility to be excessively burdensome and the modest fixed renders in cash and kind of the *bordelage* tenures appealed to them. A few *bordelage* tenures disappeared between middle of the seventeenth and the end of the eighteenth century as large upperclass *métaires* expanded. Upperclass land engrossers, nobles and bourgeois, often paid the lords with seigneurial rights over the *bordelage* tenures to free them from mortmain. Even so, *bordelage* remained the rule in Nivernais. In many lordships near Nevers in the eighteenth century, between one half and three quarters of the landmass in seigneurial tenure had the *bordelage* system.[184]

Remnants of servile customs survived under the old regime in Bourbonnais, a strip of Auvergne, in Marche and Berry. Our best information comes from Bourbonnais.[185] In the Middle Ages, the dukes of Bourbon established and maintained a fiscal system of lordship that featured seigneurial *tailles*. Some parts of Bourbonnais had mortmain, some did not, but all were subject to seigneurial *tailles*. Similar fiscal systems existed on the lesser lordships of the province.[186] After the treason of the Constable of Bourbon, François I seized Bourbonnais and annexed it to the crown properties. In 1548, Henri II abolished mortmain, the right of pursuit, and the seigneurial *tailles,* both *tailles franches* and *tailles personnelles*, in return for a modest seigneurial tax of 2 *sous* per hearth on the crown lands that formerly belonged to the Constable. The King was particularly anxious to dismantle a seigneurial fiscal system which might conflict with the royal *taille*. The system of seigneurial *tailles* with mortmain survived in a few lesser lordships in Bourbonnais and was still in existence at the end of the old regime.[187]

Until the middle of the eighteenth century, the servile customs were absolutely unassailable in law. In a very widely published case in 1738, the *Parlement* of Paris upheld the *droit de suite*. In the 1738 case, the Count of Montal from Bourgogne claimed the estate of Jean-Guillaume Moreau, a serf from Bourgogne who died in Paris where he had resided uninterruptedly for 50 years.[188] Moreau had never gone through the legal formality, *le désaveau*, required by the customary law of Bourgogne to abandon his land subject to mortmain and to shed his servile status. Consequently, in the law of Bourgogne, he remained subject to the *droit de suite*.

When Moreau died, he left an estate worth at least 150,000 *livres* principally to Parisian charitable institutions, the Hôtel-Dieu and a foundling hospital. At issue was the question of whether Moreau had the rights of a bourgeois of Paris or was still subject to the servile custom of Bourgogne. The *Prévôt des marchands* of Paris supported the claims of the charitable institutions , while the lord had the backing of the *Parlement* of Bourgogne at Dijon. The court decided in favor of the lord and upheld the servile custom. It was only after 1750 that a handful of sentences issued by the *parlements* and royal edicts modified in any significant way the legal support for these servile seigneurial practices.

The Administration of Lordship

All of the administrative and financial practices used in the management of lordships under the old regime were already well developed in the Middle Ages.[189] The widespread view that the early modern centuries brought dramatic improvements in the administration of lordship, first with the invasion of supposedly bourgeois managerial techniques in the sixteenth century and later with the advent of an equally fanciful agrarian capitalism in the eighteenth, is simply not supported by the historical evidence.[190]

The administrative institutions and the financial practices found in the estates of the princes and peers of the realm in the seventeenth and eighteenth century were identical to those found in the royal domain and in the estates of the dukes and counts of the late Middle Ages. Indeed, any of the dukes of Bourgogne from the period 1250 to 1477 would have felt perfectly at home with all of the institutions and techniques used in the administration of the estates of the princes of the blood on the eve of the Revolution.[191] Similarly, the methods of managing small and medium-sized aristocratic and ecclesiastical lordships during the old regime were the same as those used in the late Middle Ages.[192] Once again, the history of lordship under the old regime is the history of an institution with stunning, multi-secular continuity.

Fundamentally, there were only three ways of managing lordships. The lord could do the work himself, alone. He could hire a steward or intendant, *régisseur*, and pay him a salary. Or, he could put the administration of his lordship up lease and turn it over to a *fermier*.

In every age, there were always many lords who managed their estates directly without any assistance. In the sixteenth century, the *sire* de Gouberville in Bas-Normandie was a resident lord who devoted decades of his life to collecting seigneurial dues and to supervising the cultivation of his lands.[193] In the 1770s, Madame de Bellefonds managed the barony of Sennevières in Touraine in essentially the same way. She demanded homage from fief owners and formal declarations of tenure, supervised 8 *métairies*, 6 smaller *borderies*, collected tithes, *terrages*, and *corvées*.[194] In all likelihood, direct management of lordship was probably the most widespread method of noble estate administration in the early modern centuries for the simple reason that poor nobles with small estates always accounted for the majority of the French aristocracy.

Noble and ecclesiastical lords with more complex estates used either salaried general stewards or put their entire estates up for lease. Most of the magistrates in the *Parlement* of Toulouse in the eighteenth century employed hired stewards. They were resident lords with modest estates with incomes of less than 10,000 *livres* in the late eighteenth century. They were very involved with the management of their properties, but they left the drudge work of revenue collection and record keeping to the stewards.[195] Similarly, the magistrates of the *Parlement* of Bourgogne at Dijon in the late eighteenth century were deeply involved in the management of their lordships whether they used salaried *receveurs* or *fermiers*.[196] The far wealthier magistrates of the *Parlement* of Bordeaux who owned some of the most prestigious and profitable vineyards in France also used salaried intendants to manage their vineyards. But, they turned to temporary leaseholders for the collecting of the *droits seigneuriaux* in their lordships.[197]

Leaseholders who managed individual lordships and entire estates with multiple lordships appeared only in the last three centuries of the Middle Ages. These men were essentially financiers like tax farmers. Financiers wealthy enough to lease lordships or entire estates with annual revenues of thousands or tens of thousands of *livres* did not appear until the economy of late medieval France had developed to the point that it allowed men to accumulate large stocks of capital. General leasers had to have sufficient liquid capital to pay the owner the annual lease price and sufficient working capital and collateral to carry the financial load of managing the property for the duration of the lease.

Although financiers who leased the management of important seigneurial estates certainly existed in the late Middle Ages, they became numerous only in with the spectacular economic growth of the sixteenth century, and ubiquitous only in the seventeenth and eighteenth century.[198] In the Ile-de-France, the most economically advanced region in France, there was a striking parallel between the rise of the financially independent *laboureurs*, the tenant farmers who leased the great grain growing domain-farms north of Paris, and the rise of the financiers who took over the management of the entire estates in which these domain-farms appeared.

At the end of the fifteenth century, the tenant farmers, *laboureurs fermiers*, lacked sufficient capital to finance the running of the domain-farms themselves without the financial cooperation of the lords. By the end of the sixteenth century and the beginning of the seventeenth, the tenant farmers were not only able to carry the financial load alone, but they were also strong enough to lease even larger domain-farms. By the early eighteenth century, the *gros laboureurs* cobbled together even larger farms to achieve economies of scale by leasing properties from several lords or bourgeois owners.[199]

Similarly, while there were relatively few financiers capable of taking on the management of the large Parisian estates in 1500, by the second half of the sixteenth century they existed in great numbers. Consequently, both ecclesiastical and aristocratic lords moved from relying mainly on hired stewards to manage their estates to lease holding financiers.[200] By the eighteenth century, the general revenue leaseholders of the princely estates were bankers of national stature with leases worth hundreds of thousands of *livres* a year. The princely estates by this time often had properties scattered all over France. While the use of general revenue leasers became more and more common with each passing decade of the old regime, it is highly doubtful that the growing popularity of general leasers amounted to an advance in bourgeois management. As a rule, salaried stewards were far more scrupulous managers than revenue farmers with short leases.

Often lords shifted back and forth from stewards to general leaseholders as central administrators for their entire estates. Stewards were unquestionably cheaper in the long run than lease holding financiers, since the salaries of even the most expensive estate managers were a fraction of the profits which the general leaseholds took every year. In the 1770s, the Marquis de Sade paid the *régisseur* of his properties in Provence 400 *livres* a year. Total revenues of this particular estate, Lacoste, were 17,500 *livres*, so the salary amounted to less than 1% of the income of the property.[201] However, general lease holding managers in the seventeenth and eighteenth centuries routinely made 25-30% even 40% above what they paid the owners for the annual price of their lease.[202] Both systems of estate management had their good sides and their bad.

Stewards were cheaper and they were more exacting administrators. But lords who used stewards had to supply the working capital and assume the financial risks for running the entire estate themselves. Also, with stewards, the annual income from the estate fluctuated with the normal vicissitudes of the economy. Financiers were expensive, but they provided the working capital, assumed all of the financial risks, and more importantly paid an agreed annual income up front. Not infrequently, the financiers also lent money to the lords. For lords with a penchant to outspend income, the short-term advantages of using general estate leasers were obvious, but so too were the long-term financial risks. Unscrupulous general farmers took advantage of high aristocrats at court who paid no attention to their properties. During the reign of Louis XIV, members of the Delamaison family pillaged the Burgundian lordships that belonged to the famous Madame de Sévigné, whose interest in her lands never extended beyond immediate revenues.[203]

Whether lords with complex estates used central stewards or general revenue farmers, the individual properties within these states had their own officials who typically consisted of a combination of salaried or venal agents and lease holders. At the end of the old regime, the barony of Varenne in Anjou and Maine belonged to the Duke of Choiseul, peer of the realm and Naval Minister for Louis XV. Varenne had a salaried *régisseur* who corresponded frequently with the duke and who supervised no less than 129 leases for the domain lands and *droits seigneuriaux* in the barony.[204] At the level of an individual lordship, there was no difference between the way properties were managed, whether they belonged to modest provincial squires or princes of the realm.[205] At the ground level, all lords in France used essentially the same stock of managerial techniques and employed the same sorts of hired officials and leaseholders. Virtually all lords used either short-term lease holders or sharecroppers for their domain-farms.[206] Likewise, most lords turned to lease holders to collect the seigneurial dues and the tithes. In some cases, these revenue leaseholders in the individual lordship also held leases for the domain-farms; sometimes, they were the *procureurs fiscaux* of the seigneurial court.[207]

What distinguished a marquisat, a county or a ducal peerage from a modest provincial aristocratic property was not the way individual lordships were administered, but the administrative and financial superstructures of the princely estates. Once again, the higher administrative and financial structures of the old regime titled lordships perpetuated the institutions found in the royal domain and in the late medieval principalities. A comparison of the institutions in the relatively modest *comté* of Dammartin-en-Goël in the Ile-de-France in the 1490s with those found at the royal palace at Versailles, in the bishoprics and ancient monasteries, and in the estates of the Count of Artois or the Duke of Bourbon-Penthièvre in the late eighteenth century would show hardly any differences at all.[208] Likewise, there were no important differences between the higher administrative practices found in the estates of peers of France and in the titled lordships of the Rhenish princes of the Holy Roman Empire.[209]

The basic administrative structure of an old regime principality included a central administrative and financial institution called a *conseil*, staffed with either salaried or venal office holders.[210] The Count of Artois's *conseil* in the 1770s and 1780s had 40 officials. The princely *conseil* was itself only part of the larger *maison du prince*. Justice had its own separate administrative hierarchy that came under the jurisdiction of the *Parlement* of Paris and the *Conseil du roi*. The princely *conseils* functioned essentially the same way as the medieval *chambres des comptes*. The head of the *conseil* was the *régisseur, intendant, surintendant de finances, chancelier-surintendant des finances* etc. who was either a salaried general steward or a general leaseholder. At Versailles, the administrative head was a *governeur*, a salaried official in the early eighteenth century, but after 1741 a *fermier général*. [211]

The most elaborate principalities had a regional financial and administrative apparatus that mirrored that found in the royal fiscal administration: regional *bureaux des finances* staffed with *trésoriers* or *receveurs*. The Count of Artois had three regional *intendants des finances*. The principalities also had a separate administrative and financial apparatus for the forests. Some principalities retained the old term *gruerie* for the central forest administrative body, but most employed the royal nomenclature and called them a *maîtrise des eaux et forêts* or a *Table du marbre*.

Innumerable high aristocratic families below the level of the princes, especially those who lived at court from the late seventeenth century, found it imperative to have at least a simplified higher administrative and financial apparatus for their far-flung properties. The accumulation of multiple large lordships in the hands of the aristocratic families at the peak of the noble hierarchy began in the late Middle Ages and accelerated between 1500 and 1789. [212] The Saulx-Tavanes lived at Versailles and Paris, but had properties scattered from Normandie to Bourgogne. Their central administrative apparatus was relatively simple: one salaried general *receveur* in Paris, and 4 salaried regional *receveurs*. [213]

Without any doubt, the administration of lordship was one of the biggest and most profitable businesses in old regime France. The administration of lordship provided employment to tens of thousands of venal, salaried and lease-holding officials. These men came from a wide social spectrum of commoners that extended from eminent financiers of national stature to simple peasants. There were positions for men of every financial stature. For them, lordship was a business to be run for profit to facilitate enrichment and upward social mobility. They were or hoped to be notables, eventually even nobles. The administration of lordship was simply one of the easiest and most readily available businesses, one of many economic endeavors in which they were engaged.[214]

The administration of lordship brought good profits from the sale of agricultural commodities and from lucrative subletting, while it provided abundant opportunities for the establishment of remunerative loans and *rentes*. Debts led to foreclosures and land transfers, new *métairies* and the expansion of landed estates, always the foundation of wealth and prestige in old regime France. As near as we can tell, the men who administered lordships were unsentimental and untroubled by moral scruples about the social value of the *seigneurie*. When the Revolution swept aside lordship, this class of men did not disappear with it or long mourn its departure. They were ambitious opportunists. Many bought *biens nationaux*. And, of course, even after the elimination of lordship and the tithe during the Revolution, there was still plenty of work left in the management of upperclass properties.[215]

Justice and Governance

Justice was one of the fundamental attributes of lordship. At the end of the Middle Ages, the seigneurial tribunals were already integrated into the hierarchy of royal law courts. This hierarchy extended from the seigneurial courts in the villages and towns through the intermediate range of royal courts, the *bailliages* or *sénéchaussées*, to the *parlements*. From the mid-sixteenth century, yet another layer of royal appeals courts appeared, the *cours présidiaux*, between the *bailliages* and the *parlements*.[216]

Although reforms introduced in the *bailliages* and *parlements* in the last two centuries of the Middle Ages produced a considerable upgrading of the procedures and the legal training of the personnel of the royal courts, the seigneurial courts lagged behind. While the late medieval lordships had very sophisticated institutions for the management of fiscal affairs, they had only rudimentary institutions for the administration of justice.[217] The principal seigneurial administrator was the provost whose main task was the collection of seigneurial revenues. Although some lordships had judges, many lordships still left the administration of justice to the provosts, many of whom were tax farmers who leased their positions.

Whether staffed with judges or with provosts, the seigneurial courts still employed the ancient customary procedures. For centuries, seigneurial justice had been community based justice in which the elders of the village or town sat in judgement of their neighbors. In these customary procedures, a seigneurial official presided, but it was the community leaders who rendered judgement. This same type of community based justice was also enshrined in the hundreds of charters that regularized municipal and village institutions in the medieval lordships. Where formally installed municipal and village officials existed, it was the *consuls, jurats, échevins*, etc. who rendered judgement. While the rough and ready justice of the seigneurial courts was probably neither better nor worse than the justice meted out by the more sophisticated higher royal courts in the late fifteenth and early sixteenth century, the ancient procedures of the seigneurial courts certainly looked archaic in an age of rapid institutional modernization.

Through a series of ordinances in the sixteenth century, the monarchy dramatically reformed seigneurial justice. A cluster of edits and ordinances reformed the courts and their civil procedures: Villers-Coterêts, 1539; Orléans, 1545; Moulins, 1566; Blois, 1579; and finally Paris, 1667.[218] These ordinances prohibited the community based system of justice and conferred judicial authority on a legally trained judge whose credentials had to be approved by the regional royal court of appeal. The old style community based justice handled by men without formal legal training survived only in provinces added to France after the sixteenth century reforms such as Béarn, Artois, Alsace and Lorraine.[219]

At the same time, the royal ordinances reformed the court procedures by laying down a set of standards applicable to the entire realm. Civil procedures featured written depositions and proofs along with a formal written recommendation by the public prosecutor to the judge. In simple cases, the judge just confirmed the opinion of the *procureur d'office* with an official sentence. The most comprehensive ordinance dealing with criminal affairs appeared under Louis XIV in 1670. Among other things, it called for a preliminary investigation and judgement to determine if there was sufficient material for a formal trial.

Although the jurists and even the royal ordinances delighted in elaborating on the distinctions between high, medium and low justice, in practice most operational seigneurial courts handled the full range of civil and criminal cases allowed by royal law.[220] The seigneurial courts exercised jurisdiction over cases involving real property, damage caused by animals, contracts, debts, successions, guardianship, inventories after death, and seigneurial dues. Also, they often had full authority over markets, the dump, and public health.

Throughout France, the seigneurial courts mainly handled civil cases. At Coulanges-la-Vineuse in Bourgogne, civil affairs constituted more than 90% of the business of the court.[221] Many of the affairs that came before the court were not trials, but what the jurists called *jurisdiction gracieuse* such as the appointment of guardians, selection of experts to draw up inventories after death and the like. *Affaires de famille* often accounted for half the annual business handled by the court. Successions, even estates that were worth virtually nothing, often led to familial disputes, verbal insults, assault and battery, and conflicts over guardianship. All family dirty laundry was gladly washed in front of the judge.[222]

After the sixteenth century reforms, seigneurial judges handled the civil cases in first instance, but lost some of their criminal jurisdiction. At the end of the Middle ages, royal edicts had already reserved some criminal cases to the jurisdiction of the royal courts. The list of criminal cases reserved for the royal courts expanded considerably under the old regime. Enumerated in detail in the 1670 royal criminal ordinance and expanded further thereafter, the list of royal cases included treason, sacrilege with breaking and entering, rebellion against royal officials, popular sedition and popular uprisings, counterfeiting and passing counterfeit money, illegal assembly, heresy, public disturbances of religious ceremonies, abduction and rape.[223]

It had also been evident for some time that the lordships were not up to the task of maintaining law and order. Indeed, the local lordships had never developed truly effective police forces. To fill an institutional void that had become all the more apparent with rapid population increase, the monarchy intervened. Ordinances from the reign of François I formalized the jurisdiction of the royal police force, the *marchéchaussée*, in minor criminal cases.[224] The *gens d'armes* of the royal *maréchaussée* dated from the Hundred Years' War. They policed the roads and protected the people from the depredations of

soldiers. The royal *prévôtés des maréchaux*, the courts of the mounted constabu-
lary, also handled crimes committed by vagabonds.[225]

As was so often the case in the old regime, implementation of the reforms in
criminal and police jurisdiction fell far short of their stated goal. Even after a
considerable expansion of the *maréchausée* in 1720, the seigneurial courts still
handled at least some of the criminal cases theoretically reserved to royal
officials.[226] Criminal cases that went as far as a formal investigation were very
unusual. Most misdemeanors were handled in a summary fashion with a fine or
a warning. The seigneurial courts handled the most benign misdemeanors, verbal
and physical battery that stemmed from familial disputes or drunken brawls.
More serious cases went automatically to the higher royal courts.

The seigneurial courts did their best to promote private settlement of the
minor misdemeanor cases, in part to lessen their own work load, in part to
protect the local individuals concerned from what inevitably would be a much
more severe punishment if the case passed into the hands of the royal officials.
Everyone, the judicial officials as well as the parties involved, viewed private
settlement, usually with compensation of some sort, as the best way to handled
misdemeanors.[227]

Taken as a whole, the royal reforms did not set out to eliminate the
patrimonial courts of the lordships, but to upgrade them and to supplement
deficient or non-existent seigneurial institutions with royal institutions. In effect,
the old regime reforms transformed the seigneurial tribunals into royally
regulated, public institutions. The lords continued to appoint the judges and the
other judicial officials, but these men now served as public judicial agents.
Typically the seigneurial courts had a judge, called variously *juge, prévôt, bailli,
sénéchal, vigier*, etc., a chief assistant called a *lieutenant*, and a *procureur fiscal*
or *procureur d'office* who served as the public prosecutor.[228] All of these men
were legally trained professionals. There were also a number of lesser officials
such as the scribe, *greffier*, who frequently leased his position, and deputies,
sergents, who served papers and carried out court instructions.

The seigneurial courts were the indispensable tribunals of first instance and
it was not until the very eve of the Revolution that royal ministers seriously
considered eliminating them. In the territory of what became the *département* of

Yonne in Bourgogne, there were 4 royal *bailliages*, less than a dozen royal *prévôtés* (royal seigneurial courts), and several hundred seigneurial tribunals.[229] In the *bailliage* of Châtillon-sur-Seine in Bourgogne, there were 61 functioning seigneurial courts at the end of the old regime that handled 354 cases in 1750 and 748 in 1789.[230] In Dauphiné, there were 420 lords with rights of justice at the end of the eighteenth century.[231] Everywhere in France, the number of noble fiefs without rights of justice far outnumbered those entitled to maintain law courts. Fiefs with rights of justice and operational courts exercised jurisdiction over large, in some cases, huge areas.[232] Without the seigneurial courts, the intermediate royal *bailliages* would have been overwhelmed. In Bretagne, seigneurial courts probably handled 90% of the judicial case load in the province.[233]

Although precise figures are hard to find, there is no doubt that the number of functioning seigneurial courts increased substantially under the old regime, most notably in the sixteenth and seventeenth century.[234] Much of this increase occurred spontaneously as petty fiefs or clusters of common and noble lands evolved into substantial lordships. Justice was a major attribute of true lordship, and ambitious men simply set up courts as they expanded their properties, much as they had in the Middle Ages. Since the new seigneurial tribunals rendered vital public services, the kings did not go out of their way to roll back these "usurpations".

In the sixteenth and seventeenth century, the kings routinely created new seigneurial courts and supported the restoration of those that had decayed.[235] In Normandie, fiefs elevated to the status of lordships received rights of justice.[236] In Languedoc and in Gascogne, fiefs detached from the royal domain were fitted out with seigneurial courts, but in the eighteenth century portions of the royal domain transferred to *engagistes* normally did not include rights of jurisdiction.[237] More spectacularly, the Canal du Midi, established by royal edict in 1666, was a direct fief of the crown with high, medium and low justice. The canal had a very active seigneurial court with six chambers at Toulouse, Castelnaudary, Trèbes, le Somail, Béziers and Agde, that exercised full jurisdiction in civil and criminal affairs over the 200 km long canal.[238] In 1784, the Count of Galissonnière, who was the royal *sénéchal* of Anjou, reestablished his seigneurial court at Guerche. In a seigneurial ordinance, he explained that he was restoring the court in order to provide his subjects with a local tribunal so that they would no longer have to put aside their work and travel long distances for justice.[239]

The kings confirmed the status of seigneurial *bailliages* in ancient titled fiefs like the *comté* and later *duché* of Nevers. On the eve of the Revolution, the *bailliage* in the ducal peerage of Nevers served as a court of appeals for 19 *châtellenies* and another 1004 ordinary seigneurial tribunals.[240] Similarly, the kings established new *bailliages* for fiefs newly elevated to the rank of peerages. In 1711, Louis XIV authorized the establishment of a seigneurial *bailliage* when he elevated Rambouillet to the status of a ducal peerage for his legitimized son, the Count of Toulouse.[241] In addition, the multiplication of robe nobles in the various royal tribunals led indirectly to a strengthening of seigneurial justice. Normally, the royal magistrates were second to none in the punctilious exercise of justice in their lordships.[242]

After the reforms of the sixteenth century, the judicial personnel of the seigneurial courts functioned as part of the royal apparatus of justice. The polemic literature of the old regime and many of the narrative sources written by royal judicial officials and the intendants depicted the seigneurial judicial officials as ignorant, uncouth, corrupt and incompetent. At the beginning of the seventeenth century, the very influential jurist Charles Loyseau penned a damning assessment of seigneurial justice that was quoted right down to the Revolution.[243] However, virtually all of the recent studies based on a fuller range of documentation paint an entirely different picture.[244]

At their best, the leading judicial officials of the seigneurial courts functioned as public-minded civil servants answerable to higher royal authority, not as lackeys of the local lords. In their minds too, they were royal servants more than employees of the lords. According to the prevailing royal legal theories of the old regime, the judges of the seigneurial courts derived their authority from the king himself since it was the king who had delegated judicial authority to the lords.[245] Pluralism was common and many men performed judicial functions in a number of local seigneurial courts. The seigneurial judges and procurators also normally held offices in the royal *bailliages* and *cours présidiaux*.[246] This widespread pluralism meant that the officials of the lower royal courts and the seigneurial courts formed a single professional class. Within the jurisdiction of the presidial court of Angers at the end of the old regime, there were 300 seigneurial courts staffed by 40 royal lawyers who also served in the royal tribunals.[247] In Velay in 1789, there were only 45 men for the entire province who served as judges in all of the seigneurial courts.[248] For ambitious men, a judgeship in a significant seigneurial court was often the starting point for a *cursus honorum* that led to more prestigious royal judicial offices.[249] Finally, pluralism also insured a great degree of uniformity in the administration of local justice.[250]

The criticism of the fees charged for justice under the old regime was not limited to the seigneurial courts, but was also levied at the royal tribunals. However, the costs of litigation revealed in the documentation suggest that the fees in the seigneurial courts were quite modest, typically in the range of 1 to 15–20 *livres*.[251] These sums did not go directly to the judicial officials, because they had expenses to pay for paper, for witnesses, for medical or expert opinion, etc. Seigneurial justice was certainly not a money-making operation.[252]

The seigneurial courts habitually acted with meritorious speed in disposing of the cases that came before them.[253] At Coulanges-la-Vineuse in Bourgogne in the eighteenth century, the seigneurial judge could often handled 40 to 50 cases in a day since the *procureur d'office* had already done all of the investigation and prepared all of the paper work.[254]

Naturally, the judges and procurators in the seigneurial courts upheld the entire apparatus of local lordship since lordship was an integral part of the institutional infrastructure of the old regime monarchy. The judge presided over the plenary session of the seigneurial court, the *assise*, where the seigneurial and royal police regulations were read and where subjects of the lordship stepped forward to declare any changes in property ownership.[255] Nevertheless, cases that involved the lords' authority directly, such as the collection of arrears of *cens*, never accounted for more than a minor part of the total case load in the seigneurial courts.[256] At Coulanges-la-Vineuse in Bourgogne, litigation involving the lord's rights amounted to only 1–2% of the cases in the eighteenth century.[257]

The seigneurial judges and procurators were normally highly respected members of the local communities who were seen more as public servants than as simple agents of the lords. At the beginning of the Revolution, many former seigneurial judges, lieutenants, and procurators were elected by the local communities to staff the courts of the justices of the peace and to fill the offices of the new communes, the term given to the new village and municipal governments.[258]

In addition of the administration of justice, the judicial personnel of the seigneurial courts played a role in local governance in the towns and villages. As was the case with the administration of justice, the practices of the medieval lordships in local governance had been summary and in fact deficient. The medieval lordships had always been first and foremost fiscal institutions. If justice was a secondary assignment for seigneurial officials who were essentially revenue collectors, then local governance was no more than a tertiary concern for them. Village and towns developed institutionally within the larger framework of the medieval lordships. When suitable men were available in sufficient numbers, lords and their agents gladly let them handle their own communal affairs. As often as not, the lords and their agents were content with a supervisory role that left the drudge work of local administration to communal officials.

While the towns in every province of France had fairly well-developed administrative institutions by the end of the Middle Ages if not earlier, the same was not true of the villages and hamlets where the vast majority of the population lived. There was great regional diversity.[259] In areas with predominately dispersed settlement in small villages, hamlets and isolated farms, a vast area that encompassed much of Normandie, Bretagne, the Pays de la Loire, and central France, often there were no permanent administrative institutions at all in the villages. Areas with concentrated population, Picardie, the French Low Countries, Champagne, Bourgogne, Alsace, Lorraine, Aquitaine, Languedoc and Provence, had very well-developed systems of village administration that were virtually identical to those found in the towns.

The Ile-de-France and parts of Haute-Normandie certainly had concentrated settlement, but village administration collapsed in the best grain-growing regions under the old regime, while it survived in the viticultural areas.[260] In the grain-growing areas, upper class investors, nobles, bourgeois, and clerics, bought up the land for large farms and in the process largely eliminated the class of property-owning village notables, the bedrock of village administration everywhere. At the same time, massive population increase produced a swollen and impoverished landless class. Consequently, there were too few substantial, property-owning residents left in the villages to form a vibrant village administrative class. Village administration survived better in the viticultural regions precisely because every community had a large class of resident, property-owning vinedressers.

The medieval arrangements for local administration continued in the sixteenth and the first half of the seventeenth century. But as was the case with seigneurial justice, the deficiencies of village and town administration became more and more apparent with the passage of time. Monarchical intervention in local governance began in earnest under Louis XIV. From the 1660s, Louis XIV's intendants took over control of village and municipal finances which were in a deplorable state. In the interests of law and order, Louis XIV also unified the police authority of the towns with a new royal official, the lieutenant general of police. Many of the deficiencies of municipal policing stemmed from the multiplicity of lordships that typically divided the physical territory of many of the realm's major cities. These divisions and the conflicts of jurisdiction that flowed from them stood in the way of maintaining simple law and order. Louis XIV started by naming a single royal lieutenant general of police for Paris in 1667, a city which had no less than 25 lords who exercised high justice.[261] From the 1690s, the king extended this reform to the major towns in the realm.

The new lieutenants general of police took over many of the tasks heretofore performed by the seigneurial and municipal officials, especially the sensitive issues that directly affected public order such as the control of bread prices. While the seigneurial and old municipal officials lost much of their police authority in the cities in the eighteenth century, they survived as the indispensable local police agents in the villages where the bulk of the French population lived.

Finally from the 1690s too, Louis XIV also installed royal mayors in towns and villages with a formal municipal organization and permanent *sydics* in the villages where no formal apparatus of administration existed. There is no denying that the king designed these new venal offices in part to garner revenues to finance his wars. But, he also intended to facilitate better local governance by instituting a single local royal official answerable to the intendants and their subdelegates.

The reforms of the era of Louis XIV were far more effective in the areas of local finances and police affairs than they were in upgrading local governance. Often entire provinces or individual cities and towns succeeded in blocking the establishment of the royal mayors and *syndics* by paying what amounted to bribes to the king. Even where they appear, the new mayors and syndics did not in practice spearhead a major upgrading of municipal and village governance. Although some particular aggressive intendants in the eighteenth century went out of their way to sweep aside the supervisory authority of the seigneurial officials in local governance, this was unusual and ultimately fruitless.[262]

Virtually everywhere, local notables and seigneurial judicial agents worked together in a spirit of cooperation in carrying out the tasks of local governance. The judicial officials were more or less active depending on the ability of the local men to perform the tasks. Even where the administrative systems in the smaller towns and villages of France were well structured, they were often too weak to manage their own affairs without the aid of the seigneurial officials. Town and village assemblies met infrequently and kept only the most summary minutes of their deliberations, if that. Moreover, they were staffed with untrained, often nearly illiterate local men, who served part-time. As permanent institutions that functioned on a regular basis, the town and village administrations were far inferior to the seigneurial courts.[263]

Indeed, the officials of the seigneurial courts still served in the eighteenth century as the most effective agents of local administration, not only in the villages but also in many towns.[264] The judicial reforms of the sixteenth century which clearly separated justice from revenue collection in the lordships may well have facilitated the expansion of the activities of the professionally trained legal personnel of the courts in local administration. The records certainly suggest that if anything the role of the seigneurial judges, lieutenants and procurators in the administration of the villages and many towns increased rather than decreased under of the old regime.

The royal reforms, especially the ordinance of Moulins in 1566, clearly transferred jurisdictional authority in civil cases from village and town officials to the legally trained professionals in the seigneurial courts. However, the royal reforms did not confer sole jurisdiction in police and minor criminal affairs on the seigneurial courts. Often, the lines of authority in minor criminal and police affairs were very blurred even where municipal bureaus of police existed.[265] As a rule, the local officials acted as auxiliaries to the judges, lieutenants and procurators.[266] In eighteenth century Gascogne, for example, towns and villages with a formal consular government maintained municipal courts with jurisdiction over minor criminal and police affairs, while villages without a consular system relied on the seigneurial judicial officials for these matters.[267] In general, local officials often enforced the established customs, even modified them when the need arose, but they remained subordinate to the judicial officials because they lacked full jurisdictional authority.[268]

In practice, the officials of the seigneurial courts remained active as *ex officio* members of the various municipal committees that managed public properties, enforced local agrarian regulations, maintained law and order, managed church property, and supervised local charity. In Bourgogne, a province with particular strong town and village administrative systems, many of the tasks of local governance still fell by default to the staff of the seigneurial courts. At Coulanges-la-Vineuse in Bourgogne, a small town with 1478 inhabitants at the end of the old regime, there were 4 *échevins* elected by the general assembly of the town as head administrators, but in practice the seigneurial officials did much of the work.[269] The *procureur fiscal* served as an *ex officio* administrator of the *fabrique*, the institution which managed the church property, the school, and the hospital. The *lieutenant* of the seigneurial court supervised the administration of the town budget. The *bailli*, judge, or the *lieutenant* presided over the meetings of the town assembly and the *procureur fiscal* set the date of the vintage. Likewise, the *échevins* always turned to the judicial officials of the seigneurial court when the need arose to order recalcitrant inhabitants to clean the streets in front of their houses, to tear down dilapidated buildings, or to perform public labor services for the repair of the streets. Indeed, the seigneurial court supervised and implemented through its officials all of the police activities in the town.

The great reforming ministers of the eighteenth century, Maupeou, Turgot, Malesherbes, Necker, Calonne and Loménie de Brienne, were fully aware of the weaknesses of local governance, but they were powerless to carry out truly effective reforms. Consequently, the seigneurial courts continued their work in local administration until the Revolution instituted more modern institutions staffed by salaried officials of the state.

All told, the monarchical reforms that affected seigneurial justice and local governance under the old regime had the effect of dramatically improving the quality of work in exactly the spheres where lordships had always been strongest. The seigneurial courts remained the principal courts of first instance for the full range of civil affairs and for minor criminal affairs. The other monarchical reforms in criminal jurisdiction, local policing, and the supervision of local governance were more or less successful in precisely those areas where the lordships had never had great strength.

CHAPTER TWO

Regional Patterns of Lordship, I

Ecclesiastical Lordships

The Catholic church was one of the major lords in France. The lordships belonged individually to each ecclesiastical institution rather than to the French Catholic church as a whole. Although there was a central fiscal apparatus that handled the assessment and collection of royal taxes levied on the church, there was never any centralized administration for the properties of the church themselves. Each institution managed its own affairs.

At the end of the old regime, there were 139 bishoprics and archbishoprics, an equal number of cathedral chapters, another 500 collegial churches.[1] There were over 1000 monasteries in the eighteenth century. The clergy of France eliminated some of the decayed houses. Loménie de Brienne was particularly active in this movement and between 1766 and 1789 at least 450 minor houses disappeared. There assets were transferred to more robust abbeys. Even with this pruning there were still well over 750 ancient monasteries of monks in 1789, about half that number of female convents, hundreds of church affiliated hospitals, and several hundred more male and female service-oriented houses founded after 1500.[2]

In the late eighteenth century, Necker estimated the total net income of the Catholic church at 120,000,000 *livres.* Talleyrand, a bishop and an important financial official of the church, put the figure at 150,000,000, while Dupont de Nemours gave an even higher estimate of 180,000,000.[3] Gross revenues may have been as much as twice net, since administrative costs, essentially the share taken by tax farmers, often absorbed nearly 50% of gross proceeds in the seventeenth and eighteenth century.[4] The church's net revenues amounted to about 80% of the total income from all of the royal direct taxes, the *taille*, the *capitation,* and the *vingtième.* By any standard, the ecclesiastical revenues were enormous. Roughly two-thirds of the total income of the church came from the tithe and the final third from domain lands and seigneurial dues.[5] In the Midi, where the church owned very little domain land, tithe revenues routinely accounted for 75–90% of ecclesiastical incomes in the eighteenth century.[6]

The tithe was the most valuable, most contested, and most hated asset of the church. Some tithes established in the Middle Ages remained in the hands of laymen even at the end of the old regime. In the eighteenth century, the diocese of Poitiers had 719 parishes. In the 500 parishes for which records have survived, lay ownership of tithes appeared in 114 parishes.[7] It was highly unusual, but not completely unknown, for laymen to establish tithes on new tenures in their lordships in the early modern centuries. In Lorraine, however, lands in the ducal domain cleared between the sixteenth and the eighteenth century paid tithes to the duke, not to the church.[8] Nevertheless, the vast majority of the tithes belonged to ecclesiastical bodies.

Protests, litigation, and even flat refusals to pay the tithe occurred in the Middle Ages and resumed in the late fifteenth and early sixteenth century, decades before the appearance of any significant penetration of Protestant ideas[9]. As population recovered and even surpassed its pre-Black Death levels, agricultural prices and prices for land rose, while wages started their long decline. The periodic famines which were so characteristic of France in the sixteenth century fueled the anti-tithe protests as did the steady expansion of upperclass land ownership. Unlike seigneurial renders and *cens* which were widely considered as related in some way to a transfer of land, the tithe was resented as an unjust and confiscatory feudal tax. Opposition to the tithe also fed on the widespread but historically erroneous conviction that the tithes were being diverted from their intended use. Tithe revenues were not used primarily to support the local churches but drained off for the benefit of the least useful members of the ecclesiastical community, the high-living bishops, commendatory abbots, and canons.[10]

Some very significant episodes of violent opposition to the tithe occurred in Languedoc, Lorraine, the Ile-de-France, Picardie and elsewhere in the sixteenth century. The kings issued ordinances and edicts in support of the tithe and deployed force when necessary to enforce the law.[11] With royal support, revenues from the tithes recovered and expanded in the seventeenth century with the on-going clearance of new lands for cultivation.[12] Revenues from the tithe increased even more dramatically in the eighteenth century as grain prices rose. The church could not have maintained let alone expanded its tithes without the full support of the kings and the royal courts.

The kings of the old regime supported the tithe for the same reasons that kings of the Middle Ages had. The kings always derived substantial revenues from the church in one way or another. The wealthier the church, the more revenue there was to drain off. Moreover, tithes were the least threatening form that the ecclesiastical wealth could take. Finally, innumerable institutions which performed essential services, most notably hospitals and schools, held tithes as part of their endowments.

The institutional consolidation of the monarchy in the seventeenth century ended for the most part the violent anti-tithe protests. The full support of the monarch for tithes made open protest both pointless and dangerous. Henceforth, opposition mainly took the forms of petty deception and an endless stream of litigation.[13] From the middle of the eighteenth century, the volume of litigation rose to flood levels.[14] But, it was not until the monarchy collapsed in 1788–1789 that violent anti-tithe insurrections finally removed this hated ecclesiastical tax.

Prior to 1788–1789, it was pointless to contest the legitimacy of the tithe itself, but there was always room for litigation over actual assessment. The laws were neither clear nor uniform and rates varied enormously. Although there were a handful of royal ordinances that dealt with the tithe, the legal foundation of the tithe, like the legal foundation for lordship itself, lay in the customary laws and practices.[15] When disputes arose over the tithes, the royal courts examined the written records and even held special judicial inquiries in which the elders of the community gave testimony.[16]

Each tithing district and each ecclesiastical lordship had its own customs. Rates of 1/11 and 1/12 were common in northern France, while the rate of 1/8 was widespread in Languedoc and Gascogne. By contrast, rates in western and central France as well as in Provence were generally low, even as low as 1/22 and 1/40.[17] In the Ile-de-France, tithes on grains, the most valuable agricultural products, were assessed at 1/12, but tithes collected on the common wines were rarely more than 1/40.[18] In Normandie, the great tithe on wheat, rye, barley and oats was 1/11, but the tithe on flax, hemp, clover, and livestock was 1/13.[19]

Litigation arose when new lands came into cultivation, when new crops appeared, and when cropping practices changed. In some instances, landowners and tithe collectors negotiated amicable new rates. Such was the case in the Pays d'Auge, a region of Normandie which in the seventeenth and eighteenth century phased out grain cultivation in favor of pasture for livestock. Since the transformation of the agricultural system here was essentially the work of the upper classes, the nobles and bourgeois involved took a businesslike approach to the problem of the tithes and worked with the tithe collectors to replace the proportional tithes on grains with annual fixed cash payments.[20] In Languedoc, as indeed in most areas of France, innumerable negotiated arrangements concerning the tithe appeared during the old regime.[21]

In general, tithes were always due on the major grains, wheat, rye, oats, and barley. The spread of maize from the early seventeenth century and of potatoes in the late eighteenth century produced a concomitant outpouring of litigation.[22] The church mobilized every legal weapon in its ample arsenal to impose tithes on these new crops, achieved some limited successes, but in the process blackened its reputation as grasping and heartless.[23] Since hayfields were not uniformly subject to tithes, there was also ample room for litigation over whether the church could collect tithes on the new fodder crops such as sainfoin and alfalfa.

The greatest diversity reigned in the question of the lesser tithes on minor crops and on animals. Fruit trees were usually exempt as too were small gardens used to supply the family table.[24] However, the commercial gardens that ringed Paris paid tithes. Tithe collectors also kept a sharp eye for field crops cultivated in gardens as a way of avoiding payment.[25] Normally work animals were not tithed, but there were exceptions. Tithes on lambs were widespread, but not universal, and tithes on ewes were assessed in wool and sometimes cheese.

The second most important source of income for the church was its directly owned domain lands. Estimates of the total landed properties of the church based on the inventories drawn up in the early years of the Revolution placed the total between 6 and 10% for the entire realm, but there were enormous regional variations. In the northern part of the Ile-de-France, in Beauvaisis, Picardie, Laonnois and Cambrésis, as well as in Hurepoix located south of Paris, the church owned nearly 40% of the land, 19% in Bourgogne, 18% in eastern Champagne, less than 10% in Touraine, less than 4% in the *bocage* areas of western France, 5–6% in Bordelais, Gascogne, Languedoc, Provence, and Lyonnais and in some parts of the Midi only 1–2%.[26] These regional variations were already in place in the Middle Ages and reflected the uneven distribution of wealth, population densities, and consequently royal, princely and aristocratic patronage north and south of the Loire.

In the Midi, the church owned little land directly and consequently derived most of its revenues from the tithe. In Bordelais, none of the major ecclesiastical bodies owned significant domain lands. At the end of the eighteenth century, the archbishop of Bordeaux drew only a little more than 1/6th of his modest income of 65,777 *livres* from domain lands. The reserved lands of the cathedral chapter of Saint-André of Bordeaux consisted essentially of urban properties near the cathedral and cloister. Neither the collegial church of Saint-Seurin nor the abbeys of La Sauve-Majeure and Sainte-Croix at Bordeaux owned extensive domain lands.[27] Similarly, the temporal possessions of the cathedral chapters and the collegial churches in Agenais and Périgord consisted of tithes, a few scraps of domain land, lands in tenure that paid *cens*, and a few modern *rentes*. Tithes normally accounted from between 75% and 90% of total revenues in the eighteenth century.[28]

There was no ecclesiastical institution in the Midi with wealth comparable to that of the great bishoprics, cathedral chapters and monasteries in northern France. The wealthiest church in the Midi in the eighteenth century was probably the archbishopric of Auch with 150,000 *livres* of income drawn essentially from the tithe. The revenues of the bishops of Oloron, Lescar and Dax were 13,000, 15,000 and 18,000 *livres;* the bishops of Bayonne, Lectoure and Lombex had 20,000 *livres* each; and the bishops of Aire and Saint-Bertrand-de-Comminges had 30,000 *livres* each.[29]

The third major source of income for the church was seigneurial dues and fees. For ecclesiastical lordships as indeed for noble, princely and royal lordships, *droits seigneuriaux* were normally the least important source of income. At the end of the eighteenth century, the major ecclesiastical lordships in Paris, principally the archbishopric, the cathedral chapter of Notre-Dame, and the abbeys of Saint-Germain-des-Prés, Sainte-Geneviève, and Saint-Martin-des-Champs, had total revenues of 3,220,000 *livres*.[30] Rural domain lands brought in 35% of the total, leases of urban properties produced 27% and *droits seigneuriaux* around 30%. The *lods et ventes,* transfer fees for real property, were by far the most productive *droits seigneuriaux* and accounted for 27% of total revenues. This very strong showing of *lods et ventes* in the Parisian ecclesiastical houses was exceptional and was the product of the sky-high prices for urban real estate in Paris in the late eighteenth century. Excluding *lods et ventes*, the major ecclesiastical lordships in Paris drew less than 5% of their total incomes from renders and other seigneurial dues. In the Norman Pays de Caux in the seventeenth and eighteenth centuries, a more typical pattern appeared. Seigneurial dues and fees averaged around 10% of total ecclesiastical revenues.[31]

Although most of the ecclesiastical property dated from the Middle Ages, the temporal possessions of the church were not completely static during the old regime. During the Wars of Religion, the church sold some of its assets to pay for royal taxes. Between 1563 and 1588, the kings of France levied extraordinary taxes on the catholic church which came to more than 11 million *livres*. The mendicant orders, the parish churches and the Hospitalers were exempt. The monasteries, bishoprics and cathedral chapters paid the majority of the assessment. To raise such an enormous amount of money in a short period of time, the ecclesiastical institutions had to sell some of their holdings. For the most part, the ecclesiastical institutions sold their least valuable properties. These sixteenth century forced sales always stipulated that the church could repurchase its alienated properties at some later date.[32] With the support of the kings and particularly Cardinal Richelieu, the church recovered most of these properties during the peak of the Catholic Counter-Reformation in the seventeenth century.

At least some ecclesiastical bodies increased their holdings of domain lands and *seigneuries* through bequests, royal gifts, and simple purchases during the old regime. The increases in landed properties occurred in exactly the same areas where the church was already heavily endowed in 1500, mainly north of the Loire. While some expansion occurred during the first half of the sixteenth century, most of the growth came during the first two thirds of the seventeenth century.[33] Richelieu and Louis XIII favored monastic growth. Louis XIII gave significant lands to Saint-Denis, to the reformed Cistercian abbey of Trappes, and to Sainte-Geneviève. The Cistercian nuns at Port-Royal also received royal support in the construction of an estate of middling importance.

Ecclesiastical property expanded in the best grain-growing lands of the Ile-de-France in the sixteenth and seventeenth centuries despite the forced sales during the Wars of Religion.[34] The Cistercians at Plessis-Gassot received a gift of two farms with 130 ha of land in 1521. The Cathedral Chapter of Notre-Dame benefitted from many gifts in the late fifteenth and sixteenth century and in 1693 purchased a domain-farm of 193 ha for 100,000 *livres* at Belloy-en-France. In 1681, the abbey of Saint-Geneviève bought a domain-farm of 53 ha and added it to its existing property at Vémars. At Gonesse, the Carmelites bought two farms in 1632 and a third in 1677 and combined them into a single property that covered 181 ha. Similarly, the monks of Saint-Germain-des-Prés in Paris expanded their domain lands in the seventeenth century.[35] The monks were active in selling and buying properties. Often the kings forced the abbey to sell lands to the crown or to prominent aristocrats. Between 1631 and 1710, the total value of sales in the *mense conventuelle* was 424,125 *livres*, but purchases amounted to 985,127 *livres,* which left a net gain of urban and rural properties worth 525,002 *livres.*

The growth of ecclesiastical property slowed dramatically during the reign of Louis XIV. Complaints about land engrossing in both urban and rural areas, although hardly new, became more insistent. Likewise, the King and Colbert were concerned about losses of significant royal revenues from property transfer fees since lands that came into the hands of the church rarely appeared on the market again. In 1666 and 1693, Louis XIV issued edicts which sharply restricted further growth of ecclesiastical property. Renewed complaints in the first half of the eighteenth century eventually led Louis XV to issue yet another edict in 1749 which effectively ended the expansion of ecclesiastical property in

France.[36]

The expansion of ecclesiastical property north of the Loire was far from universal among the various sorts of religious institutions. In general, the archbishoprics and bishoprics experienced little change. There was some transfer of ecclesiastical assets from monastic to episcopal benefices, most notably when new dioceses were established. There certainly were several well-endowed episcopal benefices with extensive urban and rural properties, but these rarely expanded in the early modern period. As a rule, the archbishops and bishops were political appointees who drained off the revenues of their offices. Few attempted to expand the episcopal patrimonies.

The cathedral chapters, especially those whose canons were secular rather than regular clerics, were a little more dynamic than the bishoprics.[37] Regular clerics, usually members of the Augustinian order, were bound at least in theory by their vows of poverty, but secular canons took no such vow. Canons were drawn from the aristocracy and the bourgeois class as a rule. They came from wealthy families. Many were actively engaged in land speculation and not a few in usury. On their deaths, many canons left their accumulated estates to their cathedral chapters.

The cathedral chapters were usually very wealthy. The cathedral chapter of Tours had an income of 133,000 *livres* in the late eighteenth century, while the cathedral chapter of Chartes had around 300,000 *livres*.[38] Although the cathedral chapters and collegial churches certainly had landed property, normally they derived most of their revenues from tithes. Normandie had 7 dioceses and hence 7 cathedral chapters and another 18 collegial churches at the end of the old regime. Together, the chapters owned 5000 ha of land, 329 urban houses and more than 150 other buildings. Although this landed patrimony was significant, many individual Cistercian monasteries in Champagne and Bourgogne had far greater holdings. The Norman chapters derived most of their revenues from tithes. The cathedral chapter of Evreux had total revenues of 68,444 *livres*, 75% from tithes; Lisieux, had 76,662 livres, 84% from tithes; and the cathedral chapter of Bayeux had 89,726 *livres* of revenues, 91% from tithes.[39]

The ancient male religious orders surpassed all other ecclesiastical bodies in the ownership of real estate. They held at least half of the total landed patrimony of the church.[40] The Benedictines, Cluniacs, Cistercians, Carthusians and Premonstratensians had vast landed estates established in the Middle Ages. The ancient male religious orders were also second to none in rigorous estate management, but relatively few of them expanded their holdings significantly in the early modern centuries. Virtually all of the monasteries had divided their assets into two parts, *menses*, one for the abbot and the other for the monks. These ancient monasteries came in every size, from grand abbeys that had holdings equal to those of peers of the realm to modest houses with incomes similar to those of petty nobles. The tiny abbey of Belle-Etoile founded in Normandie in 1216 had total revenues of only 6296 *livres* in 1751.[41]

The monastic lordships north of the Loire were composite properties that closely resembled the aristocratic lordships. In general, the largest of the old Benedictine abbeys drew more of their income from domain lands than from tithes and seigneurial dues, while the reverse was true for the smaller monasteries. For example, the Benedictine abbey of Saint-Aubin at Angers derived 60% of its total revenues of 110,000 livres from its domain lands on the eve of the Revolution, while two smaller Benedictine abbeys in Bretagne, Saint-Georges of Rennes and Saint-Sauveur de Redon, with 70,000 *livres* and 40,000 *livres* respectively, derived less than 10% of their revenues from their domain. Both relied essentially on tithes and *droits seigneuriaux*.[42]

The patrimony of the venerable abbey of Saint-Germain-des-Prés in Paris had the typical property structure found in major Benedictine monasteries.[43] South of Paris, Saint-Germain-des-Prés owned innumerable lordships with domain lands that totaled 2000 ha. At Antony, a village that covered 860 ha, the abbey owned 350 ha, 42% of the land. The domain lands appeared as three large farms of 111 ha, 93 ha and 67 ha and another 36 ha of scattered fields, vineyards, and houses leased to 63 individuals. Nearby, the abbey owned another 340 ha of forest and a château. Total revenues from the *seigneurie* of Antony without counting the tithe levied at 1/9 were 28,046 *livres* at the end of the old regime. Strictly seigneurial renders, *cens* and other fees brought in only 1,494 *livres*, while directly owned domain lands produced the rest. Despite the minor importance of *droits seigneuriaux*, the abbey maintained rigorous administration and collection of its *cens*. There were two recent *terriers* drawn up in 1768 and

1785 and two geographically accurate atlases which showed the location, the boundaries and the size of every piece of property in the lordship.

As a rule, the Cistercian abbeys drew even less income from *droits seigneuriaux* than the Benedictines and Cluniacs. The original rule of the Cistercians prohibited the ownership of lordships and tithes. The Cistercian abbey of Morimond in Champagne retained most of its medieval structure. The abbey had 3700 ha of land organized into 17 domain-farms or *granges*. Although the abbey had tithes that brought in good revenues, it collected few renders, *cens* and seigneurial fees. In the 1760s, the abbey had a total income of about 60,000 *livres*. Fully 76% of its revenues came from the lease of its landed properties while the remaining 24% came from the tithe.[44]

In Alsace, yet another pattern prevailed. Ecclesiastical institutions owed between 1/4 and 1/3 of the land, but this rarely took the form of the classic French domain-farm. Rather, Alsace followed German practice. Most of the church's land consisted of innumerable tiny plots and farms interspersed haphazardly with peasant tenures. These domain lands were let on leases which were often indistinguishable from perpetual tenures and which produced very modest incomes.[45]

The kings distributed most of the ancient male monasteries as patronage offices to politically appointed bishops and even laymen who served as titular abbots *in commendam*.[46] Cardinal Richelieu was the commendatory abbot of 71 abbeys. Mazarin was equally shameless. At the beginning of the Revolution, the Cardinal de La Rochefoucauld was the archbishop of Rouen as well as the commandatory abbot of several major monasteries, most notably Cluny in Mâconnais and Fécamp in Normandie. His total income of more than 400,000 *livres* came mainly from the monasteries.[47] The spiritual life of the monasteries suffered more from the commendatory system than the temporal. Normally, monasteries *in commendam* were administered by professional estate managers. On the rare occasions when the commendatory abbots became more directly involved by using supervisory stewards or intendants, the result was usually more rigorous management.[48]

The ancient male monastic orders were arguably the most corrupt and politically abused institutions in a church characterized by aristocratic exploitation. Even the introduction of monastic reform in the Benedictine houses in the form of the order of Saint-Maur had little real impact on the spiritual life of the monasteries, but it often tightened up estate administration.[49] Normally titular abbots simply drained off the revenues of the abbatial *mense* and took no part in the religious life of the monastery. Monks in charge of the conventual *mense* often behaved similarly. Old noble families and robe nobles from the *Parlements* routinely installed their lesser children as monks in the wealthiest monasteries where they lived a life suitable to their birth.[50]

Some of the old monasteries were among the wealthiest property owners in the realm.[51] Among the Benedictine houses, Saint-Ouen of Rouen had 4000 ha of farmland in 27 farms, 1400 ha of forest and 77 houses in Rouen. Fécamp, also in Normandie, had holdings that were comparable as did Saint-Bénigne in Dijon. The leaders among the Cistercians were Cîteaux and Clairvaux. Clairvaux had innumerable domain-farms or *granges*, 9000 ha of forests, iron foundries, and urban properties in Paris, Troyes, Reims, and Dijon. Also near the top were the venerable Benedictine abbeys in Paris, Saint-Denis, Saint-Germain-des-Prés, Sainte-Geneviève, and the priory of Saint-Martin-des-Champs.

The knights of Saint-Jean of Jerusalem, popularly referred to as the Order of Malta or the Hospitalers, had old-fashioned lordships scatter all over France which, according to estimates made by the Constituent Assembly in 1790, brought in revenues of 4,284,650 *livres.*[52] The holdings of the Order of Malta were stable during the old regime. Although domain lands predominated in some *commanderies* of Malta, in general the assets of the Order consisted of tithes, *droits seigneuriaux*, and domain lands in declining order of importance. The *commanderie* of Poët-Laval in Dauphiné was typical. In the eighteenth century, tithes brought in a little more than a third of the total revenues, tithes and *droits seigneuriaux* together came to 70% and the remaining 30% came from domain lands.[53] At Pézenas, less commonly, the *commanderie* of Saint-Jean drew most of its revenues from its domain.[54]

The old female religious orders were less numerous and usually far less wealthy than their male counterparts.[55] The female Benedictine abbey of Notre-Dame de Montivilliers founded in 682 in Haute-Normandie had a patrimony that consisted essentially of seigneurial dues and tithes.[56] The Benedictine nuns of

Sainte-Croix at Poitiers managed their patrimony carefully and had respectable revenues of around 25,000 *livres* in the eighteenth century.[57]

Unlike the old monasteries, hospitals were very dynamic and routinely expanded their assets. At the end of the old regime, there were nearly 2000 hospitals in France.[58] Some of these charitable institutions were extremely old while others appeared only after 1500. Although there were some purely secular hospitals, most were affiliated with the Catholic church in one way or another. Many had a religious personnel composed of Augustinian nuns or Sisters of Charity.

The wealthiest hospital in France was the Hôpital Général of Paris which had annual revenues of around 1,850,000 *livres* in the middle of the eighteenth century. The Hôtel-Dieu of Paris had revenues in excess of 1,300,000 *livres* in the 1780s. Major hospitals in even modest provincial capitals such as Grenoble, Troyes, and Montpellier had over 100,000 and in some cases over 200,000 *livres* of income. Hospitals in even smaller towns still had significant revenues. The Hôtel-Dieu of Amiens had 64,000 *livres* a year while the Hôtel-Dieu of Chateaudun had 30,250 *livres*.[59] Only the very wealthiest nobles surpassed these charitable institutions in annual income.

As a whole, the hospitals tended to have more diverse and slightly more modern assets than the bishoprics, cathedral chapters and monasteries. Virtually all of the hospitals came under municipal oversight and served as public charitable institutions. As such, they had a keener interest in productive assets than in prestige properties. Tithes were always valuable, as were solid domain-farms and good rental urban properties. These old-fashioned assets seem to have produced about half of the annual revenues of the hospitals.[60] The 1749 edict prohibited the hospitals from further acquisitions of real estate. In the last few decades of the old regime, they turned to more modern assets.[61] Royal and municipal annuities were sound investments as too were private loans established as *rentes constituées*.

The Hôtel-Dieu of Lyon was a typical charitable institution with a particularly modern endowment and a very business-like administration.[62] Founded in 542 by King Childebert and affiliated with a collegial church, the hospital operated under the authority of the archbishop of Lyon until 1486 when the municipal government of Lyon took it over. From the end of the fifteenth century until the Revolution, the municipal government managed the temporal affairs of the hospital. Twelve lay rectors chosen by the municipal government from the leading businessmen of the city administered the hospital. Seigneurial properties were of minimal importance in its endowment. Between 1758 and 1767, average revenues stood at 519,800 *livres* a year. The single most important source of income was rental houses, apartments, and commercial buildings in Lyon which produced 145,700 *livres*. Rural properties, 81 farms that ranged in size from less than 10 ha to more than 100 ha, brought in 43,800 *livres*. The rest, over 300,000 *livres,* came from annuities issued by the municipal governments of Paris and Lyon, cash legacies paid in perpetuity, a share in the municipal taxes levied on wine, etc. The rural properties dated mainly from the eighteenth century. The hospital had only three rural domains in 1660, but as agricultural prices rose in the eighteenth century, the administrators acquired the rest.[63]

The bourgeois administrators of the Hôtel-Dieu of Amiens displayed the same hard-nosed concern for good returns from assets.[64] Between the beginning of the sixteenth and the end of the eighteenth century, the administrators tripled the size of the rural farmlands. With the support of the monarchy, the tithes regained their value and remained at least a minor source of income. By contrast, the lay admnistrators largely ignored the seigneurial renders and *cens*. At their peak in the early sixteenth century, *droits seigneuriaux* listed in 290 distinct entries brought in 15% of the total revenues of the Hôtel-Dieu. By 1688, only 100 of these itemized *cens* were still active and they produced only 0.5% of total incomes. In 1789, the Hôtel-Dieu collected *cens* from only a few dozen tenures worth perhaps 1/1000 of the total income of the hospital.

Finally, there were also hundreds of service oriented male and female religious orders founded in France after 1500. Some were entirely new orders, like the Jesuits, the Ursulines, the Oratorians, while others were reformed branches of orders that dated from the Middle Ages, like some Carmelite monasteries, Augustinian and Franciscan houses. There were also countless less famous orders. Most of the new orders were engaged in social services. They ran schools, hospitals, and orphanages, or they were active in missionary work.

Kings often made use of their powers under the system of commendation to transfer properties from old houses to new. For example, kings took properties from ancient monasteries to endow the new diocescan seminaries at Reims and Uzès. Royal edicts transferred part of the holdings of the abbatial *mense* of Saint-Martin-au-Bois to endow the famous Jesuit college of Louis-le-Grand in Paris. Similarly, when Mme de Maintenon founded the abbey of Saint-Cyr, Louis XIV took property of the abbatial *mense* of Saint-Denis.[65] All told, however, the new ecclesiastical houses had only modest endowments.[66]

The Royal Domain and Princely Lordships

At the end of the Middle Ages, the king of France was the most important lord in the realm. In the narrowest sense, the royal domain included all of the lordships which belonged directly to the king. These lordships appeared in every province in France, from Flanders in the north to the Foix in the south, and from Normandie, Bretagne and the Bordelais in the west to the two Bourgognes, Dauphiné and Provence in the east. Although seriously compromised by the creation of royal appanages in the thirteenth and fourteenth centuries, the royal domain recovered and expanded its holdings in the second half of the fifteenth century with the end of the appanage principalities and the death of most the great feudal lords. With the fall of the Constable of Bourbon in the 1520s and the confiscation of most of his lands, the royal domain reached its greatest extent ever.

The royal domain had thousands of lordships organized as duchies, counties, baronies and simple *seigneuries*, along with hundreds of forests, fish ponds, salt mines, iron mines, etc. Under the supervision of the various *chambres des comptes*, the royal domain still produced what were called the ordinary revenues of the crown.[67] Although the medieval kings for centuries had derived the bulk of their revenues from the royal domain, the establishment of the royal *taille* and the royal indirect taxes in the second half of the fourteenth century to finance the Hundred Years' War totally transformed royal finances. By the early 1460s the new royal taxes brought in 97% of the king's revenues and the domain only 3%.[68]

This dramatic transformation of the nature of royal revenues led the kings to adopt a new policy for the royal domain. Henceforth, the kings used the lordships and other properties of the domain to reward political supporters, royal mistresses, provincial governors, and high officeholders of the crown. They also alienated royal properties to creditors for ready cash. Louis XI led the way in the 1470s by distributing lands that he had just recovered with the death of Charles the Bold of Bourgogne to faithful supporters and royal bankers.[69] The later Valois and Bourbon kings pursued the same policies.[70]

The *parlements* and the *chambres des comptes* vehemently opposed the spoliation of crown properties and held firm to the legal fiction of the inalienability of the royal domain even though they could not prevent the kings from disposing of crown properties for political and financial reasons. Although the kings gave some properties away, usually they sold them. The ordinance of Moulins of 1566 regularized the procedure for the alienation of parts of the royal domain. The kings sold parts of the royal domain with a perpetual right of repurchase to buyers called *engagistes* who in turn paid the crown an annual rent or *cens*.[71] The kings also assigned crown properties to the princes of the blood as appanages. Lands transferred to the new appanage princes remained with their heirs in the direct male line and were technically distinct from lands transferred, *engagé*, to lesser lords, mistresses or creditors, *engagistes*.[72]

By the end of the sixteenth century, the kings had alienated virtually all of the royal domaine except the forests and the favorite royal châteaux. Henry IV and Louis XIII, or more accurately Sully and Richelieu, attempted to redeem the royal domain, but what they took back with one hand they gave with another. Richelieu and Mazarin helped themselves shamelessly to the royal domain lands and by 1661 the domain brought in only 80,000 livres, less than the income from one major titled lordship. Colbert repurchased part of the royal domain and by 1682 it brought in over 5,500,000 livres, but Louis XIV's wars soon reversed this trend. Colbert saved most of the forests whose administration he strengthened with the famous ordinance of 1669 for waters and forests.[73] Louis XV and Louis XVI acted no differently from their immediate predecessors, but Louis XVI probably added more to than he subtracted from the crown lands. Louis XVI expanded the royal holdings not as a fiscal asset but for the personal use of the royal family, most notably by pressuring the duke of Penthièvre to sell him the duchy of Rambouillet in 1783 for 16 million *livres*.[74]

A full history of the royal domaine under the old regime has never been attempted and probably could not be written because many of the documents perished in the 1737 fire at the Parisian *chambre des comptes*. In any event, such a history would document the constant flow of properties back and forth between the crown, members of the royal family, a myriad of favorites and creditors. Over the centuries, the kings transferred many of the lordships in the royal domain to the appanage princes. In 1661, Louis XIV established the appanage of Orléans for his brother, Philippe. Orléans was one of the oldest parts of the royal domain. Prior to 1661, the lands in the appanage had been in the hands of Louis XIV's uncle, Gaston d'Orléans, and so on back to the fourteenth century. The 1661 appanage covered 1/20th of the landmass of France and extended from Berry and Orléans northward through Paris and the Ile-de-France to Picardie and then eastward into Champagne. The appanage included some of the most prestigious duchies and counties in France: Orléans, Valois, Chartres, Nemours, Romorantin, Coucy, La Fère, Soissons, Laon and Noyon, as well as the Palais Royal in Paris.[75] The appanage for the Count of Artois, established in 1773, initially included the duchies of Angoulême, Auvergne, and Mercoeur, the marquisat of Pompadour, and the *vicomtés* of Limoges and Turenne. Because these lands did not produce the expected revenues of 200,000 *livres*, the king took back the forests from the duchy of Angoulême, the marquisat of Pompadour, and the *vicomtés* of Limoges and Turenne, and then transferred to the appanage the duchies of Berry and Châteauroux, the counties of Argenton and Ponthieu, and the *seigneurie* of Henrichement.[76] Royal favorites also received many lordships for the royal domain. During the reign of Louis XIV, Turenne received the ducal peerages of Albret and Château-Thierry, the counties of Auvergne and Evreux, and the barony of La Tour. Many of these properties and others flowed back into the royal domain when Louis XV purchased the *vicomté* of Turenne in 1738.[77]

In addition to the constant flow of lordships into and out of the royal domain, the kings occasionally embellished the royal residences for their own use. The most famous example of this sort of undertaking was Versailles which grew from a small royal hunting lodge under Louis XIII to the principal royal residence under Louis XIV. Indeed, the construction of Versailles demonstrated some of the most important themes in the history of lordship in northern France under the old regime. We find the step by step movement from fragmented fiefs to consolidated titled lordships. At first, royal office holders and bourgeois bought up the lands of petty medieval noble families. The new owners then fell victim to the land engrossing of the great nobles of the realm, who in turn ceded ground to the king. Running slightly behind chronologically was the on-going dispossession of peasant land holders and the concentration of farmlands and forests into larger and larger commercial enterprises.[78]

At the end of the fifteenth and the beginning of the sixteenth century, the territory which eventually became the royal estate at Versailles was highly fragmented. The king held the *châtellenies* of Poissy and Châteaufort as well as part of the forest at Cruye. The great Parisian monasteries were present: Saint-Denis at Rueil and Trappes, Saint-Germaine-des-Prés at Celle and Chesnay, and Sainte-Geneviève at Choisy and Trianon. The Célestins were established at Porchefontaine and the Collège de Montaigu at Bois-d'Arcy and Fontenay. In addition, there were no less than thirty lay seigneuries and fiefs. Already in 1500, the lesser noble families had lost most of their patrimonial holdings to Parisian investors. The old nobles held only six lordships and lesser fiefs out of thirty, royal office holders in the courts and financial bureaus owned eighteen, and a final four were in the hands of simple bourgeois of Paris. The consolidation of farmland had not yet progressed very far around 1500 and peasants still held on to roughly two-thirds of cultivated fields.

In the sixteenth and early seventeenth century, the great court nobles displaced the lesser royal officials and bourgeois as owners of fiefs and *seigneuries* which they consolidated into new titled lordships. At the same time, they bought up forests and cobbled togther old noble domain-farms and peasant holdings. By the middle of the seventeenth century, large seigneurial domain-farms covered half the land of many parishes. Some of the most illustrious nobles in France carried out this work: the Cardinal of Lorraine at Chevreuse and Meudon; several generations of Gondis at Noisy, Marly, Bailly, Versailles, and Villepruex; Servien and eventually Louvois at Meudon.

The systematic expansion of royal holdings near Versailles began rather slowly in the early seventeenth century. Louis XIII carried out the same sort of consolidation as the Cardinal of Lorraine or Albert de Gondi, but on a greater scale and with the authority to expropriate any estate he set his eyeson. Louis XIII forced Jean-François de Gondi, archbishop of Paris, to abandoned his lands. Louis XIV greatly accelerated the expansion of Versailles from 1662 with his decision to create an entirely new royal residence. The Abbey of Sainte-Geneviève lost Trianon, the nuns of Saint-Cyr gave up Guyancourt, Buc and Voisins, while the Collège de Montaigu surrendered Bois-d'Arcy. Louis XIV demolished the old village of Trianon, started the construction of the *château* in 1668 and created a new town at Versailles in 1671.

In 1715, the domaine of Versailles covered fifteen parishes where the king was now virtually the only lord. The royal palace had 3500 ha of farmland and 2500 ha of forest. Organized with its own judicial *bailliage* and fitted out with entirely recast seigneurial dues, Versailles in 1715 stood as a single, unified lordship which encompassed an area that once had belonged to no less than forty distinct lordships and fiefs. Louis XV and Louis XVI expanded Versailles' holdings even further. In 1747, Louis XV added the domains of the Célestins and in 1766 annexed Clagny and Glatingny which Louis XIV had established for his mistress Madame de Montespan. Louis XVI added Meudon in 1778 which had formerly belonged to the Le Tellier family.

At the end of the old regime, the domain at Versailles was more than twice what it had been in 1715. It covered 13,000 ha, of which 6000 ha was in forest and 5000 ha in 35 domain-farms. In keeping with the economic trends in the Ile-de-France, the kings organized their domain-farms into ever larger entities. In 1727 the average size of a grain and livestock farm was 110 ha and in 1790 it was 153. The revenues of Versailles were, of course, not comparable to those of other aristocratic estates. Indeed, most of the budget of over seven million *livres* came from earmarked royal tax revenues, specifically the income from the indirect royal taxes at Versailles. But, considering only the strictly seigneurial incomes, the revenues of Versailles were fairly typical of aristocratic estates in the Ile-de-France. The forest brought in the bulk of the income, around 400,000 livres a year at the end of the old regime, the domain-farms around 120,000 livres, and the various seigneurial taxes and dues around 20,000 livres, mainly from *lods et ventes*.

The princely lordships were simply smaller versions of the great royal estates which ranged in size from the large estates of old feudal families like the Montmorency in the sixteenth century to the massive estates of the princes of the blood in the last century of the old regime. The accumulation and consolidation of landed estates, whether carried out by kings or the leading nobles of the realm, was almost always a multi-generational endeavor. The Montmorency family, one of the great noble families of France, steadily expanded their patrimony in the fifteenth and sixteenth centuries through careful marriages, strict family discipline in inheritance, and through enormous investment financed in part from royal pensions.[79] To the already considerable ancestral lands that the family owned at Montmorency, Jean II de Montmorency, 1414-70, added two new clusters of lordships thanks to two marriages, the second with Marguerite d'Orgemont that brought in a very large cluster of lands carefully assembled by a Parisian *parlementaire* family that included Chantilly. In the early sixteenth century, Guillaume de Montmorency expanded the estate with two marriages and by purchases. By the 1520s the Montmorency estate included five major *châteaux* at Ecouen, Chantilly, Thoré, Mello and La Rocheport along with three *hôtels* in Paris.

The famous sixteenth century Constable Anne de Montmorency, who died in 1567, continued this work. He managed and expanded his estate with great care over a forty year period. By the 1560s, the estate of Anne de Montmorency included dozens of *seigneuries* in the Ile-de-France, in Picardie, Bourgogne, Normandie, Champagne, Angoumois, Berry and Bretagne, seven major *châteaux* and four Parisian *hôtels*. Royal pensions and salaries of all sorts rose from 30 or 40,000 *livres* a year in the 1520s and 1530s to 50,000 in the 1550s, and still 45,000 *livres* at the time of his death in 1567. Although Anne de Montmorency received some lands from the royal domain as compensation for his services, he purchased most of the new estates. He took advantage of his high political position to watch closely the land market at the summit of French society. He made many of his acquisitions by bidding on the confiscated properties of fallen political and financial figures put up for sale by the *Parlement* of Paris. In the 1550s he spent an average of 150,000 *livres* a year on estate purchases and on clearing his properties of *rentes*.

Once lordships had reached a certain size and honorific status in the hierarchy of fiefs, they became part of a very exclusive real-estate market and circulated through marriage and purchase only among the highest noble families. Much of the Montmorency estate passed by marriage in the early seventeenth century to the princes of Bourbon-Condé: the *château* of Chantilly and its *seigneurie*, the ducal peerage of Montmorency and the duchy of Enghien-Montmorency.[80] The marquisat of Chilly followed a similar path. In the early seventeenth century, the *seigneuries* of Chilly and Longjumeau, located south of Paris in the Hurepoix, belonged to the d'Effiat family. In 1624, Marshal d'Effiat obtained royal letters patent which elevated these lands to the status of a marquisat and in 1627 he expanded the marquisat with the barony of Massy which he purchased from the Duke of Luxembourg. In 1719, the d'Effiat family died out and Chilly passed to the Duke of Mazarin.[81]

The massive consolidation of lordships by the most prominent nobles in France was certainly one of the most striking transformations of lordship in the late medieval and early modern centuries. Some of these consolidated properties eventually received the prestigious title of a ducal peerage, *duché-pairie*, and their owners became hereditary dukes and peers of the realm, *ducs et pairs*. Prior to the Hundred Years' War, there were only 12 peerages in the realm, six duchies and six counties, half held by churchmen and half by aristocratic lords. In the fourteenth century, there were thirty-four elevations. Until the beginning of the sixteenth century, only members of the royal family, members of the highest feudal and foreign noble families were elevated to the dignity of peers. The first elevation of a lesser man was in 1519 with the elevation of Artus Gouffier, *grand maître de France*. Between 1519 and 1790 there were 128 elevations.[82]

The inflation in noble titles which started in the sixteenth century and continued until the end of the old regime was at least in part associated with the consolidation of lordships at the top of the noble hierarchy. Although much of the money for the construction of these new titled lordships came from high government office in the royal household, in the central administration of state, in the provinces and from high military command positions, the lands that were elevated to the ducal peerages were overwhelmingly patrimonial, personal possessions, not grants of property from the royal domain. In one sense, the elevation of a large cluster of lands to the dignity of an hereditary ducal peerage was royal recognition for the successfully consolidation of fiefs and lordships carried out by the most wealthy and ambitious noble families of the realm.

The elevations to the dignity of ducal peerages by letters patent were far less frequent than the elevation of simple lordships into castellanies, baronies, counties, and marquisats. Titles beneath the dignity of a ducal peerage were also frequently usurped, especially in the sixteenth and early seventeenth centuries, but there were no usurpations of ducal peerages. According to the most widely accepted standards, it took three castellanies to make a barony, two baronies or one barony and 5 castellanies to make a county, three baronies and five castellanies to form a marquisat, and four counties to make a duchy. The detachment of significant lordships from a ducal peerage could compromise its honorific status and often led to the extinction of the title.[83]

Although vast by the standards of the time, the ducal peerages of the old regime were not remotely comparable in size or in power to the great medieval principalities. The average ducal peerage, its lands compacted for purposes of measurement, was equivalent to the area of two or three modern cantons or 5% to 8% of a single modern *département*. The administrative reforms of the Revolution divided the terriroty of the medieval duchy of Bretagne into five *départements*, and that of Bourgogne into four.

Both the numbers of ducal peerages and their geographical location reflected the underlying wealth of old regime France. In 1519 there were 9 living ducal peers, in 1589 there were 23. By 1661 the number had risen to 56, and 60 in 1715. There was a slight drop in the eighteenth century with 53–54 in 1774 and 58–59 in 1790. The expansion of the company of ducal peers was undoubtedly related to the increasing wealth of France over the centuries. Even more telling was the geographic location of the ducal peerages. Of the 128 elevations, 70% were located in northern France, north of a line from La Roche-sur-Yon to Lons-le-Saunier, and only 30% were in the center of France and the Midi. At the top of the list were the Ile-de-France with 16, Champagne with 16, the Bordelais and Gascogne had 12, Normandie 10, Orléanais 8, Picardie 6 but only 3 in Languedoc and 1 in Provence.[84] Although proximity to Versailles and Paris certainly figured into the locale of the ducal peerages, the geographical distribution of these titled lordships, apart from the booming Bordelais and its economic hinterland, was remarkable similar to the concentration of great lordships, royal, ecclesiastical and aristocratic, in Merovingian, Carolingian and Capetian times.

La Meilleraye, the largest lordship in Poitou offers a good example of an old regime ducal peerage.[85] The La Porte family were already well-established provincial nobles in Poitou by the sixteenth century. From a solid patrimonial base, the family expanded its holdings with the purchase of the *seigneurie* of La Meilleraye in 1574. At the beginning of the seventeenth century, the estate consisted of three lordships with seven domain-farms or *métairies* with a total of 300 ha. With a long family tradition of military service, Charles de La Porte rose rapidly under Richelieu and became a marshal of France. La Porte used his new position and salary to buy lordships and lands. Between 1634 and 1641 he spent over 500,000 livres to purchased 6 major lordships, one of which was the barony of Parthenay. A good marriage and additional royal favor led to the acquisition of three more lordships and some lesser fiefs. By 1663, the domain of Le Meilleraye was complete. In 1663, La Meilleraye was elevated to the status of a ducal peerage.[86]

The ducal peerage of La Meilleraye was a carefully constructed assemblage of fifteen formerly distinct lordships, with forests and farmland centered on Parthenay and Secondigny. The fortune of the family rose even further under Armand Charles de La Porte, who through marriage to Mazarin's niece Hortense became the duke of Mazarin, 1664–1713, and eventually royal governor of Haute and Basse Alsace. In the late seventeenth century, La Meilleraye was only one of many major seigneurial properties of the duke who was now well-established in the Ile-de-France and Bourgogne. The duke's political career faded in the 1690s.[87]

The next generation lived in Paris from the 1730s and in 1776 the Duchess of Mazarin sold the heavily indebted duchy of La Meilleraye for 1.4 million *livres* to the Count of Artois. The entire purchase price went to creditors. The Count of Artois then partially disassembled the duchy, sold off some of its assets and netted a nice profit. Prior to its dismemberment, the duchy of La Meilleraye had 1350 ha of farmland organized in 33 *métairies*, 3100 ha of forests, used for lumber and the production of charcoal for a number of iron foundries, and a very valuable base of feudal and seigneurial rights. Total revenues in 1775 stood at 61,000 *livres*, of which 41% came from the feudal and seigneurial dues. Annual cens in cash collected in 70 parishes brought in 1000 *livres*, but the proportional *terrages* collected in the major grains at 1/6 produced 7500 *livres*. Transfer fees for feudal fiefs, *rachat*, taxes for the sale of fiefs and tenures, *lods et ventes*, accounted for another 5–6,000 *livres* a year.[88]

As impressive as the ducal peerages were as newly consolidated lordships, they paled in comparison to the estates of the late seventeenth and eighteenth century princes of the blood. Certainly the Bourbon-Penthièvre were among the most successful land engrossers in eighteenth century France.[89] The Count of Toulouse was the seventh and last child of Louis XIV and Mme de Montespan, born in 1678 at Versailles. His son was the Duke of Penthièvre who still headed the family at the time of the Revolution. Thanks in part to royal generosity and public office, this legitimized branch of the royal family acquired a status and wealth in keeping with its birth. Both Toulouse and Penthièvre were extremely conscientious in the management and the expansion of their estates. From the 1680s, Toulouse had a princely administrative apparatus set up by Louis XIV that mirrored the standard system in use from the late Middle Ages to the Revolution. At the time of his death in 1737, the estate of the Count of Toulouse was estimated at 13.5 million *livres*. In 1789–90, the estate of the Duke of Penthièvre stood at 104.7 million. The fortune of the family expanded easily ten-fold in the eighteenth century and the family rose from the seventh wealthiest to the third wealthiest after the king and the Duke of Orléans.

Although royal gifts started the family on its way, Toulouse and Penthièvre purchased most of the rest. Although they lived on a princely scale, they almost always ran an annual surplus in their revenues. From the outset, the estate consisted of an assemblage of properties of different legal standings which stretched from the Ile-de-France and the northern coast of Bretagne to Beaucaire in Languedoc. The core of Penthièvre, for example, was a *domaine engagé* from the crown which Toulouse bought from his sister in 1696, but 38 additional purchases over the next 56 years had the status of patrimonial property.

Although a few lordships, such as the ducal peerage of Châteauvillain remained unchanged in the eighteenth century, as a rule Toulouse and Penthièvre carefully expanded and consolidated their holdings. Penthièvre was elevated to a ducal peerage in 1698, Arc and Châteaudvillain in 1700 and Rambouillet in 1711. The elevation to the status of a ducal peerage of course conferred immense prestige, but it also simplified at a stroke the feudal hierarchy. All of the properties in a ducal peerage, whatever their origin, now formed a single fief held directly from the crown. At Rambouillet, the elevation authorized the establishment of a seigneurial *bailliage*, just as the royal consolidation of Versailles resulted in the creation of a judicial *bailliage* there.

Rambouillet was a model of aristocratic consolidation that took forty years to accomplish, 1706 to 1746, executed through a dozen major purchases and another 150 smaller ones. Toulouse and Penthièvre used every opportunity and legal procedure to expand this estate: direct purchases, foreclosure, and *retrait féodal*, the preemptive right of a lord to acquire any fief dependent on his lordship that was put up for sale. They created an immense park near the *château* and pieced together one of the largest forests in France, built grain farms, renewed the *terriers* and collected every single *droit féodal et seigneurial*.

Toulouse and Penthièvre always bought with an eye for profit. They bought forests at Rambouillet, Vernon, Gisors, and Brie, precisely where the French forests were most valuable. They were well-established in the best grain growing regions of the Ile-de-France and they were among the major owners of iron foundries in the realm. In Breton duchy of Penthièvre which had neither minoral nor agricultural wealth, they invested in seigneurial dues.

The total territory of Rambouillet in the 1780s was 23,000 ha: 11,000 ha of forest, 2000 ha of arable land, and 10,000 ha of seigneurial tenures.[90] Rambouillet was the center of the life of the family in the eighteenth century, where they lived, where they were buried, and where the single most important source of their revenue was located, their huge forest. The immense success of the family in constructing Rambouillet attracted the attention of Louis XVI and it was with a heavy heart that Penthièvre agreed to sell Rambouillet to the king in 1783 for 16 million *livres*.

The distribution of annual revenues in 1781, prior to the sale of Rambouillet, was fairly typical of high aristocratic incomes in the late eighteenth century. The total was around 6 million *livres,* of which 32% came from high office and 68% from the patrimonial domain. Looking at the domain revenues alone, the forest brought in 48.8%, the domain-farms, foundries, glass works, etc. accounted for 34.5%, and the feudal and seigneurial revenues came in last at 16.7%.[91] As immense as Rambouillet was, in 1781 it produced only 14% of the Duke of Penthièvre's total income, 842,644 livres out of 5, 930,621.[92]

The careful preservation and restoration of the feudal and seigneurial revenues was a constant feature of the management of the Bourbon-Penthièvre family from the 1690s to 1790. As was almost always the case, the management of seigneurial revenues was consistently more difficult than the management of the forests and domain-farms. The last eighteenth century *terrier* filled 16 folio volumes when completed and was the culmination of six decades of meticulous work.[93] The records of the ducal council in the eighteenth century show that 13% of its sessions were devoted to litigation, 3% to the purchase and sale of lands, 8% to the management of the forests, while 27% of its sessions dealt with feudal and seigneurial affairs.[94]

The dukes of Orléans were also impressive estate builders who used their royal pensions and the revenues from their holdings to construct a massive patrimonial estates along side their royal appanages lands. Between 1661 and 1790, the Dukes of Orléans purchased lordships, forests, seigneurial and feudal rights which effectively doubled the size of their total estate. In 1790, the appanage covered 1/20 of the landmass of France, while the patrimonial lands were at least that large if not larger. By conservative estimates, the estate of Philippe Egalité encompassed 1/10 of the land of France. Total revenues of the estate were about 9 million *livres,* 1/3 from royal pensions and the rest from the landed estate.[95] The princes of Condé and Conty constructed similar patrimonial estates to supplement their appanage holdings.[96] Finally, the Count of Artois was also an ambitious estate builder, but unlike Penthièvre, Condé, and Conty, all of whom financed acquisitions largely through their own revenues, Artois borrowed massively and spent with abandon, confident that his indulgent brother, Louis XVI, would eventually pay his bills.[97]

Northern France

Ile-de-France

Under the old regime, the Ile-de-France widely conceived was the center of the political, economic and social life of France. This area, the territory of the *gouvernement* of Paris, included not only Paris but the *élections* of Senlis, Compiègne, Laon, Pontoise, Beauvais, Mantes, Dreux, Montfort, Etampes, Melun and Nemours. The most dramatic changes in lordship in the Ile-de-France between 1500 and 1789 were the massive consolidation of lordships at the top end of the noble hierarchy and the equally massive construction of domain-farms from fragmented peasant tenures. Both of these changes were the result of general political, demographic, economic and social forces rather than any specific alteration in the system of lordship itself. Although both of these changes in lordship appeared in every province in France under the old regime, nowhere were they more apparent and more pronounced than in the Ile-de-France.

The accumulation of lordships and fiefs at the high end of the noble hierarchy was already apparent at the close of the Middle Ages. Between 1350 and 1450, the driving forces behind these changes were demographic contraction and economic crisis.[98] After 1450 and with only brief interruptions until the end of the old regime, the driving forces were economic and demographic growth and the explosive expansion of the royal government.[99] The massive increase in the size of the royal administration and the proliferation of ennobling offices drew nobles and notables in ever greater numbers into royal service. For these men, lordships were an indispensable component of the noble lifestyle. Likewise, the revenues from royal office and royal gifts greatly facilitated the expansion of their estates.

Although the consolidation of lordships continued down until 1789, the most dramatic changes occurred between 1500 and 1700. The most successful and ambitious men little by little replaced the declining old-noble families, swept fiefs into lordships, lordships into baronies, counties, marquisats and even ducal peerages. At the pinnacle of society, the princes of the blood and the kings themselves carried out similar work. The most eminent men in the realm consolidated lordships in the Ile-de-France: Montmorency and the Cardinal of

Lorraine in the sixteenth century; Villeroy, Le Tellier, Louvois, Lamoignon and the Phélypeaux in the seventeenth. In the middle of the seventeenth century, the Grand Condé, heir of the Montmorency, owned the duchy d'Enghien which encompassed some 80 fiefs and seigneuries.[100] The ducal peerage of Villeroy, elevated in 1663 for Nicolas de Neufville, a marshal of France, pulled together sixteen lordships.[101] Naturally, these men applied the most sophisticated managerial practices to their properties.[102]

At the same time but at a slower pace, upperclass investors of all sorts, ecclesiastics, nobles and commoners, expanded existing domain-farms and created entirely new ones from fragmented peasant tenures.[103] The driving force here was the massive expansion of the Parisian market. Around 1550, the population of Paris was about 200,000; in 1650 over 400,000 and in 1789 nearly 600,000. Although there were complex regional patterns, in general the population of the Ile-de-France as a whole moved in the same direction. The insatiable demand for basic food-stuffs, for bread-grains, for meat and cheese, for oats and hay for horses, etc. drew investors into farmland. Upperclass investment displaced simple peasants first in the valuable grain fields of the *plaine de France* north of Paris and only later in the poor soil regions of Hurepoix and southern Brie. Peasant indebtedness and the fragmentation of family farms into shares for all children paved the way for the implosion of the middle ranges of the peasant social hierarchy, the polarization of peasantry, and the proliferation of landless rural inhabitants.[104] Land investors benefitted from this process of peasant impoverishment, but they did not directly cause it.

What massive upperclass investment in farmland meant for lordship was that noble, ecclesiastical, and bourgeois owners replaced peasant farmers as the owners of most of the good farmland in seigneur tenures. By the end of the seventeenth century, it was not at all uncommon for non-cultivators to own two-thirds or three-quarters of the farmland in the legal territory of a village. A 1717 survey of ten villages near Gonesse in the *plaine de France*, the best grain producing region in the kingdom, showed that 22% of the land belonged to the church, 47% to nobles, 21% to bourgeois of Paris, and only 10% to peasants and *taille*-paying commoners. For the *plaine de France* as a whole, the share of the church was even higher: 40% at the end of the sixteenth century and half in

1717 [105] In the Vexin region near Pontoise, three-quarters of the land belonged to the clergy and the nobility at the end of the eighteenth century.[106] Consequently, it was members of the upperclasses who paid, directly or indirectly, the bulk of the old seigneurial renders and tithes. Most of the inhabitants of villages in the Ile-de-France by 1700 or 1750 were landless or nearly landless day laborers who were under the jurisdiction of the lords, but who paid virtually no seigneurial land dues at all. The heavy *champarts* and tithes, the ancient seigneurial *tailles*, even the lingering *corvées* fell on the upperclasses.

The typical upperclass domain-farm, whether it belonged to an ecclesiastical establishment, a noble, or a bourgeois, consisted of a jumble of fields with diverse legal standings. Some fields came from old fiefs and were free of seigneurial renders, but others owed renders and *cens*, often to various lords. The legal status of the lands remained unaltered unless changed by a specific and very expensive buy-out, even when the new domain-farm was physically consolidated. Since virtually all of the upperclass farms were leased to tenant farmers, the seigneurial renders were simply a cost of doing business, paid by the tenant farmer in the name of the legal owner to the appropriate lord or lords. The 1782 lease of the Frémigny domain-farm at Soisy-sur-Ecole which belonged to the Count of Cély specified that the tenant farmer was responsible for paying the seigneurial renders and the tithe.[107]

In other ways, lordship in the Ile-de-France remained fundamentally unaltered between 1500 and 1789. The reformed customary law of the *prévôté et vicomté* of Paris and the dozen or so other customary laws of the Ile-de-France compiled in the sixteenth century made no significant changes in the seigneurial system. However, there were some minor differences in the seigneurial dues from one small area, or *pays*, to another in the Ile-de-France. These regional variations were already well-established at the end of the Middle Ages and they survived until 1789, in part from legal conservatism, in part because they were rooted in significant differences in the regional economies which in turn flowed from differences in topography, soils, and climate.[108] In the flat, loamy soil areas which stretched in an arc northwest to northeast of Paris and which formed the richest grain growing district in France, lords collected the *champart*, the proportional render in grain, usually assessed at 1/11.[109] Indeed, lords often maintained special records to facilitate the collection of these very valuable renders.[110] In the areas of poorer soils that ran in an arc southeast to southwest of Paris, *champarts* were uncommon and the principal renders were assessed in fixed rates of grain or more commonly in *cens* payable in cash. Finally, in the immense viticultural regions which lined all of the river valleys in the Ile-de-France, renders were normally assessed in cash.

The seigneurial duties of the county of Dammartin-en-Goële were typical for the rich *plaine de France* north of Paris.[111] Lands in the *comté* were subject to minor *cens* in cash, a seigneurial *taille abonnée*, assessed at a fixed rate in cash per *arpent* of cultivated land, and most importantly a *champart* of 1/11 on the major grains. In addition, there were taxes collected on wine sales, tolls on the roads, banal ovens and banal mills. The pattern was much the same in the *seigneurie* of La Bussière near Souppes-sur-Loing, which belonged to the canons of the Sainte Chapelle in Paris.[112] But, in the poor-soil region of Hurepoix south of Paris, the *cens* were mainly in cash and *champarts* were rare. The seigneurial dues at Antony, a village under the authority of the Abbey of Saint-Germain-des-Prés, included 38 *redevances foncières*, 37 assessed in cash and only 1 in grain.[113] Similarly at Sucy in the Val-de-Marne, the *censier* of 1412 for the Cathedral Chapter of Notre-Dame de Paris showed that virtually all of the *cens* and the *taille* were assessed in cash.[114] Similarly, the *cens* in the *seigneurie* of Fleury-en-Bière near Fontainebleau and Melun were very light and almost totally in cash in the seventeenth and eighteenth century.[115] Finally, tithes and *cens* were light n the vineyards which lined the river valleys near Paris and which produced an ocean of common wine for the Parisian market. Tithes assessed on wines at the press were rarely more than 2–3%, compared to 1/11 or 1/12 for the tithe on grains. Also,the seigneurial *cens,* once collected in kind, had been commuted into a modest and uniform tax in cash of a few *deniers* or *sous* per house or unit of land.[116]

Remarkably, neither the consolidation of fiefs and lordships nor the growth of commercially oriented farms had any significant impact on the internal structure of lordship or the grid of seigneurial dues. Each fief and lordship retained its own distinctive seigneurial institutions and traditions in place at the close of the Middle Ages even when it was bundled together into a newly elevated county marquisat, or ducal peerage. Engrossing lords almost never recast the seigneurial structures of their consolidated properties into a new and simplified system. Political and legal constraints prevented them from behaving like the sovereign lords of the Middle Ages. Louis XIV's recasting of the seigneurial system at Versailles was highly unusual, the act of a king, not of a lesser old regime lord.[117] Likewise the total transformation of the ownership of tenures made no impact on the underlying grid of seigneurial payments. Actual working farms and land ownership were distinct entities which like transparencies lay one on top of the other.

Nevertheless, lords often made piecemeal changes which had the cumulative effect of obliterating almost completely from the seigneurial *terriers* any sense that there once had been a single, comprehensive fiscal system for the lordship.[118] These changes certainly reinforced the notion that the seigneurial dues were tantamount to land rentals, established by contract for a specific tenure, rather than taxes which a lord collected from his subjects. Indeed, new tenures were often put up for bid and at the very least were subject to negotiated new rates. Geographically, the piecemeal upgrading of the annual *cens* or renders occurred mainly in the viticultural regions and in the poorer farming zones, rather than in the areas where the *champart* was the standard. As an annual render, the *champart* could hardly be improved.

The piecemeal upgrading of annual payments added greatly to the cost of seigneurial record keeping and collection in the Ile-de-France. Lords of the Middle Ages simply could not afford the massive, individualized accounts for each and every tenant which was one of the main reasons they often established and then rigorously maintained standard fiscal grids for their lordships. Lords of the early modern period were able to afford more voluminous records. Also, early modern lords were less reliant on the seigneurial dues than their medieval counterparts. While it is true that the greatest lords of the Ile-de-France, the abbeys, already drew the bulk of their revenues from the domain lands in the Middle Ages, the disparity between domanial and seigneurial revenues certainly grew between 1500 and 1789. More than ever before, domainial revenues subsidized the management of seigneurial revenues.

Nevertheless, some seigneurial renders and fees were well-worth collection, especially the tithes and *champarts*, whose volume and value increased significantly between 1500 and 1789. Also, the *lods et ventes*, the seigneurial transfer fee of 1/12 or 8.33% on the price of tenures that changed hands through sale, became one of the most lucrative sources of seigneurial revenues in the eighteenth century. The establishment in 1703 of the royal tax on all real estate sales, the *centième denier* of 1%, and the creation of a new royal fiscal bureaucracy, the *Côntrole des actes*, greatly facilitated the identification of land sales in the lordships.

The evidence for the dramatic increase in revenues from the *lods et ventes* in the city of Paris in the eighteenth century is particularly striking.[119] Prior to the *centième denier*, seigneurial officials had the greatest difficulty in tracking down sales in their lordships. During the sixteenth and seventeenth centuries, buyers and sellers regularly resorted to fraudulent transactions to cover up actual sales. For the archbishopric of Paris, the largest lordship in the city, revenues from the *lods et ventes* stood at 30,000 *livres* in 1630 and in 1665-67. In 1715, the figure was 60,000 but in 1720 rose to an astounding 850,000 *livres*, then fell back to about 60,000 *livres* until the 1760s. From the mid-1760s, revenues from the *lods et ventes* rose dramatically with the steep rise in urban real estate prices and the increased frequency of sales. In 1784-1786, revenues averaged 350,000 *livres* a year and hit 475,000 *livres* in 1787. During the 1780s, the abbatial portion of the property of the monastery of Saint-Germain-des-Prés collected 182,000 *livres*, the royal domain 100,000 *livres*, and even lesser lords such Saint-Martin-des-Champs took in 35,000 *livres* from the *lods et ventes*. For the principal ecclesiastical lordships in Paris, total revenues in 1790 were 3.2 million *livres*: 35% from a variety of rural sources which included domain-farms, seigneurial renders, and tithes; 27% from annual non-seigneurial rentals charged for houses in Paris; and 26% from *lods et ventes*.[120]

Prior to the *centième denier*, lords regularly offered substantial rebates to encourage payment. In the eighteenth century, rebates still existed for those who stepped forward and paid willingly, but they were considerably less generous than in the past. In the royal domain in Paris, the royal *Conseil* established a sliding scale in 1771 for rebates for the *lods et ventes*: no rebates for properties sold for less than 12,000 *livres*, but rebates rising from 1/6 to 1/4 and even 1/3 lui the most expensive properties. With an official rate of 8.33%, this meant that an average priced property which sold for 22,000 *livres* in Paris was assessed a rate of 7.75% at the end of the old regime.[121]

Although individual lordships occasionally suffered from the negligent behavior of their owners, as a rule lords in the Ile-de-France throughout the early modern centuries managed their lordships with great care.[122] There never was a time between 1500 and 1789 when seigneurial administration as a whole was slack. Consequently, the often-cited renewal of *terriers* in the three or four decades prior to the Revolution was only the last phase of a perpetual process of record updating which had been in operation since the Middle Ages. Lords renewed their *terriers* on a regular basis and kept other special registers to facilitate the collection of their *droits*. The Cathedral Chapter of Notre-Dame de Paris, for example, maintained an unbroken run of registers that covered the years 1518 to 1790 in which it recorded the investiture of all new tenants and the collection of *lods et ventes* in its lordships.[123]

Although lords frequently shifted back and forth between a salaried general intendant, *receveur*, and a single financial manager, *fermier général*, who leased the entire lordship, these changes at the very top of the seigneurial administrative system did not alter the rest of the middle and lower echelons of the apparatus.[124] Lords applied standard administrative practices that varied little between 1500 and 1789. The managerial system used in the country of Dammartin-en-Goële in the 1490s and that employed three centuries later in the estates of the Duke of Penthièvre and the Count of Artois was virtually identical. Naturally, the eighteenth century princes of the blood had a more fully developed higher administrative apparatus than that required for a single county in the fifteenth century, but the actual management of the lordships was very similar. In every instance there was a strict separation of both the judicial apparatus and the forest administration from the management of the rest of the property. Likewise, most of the collection of revenues was in the hands of individual contractors who bid on individual accounts.[125]

Southern Low Countries

The southern Low Countries, the present *départements* of *Nord* and *Pas-de-Calais*, became part of France through the 1659 Treaty of the Pyrénées and the 1678 Treaty of Nimègue. The newly annexed territory contained several small and historically distinct provinces that stretched from west to east: maritime Flanders, interior or Walloon Flanders, Artois, Hainaut and Cambrésis. Maritime Flanders was Flemish and much of its territory had recently been reclaimed from the sea. The other provinces were French and had a much older history of settlement. In the late Middle Ages, most of these provinces were under the authority of the dukes of Bourgogne. At the end of the fifteenth century, this area passed to the Hapsburg, and in the seventeenth century it came under the control of the king of France, Louis XIV.[126]

The southern Low Countries as a whole demonstrated the remarkable tenacity of lordship which loosened its grip only in the most extreme conditions. This tenacity was in part the result of ancient settlement and an unbroken, multi-secular tradition of careful management of lordship by princes, aristocratic lords, and ecclesiastics.[127] In part also, the tenancy of lordship flowed from the unusually strong position of the church. Bishoprics, cathedral chapters, lesser chapters, and ancient monasteries, historically the most conservative of lords, were more in evidence here than in any other region of France. The Bishopric of Cambrai and the cathedral chapter of Notre-Dame de Cambrai, the abbeys of Saint-Vaast, Saint-Amand, d'Anchain, Saint-Sépulcre, and Saint-Aubert were among the most important land owners and lords of the region. Although none of the ecclesiastical lordships in the southern Low Countries had the wealth of the bishoprics and monasteries of the Ile-de-France or Normandie, collectively they exercised an enormous influence. For the region as a whole, the directly owned domains of the church amounted to no less than 20% of the land and in Cambrésis, 40%.[128]

Everywhere, lordship still provided the institutional foundation for local governance and the administration of justice. Even the cities were under the supervisory authority of the lords, although in practice they operated as largely self-governing communities.[129] Medieval charters that remained in force until the

Revolution carefully delineated the powers and responsibilities of mayors, aldermen and an array of municipal institutions and offices. The lords were unusually strong in the villages too. The rural villages, with or without charters, had a simplified version of municipal governance.[130] The lord or principal lord nominated the mayor. The mayor was often a peasant tenant farmer who leased the entire *seigneurie*, worked the domain-farms, and collected the seigneurial dues. The French royal edicts that required all seigneurial judges to have legal training were not rigorously applied here after annexation. While legal professionals staffed the law courts in the cities, in the villages it was often the lord's tenant farmer who served as mayor and administered justice jointly with the village elders in an arrangement that prolonged the medieval practice of community based justice.[131]

The regional variations of lordship appeared at the level of the land duties and the tithe and were the result of historically different patterns of economic and demographic development. The first and geographically most extensive model of lordship appeared mainly in the southern three-quarters of the region: in the southern two-thirds of Artois, in the whole of Cambrésis, and the northern part of Hainaut.[132] This was flat open country that had always been admirably suited for large scale sheep and grain farming and which never experienced a wrenching reorientation of its agricultural economy. The early modern centuries brought population increase and a further concentration of lands in the hands of the upper class investors: the ecclesiastics, the aristocratic lords, and bourgeois land engrossers.[133] These changes were not powerful enough to disturb the medieval structures of lordship.

The *terrages* of 1/11 and tithes of 1/12, the banal ovens and the mills survived largely unaltered.[134] The *terrages* and tithes were extremely valuable and the lords managed them with great care even though they typically drew most of their revenues from their domain-farms. The survival of largely unaltered tithes and renders paid in kind was very similar to what occurred in the excellent grain growing region north of Paris, the *plaine de France*, and for the same reasons. The principal difference was that Cambrésis, northern Hainaut, and southern Artois sold grain to the towns of the southern Low Countries, whereas the *plaine de France* sold mainly to Paris.

The second pattern of lordship occurred in Walloon Flanders and northern Artois, an area which constituted the southern tip of a larger zone of intensive Flemish agriculture and extremely dense population in the Southern Netherlands. Walloon Flanders with its capital Lille and northern Artois were part of a region that for the better part of five centuries prior to the French Revolution experienced repeated tectonic shifts in its economic base. These major shifts in economic structure and land use had the force of several earthquakes that simply pulverized the old system of land renders and seriously weakened the tithes.[135] The liquidation of the old land renders began in the late Middle Ages in Walloon Flanders with the collapse of the textile industry and the shift eastward of the economic center of gravity to Brabant. In a setting of general economic and demographic depression, farmers simply refused to take over the abandoned tenures with their heavy renders in kind. Farmers demanded better and lower rates. Legally, lands that had previously been perpetual tenures with fixed or proportional renders became part of the lords' domain lands let out on temporary leases with negotiable rentals.

During the early modern era, the liquidation of the old tenures and their renders in kind continued, but for different reasons. The slow economic recovery of the region, the spread of the rural textile industry, and the concomitant growth of population densities in both urban and rural areas produced an entirely new set of economic opportunities for agriculture. Walloon Flanders and northern Artois moved towards ever more intensive agriculture on very small plots of land for the production of an array of industrial crops such as oil-seeds, flax and hemp, hops, fodder and root crops, dairy products and the like. The old system of seigneurial renders that featured *terrages* on grain production simply collapsed with the radical transformation of the agricultural economy.

Legally the liquidation of the old system proceeded by several different routes. On new tenures, the old renders were abandoned for fixed payments, often in cash. On old tenures, the renders were commuted. With ever greater bourgeois investment in land and subsequent leasing to peasants, bourgeois investors and even aristocratic lords approached the *seigneur* and bought out the annual land dues of all sorts by offering an indemnification that was typically 20 or 25 times the value of the annual dues. By the end of the old regime, upwards ᵒf half the agricultural lands in the most intensively cultivated regions had been cleared of all seigneurial renders and dues, although they, their owners and their cultivators still remained under the jurisdictional authority of the lords.

Liquidation of the medieval fiscal system of lordship also occurred in the south and southeast of Hainaut. This part of Hainaut did not adopt the intensive Flemish agricultural system, but simply shifted from grain farming to pasture and livestock. This change in land use began in the late Middle Ages and continued in the early modern eras.[136] Although the economic pressures were simpler, the legal procedures for liquidating the old renders in parts of Hainaut were the same as in nearby Walloon Flanders and northern Artois.

Finally, a third model of lordship appeared in maritime Flanders, an area reclaimed from the sea by stages from the high Middle Ages to the seventeenth and eighteenth century. The reclamation process was extremely costly and simply beyond the financial capabilities of capital-poor peasants. Maritime Flanders had fertile but heavy soils most suitable for mixed livestock and grain production in large farms with heavy plows and abundant draft animals.[137] Initially, it was princely, ecclesiastical and aristocratic lords who constructed domain-farms rather than perpetual tenures from the newly reclaimed lands. Eventually bourgeois investors joined in. Although some traditional tenures appeared, much of the land mass of maritime Flanders was never subject to the renders and dues that were a stock feature of perpetual seigneurial tenures.[138]

Not surprisingly, significant changes in the economic use of farm land also affected the tithe. Historically, the great tithe on grain fields was the most valuable and durable of the various categories of tithes. The lesser tithes on the secondary crops and livestock were always more difficult to collect, less valuable, and frequently hotly contested. The great tithes survived easily in the areas of traditional grain farming , but collapsed where dramatic changes in land use occurred. Land owners and their tenants evaded and even flatly refused to pay tithes on the new crops. Although the tithe collectors, mainly the ancient monasteries, the bishoprics and the cathedral chapters, pursued their litigation until the last day of the old regime, in practice they were unable to enforce regular collection of tithes on the industrial crops and dairy products in the areas that adopted intensive Flemish agriculture.[139]

CHAPTER THREE

Regional Patterns of Lordship, II

Eastern France

Champagne

The province of Champagne was a conglomerate of various poor soils regions on the eastern border of the Ile-de-France. Champagne was always less densely populated, less urbanized, and less economically developed than the Ile-de-France. Much of its land was cleared very late, between 1050 and 1300, and finally between 1500 and 1650.

The seigneurial institutions of Champagne in the early modern centuries perpetuated with timely updates a number of distinct historical deposits which like geological layers settled on top of, or next to, each another in the Middle Ages.[1] The core settlements in the valleys still had traces of the ancient seigneurial *mansi* structure that had given way to individualized *censive* tenures. Later, the Cistercians constructed immense *granges*, while the rivalry of the Capetian kings of France and the counts of Blois-Champagne produced two more fiscal systems of lordship. Acting either alone or in joint lordship with an ecclesiastical institution, the kings and counts organized territory with new or newly organized settlements. The kings of France used a variant of the charter of Lorris, while the counts of Champagne favored a version of the charter of Beaumont. Finally, the political struggle for control of territory led first to the widespread imposition of servile controls and then to their partial liquidation.[2] The institutional expressions of these historical developments were still very apparent in 1500.

For the most part, the economy of Champagne functioned well-outside the economic radius of Paris. At the end of the Middle Ages, Champagne was one of many poor soil areas that had a hard time holding on to its peasant population. The Ile-de-France was attractive, while Champagne was repulsive. To retain population and to cut administrative costs, lords liquidated most of what was left of medieval serfdom.[3] The Capetian kings and the counts of Blois had cleared most of Champagne of serfdom before the close of the thirteenth century. At the end of the Middle Ages, servile burdens lingered mainly on the lands of the bishoprics, cathedral chapters, and the ancient Benedictine and Cluniac monasteries. For Champagne as a whole, serfdom affected only a small part of the province.[4] The geographical marginality of serfdom weakened the grip of the lords further since peasants tended to flee or avoid servile villages. Between 1450 and 1520 a final wave of manumission eliminated most of the controls. In the county of Bar-sur-Seine, 57 villages were freed from servile burdens, 26 or nearly half at the end of the fifteenth and the beginning of the sixteenth century.[5] Manumission was never free, and as population recovered lords became more demanding. The charters of manumission eliminated *mainmorte* and *formariage*, but sometimes required residence. The charters contained a detailed inventory of the entire fiscal apparatus of lordship as well as the replacement taxes for the elimination of serfdom.

Lords and their subjects often agreed to both an initial price for the redemption of the servile burdens and to an annual tax. This annual tax took several forms. In many cases a new seigneurial *taille* appeared in place of the servile burdens, assessed either globally on the entire village community or individually per hearth. These new *tailles* were collectable either in cash or in agricultural products. Typically, the new *tailles* replaced all previous *tailles* and bundled the payments into one. Occasionally, a proportional tax on some or all crops replaced serfdom or a fixed tax in cash or kind per unit of cultivated land. In a minority of cases, 30% of the charters, lords required residence of all property owners in the village or at least in the lordship.

The elimination of serfdom did not normally involve a total recasting of the seigneurial systems in operation in the villages. Lords had imposed servile controls everywhere in Champagne, regardless of what underlying fiscal system of lordship was in use. Consequently, the elimination of serfdom normally did not disturb the basic outlines of the old fiscal bases of lordship. Rather, manumission adjusted these underlying systems.

The geographically most important systems of lordship in Champagne were those inspired by the charters of Lorris and Beaumont. These survived in the early modern era and expanded with new clearings and new tenures, most notably in the sixteenth century. The demographic and economic forces in operation in Champagne were mainly indigenous. First abandoned lands were resettled, then in the sixteenth century isolated farms and hamlets expanded into villages. The old fiscal systems of lordship remained in use and spread to every new field that was cleared and cultivated. Tenures derived from the old *mansi* retained their *cens* in cash supplement with a substantial new seigneurial *rente*, usually in cash too. The charter of Lorris featured fixed payments, normally in grain, per unit of cultivated land or per plow team in which case it was called a *droit d'accensie.* Beaumont favored a proportional render, called variously a *champart, terrage,* or most often *tierce.* The rates were relatively low in the fifteenth century, 1/11, 1/12, 1/13, even 1/21 for grain lands, but as population expanded and demand for land grew the rates rose to 1/9 for both grain fields and vineyards.[6] *Terrages* or *tierces* were still in widespread use in the lordships on the eve of the Revolution. Indeed, when peasants started planting potatoes, lords demanded *terrages* and the church demanded a tithe. In both cases, the courts upheld the lords.[7]

The popular vineyards expanded with population and served mainly the local markets, not a distant export market. Lords assessed various sorts of renders or dues on the vineyards. In some places there were taxes in cash, elsewhere, proportional renders. Some villages owed the *muage*, essentially a *taille* payable in wine, assessed either on the entire village or on individual holdings.[8]

Champagne also had a remarkably well-preserved stock of seigneurial taxes on grain, flour and bread collected in every market town in the province. These withstood the reforms of Turgot and the physiocrats since they were universally regarded as legitimate property rights that could not be abolished without compensation. On the eve of the Revolution, towns collected these taxes as did the most eminent lords: the Archbishop of Reims, the Abbé de Saint-Rémi, the Duke of Orléans, the Count of Brienne.[9]

The tithe was nearly universal which is not surprising given the great presence of the ancient ecclesiastical institutions and the enormous importance of joint lordships, *pariages*. The foundation charters for these medieval joint lordships always established tithes.[10] As a rule, only the lands of the Cistercians and the Knights of Malta were exempt from the tithe. Frequently, the revenues from the tithe in many villages far exceeded the total of all of the direct royal taxes at the end of the old regime. At Balesmes, the tithe stood at 3600 livres and the royal taxes at 2500; at Chalindrey, the figures were 5868 and 3529; at Chassigny, 2655 and 2592. The canons of the cathedral chapter of Langres had total revenues in excess of 200,000 livres of which roughly 60% came from the tithe collected in 59 parishes.[11]

There were some changes in land ownership in Champagne in the early modern era. Population increase led to a proliferation of peasant vine dressers, a class that often constituted half the rural population in many villages. In the grain and livestock farms, there was the normal polarization between rich *laboureurs* and poor *manouvriers*, or yeomen and cottagers. From the sixteenth century petty bourgeois investors in the towns bought up tenures in villages where residence was not required. By the end of the old regime, bourgeois ownership of land and peasant ownership, both in tenures, was about equal, 20% each. The bourgeois domains rarely exceeded 30 ha, were usually very fragmented, and were leased in small lots rather than as consolidated farms.

All told, Champagne experienced only a modest variety of land engrossing and consolidation, *remembrement*. The poor soils of Champagne were not suitable for large scale production of grain and livestock for export. Significantly, nobles in Champagne hardly bothered with this sort of land enterprise. Most of the domain-farms of the lords and the *granges* of the church were not assembled piecemeal from peasant tenures after 1500. Rather, they were either block farms carved from the reserve lands which, whether established in the Middle Ages or in the early modern centuries, stood clearly apart geographically from the fragmented tenures in the village *finages*.[12]

What attracted noble interest in Champagne were the lordships and the forests.[13] Parts of Champagne were heavily forested and endowed with rich iron deposits. The noble class in Champagne underwent wave after wave of renewal from the end of the Middle Ages until the Revolution.[14] With each wave, the new lords consolidated fiefs and lordships further. Here as elsewhere, service to the king and royal gifts help finance this work of *rassemblement*.[15] Great lords eliminated lesser lords and absorbed their fiefs into ever larger feudal entities which in time were elevated to counties, marquisats and ducal peerages. Noble families of national stature succeeded each other here century after century: Anne de Montmorency and the duke of Nevers in the sixteenth century, Chancellor Brûlart in the seventeenth, Béthune, Choiseuil, Marshal de Broglie, the Duke of Penthièvre and the Count of Artois in the eighteenth. The Duke of Penthièvre owned nearly 12,000 ha of forest that stretched from Arc-en-Barrois to Châteauvillain, while the Count of Artois received 120,000 *livres* from his forests in Champagne.[16] At the end of the old regime in the part of Champagne which became the *département* of Haute-Marne, nobles owned 30% of the land directly, clergy 18%, bourgeoisie 18%, peasants 17%, while common land accounted for 17%.[17]

Noble interest in the forest stirred from the sixteenth century. Lords took advantage of every opportunity to bring more of the forests under their control. Lords bought forests, took them as payment for debts, pressed for *cantonnement* and *triage,* took forest for the liquidation of serfdom and for the elimination of residence requirements in the villages.[18] As late as 1777, the Marquis of Baillet abandoned his right to confiscate the property of non-residents at Givry-en-Argonne, the *droit de déchéance,* in return for the surrender of 22 *arpents* of communal forest[19].

Noble interest in vineyards was uncommon before the eighteenth century. As the market for the quality wine of Champagne grew in the eighteenth century, nobles joined the Benedictines and the Cistercians in lavishing care on newly improved and expanded vineyards. Great nobles were also found among the most vocal opponents of the tithes on vineyards. With no apparent sense of hypocrisy, the Marquis of Sillery denounced the ecclesiastical tithe collectors and financed lawsuits against them.[20] In fact, nobles in Champagne often owned between 1/3 and 1/2 of the tithes.[21]

Ecclesiastical lordships owed forests too and they far surpassed the aristocratic lords in the ownership of domain-farms. Champagne had hundreds of ancient and well-endowed churchs. The ancient monasteries included the abbeys of Pothières, Saint-Pierre de Molesme, Saint-Michel de Tonnerre, Saint-Victor de Montiéramy, Auberive, La Crête, Montier-en-Der, Morimond, Clairvaux, and Quincy. There were bishoprics and cathedral chapters at Langes, Troyes, and Châlon-sur-Marne. As a rule, these ecclesiastical lordships were managed with great care.[22] The most characteristic ecclesiastical domain-farm was an immense medieval *grange*. At the end of the Middle Ages, ecclesiastical lords chopped a few *granges* into peasant tenures, but this was uncommon.[23] Most of the medieval *granges* survived. The county of Bar-sur-Seine had no less than 70 monastic *granges* with an average size of 80 ha. By contrast, the aristocratic domain-farms covered on average only 20 ha.[24]

Bourgogne

Bourgogne was an economically backward province with relatively light population, poor soils and marginal fertility that was just a little too remote to be of direct interest to the noble families of national stature that flocked to the Ile-de-France. Although the Montmorency and the Louvois had estates in the northern tip of Basse-Bourgogne, it was mainly local men who influenced the evolution of seigneurial institutions in Bourgogne under the old regime.

The principal changes in lordship in Bourgogne between 1500 and 1789 were local variations on the themes of consolidation of fiefs and farm lands. Although some ecclesiastical lords expanded their holdings, the most significant changes were the work of the local robe nobles, especially the *parlementaires* of Dijon. In Bourgogne, as elsewhere, the noble class underwent a constant renewal over the centuries. Some old noble families like the Saulx-Tavannes survived through good marriages with rich bourgeois heiresses, and some old *chevaliers* shifted base by acquiring high royal office. But many of the robe nobles rose from bourgeois backgrounds in the sixteenth and seventeenth centuries.

The *Parlement* of Dijon had more than one hundred magistrates. In addition Bourgogne had a *Bureau des finances*, a *Table de marbre* for the administration of the forest, a *Chambre des comptes*, a *Chambre des monnaies*, nineteen royal *bailliages*, six of which were *cours présidiaux*, etc.[25] Without significant competition from noble families of national stature, the noble royal office holders led the way in sweeping up the debris of fiefs into consolidated lordships and in pulling together peasant lands into larger domain-farms.[26] Likewise, it was the robe nobles who carefully preserved the archaic seigneurial institutions of Bourgogne.[27]

Bourgogne enjoyed almost a century of vigorous economic and demographic growth from about 1480 to 1570 and then experienced over a century of tribulation, 1570 to 1680.[28] Until the annexation of Franche-Comté in 1678, Bourgogne was on the political and military border that separated the kingdom of France from Hapsburg territories. The Wars of Religion, the Thirty Years' War, and the Fronde all disrupted the province and plunged individuals, cities and villages into debt. These debts in turn often led to the alienation of lordships, lesser fiefs, tenures and common lands. The transfer of individual properties from old nobles and unfortunate peasants to engrossing lords and bourgeois unfolded here as it did everywhere in France mainly in the sixteenth and seventeenth centuries. Many villages surrendered commons and forests to lords and other creditors to clear up debts. However, the villages certainly did not loose all of their communal properties. Indeed, the communities in Bourgogne were still among the best endowed with communal lands in France at the end of the old regime.[29]

The vineyards of Bourgogne also expanded considerably between 1500 and 1789, although the massive growth came later in the nineteenth century.[30] The medieval centuries produced a rich deposit of vineyards that appeared in clumps along the hills from Auxerre in the north, past Dijon in the center, to Mâcon in the south. Most of the new turnips, growth was the work of peasant *vignerons* who produced common wines, but the quality vineyards expanded too. Aristocratic lords and bourgeois took up the work begun by the ecclesiastical lords in the Middle Ages.[31]

Lords in Bourgogne always depended mainly on their domain lands for their revenues.[32] The Burgundian estates of the Saulx-Tavannes family were typically of the high aristocracy. Revenues came principally from the forests, secondly from small domain-farms, and at a distant third from seigneurial dues.[33] In a sample of lordships in the north of the province in Auxois, *droits seigneuriaux* brought in on average 30% for small lordships, but substantially less for major ones.[34] For the barony of Marigny-sur-Ouche, seigneurial dues accounted for only 1000 *livres* out of a total income of over 16,000 *livres* in 1782.[35]

On the eve of the Revolution, nobles owned 30% of the land directly and the church nearly 25%. Nevertheless, the land engrossing of Bourgogne was on a modest scale in keeping with the general mediocrity of the provincial economy. Bourgogne was an area of small scale or *petite culture* agriculture. The seigneurial domain-farms were commonly 12 to 20 ha in the bottom lands, 40 to 50 ha in the *bocage*, and were in no way comparable to the massive, economically progressive farms of the best zones of the Ile-de-France. Likewise, the consolidated lordships were also of modest proportions. Between 1519 and 1790, there were 16 elevations of lordships to the status of ducal pecrages in the Ile-de-France, 16 also in Champagne, but only 3 in Bourgogne.[36] Bourgogne and Mâcon had a plethora of petty lordships with titles more impressive than revenues and a truly astonishing number of ecclesiastical lordships.[37]

The seigneurial institutions of Bourgogne were certainly burdensome. Renders were mainly assessed in kind either as a fixed amount per unit of land or as a proportional tax, the *tierce*. Annual seigneurial *tailles* were common, as were *corvées*. The tithe was nearly universal. The inhabitants of the *seigneurie* of Saffres in Auxois were subject to *mainmorte* and *formariage*. They paid an annual *taille abonné*e of 120 *livres*, a consolidated tithe and *tierce* of 2/13, an additional 21.5 *boisseaux* of wheat for the rights of open pasture, 2 *boisseaux* of wheat per household in lieu of the suppressed banal oven, and they performed *corvées* for the vintage, plowing, harvesting, and cutting of the hay. There was also a marriage tax of a hen and a cake, a banal mill, and the occasional *droit d'indire*, the local term for the occasional *taille aux quatre cas*, collected most commonly for the marriage of the lord's oldest daughter, at double the value of all the annual payments.[38]

In 1782 in the *seigneurie* of Brandon near Creusot, the Marquis de Beaurepaire, a modest *captaine d'infanterie*, demanded the *droit d'indire* on the occasion of his daughter's wedding. The 75 households of the village paid double the 1781 assessment which came to 792 measures of wheat, rye and oats, 83 hens, 75 *corvées* of manual labor, 6 *corvées* of hauling, 276 eggs, some wax, and 212 *livres*. The total, evaluated according to the official prices of the *mercuriale* came to about 1264 *livres*, which was more than the total for the royal *taille*,

1204 *livres*.[39] Similarly, in 1784 a member of the Saulx-Tavannes family became a knight of the Holy Spirit. The Count of Saulx-Tavannes demanded the *droit d'indire*. Most of the inhabitants of the lordship paid, but those of Arc-sur-Tille refused. They argued that the tax had never been demanded in these circumstances before. They lost their case initially in the royal *bailliage* and then again on appeal to the *Parlement* of Dijon which ordered them to pay in 1787–88.[40]

When new villages appeared, lords typically fashioned schedules of seigneurial dues which closely resembled the medieval fiscal systems of lordship. Similarly, the new villages, although far less numerous than new monastic *granges*, resembled their medieval predecessors in that they normally had a planned geometric layout.[41] The Cistercians of Cîteaux had a *grange* at Crepy which appeared in the twelfth century with lands in part taken from a ninth century *villa*. From 1380, the Cistercians turned to tenant-farmers and throughout the sixteenth century Crepy was a leased domain-farm. The troubles of the late sixteenth century undermined the operation and in 1612 the Cistercians transformed most of the old *grange* into a new village. They divided the land into 18 sections and found inhabitants immediately for 14. Each household paid annually 10 *sous*, a *boisseau* of wheat, a fat hen, and a *tierce* of 1/9 on all grains, legumes, hemp, and vineyards. The tithe was 1/12 on field crops, vineyards, lambs and fleeces. The rate at the banal grape press was 1/12. For the banal oven, there was another annual tax of 10 *sous*. Finally, there was one *corvée* a year. Despite the great weight of these seigneurial taxes, the village prospered.[42]

The seigneurial dues certainly did not diminish in Bourgogne under the old regime. In fact, they often increased, especially during the century 1560–1660. These increases were not the work of malicious lords who had scoured their medieval records in search of ancient dues that could be turned to account. Rather, they flowed directly from the indebtedness of peasant families and villages that resulted from war and massive royal tax increases. Aristocratic and ecclesiastical lords came to the assistance of their desperate tenants. Although it would be naïve to suggest that there was never an element of calculation involved in the actions of the lords, it is also clear that in lending to borrowers reduced to pemury lords were certainly not making safe investments. Repayment came only at the cost of lengthy litigation. Lords did not have a free hand. The creation of new rents was supervised by the royal courts, especially by the *Parlement*. While the lords sometimes received part of the communal forests, they frequently were forced to take nearly worthless scrub pastures in payment for bad debts.[43]

The new rents took several legal forms.[44] Some were non-seigneurial *rentes*, that were either perpetual or temporary. Others were indeed increases in existing seigneurial dues. Yet frequently the *rentes* of very different legal standing went by the same, medieval, terms: *taille, dîme, cens,* etc. The evidence for the tithes, *dîmes*, is particularly clear. In the bottom lands near Dijon, double tithes were frequently established to liquidate village debts. Hence it was not uncommon for a single lord, aristocratic or ecclesiastical, to collected old tithes and new merged together for convenience. Massive village debts on occasion also led lords and their tenants to recast entirely the fiscal base of the lordships. In 1612, the inhabitants of Vernois and their lord agreed to eliminate all existing renders and dues for a new annual *taille*.[45] Likewise, new or increased proportional renders, the valuable *champarts* or *tierces*, multiplied in the seventeenth century for the cancellation of debts.[46]

Seigneurial justice was also very well preserved in Bourgogne and functioned continuously until the Revolution. The *bailliage* of Châtillon-sur-Seine had 61 functioning seigneurial courts in the second half of the eighteenth century. In 1750, these courts held 162 sessions and heard 354 cases; in 1789 they held 384 cessions and heard 748 cases.[47] Far from fading, the seigneurial courts remained a vital venue for the petty affairs of the rural inhabitants. In the barony of Marigny-sur-Ouche and in the small lordship of Magny-sur-Tille the seigneurial courts functioned regularly from the sixteenth to the end of the eighteenth century.[48]

The seigneurial institutions varied slightly in the three geographical zones in Bourgogne.[49] The most attractive areas were the flat lands that ran along the rivers, principally the Saône and the Yonne. The main towns, Dijon, Chalon-sur-Saône, and Auxerre, were found here as were the most attractive farm lands. These regions had concentrated villages with regulated two and three cycle farming. The cities began to emerge from serfdom with charters in the late twelfth century, while most villages shed serfdom in the rebuilding phase at the end of the Middle Ages and the beginning of the sixteenth century. The second zone consisted of the hillsides along the rivers that lent themselves readily to viticulture. Serfdom faded here very quickly too.

Finally, the third zone located on the western border of the province had heavy and impermeable clay soils, dispersed population and fenced or hedged farms, *bocage*. It was here that serfdom lingered longest. Roughly a third of the communities in Bourgogne were still subject to mortmain at the end of the old regime. Although pockets of serfdom appeared here and there all over the province, the heaviest concentrations of servile communities were in the west, in Châtillonnais, Auxois, Morvan, Autunois and near the border with Nivernais.[50]

Most villages shed mortmain at the end of the Middle Ages and the beginning of the sixteenth century, at a time when the Black Death, the Hundred Years' War, and the fighting occasioned by the death of Charles the Bold thinned the population. Survivors left burdensome tenures for freer lands. Serfdom lingered in the least appealing farming zones where there was little competition for land. After 1550, there were relatively few acts of manumission, about 40 acts of collective freedom for entire villages in the seventeenth century, and about 30 for the eighteenth. The pace did not increase in the eighteenth century. Individual acts of manumission were even less common.[51]

Although rare when measured against the hundreds of villages in the entire province, the acts of collective manumission nevertheless provide striking examples of seigneurial hard bargaining, not to say simple rapacity. In return for the abolition of mortmain, lords normally demanded increases in the remaining seigneurial dues: a doubling of the seigneurial *taille*, significant increases in renders in grains, a new annual payment in cash, etc. To be freed of mortmain, the inhabitants of the lordship of Trouhans in 1655 promised to pay their lord, a magistrate in the *Parlement* of Dijon, a perpetual double tithe of 2/15 and to cut the hay of one of the lord's fields every year. Within just a few years, 1663, they decided that the price of freedom was too high and petitioned first their lord and then the intendant to liberated them from this onerous new tax. These efforts to break a good contract failed and the inhabitants of Touhans paid the double tithe right down until the Revolution. About a century later, the price of freedom had nearly doubled. In 1758 The tenants at Clamerey agreed to pay a new proportional render, also called a tithe, of 1/8 on all of the fruits of the earth, on grains, legumes and even on turnips.[52]

Villages with common pastures and forests often purchased manumission by surrendering part of the common lands to the lord. In 1746, twenty families at Clomot gave up two-thirds of their common lands to their lord. Similarly, in 1782 the inhabitants of Chamesson purchased freedom from mortmain by handing over half of the village forest, a block of 112 ha, to their lord, Nicolas Brulart, first president of the *Parlement* of Dijon. There was a similar agreement at Blangey negotiated with the lord, a president of the *Cour des Aides*, that involved the surrender of 28 ha of communal forest in 1732.[53]

For the villages that remained subject to mortmain, the most obvious effect of this servile restriction was to block the normal transformations in the ownership of land and social structure that occurred elsewhere in villages: land engrossing by outside non-peasant investors, noble and bourgeois, and extreme social polarization of the peasantry.[54] In a sense backwardness reinforced backwardness. Serfdom collapsed in the most attractive farming areas where outside investment simply could not be forestalled, but survived where efforts to skirt the rules of mortmain were infrequent enough to be dealt with by vigilant seigneurial administration. Lordships that preserved mortmain in Bourgogne in the early modern centuries held on to this archaic institution only by monitoring land transactions and by undertaking nearly constant litigation.[55] At the end of the old regime, even lords from the highest echelons of the nobility, such as the Princess of Nassau and Bertier de Sauvigny, intendant of Paris, had their agents and seigneurial officials enforce the servile regulations to the letter.[56]

Lorraine

In the early modern centuries, Lorraine went its own way, just as it had in the Middle Ages. Although the seigneurial institutions of Lorraine bore a familial resemblance to those in the rest of France, a particular combination of political, economic and demographic forces gave lordship in Lorraine its own distinct physiognomy.

The troubles of the late Middle Ages had redounded to the benefit of the duchy which in the fourteenth and fifteenth centuries annexed the territories of a number of counties, baronies, castellanies, and lesser lordships that were unable to weather the storms. By 1500, most of the top echelon of aristocratic lordships had disappeared apart from a few, non-resident German princes such as the counts of Créhange, Sarrewerden, and Salm. What was left was a much enhanced duchy, a multiplicity of medium and small aristocratic lordships and minor fiefs, and the ancient ecclesiastical lordships. For Lorraine as a whole around 1500, the duchy held about 28% of the lordships, the lesser aristocratic lordships had 24%, and the church controlled 48%.[57]

The duchy of Lorraine consolidate institutionally only in the fifteenth century. A major part of the territory in the west of the province, principally the county of Bar, was a fief of France. The duchy itself was a principality of the Holy Roman Empire and the main cities, Metz, Toul and Verdun, were Imperial bishoprics. Although much reduced in size, the bishoprics with their cathedral chapters and ancient abbeys still occupied the lion's share of the territory in the united principality of Bar-Lorraine. In the early modern era, Lorraine passed under the political influence of France. In 1552, Henri II established a royal protectorate over the bishoprics which evolved to full annexation in 1648. Louis XIII and Louis XIV placed Lorraine under military occupation; and finally in 1766 Louis XV annexed the entire province to the crown.

Between 1500 and 1766, the duchy operated institutionally like a medieval principality comparable to Burgundy or Bretagne in the fourteenth and fifteenth century. Lorraine had an Estates General that regularly voted taxes or subventions, but the dukes continued to derive most of their revenues from their own domain lands.[58] Ducal salt mines, ducal forests, ducal domain-farms and the seigneurial dues on ducal lordships normally brought in more than half the annual revenues of the duchy. The heavy reliance on the ordinary revenues of the duchy explains the enormous care which the dukes lavished on their patrimonial domain and their sustained efforts, in good seasons and bad, to expand their holdings. Similarly, the dukes exercised a wide and lucrative protection over the ecclesiastical lordships and lent their very considerable legal support to the maintenance and the expansion of the tithes that were normally collected at 1/11.[59]

Between 1500 and 1789, Lorraine experienced first a period of recovery and growth that lasted until the 1560s, then an era of warfare and depopulation during the Wars of Religion, another period of rebuilding and recovery that extended until 1630, followed by decades of massive destruction and depopulation caused by the Thirty Years' War, Louis XIV's wars and French occupation, followed by a final wave of rebuilding, recovery and growth in the eighteenth century.[60] During each phase of reconstruction, lords consulted their ancient titles and *terriers* and strove to re-establish their lordships as they had been earlier.[61] Just as in the late Middle Ages, so too in the early modern era it was only the strongest lordships which survived the repeated cycles of devastation and rebuilding. The dukes led the way in rebuilding abandoned villages and in founding new ones, often in joint lordship with the church.[62] Although there were some temporary losses, on balance both the church and the duchy increased their holdings of lordships and domain lands while the lesser aristocratic lordships lost ground.

The fundamental demographic and economic structures of Lorraine certainly affected lordship in the province. Lorraine was lightly populated and economically underdeveloped. The towns were all small and had only a few thousand inhabitants each in the sixteenth century. At the end of the old regime, Nancy, the administrative capital, as well as Toul and Verdun, stagnant episcopal cities, had less than 10,000 inhabitants each, while Metz with about 30,000 was still a somnolent river port with at best lackluster commerce.[63] Lorraine exported a little salt, grain, lumber, iron, and wine. There was also a fairly lively transit trade, but it had little local impact.[64] In fact, most of the province lived in a state of virtual economic autarchy in which the most traditional food stuffs and commodities circulated in a number of inter-provincial local markets.[65]

Without any doubt, the most important economic activities in the province were the administration of the lordships, whether ducal, episcopal, monastic or aristocratic, the local grain trade, itself partially seigneurial, and private lending.[66] Ducal ennobling office and venal patents allowed a few men to claw their way into the lowest echelons of the nobility.[67] The only significant consolidation of lordships in early modern Lorraine was the work of the dukes. The economy was not immobile, since it underwent repeated cycles of devastation and rebuilding, but there was no economic development, and no dynamism. Lorraine lived in the sort of pre-industrial world described by Malthus and Ricardo in which demographic growth brought impoverishment for the masses and the small profits of economic backwardness to a few.[68]

Land engrossing was on a very modest scale. In villages where mortmain had been abolished and purchases by non-residents were tolerated, peasants lost some land to bourgeois investors. But only exceptionally did the non-peasant investors create substantial domain-farmers.[69] Land ownership changed, but often neither the social composition of the village nor the physical structure of farms underwent much alteration. The normal procedure simply involved the loss of ownership by the peasant families who stayed on as tenant-farmers. The investors became the legal tenants, while the old owners paid absentee landlords new rents in kind that were substantially higher than the old seigneurial renders. These rents in grain and wine supplied the tables of the bourgeois investors and provided a little extra for sale in the local markets. The few new domain-farms that appeared in the early modern centuries, whether they belonged to nobles, ecclesiastics, or commoners, were small, rarely more than 40 ha and normally less, and often composed of scattered fields that had not been physically consolidated.[70]

After every phase of devastation and depopulation, the dukes, the clergy and the lesser aristocratic lords strove to re-established tenants in their lordships.[71] Most villages were nucleated settlements and with every wave of rebuilding the village territory, the *finage*, took on a neater and more geometric layout.[72] With each rebuilding, there was some sorting out of lands and exchanges. The result was that by the middle of the eighteenth century, Lorraine had the most perfectly sculpted, geometrically balanced three-field village territories in France.[73] But institutionally, the systems of lordship in the villages had changed little.

Lordship remained a fundamental institution in the villages.[74] Village mayors drawn from the resident property owners served as agents of the lordship in the assessment and collection of seigneurial dues and the performance of *corvées*. Likewise, the apparatus of seigneurial justice with the annual assizes functioned right down to the Revolution.

A significant minority of villages in Lorraine were still subject to mortmain in the early modern centuries.[75] Most of the charters of emancipation dated from the Middle Ages. The next wave of manumissions occurred at the end of the fifteenth and the beginning of the sixteenth centuries, and the last during the reconstruction after the seventeenth century troubles. Most of the territory of the old county of Bar was free of serfdom, as was the territory under the jurisdiction of the municipal government of Metz. Serfdom had also largely disappeared in the territory of the bishopric of Toul. Elsewhere, in the bishopric of Verdun, on the lands of the cathedral chapter of Verdun, in many of the ancient abbeys and in both French and even more importantly Germanic sections of the duchy, serfdom survived right down to the Revolution.

The legal customs of serfdom in Lorraine lacked the uniformity found in provinces where political and legal unification had developed early. Lorraine was politically fragmented until the fifteenth century and so too were its legal traditions.[76] In general, *formariage* faded after the sixteenth century. The bedrock of the institution everywhere was real mortmain according to which landed estates located in villages with *mainmorte* escheated to the lord in the absence of direct heirs living in common with the deceased tenant. *Forfuyance*, initially understood as mandatory residence for real-property owners, had evolved in the hands of the jurists to mean the *droit de suite*, itself understood not as the right to retrieve the person of a serf who had left the village, but to claim ownership of his property at his death. The jurists distinguished between real and personal *forfuyance*, the first the right to claim real-estate, the second to claim movables or chattel.

Not surprisingly, the most rigorous forms of serfdom survived in the ecclesiastical lordships, in the ancient female Abbey of Saint-Pierre de Remirement and in the Cathedral Chapter of Verdun.[77] Duke Leopold's bumbling efforts to abolish mortmain on the ducal domain at the beginning of the eighteenth century as a money making project failed miserably and was finally abandoned in 1719 when the tenants refused to pay the extortionate price of freedom. In the end, Leopold abandoned without payment the right to claim the chattels of non-resident serfs, the least remunerative of the rights, and left the rest of the institution intact.[78]

Lorraine had three major fiscal systems of lordship on its small territory: two were the result of deliberate reorganization and normally had charters while the third was an unreconstructed jumble of seigneurial taxes that had accumulated over the centuries.[79] Serfdom was independent of the underlying fiscal structure of the lordship and although it normally disappeared with a comprehensive recasting of the fiscal system this was not always the case. Similarly, serfdom and unreconstructed fiscal systems often went together, but in the territory of Metz and Toul, lordships were free of serfdom but typically had unreconstructed dues and obligations.

The two reconstructed systems of lordship were already widely used in the Middle Ages.[80] In lordships recast or newly founded with the charter of Beaumont, or the local variant of it called Sainte-Croix, the principal seigneurial obligation was a proportional render, a *terrage*, of 1/11. This system was found where the villages had a single or only a few lords.[81] In villages where seigneurial authority was highly fragmented and where consequently the difficulties of collecting and dividing a proportional render were too great, lords opted for a fixed tax called an *assis*, normally assessed in kind or in cash at a fixed rate per unit of farmed land, often a standard notional unit, the plow. As a fiscal unit, the plow was normally defined as the cultivated land worked by a heavy plow drawn by 4 horses. The actual assessment was either a multiple or a fraction of the fiscal plow and depended on the size of the holding. In both of these reformed systems, many ancient obligations that usually included some or all of the *corvées* and the seigneurial *tailles* were eliminated.

The final unreconstructed system was the fiscal equivalent of an archeological dig in which age after age new seigneurial taxes had piled up. In the ecclesiastical lordship at Vergaville which belonged to the small Benedictine female convent of Saint-Eustasse, seigneurial taxes derived from the ancient *mansus* and mentioned specifically in the foundation charter of 966 where still collected on the eve of the Revolution.[82] After the inflation of the sixteenth century, the old taxes specified in cash had lost all but symbolic value. There were two annual seigneurial obligations, however, that could be updated to produce acceptable levels of income for the lords: arbitrary *tailles* and *corvées*. Lords increased arbitrary *tailles à volonté* or the *Schafft* to keep pace with changing economic times and they used periodically updated schedules to assess

the value of *corvées* in cash Hence the characteristic feature of the unreconstructed lordships was the predominance of the *tailles* and the *corvées* in the
revenue accounts.[83]

The county of Bitche, which belonged to the counts of Zweibrücken before
it passed to the dukes of Lorraine, had the unreconstructed system of lordship.
Bitche had a very important reserved domain that included forests, iron
foundries, glass works, at least 35 grain mills, thermal baths and several domain
farms. Yet, 70% of its revenues came from the tithe and from seigneurial dues,
most notably an arbitrary *taille* assessed globally on each village and town.[84]

Although the various fiscal systems of lordship in Lorraine were all strictly
maintained and periodically rebuilt, they normally brought in far less income than
the directly held domain lands.[85] The most remunerative system was unquestionably the one with the *terrage*; the least valuable, the unreconstructed fiscal grid
with the *tailles* and corvées.[86]

Alsace

Alsace became part of France in a two stage process that occurred during the
reign of Louis XIV: the first by the 1648 Treaty of Munster and the second in the
early 1680s by military occupation, subsequently recognized by international
treaties.[87] French policy from 1648, confirmed in the 1680s by royal decrees and
throughout the eighteenth century by the decisions of *Conseil souverain* at
Colmar, upheld the existing legal traditions in this Germanic province. Apart
from royal decrees that sought to limit undefined *corvées*, French annexation did
not disturb Alsatian lordship. Indeed, the king supported the integral rebuilding
of Alsatian lordship in the late seventeenth and early eighteenth century.[88]

Alsace had two counties, Nordgau and Sundgau, with capitals at Strasbourg
and Haguenau, two bishoprics, Strasbourg and Bâle, two cathedral chapters, and
a multiplicity of ancient monasteries such as Wissembourg, Munster,
Marmoutier, Murbach, Neuwiller, etc. The imperial properties were located
mainly in the Nordgau, whereas the patrimonial properties of the Habsburg were
in the Sundgau. Many aristocratic lordships rose by usurping lands from either
the emperors or the church. There was certainly some concentration of lordships
at the top of the princely hierarchy in the late Middle Ages. Significant parts of

the territory of Alsace were in the hands of German princes: the Elector of the Palatinate, the Margrave of Baden, the Count and later Duke of Württemberg, the Count of Hanau-Lichtenberg etc. But, there was also fragmentation at the bottom, most notably with the solidification of the imperial knights. The imperial knights, found mainly in the Nordgau, typically held fiefs, collected renders, but often did not exercise jurisdiction.[89] After 1648, Cardinal Mazarin helped himself shamelessly to the former Habsburg patrimonial lands which passed to his heirs after his death.[90]

The Protestant Reformation had hardly any impact on Alsatian lordship. Lordship and tithes went on as before. During the Reformation, Bâle embraced Protestantism and the municipal government took over the lordships of the bishopric, the cathedral chapter, and most of the monasteries. Bâle joined the Swiss Confederation, but many of its holdings were in Alsace. Every imperial city in Alsace, the Decapol headed by Haguenau and Colmar, as well as Strasbourg, owned lordships, exercised seigneurial jurisdiction over an extended hinterland, the *Rechtspflege*, and collected seigneurial dues.[91]

Alsatian lordship ultimately derived from the same stock of late Roman, Merovingian and Carolingian traditions as lordship in France. Alsace was a heavily forested, poor soil region, with light population. The province had a remarkably durable deposit of Carolingian *villae* and *mansi* that still served as the fiscal base of lordship in some regions well into the early modern centuries.[92] There were also more recent fiscal systems of lordship devised for clearings carried out between the late twelfth and the mid-fourteenth century that from the outset had renders assigned to individual holdings.[93]

Likewise, Alsace had its share of bad customs with taxes for hospitality and extraordinary taxes for protection, the *Schirmgeld* or *Gewerff*, the German equivalents of the seigneurial *taille*.[94] Occasionally, as in the Hapsburg lordships of the Sundgau, there was evidence of entirely recast fiscal structures in which the older layers of duties had been eliminated in favor of simplified assessments in cash and kind.[95] Finally, medieval lords mobilized the same servile controls as their French counterparts to protect the integrity of their lordships: *mainmorte, formariage*, mandatory residence. As in France, most of these servile controls shriveled to vestigial forms, most notably a mortuary fee, by the end of the

Middle Ages

What medieval Alsace did not have, and what even the early modern centuries did not produce, was a strong and unifying principality. After the collapse of the Zähringer family in the early thirteenth century, the only noble family with a large enough base to attempt to construct a real principality was the Habsburgs. The Habsburgs had their territorial base mainly in the south, in Haute Alsace. The Habsburgs acquired willy-nilly additional lordships in Alsace and in the nearby Brisgau. They managed their individual lordships with great care, or more commonly pawned them to creditors who did this work. They even, belatedly, erected a higher seigneurial administrative apparatus with provosts and bailiffs, a central counsel and a chamber of accounts. These high administrative institutions for their lordships copied Burgundian and French royal practices and appeared 200 to 300 years later than in France, during the reigns of the emperors Maximilian I, Ferdinand I, and Maximilian II, from the 1490s to the 1570s.[96] But, the Habsburgs never seriously attempted to construct a real sovereign principality in Alsace.[97] The absence of a territorial principality that claimed and exercised sovereign authority had a profound and durable influence on the political and institutional development of Alsatian lordship.

Where strong principalities appeared in France, the king and the princes claimed for themselves the exclusive right to impose new taxes which characteristically took the form of state taxes assessed on the entire landmass of the principality or domain and on all of the inhabitants, even those on noble and ecclesiastical lordships. In France, lesser lords where hemmed in by the higher political and institutional authority of the prince and his state. Specifically, this meant that French lordships beneath the status of sovereign principalities could not expand and modernize at will their fiscal base. They were limited to traditional renders and dues. The more comprehensive seigneurial taxes, the *tailles*, that encompassed all residents of a given area regardless of tenurial holdings, were strictly limited by custom. Politically, it was the power of the king which settled the issue of control of the potential fiscal base. Tactically, the king and the royal courts in the early modern centuries used the customary laws as a brake on lordship. For example, lords could typically claim the extraordinary seigneurial *taille* for the widely recognized "four cases", such as the marriage of a daughter, but they could not just impose a new tax, a *taille*, to defray the costs of their household. Control of the fiscal base had been decided in favor of the king of France by the end of the Middle Ages.

However, in Alsace, lesser lords were not hemmed in by an overarching princely state. They could and did pile new taxes on top of old, direct and indirect.[98] Imperial decrees of the late fifteenth and early sixteenth century specifically recognized the fiscal authority of the lords to impose new taxes for legitimate expenses. Likewise, the imperial supreme court, the *Reichskammergericht*, confirmed these rights. After annexation to France, royal decrees and the jurisprudence of the *Conseil souverain* likewise confirmed the wide taxing power of Alsatian lords.[99] In one of its last meetings after French annexation, the Estates of Basse-Alsace recognized the right of lords to assess extraordinary taxes to defray the costs of rebuilding their lordships.[100] Similar arrangements existed elsewhere in the German Rhineland region for the same political and institutional reasons.

The fiscal burdens of Alsatian lordship divided into two parts from at least the thirteenth century.[101] The first part consisted of the renders in cash and kind assigned to individual tenures or to fiscal units which encompassed various land holdings. This layer of lordship, *Grundherrschaft*, and taxes, *Grundzins*, in French *redevances foncières seigneuriales*, was restored after every wave of devastation and depopulation: at the end of the Middle Ages and after 1660 in the wake of the Thirty Years' War.[102] While not always absolutely immutable, this layer of seigneurial taxes was usually light and designed to attract and hold settlers in an area which was not particularly attractive to farmers. This was the bait used to settled the lands.[103]

The second part of Alsatian lordship, *Landherrschaft*, what modern French historians call the *seigneurie banale*, had its own fiscal institutions that consisted of direct and indirect taxes which lords could increase largely at will. These taxes included indirect levies on wine and commodities sold in the market, income taxes assessed on the wealth of all of the inhabitants of the lordship, and the like. This layer of seigneurial taxes almost always brought in more income than the land renders.[104]

In the century prior to the German Peasants' War which deeply affected the territory of Alsace, lesser counts, robber barons, grasping cathedral chapters, bishoprics and monasteries imposed without restraint new direct and indirect seigneurial taxes.[105] Whereas the payment of new taxes to the King of France eventually resulted in the establishment of peace, law and order, in Alsace the new seigneurial taxes of the fifteenth and early sixteenth century, like the bad customs of the earlier Middle Ages, simply financed endless petty feudal warfare that diminished rather than enhanced the security of the region.[106] This growing frustration spilled out in decades of unrest that culminated in the Peasants' War of 1525.[107] The Peasants' War, however, was a resounding failure for the rebels that only strengthened the authority of the lords. Indeed, with the support of the emperor and the imperial court, lords imposed new taxes to amortize the debts and fines that flowed from the recent uprising.[108]

Even after annexation to France, Alsatian lords continued to exercise far wider fiscal authority over their subjects than lords in the rest of France.[109] In a sample of twenty-eight lordships in the Alsatian plaine in the late seventeenth and eighteenth century, the two levels of seigneurial dues were clearly evident. The lower level contained layer upon layer of ancient medieval dues that had been carefully reestablished with resettlement and which often included modest payments in lieu of mortmain. Added together, these dues produced very little annual revenue. The real money came from the higher layer of seigneurial taxes, the *Beet* and *Schatzung*, two terms among many for varieties of annual seigneurial *tailles*, and from payments in lieu of *corvées*.[110] At Ittlenheim which was part of a divided seigneurie that belonged jointly to the Bishop of Strasbourg and the municipal government, the magistracy of Strasbourg, resettlement was turned over to a professional land manager and recruiter. The resettlement occurred between 1694 and 1726 and involved about a dozen families. In the long list of seigneurial payments due, only two produced significant revenues: the annual *taille*, which brought in 33 florins and 20 sacks of rye, and payments in lieu of *corvées*, which produced 118 florins.[111]

At the time of the reconstruction of Alsace, the Duke of Mazarin-La Meilleraye, the provincial governor of Alsace and the owner of the bulk of the Hapsburg lordships, was one of the most hard-faced seigneurial administrators. His demands for redemption payments for *corvées* from his subjects were supported by the royal *Conseil d'État* in 1698 but vigorously opposed by the intendant who was horrified at the sums involved. Mazarin demanded 600,000 *livres,* roughly twice the entire provincial assessment for the royal direct taxes. There were uprisings against the Duke, and royal troops had to be sent to restore order.[112] During the second half of the eighteenth century, aristocratic and ecclesiastical lords, led by the Bishop of Strasbourg, the Duke of Württemberg, and the Duke of Mazarin, dramatically increased the annual assessments for *tailles* and *corvées* in their lordships.[113] Alsatian customs usually placed no limits on the number of annual *corvées* which lords could assess on their subjects. Like the ancient Roman *munera sordida* which it resembled, the Alsatian *Frondienst* was often assessed at will.

Another peculiarity of Alsatian lordship flowed from the insurmountable mediocrity of the local economy and the enormous solidarity of the peasant villages which in part derived from very traditional pre-industrial economic arrangements. Lands in Alsace lent themselves best to subsistence and small scale peasant agriculture, *petite culture.* The towns were very small and offered only narrow markets for the most common agricultural products. Even after decades of demographic growth in the eighteenth century which roughly doubled the population of the province, Strasbourg, the largest town, had barely 50,000 inhabitants on the eve of the Revolution.[114] Likewise, prior to the abolition of feudalism by the French Revolution and Napoleon, commerce on the lower Rhine was choked by a multiplicity of tolls.[115]

The market forces for the construction of larger-scale domain farms were largely absent. Although a few isolated and consolidated medium sized farms appeared here and there, they were highly unusual.[116] Peasants owned at least 50% of the cultivated land in the province and farmed the rest which belonged in roughly equal shares to the church, the nobles, and bourgeois investors. Although legally, the upperclasses owned upwards of half the farmland, physically this farmland was normally indistinguishable from, and intermixed with, peasant tenures.[117]

In Alsace, most peasants lived in nucleated villages whose size expanded and contracted with the demographic cycles. The village, *Ding,* had its own administrative syndic, *Heimburg,* its budget and, frequently, its common lands.[118]

The involuted village likewise served as the physical base for lordship. Seigneurial taxes were often levied on the village as a whole, or on fiscal units within the village. Although typically divided economically into yeomen and cottagers, the peasant inhabitants were bound together by particularly strong habits of village solidarity and by extreme hostility to outsiders.

These social, economic and physical features of the Alsatian villages had a direct and powerful impact on lordship which expressed themselves in the same ways over and over again with each cycle of strong demographic growth in the thirteenth, the sixteenth, and the eighteenth century. In the rebuilding of Alsace in the second half of the seventeenth century, labor was scarce and land was abundant. Lords generously offered tenants land at low rates. For the resettlement projects, lords employed indifferently perpetual seigneurial tenures and short term leases. The whole point was to get farmers back on the land and hold them there. Lords were not in a position to be demanding. Demographic and economic recovery was relatively quick, but still took a generation or two to produce significant results.

For the peasants in the Alsatian villages, the most important thing was to establish familial control of farmland regardless of what legal arrangement had been initially used. For lords, the important thing was to have inhabitants in their lordships. With demographic growth came division of farmlands. Leases tacitly renewed became *de facto* perpetual tenures with immutable renders.[119] Even domain-farms that where physically distinct from the village *finage* followed the same path through sub-leasing into perpetual peasant tenures. The *Conseil souverain* at Colmar followed the earlier jurisprudence of the *Reichskammergericht* of Speyer and considered any tenure whose rental had not been changed in 30 or 40 years to be a perpetual emphyteutic lease with an immutable annual payment. Bourgeois investors who bought lands in the villages or acquired them through foreclosure were forced by village solidarity to release these to village residents or face the threat of boycott, arson, or worse.[120] With time, virtually all arrangements that affected lands became *de facto* perpetual tenures that were highly fragmented.[121]

This cycle played out three times in the pre-industrial era in Alsace and each time produced the same results, one of which was the emergence of the *Träger*, the chief tenant in charge of collecting the rents from the sub tenants and handing the proceeds over to the appropriate authority.[122] The Alsatian *Träger* appeared first as the collectors of seigneurial dues for the medieval *mansi, Hube*, or *Mentag*. They multiplied in the sixteenth century with the informal divisions carried out in the re-established *Hube, Mentag*, in the individualized tenures, and even in leased domain-farms. Likewise, they proliferated in the eighteenth century on land holdings of all sorts.

Alsatian land law was notoriously vague.[123] Since there had never been a comprehensive Alsatian principality and no Alsatian provincial high court prior to annexation, not even intermediate courts comparable to the French royal *bailliages*, there were no general customary laws, and not even any regional laws.[124] Each lordship and village had its records and its customs, its *Weistümer*. Practice and possession, not logic, established Alsatian land law. Specifically, the strength and the immobile social cohesion of the Alsatian villages transformed every landholding into a peasant farm that payed fixed rentals in sacks of grain, *Gülten*, to outsiders: nobles, ecclesiastics, and bourgeois.

Even the sale of church properties during the Revolution made scarcely a dent on village solidarity and the death-grip of the peasantry on the farmland. The only difference was that the sacks of grain previously paid to ecclesiastical officials now went to private individuals. The legal status of the lands and the nature of the rentals remained as vague after the Revolution as before.[125]

A final peculiar and durable feature of Alsatian lordship was the maintenance of medieval village governance and village-based justice.[126] The basic cadre of seigneurial officials in the Alsatian villages were normally recruited from the village inhabitants. The *Schultheiss* represented the lord who exercised the rights of justice, while the *Meyer*, the mayor or mayors in the event of a divided lordship, was responsible for the collection of the lower range of seigneurial revenues. There were also sergents, communal agrarian guards, herders, etc. The French regulations which from the sixteenth century required a licensed legal professional to serve as judge in the seigneurial courts were issued, but not enforced in Alsace. Normally, the village court, *Gericht*, handled the routine judicial work. Just as in the Middle Ages, the chief seigneurial official, the *Schultheiss*, a resident village notable who usually served for life, provided over the village tribunal and confirmed the judgment which other village notables rendered collectively. These same village seigneurial officials expanded and amended the ancient village customs, the *Weistümer*, with appropriate new regulations, *Dorfordnungen*.

Lyonnais

There were no significant changes in lordship in the Lyonnais region under the old regime. The institutions and practices in place by the end of the Middle Ages remained in force until the Revolution.[127] As a thoroughly marginal region in the Middle Ages, Lyonnais had never been of much interest to the kings of France, the Emperors of the Holy Roman Empire, or local princes. Consequently, the archbishop of Lyon, the Cathedral Chapter of Saint-Jean together with a clutch of collegial churches and abbeys retained control of virtually all of the lordships of any importance. These ecclesiastical institutions were of unimpressive stature when compared to the great bishoprics, chapters and abbeys of northern France and the Empire. The ecclesiastical lords of Lyonnais had petty lay vassals in abundance, but typically they held only minor fiefs without rights of justice.

By 1500, lords had commuted most of the proportional renders, the *tâches*, to fixed renders in kind or simple cash *cens*.[128] The ecclesiastical lords were far more interested in the tithes than in the seigneurial renders. The overwhelming dominance of the ecclesiastical lordships had greatly facilitated the spread and regularization of the tithe in Lyonnais.[129] Disputes over the tithes were a constant feature of Lyonnais from the thirteenth century through the end of the eighteenth century, but there were three periods when these disputes grew to the level of generalized anti-tithe movements: in the late fifteenth and early sixteenth century, during the Wars of Religion in the second half of the sixteenth century, and finally in the second half of the eighteenth century.

In the period from about the 1470s to the 1520s, tithe disputes appeared as the population and economy of Lyonnais grew beyond previous medieval levels. The ecclesiastical lords negotiated shrewdly.[130] Often they abandoned the very high rate of 1/10 for 1/11, the rate that became the standard for the region. Occasionally, they agreed to transform the proportional tithe into a fixed payment, normally in kind. In return for these minor concessions, they usually succeeded in extending the tithe to all territories and virtually all crops within the tithing districts. In all likelihood, the ecclesiastical lords lost nothing with these changes and may well have gained.

During the Wars of Religion, the spread of Calvinism led many peasants to believe that the tithe would be abolished as the church was reformed. This was certainly not the intent of the leading Protestants. More importantly, the kings of France supported the tithe here and elsewhere in France with the full weight of their authority, political, military, and judicial. By the early seventeenth century, the tithes were all re-established. Likewise, the disputes of the last decades of the old regime failed to undermine the tithe because the entire legal, administrative, and political apparatus of the monarchy supported the church. Here, as elsewhere, the disputes arose mainly because of on-going changes in land use and cropping practices.[131]

Lordships and the tithe were as firmly planted in Lyonnais in 1780 as they had been in 1500. Virtually all of the lesser towns, and nearly all of the villages and hamlets were still under the authority of seigneurial officials and seigneurial judges at the end of the old regime.[132] In Lyonnais, most lordships with rights of justice belonged to the church, whereas in Beaujolais, aristocratic lordships with justice were common.[133]

Although ubiquitous and immovable, perhaps the most striking thing about lordship in Lyonnais under the old regime was its thoroughly marginal importance when measured against the quite dramatic economic and social changes which occurred here between 1500 and 1789.[134] Lordship was a stable and largely static institution in a region teaming with new life. Lordship was neither strong enough to stand in the way nor flexible enough to participate in the great changes that occurred.

In the sixteenth century, Lyon became for a while a major French and European commercial and banking center thanks to its fairs.[135] By the early seventeenth century, Lyon's days as an international economic center were over, but by this time the silk industry, founded in the late fifteenth century, had grown to national and international proportions. The expansion of the silk industry accelerated in the late seventeenth and eighteenth century thanks to Colbert's protectionism. Industry spilled out into the countryside in silks, toiles, even

ꞬꞬꞬꞬ The production of raw silk became a growth sector, as too did the transportation of all sorts of commodities and manufactured goods, from foodstuffs to coal and textiles. Non-agricultural workers and their families clustered in the growing villages and towns. By the end of the old regime, Lyonnais was one of the most densely populated and industrialized regions in France.[136]

Finally, Beaujolais became in the eighteenth century a growing supply region for common wines for the Parisian market. Bourgeois investment in the Beaujolais vineyards was certainly on a great scale, but it rarely disturbed the seigneurial institutions.[137] Normally, bourgeois simply bought up peasant tenures and established peasant sharecroppers who in turn paid *rentes* in kind to the new landlords. The bourgeois investors became the legal tenants of the *seigneuries*, but in practice it was the tenant farmers who handled the payment of the old seigneurial renders and tithes. Occasionally, bourgeois cleared their vineyards of seigneurial renders by offering impecunious lords ready cash. However, these transactions almost never occurred in ecclesiastical lordships, but rather on the petty aristocratic fiefs.

Lordship neither contributed to nor benefitted much from this growth and development in Lyonnais under the old regime. There were several reasons for this remarkable marginality. First of all, the soils were extremely poor and the climate was high capricious. Agriculture in Lyonnais fell well below the bar of even honest mediocrity. The soils were the despair of farmers and the city fathers alike who were charged with feeding the teaming multitudes in the urban center. Observers bemoaned the sterile and ungrateful soils. Lyon could not feed itself from the agricultural resources of the Lyonnais and depended on grains, livestock, and even wine that traveled south on the Saône from Bourgogne and Lorraine.[138]

Agriculture in Lyon was essentially low yield, small-scale mixed farming, *petite polyculture,* that remained overwhelming the concern of peasant owner-cultivators and dirt poor sharecroppers. Urban investment in the countryside was of minor importance throughout the period 1400-1789. Bourgeois investment as measured by estate inventories was typically far more concentrated in urban than in rural properties, by a proportion of three or four to one.[139] Likewise, investments in rural *rentes* paid in agricultural products were often more important than direct investments in land. The purpose of these *rentes* was to supply the urban investors with food for their tables, not commodities to sell in the market.[140] The construction of bourgeois, ecclesiastical and aristocratic domain-farms, so common in the agriculturally richer areas of France, was conspicuous by its absence in Lyonnais. Indeed, the agricultural resources of Lyonnais were so poor and uninviting that Lyon stood next to a rural country-side, but did not dominate it as a food-supply zone.[141] In this respect, Lyon resembled Marseille, rather than Paris, Bordeaux or Toulouse.

The behavior of the *Hôtel-Dieu* of Lyon, said to have been founded by King Childebert in 542, was a perfect reflection of the investment priorities of the non-peasant population in Lyonnais.[142] The *Hôtel-Dieu*, managed from the early sixteenth century by municipal officials of Lyon, regularly received pious bequests in the form of rural properties, which it unloaded as soon as possible for more profitable investments. The hospital was one of the major real-estate owners in the city and drew nearly 150,000 *livres* a year from the rental of houses, apartments, stores and the like at Lyon, roughly three times the revenues of less than 50,000 *livres* that it drew from its rural rents. Total revenues of the hospital in the 1750s and 1760s averaged over 500,000 *livres* a year.

In Beaujolais, however, more compact domain-farms appeared than in Lyonnais. From the late seventeenth century, the Parisian market for wine made Beaujolais an attractive area for bourgeois investment. Consequently, in Beaujolais the normal pattern of changes in landownership unfolded. Upperclass investors from Lyon created compact farms, in this case vineyards, from the lands of indebted peasants and from lands brought into cultivation for the first time.[143]

Another important reason for the marginality of lordship in Lyon was the absence of an important noble class. The nobility of Lyonnais consisted almost entirely of petty vassals of the church whose noble properties included noble domain-farms, some minor revenues from seigneurial renders, but rarely rights of jurisdiction. Consequently, the raw material for the construction of significant aristocratic lordships simply did not exist. There was only one elevation of an aristocratic lordship to the status of a ducal peerage in Lyonnais under the old regime, and this was on the periphery of the province.[144]

Lyonnais did not experience the dramatic renewal and upgrading of the cadre of lords by additions of fresh wealth and blood which was the normal pattern in old regime France. The nobles of Lyon were wealthy urbanites most of whom did not own significant lordships. Many nobles acquired their status through municipal offices and through the purchase of petty royal offices. A few men purchased patents of nobility and became *secretaires du roi*, but the nobility thus purchased was itself of marginal value that normally yielded more derision than admiration. In the countryside, old noble families certainly disappeared and new families replaced them. However, it was usually not the most dynamic families in the province who merged into the rural nobility, but rather peasant and petty bourgeois families of modest means and modest social aspirations. Lyon was a commercial, banking, and industrial city whose leading inhabitants were and usually remained bourgeois, not noble.[145] The institutional base for the renewal of the nobility was also absent. There was no *Parlement*, no *Chambre des comptes*, etc. A *Cour des monnaies* appeared in the early eighteenth century, but that was hardly enough to give Lyon a class of ambitious ennobled noble officials anxious to embellish their status with rural *seigneuries* and noble domain-farms.[146]

Dauphiné

Remote, lightly populated, and backward in every way, the Alpine province of Dauphiné was largely ignored by the outside world.[147] With annexation to France in 1349, the kings succeeded the dauphins, but the forbidding topography of Dauphiné stood in the way of strong political and institutional unification. The most vital units were always the local communities which typically lived a largely self-sufficient existence. The lordships of Dauphiné were nearly as numerous as the communities themselves. Although they were usually small, the lordships of Dauphiné were still remarkably durable. No force, indigenous or exogenous, disturbed the institutional arrangements of lordship either in the Middle Ages or in the early modern era.[148] Indeed, all of the seigneurial institutions that remained so forcefully in place until the Revolution, were already well-established by the thirteenth century.

The overwhelmingly dominant pattern of habitation in Dauphiné was dispersed settlement in small villages and hamlets, the *mas*. This was just the sort of settlement that had led the Carolingians to establish abstract fiscal units of assessment, the *mansi*, that pulled together for taxing purposes a cluster of households. Dauphiné had its share of Carolingian *mansi*. It was only in the valley of the Isère near Grenoble, the area called the Grésivaudan, and along parts of the flood plain of the Rhône, notably near Vienne, that collective fiscal units of assessment for seigneurial dues fragmented into individualized *censives*. Elsewhere, the *mansi*, and a number of later fiscal systems of lordship that imitated the *mansi*, survived.

The typical institutional expression of lordship consisted of the juxtaposition in a small area, often in the same lordship, of several different types of fiscal units that corresponded to the stages of settlement and land clearing in the province.[149] Next to the *mansi* of the Carolingian and early Capetian era, there were smaller units, the *cabanneria* and the *borderia*, respectively half and a quarter of a *mansi*, that dated from the clearings of the twelfth and early thirteenth centuries. Next to them were the *albergements* that proliferated from the thirteenth century and which increased in number again in the early modern period.[150] In Queyras, high in the Alps, there were 7 *allodia*, 8 *mansi*, 36 *cabanneria*, 6 *borderia*, and 6 *quarteria*, which were domain-farms. In Queyras as well as in Oisans, these fiscal units of lordship appeared in seigneurial records of the thirteenth, the seventeenth, and the eighteenth centuries.[151] All of these institutions functioned in essentially the same way. They were units of collective assessment for seigneurial taxes that normally were unaffected by the divisions of property within them. Indeed, it was precisely because population increase and land division was so timid in most of the province that these abstract fiscal units survived century after century.

There were some minor differences in the seigneurial dues or taxes assigned to these units that reflected their historical origins and development.[152] The *mansi* normally had fixed assessments in cash and more commonly in kind that were then divided among the actual inhabitants and farmers. The *cabanneria, borderia* and the *albergements* normally had proportional renders, the *tâches*, collected at rates that varied from place to place from a low of 1/20 for all crops to a high of 1/6 or so assessed only on the major grains and grapes. On top of this layer of seigneurial dues, there were a variety of collective assessments of various dates: ancient taxes for hospitality, for castle guard duty, layer upon layer of seigneurial *tailles*, payments in lieu of *corvées* and the like.[153] Some communities had simplified this array of seigneurial taxes by agreeing to a single new seigneurial *taille* of a stated amount, while others retained the full range of dues.[154] Naturally, there were also banal mills, indirect taxes collected in the markets, even tolls and taxes on transhumant livestock.[155]

In the *seigneurie* of Saint-Martin-de-Belleville in the high valley of Tarentaise, each *mas* in the lordship bore renders that consisted of a small cash *cens,* a *terrage* or *tâche* of three *setiers* of grain, half rye and half oats, and a payment of 12 deniers for the rights of hospitality, all subdivided among the actual tenants.[156] On the small fief owned by Fazy de Rame near Embrun, the various medieval assessments gave way to a single collective payment of 210 *setiers* of grain, two-thirds in wheat and one third in oats. This commutation occurred at some time during the fourteenth century and was in full operation at the end of the fifteenth and the beginning of the sixteenth century.[157] Often, but not always, the commutations of old dues into a single seigneurial tax appeared in charters that recognized town and village rights of internal self-governance.[158]

The most remote settlements in the high Alps, which for many centuries had escaped seigneurial taxation, also had a variant of the basic pattern of collective assessment. In some cases, the term used was *allodia,* which indicated that originally the communities were independent and untaxed.[159] In other cases, the term *allodia,* was not used, but the underlying reality was the same. Perhaps the most famous example of this was the 1343 contract between five Alpine communities of the Briançonnais and the last Dauphin, Hubert II, which established a single comital *taille* for the region. This arrangement lasted without alteration until the French Revolution.[160]

In the century and a half prior to the reign of Louis XIV, 1500 to 1660, the province suffered grievously from troop movements and the forced lodging of soldiers. Many communities fell hopelessly into debt and borrowed heavily from lords who often were the only ones with money to lend. Communal debts in turn led to the establishment of new taxes to service these debts. Although many of these *rentes* or *tailles* were legally not seigneurial taxes, they were nonetheless paid to lords. In the eyes of the village inhabitants, these new *rentes* established in the seventeenth and eighteenth centuries were just another seigneurial tax assessed on the community as a whole.[161]

Concentration of lordships at the top of the noble hierarchy certainly occurred to some extent in Dauphiné, as can be seen by the elevation of four clusters of lordships to the status of ducal peerages.[162] Nevertheless, the vast majority of lordships were very small and encompassed only one or two communities. These communities in turn were assemblages of hamlets and villages. For the roughly 1000 communities in the province on the eve of the Revolution, there were 420 lords with rights of justice and another 1000 nobles who collected some seigneurial dues but who did not have rights of justice.[163] Many of these minor fief holders were the direct descendants of the medieval castle guards, *militi castri*, and the hereditary fiscal agents, *ministri*, all of whom were remunerated with shares of the revenues of the fiscal units in the lordship.[164] In more progressive provinces, these parasitical agents had disappeared through repurchase by the end of the Middle Ages. In Dauphiné, especially in the high mountains, they survived.

The old comital domain of the dauphins, purchased by the king of France in 1349, was itself a thing of shreds and patches. Hardly more than 10% of the communities in Dauphiné had the king as their direct lord. Most of these lordships were in the hands of petty *engagistes* who in effect paid the king a rent for the right to collect these seigneurial dues. The church also cut an unimpressive figure.[165] The bishoprics of Grenoble, Vienne, Embrun, Die, and Valence were all poorly endowed. Finally, the robe nobles of the *Parlement* of Grenoble, a tiny town with scarcely more than 20,000 inhabitants at the end of the old regime, were arguably the poorest ennobled magistrates in the realm. The *Parlementaires* certainly acquired lordships, but they were hardly the men to carry out significant upgrading of lordships in Dauphiné.

Similarly, there was some expansion of seigneurial domain-farms. By the late eighteenth century, nobles owned as much as 65% of the cultivated lands in the most desirable sections of the plains of the Rhône and the Isère.[166] Yet, the typical noble domain-farm in Dauphiné on the eve of the Revolution was still a small, polycultural operation of 20 to 30 ha in the hands of a poor sharecropper.

All told, the most striking thing about lordship in Dauphine in the early modern period was its immense multi-secular immobility.[167] The seigneurial courts were ubiquitous and still handled the great majority of cases in the province.[168] There were over 400 seigneurial courts with full rights of justice, high, medium and low, for about 1000 communities in the province.[169] The villages and hamlets were still under the tutelage of the seigneurial officials, most notably the judge or *châtelain*, who presided over the meetings of the village consuls or *syndics*.[170] For the most part, the seigneurial dues did not change in the early modern centuries. They were still collected overwhelmingly in kind, in grain, on the eve of the Revolution.[171] Often, the totals collected for seigneurial dues in the communities exceeded the totals for the royal *taille*.[172]

CHAPTER FOUR

Regional Patterns of Lordship, III

Western France

Normandie

After the reconstruction of the province in the wake of the Hundred Years' War, Normandie experienced rapid economic and social change which began in the early sixteenth century and continued down to the Revolution and beyond.[1] Thanks to the river traffic on the Seine and the enormous demand of the Parisian market, patterns of landholding and employment evolved dramatically. In upper or Haute Normandie, the northern and eastern parts of the province, peasant subsistence agriculture largely disappeared in favor of commercial agriculture on ancient seigneurial domain-farms and new farms pieced together by lords, bourgeois, and ecclesiastical institutions. In response to Parisian demand, grain farming faded in favor of grassland for fattening livestock in the Pays d'Auge and for dairy products in Bessin and Bray.[2] Grain farming survived and took on a clearly commercial stature in the Pays de Caux and Vexin, but produced mainly for the burgeoning markets in Haute Normandie. In the most economically advanced regions of Normandie at the end of the old regime, 80% of the land belonged to members of the upper classes in medium-sized farms worked by market-oriented tenants farmers.[3]

At the same time, Normandie became a major center for the rural textile industry, initially for woollens, linen and flax, and then, from the late seventeenth and eighteenth century, for cotton. The availability of employment in the textile industry and in a variety of fields that served the expanding traffic of the province produced a dense non-agricultural rural population. By the late eighteenth century, 50% to 80% of the rural population in some regions consisted of landless cottages employed in the industrial, artisanal and tertiary sectors of the economy.[4]

The dramatic changes in the patterns of landownership in the most economically advanced areas of Normandie meant that the great majority of the seigneurial renders as well as the tithes fell on lands that belonged to members of the upper classes. These feudal burdens were widely viewed as just a minor cost of production for the tenant farmers who actually worked the upper-class properties.[5] The majority of the rural inhabitants in Normandie paid no seigneurial dues assessed on land and no tithes. Consequently, the disorder that occurred at the end of the old regime and the beginning of the Revolution centered around the price of bread rather than the seigneurial system.

In the midst of very significant changes in the socio-economic structures, lordship in Normandie early modern era displayed both great continuity and some alterations. Continuity appeared at the base, in the fiscal aspects of lordship. Although they were normally subdivided, the ancient Norman tenures or *fieffes* survived as the legal basis for the assessment of *cens* and various renders. The oldest Norman tenures, the *villenages, bordages, vavassories, sergenteries*, as well as the *hostises, censives, tènements*, and *masures*, which appeared from the middle of the twelfth century, survived in the Norman lordships as fiscal units in the land registers, the *censiers*, until the end of the old regime.[6]

Similarly, the local system of collection of the seigneurial dues in which a single tenant was designated each year as the *prévôt* with the responsibility of supervising the actual payment of the dues by each tenant survived and even expanded.[7] Initially, the obligation of *prévôté* appeared mainly in the oldest Norman tenures. This system, described in detail along with the annual meeting of the seigneurial general assize in the reformed customary law of 1583, soon spread to most lordships of any size regardless of what the fiscal units of tenure were.[8]

The collection of seigneurial dues at the assize, *l'assemblée des gages-pleiges*, was an annual ritual that functioned with liturgical regularity all over Normandie even on the eve of the Revolution. The threat of stiff fines and even confiscation of tenures insured attendance, declaration and payment. In 1786,

Charles-Antoine Morel, a lawyer in the *Parlement of Rouen* and the *sénéchal* or chief judicial official in the barony of Marcey, called a general assize of all tenants.[9] The barony, which belonged to Jean-Louis Carbonnel, a member of an ancient Norman noble family, encompassed parts of 40 villages in Basse Normandie. The assize met on November 12 and elected André Laîné, a twenty year old, as *prévôt*, the official responsible for the collection of the seigneurial taxes. For this burden, the new *prévôt* received 1/10 of the proceeds. After the election of the *prévôt*, the tenants made their formal declarations of what they owed for seigneurial taxes on their tenures. The *procureur-receveur* of the barony checked the accuracy of these declarations against an abstract of the land register of the barony. The renders and taxes fell due at various times during the year. Although the *prévôt* was legally responsible for the collection of the various taxes and for any non-payment, he pressured the elders of the villages who bore joint responsibility for payments within their communities. When the accounts for the year were closed on August 18, 1787, the total value of the seigneurial dues according to the official prices used was 5,273 *livres* 19 *sous* 2 *deniers*. Roughly 10% of this total came from taxes assessed in cash, while 90% came from renders in kind, in oats, wheat, poultry, sheep, pepper, etc. For his good work, the *prévôt* received a payment of 527 *livres*, substantially more than a common laborer earned in an entire year.

Another element of multi-secular continuity was the preservation of most of the ancient renders and taxes. Neither the disorders of late Middle Ages nor the skyrocketing inflation of the sixteenth century seriously weakened lordship in Normandie.[10] There was no economic crisis of feudalism here.[11] Both ecclesiastical and aristocratic lords were perfectly capable of adapting their lordships to changing economic conditions. While it is true that the fractional shares of poultry and even some of the assessments of measures of grain were commuted into cash payments in some lordships by the end of the Middle Ages, payments in kind certainly did not entirely disappear.[12] They survived largely intact in Basse Normandie and were less common but not unknown in the more economically advanced Haute Normandie.[13] Although payments often continued to be listed in kind, normally the actual collection was in cash according to official prices drawn up each year for the commodities. This arrangement protected at least some of the annual seigneurial dues from the forces of inflation.

Commutations from payment in kind to payment in cash occurred in the early modern centuries, but comprehensive recasting of the fiscal structures of lordships was unusual. Such a recasting occurred in 1535 in the Pays de Caux when the *seigneurie* of Saint-Martin-aux-Chartrains and d'Englesqueville scrapped the ancient fiscal system of *villenages* with its renders in kind that included a *champart* of 1/6 in favor of a uniform rate of 2 *sous* 6 *deniers* per *vergée* of arable land.[14] The more common examples of fiscal recasting involved the elimination of the payments in kind for the tithe in favor of a simple cash tax. This sort of change occurred when cropping patterns underwent significant and widespread alteration. The records of the priory of Sainte-Barbe at Bonneville-la-Louvet in the Pays d'Auge show that as grain farming retreated in favor of pasture a number of arrangements between the tenants and the priory little by little transformed the tithes collected in grains to fixed annual rents in cash. There was some litigation, but as a rule the conversions occurred without trouble by mutual agreement.[15]

River tolls and urban market fees even when collected at ancient rates produced very significant revenues for lords lucky enough to own them. The most striking example of this sort of seigneurial revenue was the *vicomté de l'eau* of Rouen, a prestigious fief that consisted of the right to collect the ancient ducal tolls and taxes on merchandise passing through Rouen.[16] From 1717, this viscounty belonged to the princes of Condé. Although the tax rates were low, for example a mere 5 *sous* per hundred *livre* bale of cotton whose value fluctuated between 110 and 275 *livres* in the decades before the Revolution, the enormous volume of traffic passing through Rouen on the Seine meant that the total revenues of the viscounty reached 100,000 *livres* at the end of the old regime. Similarly, the counties of Eu, Tancarville, and Lillebonne, the principality of Yvetot, the barony of Fécamp, and abbey of Montivilliers collected tolls and market taxes in multiples of 10,000 *livres* a year in the seventeenth and eighteenth century. In 1778, the principality of Yvetot, centered in a bourg that was a manufacturing center, collected 76% of its revenues, 36,237 *livres* out of a total of 47,382, from market taxes.[17]

Although the fiscal system of lordship in Normandie survived with only timely updates, seigneurial dues normally accounted for only a small part of the total revenues of lordship. Lords normally drew the majority of their revenues from their domain lands. For 28 large lordships in upper Normandie in the late eighteenth century, 17% of total incomes came from seigneurial dues while 83% came from non-seigneurial holdings such as domain-farms and forests.[18] For twenty aristocratic and ecclesiastical lordships in the Pays de Caux for the period 1650–1789, *droits seigneuriaux* accounted for 20 to 30% of the revenues.[19] The fiscal revenues of lordship bulked larger in the accounts of the ecclesiastical lordships than in the aristocratic properties, but even here it was normally the tithe revenues, not the income from *cens* and renders, which were most important.[20]

Not surprisingly, Normandie was a model case for the Gregorian reform movement which transformed the tithe in the high Middle Ages into a comprehensive ecclesiastical tax of universal incidence. Rarely in the hands of laymen and collected at a pitiless rate of 1/11th, the tithe provided abundant revenues for the entire church. Bishoprics, chapters, collegial churches and monasteries controlled the great tithes on the four major grains, while the *vertes* and *menues dîmes* partially funded the parish churches. There were tithes on sheep collected in lambs and fleeces, tithes on swine and poultry, tithes on hemp and flax, tithes on hay, clover, even tithes on vegetables in the garden and occasionally tithes on forests.[21]

Seigneurial domain-farms expanded and multiplied between 1500 and 1789. Ecclesiastical and aristocratic lords as well as bourgeois who merged into the nobility cobbled together farmlands from peasant tenures and uncultivated wastes.[22] Here, as elsewhere, the principal changes in the ownership of farmland, namely the partial liquidation of the peasantry and the growth of upperclass farms, occurred between 1520 and 1720 with the most intense phase between 1560 and 1660. Lords responded both to the inflation of the sixteenth century and to the economic pull of expanding markets after 1500. In Normandie, as in England, this process of enclosure stretched over centuries and certainly did not exclude profitable investments in non-seigneurial land rents payable in kind.[23] Lords shifted from reliance on seigneurial *cens* and renders to incomes from commercial farms and forests. In the eighteenth century, the barony of Fécamp had 28 domain farms the county of Lillebonne had 18, etc.[24] While enclosure was the rule in the lordships of Normandie, *seigneuries* that were unusually well-endowed with forests, such as the baronies of Neubourg and Pont-St-Pierre, responded to the loss of income from cash *cens* through inflation mainly by expanding the commercial management of lumber sales.[25]

Social and political forces also slowly remodeled the hierarchy of Norman fiefs in line with the general trends found in the rest of the realm. Initially in the Middle Ages, the hierarchy of fiefs in Normandie differed significantly from what it was elsewhere in France. In most provinces, lordship grew spontaneously from the bottom up as the territorial and fiscal base of a governing landed aristocracy. In Normandie, the dukes of the tenth and eleventh century, acting from a position of unusual military strength, remodeled the institutions of the province from the top down to suit their political and military needs. They carved out a huge ducal domain that included all of the major towns, the bulk of the forests, and the water ways. They also retained the ancient ecclesiastical lordships, the bishoprics and monasteries, but subjected the church to tight political control and full fiscal exploitation. With a massive direct domain and tight control of the church, the dukes insured their dominance.[26]

The early dukes divided the rest of the province into petty fiefs. The basic units were the *fieffes de haubert*, a modest holding sufficient to support an armed knight. There were also *vavassories* for non-military service. The purpose of Norman feudalism was to provide the dukes with a well-armed fighting force, not to create or promote the appearance of political rivals with a large territorial base. The knight's holdings, the *fieffes de haubert*, were not initially lordships with full rights of governance and jurisdiction, but simply assignments of fiscal resources for military service. Judicial and administrative authority remained with the dukes and their officials. For judicial affairs, there were other tenures, the *sergenteries*, with agents answerable to higher ducal officials who normally resided in the towns.[27] The province was further divided into ducal administrative units, the *vicomtés*, centered in the major ducal towns with jurisdiction over the rural areas.

In its initial form, this peculiar system did not last long.[28] Social and economic forces soon began to favor the appearance of the more normal hierarchically structured network of fiefs, lordships, and aristocrats found in the rest of France. Change set in during the late ducal period and accelerated under the Capetians, the Valois, and the Bourbon kings of France. At the base, fiefs fragmented. Medieval regulations set a limit of subdivision without loss of noble status at 1/8. By the fifteenth century, there were nearly 4000 noble fiefs in Normandie.[29] At the end of the seventeenth century, the *généralité* of Rouen had 9000 fiefs and the *Pays de Caux* had between 2500 and 3000 fiefs for 715 parishes or 3.5 to 4 per parish.[30] In the middle, medium sized lordships, cobbled together from bits and pieces of fiefs and non-noble tenures also appeared.[31] More importantly, at the top there was massive concentration of properties though the accumulation of fiefs and the on-going turnover of noble families.[32] Baronies, viscounties and counties multiplied. The largest aristocratic estates were truely immense. The *comté-pairie* of Eu, elevated in 1458, covered 105 parishes.[33] Fiefs of all sizes changed hands incessantly and new ones appeared with letters patent.[34] Ten new ducal peerages appeared in Normandie in the early modern centuries.[35] Similarly, marquisats and baronies proliferated.

The marquisat of Lonrai, located in Basse Normandie just north of Alençon, belonged in the seventeenth and eighteenth century to the highest nobility, the Matignon, Colbert, and then the Montmorency-Luxembourg. Elevated to the dignity of a marquisat in 1644, Lonrai was a conglomerate of 9 distinct lordships with 8 domain-farms, 13 banal mills, and 2 banal ovens assembled over nearly two hundred years by successive families.[36] The county of Eu belonged to the Guise-Lorraine in 1650, to Montpensier in 1660, to Bourbon-Maine in 1693, and then came to rest in the hands of the Duke of Penthièvre in the eighteenth century. On the eve of the revolution, the duchy of Estouteville belonged to the Prince of Grimaldi-Monaco, while the county of Evreux was in the hands of the Montmorency-Luxembourg.[37]

For their immense estates, aristocratic families of national stature such as the Longuevilles, Guises, Harcourts, Montpensiers, Montmorency-Luxembourg and the princes of the blood employed the standard administrative practices that were closely modeled on the time-tested procedures used in the royal domain and the principalities of the late Middle Ages. Although owners often shifted back an forth from a salaried general receiver to a comprehensive or general cash lease, the rest of the administrative procedures underwent minimal changes in the early modern period. Typically, a counsel of three or four individuals served as a court of account, a *chambre des comptes*. There were also separate administrative systems for justice and for the management of the forest lands which often had a central chamber of *eaux et forêts* with a master and various lieutenants.[38]

For the modest holdings of country squires, the direct management practiced by the famous Sire de Gouberville in the sixteenth century never completely disappeared.[39] At the base of the aristocratic hierarchy, a massive class of land-poor and even landless nobles vegetated. Many, too poor to maintain a suitable noble lifestyle, slipped downwards into the mass of commoners. There were always far more nobles than noble properties.[40] Consequently, the early modern nobility of Normandie always consisted in every age of a majority of very poor, often landless, individuals.

Another change in Norman lordship was the proliferation of rights of justice. Initially jurisdiction was in the hands of ducal and then royal officials. Every fief holder had the right to enforce the collection of seigneurial dues on his property, but otherwise Norman fiefs or lordships normally did not exercise comprehensive rights of justice, despite what the stylized paragraphs of the 1583 reformed customary law suggested. Most of the seigneurial courts with full rights of justice in operation at the end of the old regime were of relatively recent date, created in the late seventeenth and eighteenth century by the kings to satisfy the demands of the great fief holders for the normal trappings of lordship and, more importantly, created to fill a major void in the administration of justice at the local level in the province.[41]

Both titled and untitled fiefs in Normandie exercised high justice with the full range of jurisdiction over civil and criminal affairs apart from the *cas royaux* reserved for the royal *bailliages*. From the late seventeenth century, these high justices were an integral part of the monarchical system of justice for the province. They also handled simple police matters in the towns, villages and hamlets and issued regulatory writs. Lordships with high justice typically had jurisdiction over at least half a dozen parishes and handled the case load of their own territory and that of at least a couple of dozen lesser lordships without rights of justice.[42]

The creation of these highly visible and very active new seigneurial courts did not entirely eliminate the longstanding weaknesses of Norman lordship as an effective instrument for local administration. Normally, it was not noble fiefs that provided the institutional base for local governance, but the parish. The rural population of Normandie, even with the demographic growth of the early modern era, remained semi-dispersed in thousands of tiny hamlets, bourgs and small villages. These physical units of habitation were typically divided among many fief owners since the ancient *fieffes de haubert,* not to mention their fractional shares, were smaller than the territory of most early modern villages.[43]

The small and fragmented fiefs provided a totally inadequate institutional base for local governance. Consequently, the parishes, which covered entire villages or pulled together many hamlets served by default as the base for local governance.[44] Hence the familiar French arrangement in which the village mayors served both as the agents of the local residents and as seigneurial officials was uncommon in Normandie. Rural administration in Normandie remained incurably weak. Local police affairs that were usually handled jointly by seigneurial and village officials were largely ignored. The parish churchwardens were a poor substitute for the village mayors and seigneurial officials found elsewhere in France. Indeed, despite ongoing efforts by the monarchy to construct a firmer institutional base, the rural villages and hamlets in Normandie remained administratively underdeveloped.

Finally, Normandie had some of the oldest and wealthiest ecclesiastical lordships in France. Taken as a whole at the end of the old regime, they accounted for about a fifth of the lordships in the province. The hierarchy of ecclesiastical lordships in Normandie was highly polarized. At the top, the wealthy bishoprics, cathedral chapters, and the ancient Benedictine monasteries controlled the bulk of the lands, seigneurial dues and tithes. Normandie had 7 bishoprics and hence 7 cathedral chapters as well as another 18 collegial churches. The cathedral chapters were particularly wealthy. On the eve of the revolution, the cathedral chapter of Bayeux had an annual income of 89,726 *livres,* Lisieux had 76,726 *livres,* Evreux collected 68,444 *livres,* etc.[45] Revenues from the tithes far outweighed income from domain lands. At Evreux, the cathedral chapter received three-quarters of its income from tithes. The cathedral chapters and collegial churches also owned well over 5000 ha of farmland and forest, nearly 500 urban houses and other buildings. This immense patrimony supported some 300 privileged ecclesiastics.[46] At the bottom, a mass of petty monasteries, priories, convents, and other religious houses, some ancient, some that dated from the Catholic Counter-Reformation, got by with only modest revenues.[47]

The evils of the pre-revolutionary aristocratic Catholic church were fully in evidence in Normandie.[48] From the sixteenth century, and indeed even earlier, politically appointed aristocratic prelates and laymen drained off the bulk of the revenues of the bishoprics and the ancient monasteries as titular abbots *in commendam*. Excluding cathedral chapters and collegial churches, there were 67 religious establishments for men and another 68 for women in the diocese of Rouen in 1730. Almost all of the monasteries for men and a handful of the most important convents for women were under the system of titular abbots or abbesses *in commendam*.

The abbey of the Holy Trinity of Fécamp, one of the wealthiest Benedictine monasteries in the kingdom, was always in the hands of the highest aristocrats of the realm.[49] Henri de Lorraine, archbishop of Reims, became titular abbot at the age of 3 in 1617 and was followed by Henri de Bourbon, duke of Verneuil and bastard of Henri IV, as titular abbot between 1642 and 1669. At the end of the eighteenth century, the Cardinal of La Rouchefoucauld, archbishop of Rouen, 1778–1790, was the abbot of Fécamp. Similarly, the abbey of Saint-Wandrille in the eighteenth century passed from bishop to bishop in rapid succession. In 1756, Saint-Wandrille was in the hands of the Cardinal de La Rochefoucauld, archbishop of Bourges, then passed to the bishop of Digne, the bishop of Orléans, and finally came to rest in the hands of Charles Loménie de Brienne, archbishop of Toulouse. The same pattern existed for the wealthiest of the female monasteries like Montivilliers.[50]

Bretagne

Under the old regime, Bretagne retained its unique systems of land tenure. In virtually every province in France on the eve of the revolution, two-thirds, three-quarters, or more of the farmland consisted legally of seigneurial tenures, even when, as was often the case, much of this land was in the hands of nobles, ecclesiastical institutions and bourgeois. The normal French pattern was roughly one-quarter legally domain lands and three-quarters legally seigneurial tenures. In Bretagne, the proportions were reversed: four-fifths to nine-tenths domain land and only one-fifth or one-tenth seigneurial tenure.[51]

The Breton system of lordship developed and consolidated in the Middle Ages largely outside the sphere of influence of French and Roman law. French legal traditions spilled over into Haute-Bretagne which bordered France. In due course, Bretagne borrowed many of the traditions of French lordship, but never abandoned its unique systems of land tenure.

The Breton variety of perpetual *censive* tenure was the *féage*. The *féage* tenures were unquestionably numerous. For parts of the royal domain that remained under direct royal management and in royal abbeys, two edits by Henri II and Louis XIII set up procedures for the transformation of lands in *domaine congéable* to *féage* in hopes that taxes from transfer fees would increase total revenues.[52] *Féage* tenures undoubtedly outnumbered all other forms of tenure combined, but they accounted for only a small percentage of the landmass of the province. *Féage* tenures appeared in many of the towns and larger villages for the residential plots and the farmed land in their immediate environs. They were most numerous in the eastern section of the province, in Haute-Bretagne.[53] But even in Haute-Bretagne, féages did not always account for the bulk of the farmed land. Near Nantes, 5/6ths of the holdings in the vineyards, the lands in *complant*, were legally part of the noble and ecclesiastical domains, not perpetual seigneurial tenures.[54] In most of the province, Basse-Bretagne, the overwhelming majority of the farmed land, upwards of nine-tenths, consisted of properties which the lords owned directly. These properties took two major forms: *métairies* and farms in *domaine congéable* or *convenant*.[55]

From a strictly economic or agrarian point of view, the Breton *métairies* and lands in *domaine congéable* were very similar to the *métairies* and *borderies* found throughout western France, in Poitou, the *Pays de la Loire*, and the *bocage* of Normandie. Everywhere, the *métairies* were medium sized farms of 20 to 40 ha or so and the *borderies* were smaller farms of 10 ha or less. Legally, the Breton *métairies* were very similar to their counterparts in the rest of Western

France. They were domain-farms that belonged to the aristocratic lords, the church, and occasionally to bourgeois. In the early modern centuries, the tenants of the *métairies* were usually sharecroppers.

What set Bretagne apart from the rest of Western France was its system of land tenure for the smaller farms. Whereas most of the *borderies* in the rest of western France were perpetual seigneurial tenures, the Breton lands in *domaine congéable* were noble domainial property and were always listed as such in the feudal declarations of fiefs. Tenants in *domaine congéable* served at the pleasure of the lords who could dismiss them, *congédier*, at will. For centuries, these arrangements were oral contracts, *convenants*, tacitly renewed for years with the tenants or *convenanciers*. In all likelihood, lords began to use this system to bring part of the immense uncultivated lands of the province into production in the high Middle Ages. The first written evidence of *domaine congéable*, appeared only in 1388, probably two or three centuries after the system began.[56] In the castellanies of Guingamp and Minibriac in the duchy of Penthièvre, located on the northeastern coast of Bretagne, *domaine congéable* was the most common system of land use.[57]

Domaine congéable expanded as a system of land tenure in the rebuilding of the fifteenth century and continued to expand thereafter, throughout the entire early modern period, survived the Revolution, grew further in the nineteenth century, and disappeared only after the First World War.[58] *Domaine congéable* did not appear in the oldest compilations of the customary law of the early fourteenth century, or indeed in the redactions of the law in the sixteenth century. By universal agreement it was not a part of the seigneurial system, but a method of working domain land.[59] Customary law governed it, but this was the customary law of the individual lordships and local customs, *usements*, that appeared in written form only from the end of the sixteenth century. There never was any strict uniformity to the system of *domaine congéable* in the various regions of Basse-Bretagne apart from a few commonly shared features. The land belonged to the lord, the tenant served at will, and the lord could alter the terms of the contract. *Domaine congéable* was consequently very different from *féage* or *censive* arrangements which gave tenants perpetual tenure and immutable rents.

Although the old narrative sources of the early modern period and the nineteenth century described *domaine congéable* in the darkest of terms as an evil variant of oppressive feudalism, the documentary evidence suggests just the opposite.[60] *Domaine congéable* was a very malleable system. In the fifteenth century, it absorbed lands formerly under servile tenure and retained many of their features. It also absorbed lands on *féage*, and was the contract of choice for newly cleared lands.[61] With the demographic and economic growth of the sixteenth and seventeenth centuries and ongoing clearings, rentals for the *convenants* rose significantly as the tenures themselves expanded. Annual rentals in cash, in wheat and rye, in sheep, goats, butter and fish all increased.

Originally little more than a device to attract scarce labor to overabundant land, the *domaine congéable* became a valuable and flexible market lease for small farms that brought modest incomes for both the tenants, the *convenanciers*, and the owners, typically lords and bourgeois.[62] That *domaine congéable* in practice promoted modest agricultural improvement cannot be doubted. By the late seventeenth century, the market value of the tenants assets, the *édifices* or *droits réparatoires* which included the houses, the cultivated fields, some of the trees etc., was often greater than the market value of the land itself.[63]

The rights of tenants grew substantially during the early modern centuries. With time and with a more formally institutionalized legal system that developed after annexation to France, the jurisprudence of the *Parlement* of Bretagne and formal judicial inquiries, *turbes*, supplemented the earliest the *usements*. In the mature form of *domaine congéable*, the *convenanciers* had extensive property rights to the buildings, the crops, and any improvements.[64] They could sublease, divide, sell, mortgage, and transfer by bequest their tenure as long as they paid their annual rents. Simple oral installation and dismissal gave way to elaborate written contracts that by the late seventeenth and eighteenth century contained a full inventory of the buildings, trees, etc. The lord retained ownership of the land. New tenants paid an entrance fee that included a sum equal to the value of the buildings and improvements, *les droits convenanciers réparatoires*, and if the lord dismissed them, they received this sum back. Often, short term leases of 9 years replaced open ended contracts.

For lords, and indeed for any property owner, *domaine congéable*, was a flexible leasing arrangement that allowed periodic revisions of rentals in keeping with market conditions. Unlike sharecropping for the *métairies* which was an economic partnership of lord and tenant and which required both an ongoing commitment of working capital and some managerial involvement by the lords or their estate managers, lands in *domaine congéable* made no demands on either the lord's budget or his time. Rentals on lands in *domaine congéable* were modest, well below rates per ha for *métairies*.[65] The *convenanciers* as a group were comparatively well-off, and certainly in better financial shape than the cottagers and workers in the rural textile industry.[66]

Also, lords almost never dismissed their tenants in *domaine congéable*.[67] They often stayed on generation after generation and were dismissed only as the result of gross failure to pay their annual rentals. In practice, many farms in *domaine congéable* became joint-family arrangements through inheritance of shares of the lease and by marriage. Dismissal of one or more of the members of these joint arrangements normally did not involve the lord, but a family member or creditor who by buying the lord's right to dismiss through a legal contract of subrogation either simplified a complex interfamilial arrangement or foreclosed on a defaulting debtor.[68] Enterprising *convenanciers* often subleased their holding in *domaine congéable* with another contract of *domaine congéable* and charged substantially higher rentals than those they owed to the lord. This stacking of one lease on top of another developed rapidly in the eighteenth century with population pressures and rising grain prices.

In addition to *domaine congéable*, Breton lordship had some other interesting features. At the end of the Middle Ages, the titled lordships in Bretagne, some two-dozen in the fifteenth century and perhaps a dozen in the sixteenth, were monumentally large and stretched from the coasts to the high mountain ridge in the interior. Not infrequently, these lordships covered over a hundred parishes, but produced only modest revenues.[69] At the end of the ducal period in the late fifteenth century, the noble hierarchy consisted of a handful of titled magnates, a modest middle range of lordships with rights of justice and governance, and at the base, an enormous number of petty noble fief holders without rights of governance whose property consisted of a noble *métairie* and a few tenants in *domaine congéable*.[70] In the sixty parishes of the Vannetais in

1480, there were 300–350 nobles: 2 members of the high aristocracy, 50 lords of intermediate rank of whom only half maintained seigneurial tribunals, and about 300 petty nobles with a manor house, a *métairie*, and perhaps some lands in *domaine congéable*.[71]

In the fifteenth century, the ducal direct domaine encompassed many of the major towns and perhaps 30–40% of the landmass of the province.[72] The last dukes imitated the kings of France and established a new and comprehensive fiscal system that produced far more revenue than the ducal domain.[73] The fifteenth century dukes persuaded the great nobles of the province to accept the new fiscal system which taxed their tenants by awarding them large parts of the ducal domain lands as gifts and rewards for service and political cooperation.[74]

The late Valois and early Bourbon kings of the sixteenth and first half of the seventeenth century followed this same policy for a slightly different reason. For roughly two centuries, the 1480s to the 1680s, Bretagne had little strategic importance for the French kings. It was not until the War of the League of Augsburg 1689–1697, a war that brought England into continental European affairs as the perpetual opponent of France, that Bretagne assumed any real significance for the kings as a naval base against England. Prior to that, the easiest way for the kings to hold on to a recently acquired province of marginal importance was to rely on the great nobles and their networks of clients. The kings made lavish grants of crown lordships in Bretagne to the great nobles and sold other lands to finance wars.[75] Normally the kings did not fully divest themselves of all rights, but retained a perpetual option of repurchasing the alienated crown properties. Legal niceties aside, what royal policy amounted to was a massive shift of property from the crown to the high aristocracy in the sixteenth and seventeenth centuries. At the same time, the lax administration of the crown properties in Bretagne facilitated and even encouraged usurpation of royal lands by one and all on a massive scale.[76]

The ultimate fate of the former crown properties in Bretagne was not always what one would have expected. By the sixteenth century, the great nobles of Bretagne were intermarried with or had been replaced by French aristocratic families of national stature. For these families, lordships in Bretagne, even prestigious titled lordships, were normally among their least valuable holdings.

The thin and acidic soils of Bretagne were of legendary sterility.[77] Massive additions of fertilizer in the form of seaweed and ground sea shells increased productivity somewhat for lands along the northern and southern coasts, but these techniques could not be used in the interior. Vast and infertile heaths, *landes*, covered most of the interior. Bretagne had a rural textile industry, a little coastal trade, and an abundance of piracy and smuggling.

Consequently, Breton lordships were never considered prime property by the high aristocracy of the realm. Usually managed from afar by agents in Paris, many of the title lordships received at best perfunctory management. Often the new aristocratic owners of crown property imitated the behavior of the kings. When they needed money, they sold their least valuable assets. Great fiefs changed hands incessantly among the high aristocracy and many were dismembered. Although not every great title lordship in Bretagne was liquidated in the sixteenth and seventeenth century through piecemeal sales, several were: Laval, Rochefort, Largouët, Kaër, etc.[78]

The titled lordships and many of the lordships still under direct royal management retained their rights of jurisdictions, but sold many of the their landed assets which consisted of *métairies,* lands in *domaine congéable,* forest, *landes,* and grain mills. The principal beneficiaries of the liquidation of the assets of the great titled Breton lordships in the sixteenth and seventeenth century were the lords of intermediate stature and more importantly the petty knights or fief holders at the bottom of the noble hierarchy. The sale of the landed assets of the great lordships, the usurpations of crown lands, and the clearings of the sixteenth and seventeenth century provided the material foundation and revenue base for a quite remarkable growth in the number of petty Breton nobles.

These petty nobles, the *sieurs* as they were called, owned noble *métairies* and lands in *domaine congéable,* but like the original medieval knights, they were vassals, not lords, and normally exercised no rights of lordship. The noble class grew rapidly in the sixteenth and seventeenth century as old noble families established more and more branches. In the Vannetais region of Basse-Bretagne in 1480, there were 2 major titled lordships, Largouët and Rochefort, a dozen ecclesiastical lordships, about 50 medium range aristocratic lordships, and about 300 petty noble fief holders, the *sieurs.* Two centuries later in 1680, there were still 2 major titled lordships, a dozen ecclesiastical lordships, still about 50 medium sized lordships, and an astounding 500 petty fief holders.

These figures alone tell only part of the story. Although the two major titled lordships in Vannetais survived, in the late seventeenth century they were largely empty shells. The middle ranks of lordships had substantially increased their holdings, while the *sieurs* had both dramatically increased their numbers and they had greatly expanded their average holdings. Whereas a late fifteenth century *sieurie* often had only a manor house and a single *métairie*, a late seventeenth century *sieurie* had a manor house, 4 *métairies*, a few tenures in *domaine congéable*, and even a mill.[79] In 1480 and again in 1680, 80% of the land in the Vannetais belonged to the nobles. In 1480, the principal landowners were the titled lordships, Largouët and Rochefort. Two centuries later, 50% of the land belonged to 500 *sieurs*. The largest *sieuries* had manor houses which were imposing edifices and had 100 to 300 ha in *métairies, domaine congéable*, mills, even forests. Often the income of substantial *sieuries*, which did not exercise rights of governance and justice, exceeded the revenues of the middle ranges of fully-fledged lordships.[80]

On the eve of the Revolution, the great Breton lordships whose assets had not been liquidated belonged to the princes of the realm like the Duke of Penthièvre, but the ducal peerage of Penthièvre, even after its reconstruction in the eighteenth century, was still one of the least valuable properties that belonged to this legitimized branch of the royal family.[81] The shells of the once great Breton lordships whose properties had been sold off in the sixteenth and seventeenth century typically belonged to the magistrates of the *Parlement* of Bretagne, noble officeholders who ranked near the bottom in wealth and prestige among the more than 1000 *parlementaires* of the realm.[82]

The noble class as a whole shrank in Bretagne in the eighteenth century as it did in most regions of France.[83] The really vibrant parts of the Breton aristocracy consisted of the hundreds of middle rank resident lords with rights of justice and the thousands of petty noble fief holders. For both, it was normally the revenues from *métairies* and lands in *domaine congéable*, and for a few of them revenues from grain mills, that financed their modest noble lifestyle. For them, the abolition of lordship during the Revolution made little difference to what was essentially the life of the modest landed aristocracy.[84]

Pays de la Loire and Poitou

In Anjou, Maine, and Touraine, the provinces located along the middle Loire, and in Poitou, lordship displayed a quite remarkable stability in the early modern centuries that was rooted in part in the enduring physical characteristics of this section of western France.[85] The Loire and its major tributaries, the Loir, the Cher, the Vienne, the Sarthe, and the Mayenne, were at best poorly navigable a few months of the year. The river valleys had narrow bands of alluvial deposits with fertile soils that contrasted sharply with the thoroughly mediocre soils of the surrounding plains. The bulk of the population and all of the major towns clustered in the valleys. The plains, covered with forests and heaths, had only a scattering of settlements.[86]

The clearings of the high Middle Ages, interrupted by the Black Death and the Hundred Years' War, resumed in the late fifteenth century and continued until the middle of the nineteenth. Even after centuries of slow clearing, the area remained lightly populated. On the eve of the Revolution, the largest town, Orléans, had 35,000 people, while the other major cities, Le Mans, Angers, and Tour, all fell in the range of 15 to 25,000.[87] The valleys produced mainly low quality wines that moved along the rivers while the plains produced grain for local consumption and an abundance of cattle and sheep that moved on hoof to areas closer to Paris.

Home to the Plantagenêts and later the favored residence of the Valois kings from Charles VII through Francis I, the *Pays de la Loire* had an unsurpassed collection of stunningly beautiful renaissance châteaux: Amboise, Blois, Chambord, Chenonceaux, and Azay-le-Rideau. Even after the kings abandoned the Loire for Paris and Versailles, the *Pays de la Loire* continued to attract the interest and the investments of the highest nobles of the realm. Despite its mediocre economy, or perhaps because of it, the area became something of a bucolic retreat, suitable for at least a short stay in the summer.

Many of the lordships belonged to the king and the appanage princes, others to noble families of national stature. There were as many new ducal peerages created here under the old regime as in Normandie or the Ile-de-France: 7 in

Poitou, 5 in Touraine, 4 in Anjou, and 1 in Maine.[88] Touraine, which was as somnolent a place as one could find in the eighteenth century, a province with no significant commercial activity, no royal law courts, and no robe nobility, was nevertheless teaming with titled fiefs.[89] In the early 1760s Touraine had 5 ducal peerages, 7 marquisats, 3 counties, 2 viscounties, and 28 baronies. The ducal peerage of Amboise was the largest with 2 castellanies, two *prévôtés*, 146 fiefs, and a seigneurial *bailliage* that replaced the royal *bailliage*. The Rohan-Guémené owned the ducal peerages of Montbazon and Luynes along with the baronies of Sainte-Maure, La Haye, and Nouâtre, while the La Trémoille held the duchy of Loudun. The Choiseuil, d'Aiguillon and Béthune-Sully also possessed titled *seigneuries* in Touraine.[90]

In Anjou, noble families of national stature already owned most of the great lordships at the end of the Middle Ages.[91] In Haut-Maine, the barony of La Ferté-Bernard, elevated to a ducal peerage in 1540, passed into the hands of Cardinal Richelieu in 1641 and remained with the Richelieu family until the revolution.[92] The desire for prestige never diminished. In remote Bas-Maine, the marquisat of Bourg-le-Prêtre, elevated in 1768, took its place as the fourth largest fief in the region, behind the ancient county de Laval, elevated in 1429, the marquisat of Mayenne, and the marquisat of Lassy. For Bourg-le-Prête, the status of a marquisat was the reward for the patient accumulation of fiefs by several families over two centuries.[93]

The hierarchy of fiefs in the *Pays de la Loire* had the usual polarization with an immensity of petty fiefs at the bottom, a considerably smaller number of medium-sized *seigneuries* in the middle, and a handful of immense titled lordships at the top.[94] On the eve of the revolution, there were upwards of 3000 fiefs in Touraine or about 7 for each of the 422 parishes, yet only 224 lords with justice, of which 56 or about a quarter were ecclesiastics.[95] Louis de Maussabré, *écuyer*, was representative of the petty nobility with a fief that consisted of two *métairies* leased to sharecroppers, a hayfield, a handful of seigneurial tenants and total revenues of around 200 *livres* drawn overwhelmingly from the domain-farms.[96]

Throughout the *Pays de la Loire*, the fiscal grid of lordship perpetuated the institutions of the Middle Ages. Habitation took one of three major forms: small fragmented holdings near the towns and along the valleys; small peasant homesteads dispersed as isolated farms or hamlets; and larger farms located on the periphery of the peasant settlements in both the valleys and the plains.[97] For each form of settlement there was a corresponding fiscal unit of tenure: fragmented *mansi* and *hébergements* for the first; *borderies* for the second; and *métairies* or *gagnages* for the third.

The valleys had the ancient *mansi* that had fragmented into individual *censives* and the more recent *hébergements* or *albergements*, established initially as single tenures. The vineyards bore *terrages* of 1/6 and even 1/4, while cash *cens* predominated on the other small plots. The *borderie*, a small peasant farmstead, was both a form of habitation and cultivation as well as a fiscal unit of lordship. With population increase, many of the *borderies* became hamlets. Some of these hamlets were called variously *fraresches*, *frèches*, *fresches*, etc. While the lands within the *borderies* and *fresches* were often fragmented, in the eyes of the lords they remained undivided fiscal entities whose tenants bore collective responsibility for the integral payment of the annual dues.[98]

As their name suggests, the *fresches* in Anjou, Maine, and Touraine were at one point held by members of the same family, but by the eighteenth century these family ties had largely dissolved. Most of the these jointly owned tenures dated from the rebuilding of the countryside in the late Middle Ages and from new clearings in the sixteenth century. Often, the *borderies* initially bore a *terrage* of 1/6 that with time and the maturing of cultivation became a fixed annual payment in kind. *Borderies* covered about 6 to 10 ha.

The *frarêche* of la Cicogne in Touraine became the object of a lawsuit in the 1490s.[99] The land in question came into the possession of the chapter of Saint-Martin de Tours through a gift in 1233 by the chancellor of France, Guillaume de Sainte-Maure, who established a chapel there in his name. For the next two centuries, Saint-Martin worked the land as a domainial *métairie*, but the Hundred Years' War took a terrible toll on it and in 1450 Saint-Martin offered it as a dilapidated tenure at public bid. After three public announcements, only one poor day laborer stepped foreword to bid. Saint-Martin awarded Perrin Bourdebure the 40 ha *métairie* for a very low annual *cens* of 30 sous, a trifling sum, but better than nothing at a time of depopulation and low prices.

Forty years later, the population and economy of the province had recovered and the *métairie* was now a *frarêche* in the hands of 5 families who were the direct heirs of Pierre Bourdebure. Saint-Martin obtained royal letters and started a lawsuit with the intention of breaking the original tenurial contract in order to get an increased annual *cens*. Saint-Martin bribed and pressured individual family members. After many twists and turns, the royal courts refused to nullify the perpetual tenure and allowed only a very modest increase of the annual *cens*.

The *métairies* or *gagneries* were the larger units of cultivation and tenure. These normally covered between 20 and 50 ha and were mixed farming operations that combined livestock with a system of arable agriculture in which grains alternated with grasses in long fallows. Some of the *métaires* were seigneurial tenures that featured payments in kind, while others were domain-farms that belonged directly to the lords. In the four *élections* of Tour which covered 224 parishes there were 4368 *métairies* or about 20 per parish in the late eighteenth century.[100] In the *département* of La Mayenne which roughly covered the same area as Bas-Maine, there were 7,162 *métairies* and 24,418 *bordages* or *borderies* in the early nineteenth century.[101]

New contracts of seigneurial tenure drawn up for *hébergements*, *borderies* and *gagneries* on the eve of the Revolution were remarkably similar to those used in the fifteenth and sixteenth century. New tenures established in the ducal peerage of Amboise in 1775 for the Duke of Choiseul and again in 1788 for his heir the Duke of Penthièvre specified a simple cash payment of a few *sous*, a couple of chickens, along with substantial fixed quantities of wheat, rye, and oats.[102] The rents in grain were normally paid in cash according to current official prices.

Between 1500 and 1789, population increase led to the expansion of the cultivated areas in all three forms of habitation. Vineyards and gardens multiplied in the valleys, while *borderies* and *métaires* proliferated. As in the rest of France, the patterns of ownership of farmland changed. Peasant ownership in seigneurial tenure dropped to 30% or less in the plains and near the towns in the valleys, while aristocratic, ecclesiastical and bourgeois ownership rose in the same areas to 70 or 80%. Some of the advance of the upperclasses came through depopulating enclosure, but much came from the expansion of the areas under the plow [103] At the same time, the surplus population found employment in the expanding rural textile industries.

The seigneurial system in the *Pays de la Loire* was rock solid, very carefully managed, and generally not aggressive. The fiscal grid of tenure underwent only moderate adjustment between 1450 and 1789. In Bas-Maine, the annual *cens* and renders neither increased nor decreased. At most, lords simplified the administration of their properties by dropping some of the less common obligations.[104] Also lords were more likely in the eighteenth century than earlier to divide the fiscal obligation of jointly held tenures into individual shares, while they still maintained the legal principle of collective responsibility. Lords had learned that in the event of lawsuits, which commonly pitted one tenant against another in a *fresche,* it was advantageous for the purposes of collection to have a schedule of individualized shares in place.[105]

Revenue from seigneurial dues often brought in a quarter to a third of the income of the lordships in Anjou and in Maine at the beginning of the sixteenth century and in the late eighteenth.[106] Only the ancient castellanies, like Champtoceaux in Anjou which collected a river toll, derived upwards of half their income from *droits seigneuriaux*. Between 1500 and 1789 both the domainial lands in cultivation and the seigneurial tenures multiplied and expanded, but usually their relative importance in seigneurial incomes remained about the same. The seigneurial land taxes, even the fixed payments in grain and the *terrages*, took only a relatively small percentage of the total farm output in the *Pays de la Loire*. The seigneurial dues normally amounted to only 2–5% of the annual value of the market leases for *borderies* and *métairies,* although higher rates of 11–13% could also be found.[107] In short, the fiscal system of lordship was a ubiquitous, but relatively modest burden that was widely accepted as simply a part of the institutional structure of life.

There was no significant opposition to lordship in the *Pays de la Loire*. In Bas-Maine, the seigneurial archives, which are in perfect order for the entire early modern period, contain an abundance of records that flowed from regular and uncontested collection but remarkably few papers that emanated from litigation.[108] The *seigneurie* was simply an uncontested part of everyday life both as an administrative and judicial institution and as an ancient fiscal system.[109]

Indeed, seigneurial dues were regularly paid without protest. Since most of the farmland was in the hands of the upper classes, they simply specified in their leases that the tenant farmers were responsible for paying any and all seigneurial dues. Indeed, there are even cases where lords sued the tenant farmers who leased their domain-farms for failing to carry out this clause in their leases.[110]

Banal mills were common and leased to the highest bidder. While lords and their millers bore the costs of the routine maintenance of the mills, the subjects of the lordship were responsible for the periodic replacement of the millstones. In Bas-Maine, a special seigneurial assize assessed the costs of the new millstone and its installation per fief/tenure and then by individualized holdings. In the lordship of La Vaudelle, the replacement of millstones occurred in 1719, 1736, 1752, and in 1776.[111]

Lords of all stature, both ecclesiastical and aristocratic, kept their seigneurial records up to date through the periodic calling of general assizes. Unlike the Norman assizes which occurred annually, the assizes in the *Pays de la Loire* met only about once every quarter century. In Bas-Maine, these *assises de fief* were distinct from the regular sessions of the seigneurial courts. The *assise de fief* was a function of low justice, *justice foncière*, at the disposal of every noble fief owner, whereas in practice only the larger lordships maintained fully staffed seigneurial tribunals.[112] The customary law placed a limit of 29 years on the recovery of arrears of seigneurial dues, so lords normally held their assizes to avoid the prescription of their rights. Because lords routinely called an assize to update their seigneurial registers as a normal part of administration, there was no need for any spectacular effort to suddenly restore order to dilapidated lordships. The updating of the terriers occurred at regular intervals within the lordships throughout the sixteenth, seventeenth and eighteenth centuries.[113]

As an administrative and judicial institution, lordship remained highly visible in the *Pays de la Loire*. While lesser fiefs were scattered about the countryside, the major lordships, the old castellanies, were almost always centered in the urban areas since the towns and major villages had grown around them. In 1667, the *généralité* of Orléans had 580 nobles, 433 fiefs in the hands of 259 *seigneurs*, but only 87 lordships with functioning seigneurial courts.[114]

The church came well behind the nobles as a landowner in the *Pays de la*

Loire, but thanks to the tithe was still very wealthy. In Touraine, the church owned less than 10% of the land. In Touraine, the cathedral chapter was by far the best endowed establishment with 133,000 *livres* of income in 1789. Next in wealth came the abbey of Marmoutier, the most prestigious of the 17 royal abbeys in the province, with a far from insignificant 80,000 *livres* of income in the 1760s.[115]

The province of Poitou, located south of the *Pays de la Loire*, had agrarian and seigneurial structures that were very similar to those of Anjou, Maine, Touraine and Orléanais. Poitou had *borderies, métairies, freresches,* and *terrages* of 1/6. And yet, there was a difference. Unlike the *Pays de la Loire* that largely escaped the devastation of the Hundred Years' War, Poitou was one of the main centers of conflict. Whereas the *Pays de la Loire* moved without a break from the Middle Ages into the old regime, Poitou plunged into an abyss. In Poitou, the resettlement of the fifteenth and sixteenth century was less reconstruction than a totally new start which utilized familiar medieval institutions. In Poitou, the creation of domain-farms started a good century earlier than in the *Pays de la Loire*, not in response to beckoning markets, but as a consequence of massive depopulation and abandonment of farms.

Also, Poitou was even less inviting than the *Pays de la Loire*. The interior of the province consisted of an immensity of poor soils and heath while the area along the coast had poorly draining marshlands.[116] There was only one city of any significance, Poitiers. The task of resettlement and new settlement in the fifteenth and sixteenth centuries fell by default to the aristocratic and ecclesiastical lords. They created tenures in the form of *bordages* and *freresches*, new villages and domain-farms or *métairies*.

Between 1366 and 1598, the chapter of Sainte-Radegonde of Poitiers established an astounding 122 *freresches* in the lordship of Vouillé, each with a single collective annual render payable mainly in grain.[117] These *freresches* appeared first on formerly cultivated tenures and lesser fiefs that had been abandoned, then on lands that had not previously been farmed. In later centuries, the canons of Sainte-Radegonde, determined to maintain a streamlined administration of their lordship, steadfastly refused to subdivide these *freresches* even though some of these fiscal units had over 50 tenants by the end of the eighteenth century. The *freresche* of Baussay, established in 1391 for Jean and Guillaume Baussay on the territory of two small and abandoned noble fiefs, covered nearly 60 ha and in 1785 had 54 tenants who spanned the full social spectrum, from the Count of Orfeuille and prominent royal magistrates to common peasants.

In the *seigneurie* of Vaussais et Montjean, located in southern Poitou near Angoulême, at least 65% and probably closer to 75% of the lands listed in the *terrier* of the sixteenth century consisted of lands recently cleared for the first time, while only about 25% of the land figured as part of the ancient medieval core of settlements in *albergements*. The lord, the cathedral chapter of Limoges, established new tenures with a schedule of seigneurial dues that survived until the Revolution: annual payment in cash and much more important renders in wheat, rye, oats, and poultry.[118]

Nobles of greater and lesser stature and ecclesiastical lords were also active in creating new domain-farms. While there is no doubt that some of the new aristocratic *métairies* constructed in the early modern period were at least in part the result of depopulating enclosure that displaced peasant tenants, much of the land for these domain-farms came either from abandoned tenures or, more importantly, from the vast reserves of heretofore uncultivated heath.[119]

Often the nobles financed much of their estate building with the salaries and pensions they earned from royal military, judicial and administrative offices. In the fifteenth century, Yon du Fou, a petty noble from Bretagne, established himself in Poitou with monies he earned as a military captain, a master of the waters and forests, and *sénéchal* of Poitou.[120] On a much grander scale, Charles de La Porte, marshal of France and confidant of Cardinal Richelieu, assembled a vast collection of fiefs between 1630 and 1663 that became the ducal peerage of La Meilleraye. La Porte spent over 800,000 livres on this estate which when completed covered one-third of the territory of the modern *département* of Deux-Sèvres.[121]

By the end of the old regime, the patterns of landholding in Poitou were similar to those in the *Pays de la Loire*. Roughly 80% of the farmland consisted of upperclass *métairies* leased to sharecroppers: 40–45% belonged to nobles, 25 30% to bourgeois, 10% belonged to the church, while the remaining 10–20%

of the farmland belonged to the peasants in the form of small perpetual tenures, the *borderies,* or *freresches.*[122]

The seigneurial system in Poitou had the strength one would expect of a relatively new creation. The majority of the seigneurial tenures in existence in Poitou appeared after 1450. Lords, fully aware of the perils of monetary inflation had been careful to establish either *terrages* of 1/6 or fixed renders in kind. Renders in grain were always valuable and at the end of the eighteenth century took up to 20% of the gross agricultural product of the seigneurial tenures. The tithe took another 1/12.[123]

Although a majority of the lords in Poitou were resident petty nobles with small fiefs, there were a fair number of non-resident aristocrats with immense and complex titled lordships who resided in Versailles and Paris. For many bourgeois of Poitou, one of the surest paths to fortune was the profession of estate management for the aristocratic lords. While only true financiers had the capital necessary to take on the general lease of an entire titled lordship, men of lesser stature stepped forward to lease *métairies*, tithes, *droits seigneuriaux*, and the like. There were leases for men of every financial rank. For the bourgeois class, the management of lordship was a highly profitable enterprise pursued without moral scruples.[124]

Central France

Berry, Nivernais and Bourbonnais

Berry, Nivernais and Bourbonnais were all lightly populated provinces with soils of mediocre fertility. Remote and with limited economic potential, they have always been, in every age, less appealing and consequently less developed than the better endowed areas of northern France. These three provinces were also among the regions where remnants of serfdom in the form of arbitrary *tailles,* arbitrary *corvées* and *charrois*, hauling, as well as *mainmorte* and *droit de suite* survived in pockets of territory until the Revolution.

In all three provinces, the broadly similar conditions of the physical environment produced two basic patterns of settlement. The relatively fertile valleys of the Loire, the Allier, and the Cher attracted the bulk of the early settlements which with time produced highly fragmented holdings. Likewise, the majority of the important towns appeared in the valleys. Elsewhere the dominant pattern of settlement both in the Middle Ages and in the early modern centuries was dispersed habitation in isolated farms and hamlets. All three provinces experienced the multiplication of upperclass farms, the *métairies*, in Berry from the fifteenth century, in Bourbonnais and Nivernais from the seventeenth. What distinguished the history of lordship in these provinces was their slightly different legal traditions, most notably their systems of seigneurial tenure.

The retreat of the arbitrary or servile *tailles*, *corvées* and *charrois* at the beginning of the early modern era revealed the underlying fiscal network of tenures. In Berry, the towns with medieval charters paid their regulated *tailles*, while farmlands nearby typically had individualized *censives* with seigneurial taxes that consisted of minor payments in cash and kind. In south-eastern Berry, another popular medieval fiscal system lived on. Residents in the parish of Orcenais paid renders in kind for their farmlands calculated in terms of the size of the plow teams, one *boisseau* of rye for a plow team of oxen, 1/3 of a *boisseau* for those without plow animals.[125] The *seigneurie* of Saint-Germain-des-Bois, also in Berry, retained a similar fiscal system that was based on a 1202 *charte de franchise*.[126]

In the central part of Berry which was well-suited to grain and sheep farming, the noble *métairies* multiplied from the early fifteenth century, initially as in Poitou in response to severe depopulation, but increasingly from the sixteenth century in response to beckoning markets for wool.[127] Many peasant tenures disappeared into the new *métairies*. Nearby in the Sologne region of Orléanais, the expansion of the upperclass sheep farms began a little later in the early seventeenth century.[128]

Nivernais had *censives* and *bordelages*. Both multiplied in the early modern centuries. The *censives* were free tenures with fixed payments, widely used for the residential holdings in the towns and villages and for lands immediately adjacent to them. The annual payments for the old *censives* were often upgraded as they fell in with new *rentes*.[129] For farmlands of larger scale, lords preferred the *bordelage* with its renders in kind. The *bordelage* tenure of Nivernais appeared with the clearings from the twelfth century in areas not heretofore settled and hence outside the regions of the earlier *mansi* that with time fragmented into the *censives*. The early *bordelage* tenures often appeared in planned villages.[130] They typically featured renders in kind. To retain the newly arrived settlers and to encourage further clearings, lords imposed restrictions on these *bordelage* tenures: they were impartible and subject to mortmain.

In Nivernais, *bordelage* was the tenure of choice for the resettlement of abandoned lands in the fifteenth century and for new clearings in the sixteenth and seventeenth.[131] Like their medieval predecessors, the lords retained impartibility and mortmain in the new *bordelage* tenures to anchor population and encourage further clearings. Normally there were no arbitrary *tailles,* but significant payments in grain and often a sizable entrance fee. In the relatively fertile lands of the Loire valley near Nevers, the number of *bordelage* tenures grew in the sixteenth and early seventeenth centuries. Although they were often less numerous than the old *censives*, they accounted for a greater proportion of the farmed land, perhaps a third to a half of the landmass in seigneurial tenure in Nivernais in the eighteenth century.[132]

Then from the 1630s to the early eighteenth century, the *bordelage* tenures of Nivernais retreated as peasants, crushed by the massively increased burdens of royal taxation and further weakened by famine and plague, abandoned their lands. These lands passed back into the hands of lords and bourgeois investors, to men able to profit from the economic distress of the peasantry. From the *bordelage* tenures, lords and bourgeois constructed new domain-farms, *métairies*. Some of the new *métairies* swallowed up entire peasant villages. Several generations of *seigneurs* of Corvol-d'Embernard in Nivernais, created a domain-farm which by 1631 had absorbed most of the territory of the parish of Saint-Martin-des-Vaux.[133] A similar story unfolded in the lordship of Chassy-en-Morvan in the seventeenth century.[134]

The upperclass landlords in Nivernais leased their *métairies* to peasant sharecroppers. The impoverished peasants often could not afford even the modest burdens of sharecropping alone, so they formed economic partnerships that pooled the meager resources and the labor of several families. The result was the famous peasant *communautés* which were essentially economic partnerships which bound together families whose members were sometimes related or intermarried, sometimes not. Although some peasant *communautés* certainly did have impartible seigneurial tenures with mortmain as their foundation, for the most part it was not *bordelage* but the economic needs of larger farming enterprises that explains the proliferation of the peasant *communautés*. These multiplied with the upperclass *métairies* let on a sharecropping basis and then declined in the nineteenth century as less labor intensive cattle-ranching replaced grain farming.[135] Some of the peasant *communautés* lasted for generations, even centuries. The partnership of the Jault family in Nivernais ran from 1580 to 1847.[136]

As *bordelage* tenures fell into the hands of the lords and the bourgeois investors, the new owners made arrangements with the lords with jurisdiction over the lands to eliminate the restrictive features of these tenures, namely impartibility and mortmain, and to transform *bordelage* into free *censive*.[137] A similar process of purchasing enfranchisement occurred in Bourbonnais in the seventeenth century when the *bordelage* tenures and lands subject to a *taille réelle* passed into the hands of upperclass buyers.[138] For all that, many *bordelage* tenures survived as fiscal units in the seigneurial *terriers*, for lands that had been swept up into new *métairies* as well as for lands that still had peasant tenants. The elimination of mortmain on some of the old *bordelage* tenures and the general hostility of the *Parlement* of Paris to any servile restrictions produced a jurisprudence by the late seventeenth century which substantially weakened mortmain in the tenures where it still existed by allowing disposition of the tenure by written wills.[139]

Bourbonnais also had *bordelage* tenures that were impartible and subject to mortmain, but they seem to have been far less numerous than in Nivernais. Normally, the dispersed settlements, the *mas* which ranged in size from 4 or 5 ha to 100 ha or more, were unrestricted holdings or *tènements* with substantial payments in kind.[140] Here, as in most areas of central France, lords retained the *tènements* as undivided fiscal units in their records, but did not prevent actual division. Rather, they maintained the legal notion of *solidarité*, individual and collective responsibility for the annual payments.

Bourbonnais had *métairies*, many from the Middle Ages and even more created under the old regime, but also a system of tenure for smaller properties that resembled the Breton *domaine congéable*. Lords in Bourbonnais used sharecropping for their fully equipped *métairies* with oral arrangements in the Middle Ages and written contracts from the late fifteenth century. Sharecropping, of course, involved an ongoing financial involvement of the lords or their agents in the farming of the *métairies*. For smaller properties in their personal domain, lords often used an open ended contract, revocable at their pleasure, which featured a proportional payment called a *parcière* for grain lands and *carpot* for vineyards. More formal annual leasing arrangements also appeared for small properties with proportional payments that were usually called *champarts*.[141]

In Bourbonnais and Nivernais, the upperclass enclosure movement seems to have been as much the result of the implosion of the peasantry as a product of strong economic pressures of expanding markets. Nivernais exported large quantities of lumber and iron down river to Paris under the old regime, but did not produced great numbers of cattle for the market in Paris until the early nineteenth century when cattle-ranching of the *charolais* developed.[142]

In the less fertile regions outside the river valleys such as the mountains and *bocage* of Bourbonnais and in parts of Sologne where lands were less attractive to upperclass investors, the peasant tenures survived the troubles of the seventeenth century. With the population expansion of the eighteenth and first half of the nineteenth century, they became hamlets that bore the names of the families that had originally settled then in the late fifteenth and early sixteenth century.[143]

Everywhere, lordship survived as a judicial and local administrative apparatus. There were regular sessions of the seigneurial courts and annual general assizes that handled the full range of civil and many criminal affairs. The castellany of Epineul in Berry had a seigneurial *bailli*, a *procureur*, a *prévôt*, as well as a scribe and sergeants.[144] For the bourgeois class of Varzy in Nivernais, offices in the seigneurial tribunals were prized positions.[145]

Much of the territory in Berry, Nivernais and Bourbonnais was part of the royal domain and throughout the early modern centuries passed from hand to hand among the princely families of the realm. Berry was part of the appanage of Orléans, a small part of a much larger principality. The duchy of Nivernais, however, retained its individuality and continued to function as a institutionally unified principality with a chamber of accounts, ducal *bailliages*, an array of lesser fiefs with tribunals that sent cases on appeal to the duchy. The seigneurial tribunals of the duchy were very busy and performed a necessary task. This rather quaint principality of decidedly medieval allure survived because it posed absolutely no threat to the centralized monarchy.[146]

Auvergne

The immense province of Auvergne in central France sat on the remnants of an ancient volcanic mountain chain and encompassed two quite distinct regions. Basse-Auvergne in the north had the relatively fertile valley of the Allier, the Limagne, as its center with mountainous regions to the west, south and east. The largest towns, Clermont-Ferrand and Issoire, were located in Basse-Auvergne but had less than 25,000 inhabitants even at the end of the old regime.[147] Haute-Auvergne to the south was entirely mountainous with only a few relatively flat plateaux, the *planèzes*, near the base of the lava runs, most notably near Saint-Flour and Mauriac.

Remote and difficult to traverse, Auvergne displayed a quite remarkable socio-economic and institutional stability that modest population increase and even more modest commercial growth modified in detail only between 1450 and 1789. Lordship was a very visible part of the institutional apparatus of Auvergne. Likewise, the juxtaposition of small peasant farms, *héritages*, and the larger domain-farms of the nobles, the church and increasingly the bourgeois class was a permanent feature of rural life.[148]

The domain-farms which belonged to the upper classes increased in number under the old regime.[149] There were thousands of them in Haute- and Basse-Auvergne in the eighteenth century. In the most desirable areas, they swallowed up the peasant *héritages* and monopolized the valuable mountain pastures. The domain-farms were mixed operations that combined livestock breeding and grain production. In the western part of Haute-Auvergne where the natural mountain pastures were at their best, they were dairy farms with herds of cows for the production of cheese.[150] In Basse-Auvergne, lords also had smaller domain properties which they leased out in annual or open-ended contracts for a proportion of the crop, the *percière*, of 1/4 or 1/3.[151] Although the upper-class domain farms largely dominated commercial agriculture in Auvergne, small scale peasant farms still accounted for the bulk of the cultivated land. Peasant ownership fell to 20% in the areas most suitable for domain-farms, but rose to 70 to 80% elsewhere. For Auvergne as a whole, peasant ownership was not far below 50%.[152]

In the middle of the eighteenth century, Basse-Auvergne had about 400 noble families and Haute-Auvergne another 250. Although there were a few great families of national stature with lands in Auvergne, such as the Tour d'Auvergne or the Grimaldi of Monaco with the *vicomté* of Carlat, most of the aristocracy consisted of resident families of modest means: a minority of barons and marquis with respectable sized lordships and a far greater number of petty fief holders with very modest incomes.[153] In Haute-Auvergne, the nobles as a whole derived about a third of their income from seigneurial dues and the other two-thirds from their domain-farms. Roughly a third of the 265 nobles in Haute-Auvergne at the end of the eighteenth century had incomes of less than 500 *livres*, and only half of all nobles derived income from seigneurial dues.[154]

The seigneurial system in Auvergne, reconstructed virtually unchanged at the end of the Middle Ages, was simple and durable.[155] As an institution, lordship remained of fundamental importance in the rural areas.[156] Even in the towns which had a consular municipal government, lordship survived as a fiscal institution and a seigneurial official, typically a judge or *vigier*, presided over the judicial tribunal.[157] The lordships themselves were often divided, while others were assembled in the fifteenth and sixteenth century from bits and pieces of ancient fiefs. In Haute-Auvergne, the barony of Salers was divided in half in the Middle Ages and so it remained until 1789, while the nearby *seigneurie* of Mazerolles was cobbled together in the late sixteenth century from parts of no less than five fiefs.[158] These divisions and reconstructions were minor inconveniences which sound administration easily overcame.

Cultivated lands in seigneurial tenure in Auvergne bore fixed renders in kind, payable in wheat, rye, oats, eggs and poultry. Houses in towns, hayfields, and mountain pastures had modest seigneurial taxes in cash.[159] At the end of the Middle Ages, the dues payable in kind were already of far greater importance than those assessed in cash.[160] Consequently, the inflation of the early modern centuries worked to the advantage of the lords. The minor payments in cash fell to symbolic levels, while the payments in agricultural products maintained and even increased their value.[161] Lords with *seigneuries* of middle rank and higher derived a substantial proportion of their annual incomes from grain sales in the purely local markets. Much of this grain came from seigneurial dues and from impropriated tithes.[162]

With the exception of the Limagne where each plot of land had its own dues, the predominant form of seigneurial tenure was the familiar large block or composite holding, called *mas* in Basse-Auvergne and *affar* in Haute-Auvergne, associated throughout central France with dispersed settlement.[163] Reconstituted at the demographic low point in the fifteenth century or newly created from clearings later, the *mas* or *affar* remained a fiscal unit for the collection of seigneurial dues throughout the early modern period regardless of how fragmented its lands became. Lords steadfastly refused to abandon unified assessment.

The terms used to describe this legal unity of the tenure were *pagésie, solidité, solidarité*.[164] At most lords agreed to divide for ease of annual collection the fiscal burden among the various tenants. But these contracts, called *égalations, également*, which matched holdings to fractions of the entire assessment, always maintained the legal unity of the tenure. In case of trouble, each tenant individually and all collectively were responsible for payment. The lord could therefore single out the leading tenants and pursue them in court for full payment. The legal unity of the tenure was certainly not unique to Auvergne, Its survival stemmed from the generally modest population pressures in the mountainous regions of the province.

The annual payments in kind associated with the *mas* and *affar* were by far the most important seigneurial assessment. In addition, the chartered towns with the consular form of government paid an annual seigneurial *taille*, but in the rural areas annual *tailles* were exceptional.[165] Medieval Auvergne never produced a princely family strong enough to unify the province and erect a comprehensive fiscal apparatus for the rural areas. There were some exceptions.

Aiiiuci l iii souιheaatern Basse-Auvergne had a rural seigneurial *taille* of strictly local importance established by the counts oi Auvoιρno.[166] Combraille, which had been part of Bourbonnais in the Middle Ages, had the Bourbonnais system of mortmain and comprehensive *tailles*.[167] But, for most of Auvergne, it was only the episodic *taille aux quatre cas* that fell on the rural areas.[168]

The seigneurial system in Auvergne was rock solid and never underwent a period of significant generalized decay in the early modern era. Lords renewed their *terriers* as a normal part of seigneurial management and between comprehensive renewals carefully stored copies of individual declarations of tenure. The records and *terriers* of the late fifteenth and early sixteenth century, more precise than the seigneurial documents of the Middle Ages, served as the foundation for all subsequent *terriers* right down to the Revolution.[169]

Peasant and increasingly bourgeois tenants of the lordships in Auvergne normally paid their renders without protest year in and year out with at most a delay of a year or two occasioned by a bad harvest or some unfortunate event in the family.[170] The resignation of the tenants in meeting their seigneurial obligations continued even in 1789 and Auvergne escaped the Great Fear. This resignation certainly did not signal any heartfelt support for what was unquestionably a heavy burden, roughly 10% of the net taxable income, but rather stemmed from the pointlessness of refusal to pay.[171] Strict seigneurial management was the hallmark of lordship in Auvergne and behind the lords stood the full apparatus of royal justice.[172]

However, at the first sign of slack management, tenants ceased payment. To recover their revenues, lords had to turn to the royal courts and to the brutal procedures found in the laws of Auvergne. Examples of renewed vigilance within lordships that had suffered a temporary lapse in management can be found in every century of the early modern period, but the most striking examples dated from the reign of Louis XIV. In the 1660s, Louis XIV sent the *Parlement* of Paris into Auvergne to restore order. As a result of the *Grands Jours d'Auvergne*, royal officials seized many lordships, condemned the noble owners to death, assessed heavy fines, and razed castles. The royal sequestrations and the judicial sales, followed by contested ownership, plunged the lordships of the guilty parties into chaos. Tenants in the affected lordships soon took advantage of the legal turmoil and simply stopped paying their annual dues.[173]

The *Grands Jours d'Auvergne* condemned the barons of Salers in Haute-Auvergne to death and seized their lordship in the 1660s. A flurry of conflicting claims by the sons-in-law of the barons, by remote family members, and by creditors totally undermined the normal operation of the barony. The barony of Salers, heretofore a very well-managed lordship in the hands of members of the same family since the thirteenth century, all but collapsed during the reign of Louis XIV. At first only hamlets with a long history of disputed collection and a handful of notables with significant tenures stopped paying, but soon the movement spread from *affar* to *affar*. Emboldened tenants attacked the domain-farms of the barony and pillaged the seigneurial forests. Collection soon fell off without further notable incidents in what amounted to a strike of tenants.[174]

It took nearly fifty years for the new owners of the barony of Salers, the d'Escorailles, to re-establish regular collection. The lawsuits to salvage the barony of Salers carried out in the royal *bailliage*, the *cour présidial*, the *parlement*, and even the *conseil du roi*, as well as the local action by the court of the barony during the reign of Louis XIV produced a mountain of documentation that was greater in volume than the combined archives of Salers and d'Escorailles for the previous four centuries. Exemplary judicial seizures and forced sales eventually convinced the tenants by the 1740s to resume regular payment, but the new barons collected little of the half-century of arrears and judicial fines. Since it was simply impossible to seize and sell the tenures of the entire barony, the barons had to write off their losses.[175]

The disruption in seigneurial management caused by the *Grands Jours* affected only the confiscated lordships and did not spread to the rest of the province. Indeed, the d'Escorailles, who eventually established themselves as the new barons of Salers, pursued a policy of undisputed seigneurial management in other lordships which belonged to them, most notably in the *seigneurie* of Mazerolles.[176]

There can be no doubt, however, that without the unquestioned support of the royal courts that lordship in Haute-Auvergne, and indeed in every province of France, would have collapsed, The peasants of Haute-Auvergne did not participate in the Great Fear, but once it was clear that the new revolutionary governments lacked both the will and the power to collect redemption payments for the abolished seigneurial dues, the peasants went on strike again. Some strenuous efforts at collection produced a violent anti-seigneurial uprising in parts of Haute-Auvergne in 1792.[177]

Limousin and Marche

The seigneurial institutions in Limousin and Marche were similar to those in Auvergne. Lordship remained a fundamental institution for the organization of both rural and urban life. In Marche, seigneurial justice was particularly well-preserved and active.[178] Remnants of serfdom in the form of mortmain and annual seigneurial *tailles* lingered on here and there in Marche.[179] The barony of Crocq, located in the south-east of Marche on the border with Basse-Auvergne had a classic structure for the region.[180] The walled town of Crocq formed the center of the barony, but the majority of the population lived in dispersed settlements of hamlets and *métairies*. The barony had a dozen vassals with petty fiefs, a complete apparatus of justice, a seigneurial collegial church with canons, and rural priests nominated by the lord. Revenues came from impropriated tithes, a regulated *taille franche* on the town, market fees, seigneurial dues in cash, but mainly from *redevances foncières seigneuriales* paid in rye and oats. The domain properties included banal ovens and mills, fish ponds, and a forest with a regular schedule for cutting.

For other aspects of lordship, our best information comes from Limousin. Limousin had such a repellant physical environment that it was frequently called the Siberia of France by upperclass observers.[181] Vast areas were unsuitable for farming on a regular basis.[182] Cold, buried under snow for months each year, afflicted with a variety of leached out and infertile soils in the mountainous terrains and plateaux and equally infertile but soggy and impermeable soils in the valleys, Limousin was so inhospitable that in virtually every age substantial numbers of individuals fled each year in search of a better life elsewhere. The difficult physical environment made economic development impossible. For the peasants who did not emigrate, the choice was between impoverished subsistence agriculture on farms in perpetual seigneurial tenure or an equally impoverished existence as sharecroppers on the medium-sized *métairies* of nobles, bourgeois, and the church.

In the moderately fertile areas near the main towns, small tenures predominated, whereas elsewhere much larger tenures appeared in the form of a block of land or more commonly as a conglomerate of a number of fields from different parts of the countryside, from the flat lands, hillsides, valleys and the like, pulled together as a single unit.[183] Whether small or large, these seigneurial tenures typically had minor dues in cash and more important renders in rye, wheat, and oats. In the viticultural areas, payments were specified in wine or grapes. They were also subject to a modest *droit de mutation*, called an *acapt*, collected with the arrival of each new tenant and lord.[184] Although both the small and the larger tenures were often subdivided among many tenants, for the collection of seigneurial taxes and renders they remained a single fiscal unit.[185]

Limousin was hard hit by war and depopulation in the late Middle Ages. Reconstruction was slow and often tenures stood vacant for decades before new tenants appeared. Occasionally, lords such as the Cathedral Chapter of Limoges consented to a temporary reduction of *cens* for small tenures let out to individuals, but normally lords maintained the old level of *cens*.[186] Neither the farming methods nor the seigneurial dues changed. Both were geared to the physical environment that produced a largely immobile economic system in which the amount of land farmed was simply a function of the available, but impoverished, manpower. Initially, the canons of the Cathedral Chapter concentrated on rebuilding in the most favorable lands near Brive and Limoges, while they ignored the less attractive and severely depopulated eastern part of Limousin until the late fifteenth century when population there began to recover a little.

Many of the tenures established in the fifteenth century reconstruction were very large and from the outset were in the hands of several men. Four *terriers* of the Priory of la Beille in Limousin drawn up in 1431, 1464, 1488, and 1540 reveal the details of the reconstruction.[187] In 1431, four out of five *accensements* were collective and bound together groups of peasants for a single large tenure. The tenants were individually and collectively responsible for the annual payment of dues and renders. In 1464, ten of seventeen newly established tenures were collective. The collectively held isolated farms with three adult tenants recorded in the fifteenth century *terriers* appeared as hamlets in the 1540 *terrier* with eleven to seventeen tenants.

Sometimes lords in the fifteenth and sixteenth century used perpetual sharecropping arrangements to get the land back into cultivation.[188] From the late fifteenth century, lords turned away from the perpetual sharecropping tenures and as they fell back into their hands transformed them into either perpetual tenures with fixed renders or *métairies* on short-term sharecropping leases. Some perpetual sharecropping tenures survived, but by the late sixteenth century the bulk of the land was in seigneurial tenures with fixed renders and in temporary sharecropping leases.[189]

Between the fifteenth and the eighteenth century, neither the patterns of settlement and land use nor the seigneurial tenures and temporary leases changed much in Limousin.[190] In the years 1712 to 1716, the *seigneurie* of Chamboulive consisted of a small *bourg* of the small name with 11 houses assessed a *cens* of between one and five *sous* along with modest renders in poultry and grain. Most of the seigneurial *cens* came from the rural tenures: 39 *tènements* with a small *cens* in cash and fixed amounts of wheat, rye, oats, and poultry, and 8 days of labor. The total revenues from seigneurial dues for Chamboulive in 1712 were 50 *livres* in cash *cens* and grains worth 1782 *livres*.

In the *élection* of Tulle in Limousin at the end of the eighteenth century, the noble lords drew an average of 33% of their incomes from seigneurial dues. Those with total revenues of less than 1000 *livres* derived about 26% of their income from *droits seigneuriaux*, whereas lords with incomes greater than 3000 *livres* derived substantially more, 43%.[191] In 1788, the *seigneurie* of Soudeilles-Lieuteret, one of the largest lordships in Bas-Limousin, had total revenues of 9232 *livres* of which 47% come from domain lands organized as 23 *métairies*, and 53% from seigneurial dues. These seigneurial dues consisted overwhelmingly of payments in kind: 300 *livres* or 6% in cash dues and 4612 *livres* from payments in rye, oats, and wheat.[192]

Despite its irremediable poverty, Limousin sported a number of titled lordships that belonged to the high aristocracy of the realm. The Noailles owned lordships in Limousin from the eleventh century until the Revolution. In 1593, Henri IV elevated the castellanies of Larche, Terrasson, Mansac and Ayen to a *comté* for his supporter Henri de Noailles. The *comté* d'Ayen soon had an appropriate administrative and judicial apparatus with a *sénéchal* who heard appeals from lesser seigneurial jurisdictions. In 1663, Louis XIV elevated Ayen to a ducal- peerage for Anne de Noailles. The *duché-pairie* covered 30 parishes but had revenues of only 10,000 *livres* in the late seventeenth century.[193]

The *vicomté* of Turenne was the largest and most famous of these titled lordships.[194] The Tour d'Auvergne family owned the *vicomté* from the late fifteenth century until 1738 when the Duke of Bouillon sold it to Louis XV for 4,200,000 *livres*. The composition of the *vicomté* of Turenne did not change significantly between 1442 and 1738. Built essentially from lordships and lands usurped from the church in the Middle Ages, it covered 91 parishes, of which 47 were in Limousin, 32 in Quercy, and 12 in Périgord. The administrative and judicial apparatus of this medieval principality consolidated in the fourteenth and fifteenth century. It had a governor, a *sénéchal* who served as the chief judicial official, *baillis* who exercised civil jurisdiction in the castellanies, *prévôts* who handled criminal affairs, and *viguiers* at the local level who had simple police jurisdiction. The *vicomté* even had two feudal assemblies, the *états,* one for Limousin and the other for Quercy, that voted annual *tailles*.

The duchy of Ventadour belonged to the Rohan family in the eighteenth century. The *sénéchaussée* of the duchy was at Ussel, a quite unappealing little town of 2500 to 3000 with a hinterland of 52 villages, hamlets and *métairies*. Total revenues of the duchy for lands in Bas-Limousin ranged between 38,200 and 57,800 *livres* between 1771 and 1782. Most of these revenues for Rohan, the prince of Soubise, came from *droits seigneuriaux*, but these lands in Limousin formed only a small part of a much larger fortune.[195]

Rouergue
Rouergue, a remote and lightly populated province located on the south-central flank of the Massif Central, was geographically a part of central France, but historically the province functioned as part of the Midi. Rouergue had the

seigneurial institutions of Languedoc and maintained its strongest economic ties with the Midi. Although it is impossible to trace the history of lordship in the province through the early modern centuries with the studies now available, the evidence from the eighteenth century indicates that Rouergue had a remarkably well-preserved stock of medieval seigneurial institutions.[196] In a sample of 149 lay lordships from all of the province, *droits seigneuriaux* accounted for an average of 70% of total noble revenues and took 14.2% of the taxable net income on farmed lands according to the records of the royal *vingtième*. The unusually high proportion of noble revenues derived from seigneurial dues of all sorts indicates that the nobles of Rouergue must not have expended much effort to expand their domain lands in the early modern centuries.

Payments in kind in the form of fixed annual renders or more commonly *champarts* assessed at 1/4 or 1/5 on both regularly cultivated and occasionally worked lands brought in most of the seigneurial incomes. In addition, lords collected virtually every other sort of medieval levy: *corvée* labor for 4–5 days a year, fees for the use of banal mills, ovens and oil presses for walnuts, market fees, tolls on bridges and river ferries, taxes for hospitality called *albergues*, annual *tailles* or *fouages*, the occasional *tailles aux quatre cas*, fees assessed for pasturing sheep and cattle.

In the county of Rouergue which belonged to the king, royal officials still collected the twelfth century *commun de paix*, a taxed assessed to defray the costs of policing the province at the height of feudal disorder. In 1780, the *commun de paix* was leased for 2900 *livres* and collected from 2,713 villages and hamlets. This antique tax, collected at a derisory rate that average a little more than one *livre* per settlement, was very unpopular. In 1776, several parishes in the Ségala, the section of the province most suitable to grain farming, refused to pay the *commun de paix* and took their case to the royal courts. The royal *Conseil*, the highest court in the realm, sided with the king. Royal officials enforced the decision with judicial seizures of property and imprisonment, but other communities took up the tax strike in the 1780s.

There are no satisfactory studies of the ecclesiastical lordships in Rouergue under the old regime. The tithe was widespread and collected at very high rates of 1/11, 1/10 and even 1/9.[197] Although many ecclesiastical bodies undoubtedly drew important revenues from the tithe, two of the largest abbeys, the *hôpital* or *dômerie* of Aubrac, founded in 1120, and the Cistercian monastery of Bonneval, founded in 1147, derived the bulk of their revenues from their domain lands. Both Aubrac and Bonneval preserved their medieval domain-farms, *granges*, in the early modern centuries. These *granges* were mixed farming operations that combined livestock farming of sheep and cattle, the production of cheese, and the cultivation of grains. Aubrac had 9000 ha of mountain pastures, part used for its own farms and the rest leased out.[198]

CHAPTER FIVE

Regional Patterns of Lordship, IV

Southern France

Languedoc

At the end of the Middle Ages, lordship was perfectly integrated into the life and the institutional infrastructure of Languedoc. In both Haut-Languedoc, the area centered around Toulouse, and in Bas-Languedoc, the region that stretched along the Mediterranean coast, population was mainly clustered in nucleated villages and towns. Typically indistinguishable except for size, the villages and towns provided the geographical base for all of the local institutions: lordship, consular government, church parishes, the royal fiscal apparatus, and royal administration.[1]

Consular government had grown up within the larger structure of lordship. The consuls were agents of the lord, representatives of their communities, and from the fourteenth and fifteenth century agents of the kings, responsible for the collection of royal taxes. The municipal police authorities, the seigneurial judges, and the higher royal judicial courts functioned as parts of a single, hierarchically structured judicial apparatus. At Frouzins, a small town near Comminges, the municipal counsel, which consisted of the three consuls, the seigneurial *lieutenant du juge*, the seigneurial *procureur*, and five notables, worked together in the 1770s and 1780s to draw up a new *cadastre* for the assessment of royal taxes.[2] This harmonious cooperation of municipal, seigneurial and royal officials was also apparent at Gajan in Bas-Languedoc between the fifteenth and the eighteenth century and at Tourneveuille in Haut-Languedoc near Toulouse.[3]

The seigneurial courts were particularly active in Languedoc.[4] Near Toulouse, the number of seigneurial tribunals even increased in the seventeenth and eighteenth century with the piecemeal alienation of the royal domain.[5] The famous Canal du Midi, established by a royal edict in 1666 and acquired by Pierre Paul Riquet in public auctions in 1668 and 1677, was legally a lordship held in fief from the king. The seigneurial tribunal that moved permanently from Castelnaudary to Toulouse in 1690 had jurisdiction over the canal which was 40 m wide and 200 km long. The seigneurial court handled essentially commercial litigation.[6]

The operation of the seigneurial tribunals is particularly well-documented for the region of Aumeladès near Montpellier in Bas-Languedoc in the eighteenth century.[7] There were six seigneurial tribunals with fully qualified officials that served 11 *seigneuries* in the Aumeladès. For convenience, lords had combined some of these tribunals. For the larger diocese of Bézier, there were no less than 90 functioning seigneurial courts. Because the lower tier of the royal courts, the *vigueries* and *sénéchaussées*, had been unable to attract purchasers for all of their offices and were consequently not in a position to function properly, the seigneurial tribunals assumed most of the burden of the day to day case load of judicial business. The seigneurial judges and municipal consuls worked together in the administration of justice.

Although the village and town lordships were often divided into multiple shares, these divisions rarely hindered the operation of the seigneurial system. The village of Saint-Bauzille-de-la-Sylvie in the barony of Le Pouget in Bas-Languedoc owed its lords a collective render of 12 *setiers* of wheat and a goose, payable in the 1770s for 7/8ths to the baron, Jean-François Xavier Daudé, and 1/8 to the king. Like many of the larger lordships in Languedoc, the barony of Le Pouget had undergone considerable consolidation between 1500 and 1789 through the repurchase of lesser fiefs and minor shares.[8]

The seigneurial fiscal system changed in minor detail only between 1500 and 1789.[9] Tenants normally paid their annual seigneurial dues without protest, while lords or their agents routinely managed the *seigneuries* with great care. Lease contracts for *métairies* commonly contained sections that specified whether the owner or the tenant-farmer paid the annual *droits seigneuriaux*.[10]

Towns and villages often had a single, relatively modest seigneurial tax, called a *taille* or sometimes an *albergue*, payable in cash each year and assessed by the consuls or their agents on the population *pro rata*. In 1602, the village of Tavel near the Rhône negotiated an agreement with its lords, the abbey of Saint-André de Villeneuve and the Count of Rochefort, which commuted an annual *cens* of 6 *émines* of barley, a *setier* of oats, 15 *livres* of pepper, 15 *livres* of wax, and 8 rabbits to a single cash *albergue* payable in shares, 62 *livres* 8 *sous* to the abbey and 3 *livres* to the Count.[11] In addition, houses normally bore a seigneurial *cens* in cash. *Cens* in cash also fell on hayfields and frequently on vineyards, although renders in kind in grapes and wine were not unknown. The grain fields bore renders in kind that took either the form of the proportional *tasque* or *agrier*, or a fixed render.[12] While rates as low as 1/20 could be found, more commonly the rates were 1/5 and 1/4.[13]

All told, the renders in kind assessed on the grain fields were the most important annual seigneurial dues.[14] The commutation of proportional renders to fixed renders was already underway at the beginning of the fourteenth century, accelerated in the fifteenth, and continued here and there until the Revolution. Nevertheless, proportional renders remained widespread and lords frequently established them on new tenures.[15] Seigneurial taxes were normally assessed on small individual tenures. While not unknown, the system in which several co-tenants were collectively responsible, *solidairement*, for a single seigneurial assessment for a legally undivided tenure was not as common in most of Langue-doc as it was in provinces with predominately dispersed population.[16] Many tenures were also subject to a double inheritance or transfer fee, due at the death of the tenant or the lord. The *acapt* and the *arrière acapt* varied from a symbolic payment in cash to a full year's seigneurial dues.[17]

Rates for the annual seigneurial dues naturally varied from tenure to tenure. The most striking variations typically arose from special arrangements negotiated between new tenants and lords. In the most desirable farming regions near the towns where bourgeois and noble investors were most active, lords often agreed to a modest, even a symbolic annual seigneurial tax in return for a large entrance fee for the tenure.[18] Or, lords maintained substantial annual *cens* and renders, and required more modest entrance fees. In 1774, the Baron of Tournefeuille invested a tenant with a tenure that consisted of 2 ha of vineyards near Toulouse for an annual *cens* of 6 *deniers*, but a *droit d'entrée* of 2,100 *livres*.[19]

Similarly, lords who constructed *métairies* from seigneurial tenures often made special arrangements to free their lands of *cens* or to commute renders in kind to simple cash payments. In 1664, two lords, the *seigneur* of Saint-Martin de Castries and the *seigneur* d'Azirou drew up an agreement with the abbey of Saint-Guilhem to commute the *tasques* of 1/4 and 1/5 into an annual payment of 200 *livres*.[20] For Languedoc as a whole, the annual seigneurial dues probably amounted to about 10% of the major crops.[21]

Banal mills and ovens were widespread and often belonged to villages and towns that at some point in time had purchased these assets from their lords.[22] In the civil diocese of Lodève, the town of Clermont paid its lord an annual *cens* of 160 *livres* for three banal ovens. During the years 1742–1747, the lease of these communal ovens brought Clermont an annual income of 4,650 *livres*.[23] Similarly, the banal oven at Lescure near Albi brought this small town more than 1000 *livres* a year in the late eighteenth century, but most banal ovens owned by small villages brought in far less.[24]

Like most provinces in France, Languedoc saw a proliferation of noble and bourgeois domains or *métairies* in the sixteenth, seventeenth and eighteenth century.[25] The opening of the Canal du Midi at the end of the seventeenth century greatly stimulated commercial grain farming in Haut-Languedoc. In the Lauragais region near Toulouse and in parishes near the canal, noble and bourgeois investors bought up the existing farm land and cleared marginal lands for permanent cultivation. In the areas most suitable for commercial grain farming, peasant ownership largely disappeared.[26]

In Bas-Languedoc near Béziers, Pierre-Raymond de Sarret purchased the royal share of the lordship of Coussergues in 1495. Starting with a small domain of about 100 ha, the Sarret family steadily increased its direct holdings. In 1790, the domain consisted of over 1500 ha that featured a large grain farm and a massive pasture for sheep in the nearby *garrigue*.[27] In Bas-Languedoc, the *vicomté* of Plaissan, purchased by the Prince de Conti in 1765 for 388,400 *livres*, had 7 *métairies* that together covered 1577 *sétérées* of farm land, of which only 273 *sétérées* was legally noble land and the rest was non-noble *roturier* property pieced together from tenures and newly cleared land since the end of the Middle Ages.[28] Similar upperclass investment in farmland also occurred near Montpelier in the sixteenth, seventeenth century and eighteenth century.[29] However, for Haut-Languedoc as a whole and even more for Bas-Languedoc, noble and bourgeois *métairies* accounted for far less farmland than the more modest peasant tenures.

The upperclass owners of *métairies* worked their lands either with sharecropping leases or less commonly with salaried stewards called *maître-valets*. In both of these arrangements, the financial involvement of the lords and bourgeois in the farming of their lands was very significant. The *métairies* normally fell in the range of 20 to 40 ha each. At Falga in the eastern part of Lauragais, the Caffareilli family owned 11 *métairies* which together covered 280 ha in the second half of the eighteenth century.[30] Similarly, the estate of the marquis d'Escouloubre also located in Lauragais had 7 *métairies* that together covered about 250 ha in 1750.[31] For other domain lands, typically smaller than fully equipped *métairies*, upperclass investors often used the *locatairie perpétuelle*, the local phrase for *rente foncière*, which stipulated an set annual payment, usually in kind. To avoid any possibility that the *locatairie perpétuelle* would be mistaken in law as a perpetual *censive* tenure and to keep open the option for increased annual payments, eighteenth century contracts specified a formal notarized renewal of these supposedly perpetual arrangemnts every 29 years. The jurisprudence of the revolutionary and imperial eras classified the *locatairie perpétuelle* as a non-seigneurial lease.[32]

As a remote province with at best moderately fertile soils in the most favored areas, Languedoc never attracted much investment by noble families of national stature. The towns, although numerous, were small. Toulouse, the largest in Languedoc, had only about 50,000 people at the end of the old regime. Leaving aside the occasional prince such as Conti who acquired lands in Bas-Languedoc in the late eighteenth century, the top echelon of the provincial nobility in Languedoc consisted essentially of the *parlementaires* at Toulouse and the *gens de robe* affiliated with the *chambre des comptes* at Montpellier, the three royal *sénéchaussées* and lesser royal tribunals.

There was both consolidation of lordships at the top of the noble hierarchy and a proliferation of lesser lordships and minor fiefs at the bottom, most notably through the piecemeal sale of royal lordships in the sixteenth and seventeenth century.[33] The robe nobles of Languedoc, often from bourgeois families, were resident lords with modest incomes. They derived the majority of their estate incomes from their domain-farms.[34] However, *droits seigneuriaux* were far from insignificant in noble budgets. In 48 lordships near Toulouse, seigneurial dues brought on average nearly 20% of total annual incomes in the middle of the eighteenth century.[35] In 11 lordships in the Aumeladès region of Bas-Languedoc, seigneurial dues accounted for 30% of total revenues.[36]

As a whole, the lords of Languedoc were nobles of modest means and generally modest lifestyle. They exercised strict and usually personal management of their domain lands and of their lordships[37] They maintained functioning seigneurial law courts. While not immune to the allure of honorific rights, the noble lords of Languedoc normally led frugal, unostentatious lives. The Count of Villèle, later one of Louis XVIII's chief ministers, was the model of the Languedoc noble. He was prudent, frugal, even ascetic in his lifestyle.[38]

The church in Languedoc was poorly endowed with land and consequently was heavily reliant on revenues from the tithe.[39] Tithe rates in Languedoc were among the heaviest in the kingdom, 1/10 to 1/12 in Lauragais. The bishoprics, cathedral chapters, monasteries and commanderies were second to none in their determination to collect tithes on **all** fruits of the earth, not only major grains and grapes, but olives, lambs, fleeces, cheese, and even vegetables grown in the gardens. In Haut-Languedoc, ecclesiastical institutions derived between 75 to 90% of their income from the tithe.[40] At Tavel in Bas-Languedoc, an agreement of 1595 stipulated that the abbey of Saint-André de Villeneuve collected a tithe of 1/14 on all grains, lambs, wine, hay, olives, and vegetables in the village *finage*.[41]

Litigation over the tithes and even tithe strikes were already part of the history of Languedoc at the close of the Middle Ages. Disputes over tithes were widespread at the beginning of the sixteenth century and swelled into a flood during the Wars of Religion. Backed by the power of the monarchy and the *Parlement* of Toulouse, the church of Languedoc reestablished collection in the early seventeenth century. For all that, disputes did not end, picked up again in the late seventeenth century, and continued right down to the Revolution.[42] Often, conflicts over the tithe led to amicable or arbitrated agreements that eliminted the proportional tithe and replaced it with a fixed annual payment.[43]

Velay, Gévaudan and Vivarais

Velay, Gévaudan, and Vivarais, the modern *départements* of Haute-Loire, Lozère, and Ardèche, were considered part of Languedoc under the old regime. The economies of these small provinces were mainly tied to Languedoc, but geographically they formed the southeastern flank of the Massif Central. Consequently, they derived part of their institutions from the Massif Central and part from Languedoc. The consular form of government for towns and villages came from the Midi as did the traditions governing the tithe, but since the great majority of the population lived in dispersed settlements, the institutions of lordship were those of the Massif Central, not Languedoc.

Our best information comes from Velay and Gévaudan. Both provinces had remarkably stable seigneurial systems that defied the ages. In the areas of oldest settlement, the medieval *mansi* fragmented into separate tenures, often called *pagésie*, while most tenures took as their geographic base dispersed hamlets, *mas* and isolated farms, *afars*. These medieval patterns of settlement and their corresponding fiscal systems of lordship survived in both Velay and Gévaudan with only minor changes until 1789.[44] While some of the hamlets retained undivided tenures with collective responsibility for payment of seigneurial dues, the general trend was toward the division of the legal responsibility for payment, *égalation*, in keeping with the actual holdings.

Seigneurial dues were paid overwhelmingly in kind and they were heavy. For tenants, the seigneurial dues amounted to 24.48% of taxable landed revenues in 11 communities in Brivadois and between 10% and 13.46% elsewhere in Velay at the end of the eighteenth century.[45] An impressive collection of seigneurial documents has survived for the Hôtel-Dieu of Le Puy which contains a full run of *terriers* from the fifteenth century until the Revolution, abstracts of the *terriers* called *lièves*, used for the annual collection of seigneurial dues, and accounts that encompass both the lordships and the domain lands. The seigneurial dues were assessed overwhelmingly in kind and changed little

between the end of the fifteenth and the end of the eighteenth century. These
renders took the form of fixed annual dues, the common pattern in most of the
Massif Central, rather than the proportional renders of the Midi. There were
examples of proportional renders, *champarts*, but these fell on former domain
lands recently converted into large, collectively held tenures. In 1720–29, fixed
renders in kind, essentially payments in rye (60%), oats, wheat (20% each) and
barley accounted for 97% of the annual value of dues, while *cens* in cash
produced only 3%. Revenues from seigneurial dues for the Hôtel-Dieu in the
seventeenth and eighteenth centuries fluctuated between a low of 20% and a high
of 50%, but on average accounted for about a third of total income of the
hospital.[46]

In addition to the usual renders in rye, oats, wheat, eggs, poultry and wax,
lords also collected a few days of *corvée* labor and the occasional *taille aux
quatre cas*. Annual seigneurial *tailles* were unusual. Normally, seigneurial
tailles, where they had existed at all in the Middle Ages, had merged with annual
cens in cash. But, there were exceptions. The *seigneurie* of Saint-Ilpize collected
a seigneurial *taille* on a multiplicity of rural tenures and small towns. Saint-Ilpize
was a lordship detached from the holdings of the medieval *dauphins* of Auvergne
that straddled Auvergne and Velay. The *dauphins* had established an annual
taille in a fragment of the county of Auvergne at some time prior to the thirteenth
century. The *taille* in the *seigneurie* of Saint-Ilpize, payable on the feast of Saint-
André, was collected from at least the fourteenth century until 1789. In 1320 it
brought in 80 *florins d'or*, in 1359 100 *florins d'or*, and in 1725 a very sizable
14,966 *livres tournois*. Upheld repeatedly by the *Parlement* of Paris over the
centuries, this annual seigneurial *taille* was highly unusual for Velay.[47]

Lordship survived as a important fiscal system in the towns too. At Le Puy,
the urban properties often bore the same kind of *cens* and renders as rural
tenures: minor payments in cash and more substantial renders in kind.[48]
However, the most lucrative urban *droits seigneuriaux* were the transfer fees,
collected by the Hôtel-Dieu of Le Puy at 1/4 and by other ecclesiastical lords at
about 1/8, and hefty entrance fees. In 1585, the cathedral chapter of Notre-Dame
du Puy established a new urban tenure, a *bail à nouveau cens et emphytéose
perpétuelle*, that specified an annual *cens* of 20 sous and a *droit d'entrée* of 180

livres 7 *sous*.[49]

Although the seigneurial dues brought in significant revenues for both ecclesiastical and aristocratic lords, lords derived most of their income from their domains. The Carthusian monastery of Bonnefoy owned 32 domains or *granges* in Velay and Vivarais at the beginning of the eighteenth century. The typical domain was a mixed farming operation with sheep, cattle, goats, and arable farming that produced butter, cheese, grain, and livestock.[50] The domain-farm of Le Poux, one of many that belonged to the Hôtel-Dieu of Le Puy, had about 110 ha of land and was stocked with 30 head of cattle, 5 yoke of oxen, 5 bulls, a dozen hogs, 15 horses, mares and mules at the time of the Revolution.[51]

Tithes followed the pattern of Languedoc. They were both widespread and at high rates, most commonly 1/11 in Brivadois, but 1/14 in other parts of Velay, and only 1/22 in the *vicomté* of Polignac.[52]

Seigneurial justice was very active and provided essential legal services to the rural and urban population. At Tence in Velay, two lords shared jurisdiction over this small town, the bishop of Le Puy and the Jesuits, replaced from the 1760s by the priory of Saint-Martin. The bishop had two *baillis* or *juges*, one for high justice, the second for medium and low, while the Jesuits and then the priory had only one official who exercised medium and low justice. The judicial officials for the two lords took turns administering low and medium justice, a year at a time. The divided *seigneurie* and the divided jurisdiction functioned smoothly without any apparent conflict with the consular government of the town. Lordship was simply part of the institutional infrastructure of the town, no more and no less.[53]

In 1734, Velay had 204 lordships with rights of high justice. However, many of the major ecclesiastical and aristocratic lords, such as the bishop and cathedral chapter of Le Puy, the abbey of La Chaise Dieu, and the *vicomte* of Polignac, owned dozens of lordships. For convenience, many of the great lords had consolidated their seigneurial tribunals. Consequently, there were only 45 functioning seigneurial tribunals in Velay in 1789, but most of these had jurisdiction over multiple lordships and dozens of communities. Only 17 seigneurial courts served a single lordship while others served 17, 18, even 24 lordships.[54]

Provence

Under the old regime, Provence was one of the poorest, most lightly populated provinces in France.[55] The physical environment, although stunningly beautiful with its sun-drenched and picturesque terraced farms, presented obstacles to economic development that were too immense to overcome with the technical and financial resources of the time. In most of the province, the Alpine topography made transportation and hence economic integration extremely difficult. Large scale irrigation was also prohibitively expensive. Consequently, in upwards of four-fifths of Provence the tiny towns and villages lived in a setting of largely self-contained economic isolation in which each community struggled to produce the basic food stuffs.

Only two regions, the Rhône valley between Arles and Orange, and the Mediterranean coast from Marseille eastwards, had physical environments that lent themselves more readily to development. Not surprisingly, half the population lived in these two regions. The upper Rhône valley was unquestionably the most fertile area in Provence. Transportation was relatively easy, the good soil of the valley lent itself to farming on a commercial scale, but this region was isolate and the towns remained small. South of Arles the Rhône degenerated into a vast malarial swamp through which only the most intrepid sailors passed. The Mediterranean coast from Marseille eastward lent itself to commercial development too, but the towns, perched on a narrow ledge of land, had minimal ties with the interior. The economic hinterlands of Marseille, Toulon, Hyères and the other coastal towns were the Levant, Languedoc, North Africa, and Italy, not Provence.

The easily recognizable patterns of lordship in Provence in both the Middle Ages and in the early modern centuries were rooted to a great extent in the different physical environments of the province.[56] The kings as heirs of the medieval counts of Provence were the direct lords, either individually or jointly, of roughly fifty communities out of a total of six-hundred.[57] The fifty lordships of the royal domain encompassed virtually all of the major towns in the Rhône valley and the Mediterranean coast, a significant part of the interior plateaux, and many of the remote villages in the high Alpine valleys. In this comital, now royal domain, the medieval counts from the early thirteenth century had vigorously developed the upper echelon of seigneurial taxes, the indirect taxes and especially the collectively assessed *tailles* that fell on the towns and villages as a whole.[58] Often the princely *tailles, aides, albergues*, etc., replaced an array of older seigneurial taxes, most notably in the towns.

From the end of the Middle Ages, the kings shifted their attention to the new royal taxes, the royal *taille*. The strictly seigneurial taxes in the royal domain, enshrined in the various municipal and village charters, survived, but were not systematical updated. The collectively assessed seigneurial *tailles*, once of great importance for the counts, became less burdensome with inflation. The even older seigneurial taxes, especially the taxes on urban properties and the taxes on farmed land in the legal territory of the settlement, the *redevances foncières seigneuriales* such as the proportional *tasques*, either disappeared or shrank in importance. In this pattern of lordship, found mainly in the royal domain, the fiscal burden of lordship was modest.

The second pattern of lordship was the direct opposite of the first and was found in the territories outside the old comital domain and hence in *seigneuries* in the hands of lords below the rank of princes. In these *seigneuries*, the fiscal burden of lordship was significant rather than light.[59] The most important seigneurial taxes were the proportional *tasques* or fixed renders in kind collected on grain fields, vineyards, olive groves, and even gardens. Likewise, banal mills, ovens, wine and oil presses brought in considerable revenues. Seigneurial *tailles* assessed on the community as a whole also existed, but technically they belonged to the lower or older register of seigneurial taxes levied on individual communities rather than the newer layer of princely *tailles* characteristic of the old comital domain.

The foundation documents for this pattern of lordship were the ancient charters, the *terriers*, and the newer charters, the *acts d'habitation*, that lords used in the late fifteenth and sixteenth century for the resettlement of their lands. The foundation charters for the village of Lourmarin, drawn up in 1480, 1488, and 1494, by Raymond d'Agout, *seigneur* of Lourmarin, were typical.[60] These documents established a standard fiscal system of lordship for all present and future inhabitants. A fixed *cens* per house was based on the size of the hayfields, the vineyards, and the olive groves. At Lourmarin the rates were 2 chickens for the house, stable and courtyard; 8 *deniers* per *quarterée* of vineyard; 3 *gros* per *séchoyrée* of hayfield; 2 *deniers* per *éminée* of olive grove; and 2 *deniers* for the hemp patch. In addition and more importantly, there was a *tasque* of 1/7 assessed on all grains, legumes, and fruits, and a separate *tasque* of 1/5 on the vineyards. Households with wagons and plows were subject to annual *corvées*. Households without these agricultural implements owed 2 *corvées* of manual labor a year. There were also banal monopolies for the winnowing of grain, for grinding in the grain mill, and for baking in the oven. Not all settlers set up house in the village. Some established isolated farms, called *affars* or *bastides*. For them, there was a separate table of rates. For one *affar* listed in 1483, the rate was 6 *saumées* of wheat and 4 1/2 *saumées* of rye. In the middle of the eighteenth century, this burdensome seigneurial system was still in place.

The seigneurial system at Saint-Martin de la Brasque was even heavier.[61] There was a *tasque* of 1/6th on grains, 1/7th on olives, 1/9 on hemp, grapes and almonds. The fees for milling grain and baking bread were 1/16th and 1/40th. In addition, each tenant owed 2 chickens for the house, another chicken for the garden, 3 *sols* per *éminée* of hayfield, and two *corvées* with a plow a year.

Geographically, this pattern of lordship was most common in the economically underdeveloped interior plateaux of Haute-Provence, especially the *viguerie* of Apt, and occurred in 116 communities out of 582 studied in Provence.[62] Lords relied heavily on the revenues of lordship for their incomes and only the most extreme financial embarrassments led them to change this lucrative system. Also, few of the small towns and villages where this pattern of lordship survived were financially strong enough to negotiate a liquidation of the old arrangements. Typically, no modifications in the fiscal system of lordship occurred after the end of the Middle Ages and the first few decades of the sixteenth century. In many lordships in the eighteenth century, most of the feudal revenues still came from the *tasques*, the fixed *cens* and renders, and the banal machinery.[63] Between 1746 and 1748, annual revenues of the lordship of Lourmarin fluctuated between 9,500 and 15,500 *livres*. Roughly 60% of these revenues were from payments in kind for *tasques* on grains and olive oil and from fees for milling.[64]

The third pattern of lordship affected the largest number of communities, 380 out of 582, and appeared in the most economically favorable settings of the Rhône valley, the Mediterranean coast, and less commonly in the interior plateaux outside the territory of the royal domain.[65] Starting around 1500 or so with fiscal systems of lordship identical to those of our second model, the most dynamic villages and towns, which were also the settlements with the strongest consular governments, took advantage of the economic and demographic expansion of the sixteenth and early seventeenth century to negotiate more favorable terms with their lords. Some communities were able to liquidate most of the lower range of seigneurial taxes in a single transaction in return for a lump sum payment and a yearly, collectively assessed *taille*. Nearly a third of the villages and towns eliminated the *tasque* or obtained a lower fixed-rate *cens*. Often communities improved their position through a number of transactions. They bought banal ovens and mills which they then maintained as revenue producing assets for the village or municipal budget. Royal records from 1729 and 1765 indicate that the communities owned 34% of the mills and 40% of the mills, whereas lords held 45% of the mills and 44% of the ovens. Commoners owned the rest.[66]

The strength of the towns and villages would not have produced a favorable modification of the fiscal burden of lordship without the financial distress of the lords.[67] Ecclesiastical lords appeared frequently in transactions in which heavy feudal dues were sacrificed for ready cash. The archbishop of Arles, the bishop of Marseille, the abbey of Thoronnet, to name just a few, negotiated multiple agreements over *droits seigneuriaux* with their subjects in the sixteenth and seventeenth century. Lay lords in financial distress pursued the same policy. The most spectacular case stemmed from the financial ruin of the Duke of Guise. In 1660, Guise sold all of his rights at Eyguières except justice to help pay for his ransom.

More typically, the financial straits of the lords led to less sweeping changes. In the barony of La Tour d'Aigues, located not far from Apt, the 1506 *acte d'habitation* drawn up for the *vicomte* of Reillanne formed the legal foundation of the lordship.[68] In 1583, the grandson of the *vicomte*, anxious to raise money for the purchase of an additional lordship, issued a second charter that substantially reduced the rates for *droits seigneuriaux* mentioned in the 1506 charter in return for a one-time payment of 2 *écus d'or* per *saumée* of all cultivated lands. The 1583 charter made several changes. Most notably it eliminated the *tasque* of 1/7 and replaced it with a fixed render of 4 *cosses* of grain per *saumée* of field. The new fixed rate render amounted to a reduction of roughly one half the original *tasque*. Although there were many lawsuits over *droits seigneuriaux* in the eighteenth century which arose when inhabitants altered traditional cropping patterns, these two charters always figured prominently in the litigation. In the eighteenth century, the barony belonged to the Bruny family, rich merchants of Marseille, who purchased it in 1719 for 900,000 *livres*. At the time of the revolution, the baron was Jean-Baptiste-Jérôme de Bruny, *président à motier* in the *Parlement* of Aix.

For the province as a whole, the communities involved in this pattern of lordship made their greatest gains in the sixteenth and early seventeenth century. A few purchased the entire lordship and replaced their old lords as direct vassals of the king: Les Mées and Mézel in the sixteenth century, Hyères in 1626, Rustrel in 1629, Coursegoules in 1636, Gardanne in 1660, Callas in 1720, and Bayons in the late eighteenth century.[69] When the *seigneurie* of Lançon, sold by King François I in 1519, came back on the market in 1562, the town itself bought the lordship.[70] Similarly, in 1775, the small village of Bayons in Haute-Provence purchased the entire *seigneurie* of the town from its lord with the approval of the intendant.[71] The contract specified a single cash payment of 22,000 *livres* and a life annuity of 1,200 *livres*, 6 pairs of partridges and three hares. The village took over administration of low and medium justice, while royal officials assumed control of high justice. Many more communities purchased at least a partial reduction of the financial burdens of lordship. A number of communities even acquired vacant lands, *terres gastes*, from their lords.

Then from the time of the Thirty Years' War and in some cases from the era of the Wars of Religion, the burdens of increased royal taxes, the costs of billeting royal soldiers, the devastation of plagues and famines undermined village and town finances.[72] Heavily indebted communities preferred to sell assets rather than to increase local taxes. Lords and other creditors who soon became lords took back vacant lands, repurchased or established banal machinery for the first time, created new *tailles* or increased old ones, etc. Although the communities lost ground financially especially in the second half of the seventeenth century, the renegotiated systems of lordship were usually less burdensome than those where no change had occurred since the sixteenth century.

A fourth pattern of lordship appeared with the demographic growth of the eighteenth century in every region of Provence except the high Alpine valleys, but mainly in the most heavily populated areas of Basse-Provence where there was still an abundance of uncultivated land. Although there is some evidence that the demographic growth of the last few decades of the old regime produced a modest improvement in economic integration and specialization, for the most part more people meant more subsistence agriculture and more small-scale peasant farming for local or at best regional markets. Men were desperate for land to farm at any price. In this setting, the two most common ways lords in Provence increased their seigneurial revenues were the piecemeal upgrading of feudal dues one tenure at a time and the creation of new tenures from uncultivated waste lands or from relatively unprofitable domain-farms.[73]

The eighteenth century notarial records for the area around Aix are filled with contracts for new seigneurial tenures.[74] In some cases, lords came into possession of tenures that fell back into the hands without their intervention. In other cases, lords used their seigneurial right of preemptive purchase, *droit de prélation* or *retrait féodal,* to acquire lands or tenures within their lordships which came up for sale. In these transactions, lords invoked their rights, paid the specified purchase price and pushed aside the buyer. Between 1745 and 1774, M. de Gallifet, a *conseiller* in the *Parlement* of Aix, routinely intervened in sales of land in his lordship. In most cases, he let the lands out again on perpetual seigneurial tenure with a hefty entrance fee, *acapte*, and an increased annual render. For example, in 1745, Gallifet demanded an entrance fee of 400 livres and an annual *cens* of 5 *livres* for a tenure of 1.8 ha that he had recently acquired through preemptive purchase.[75] Although the tenures were usually small, the total amount of land that eighteenth century Provençal lords allocated with increased feudal burdens was far from insignificant. At Sénas between 1751 and 1771, two members of the Benault family, *conseillers* in the *Parlement*, upgraded the seigneurial dues on a multiplicity of small tenures that together covered 81 ha.[76]

More particularly, some lords established new villages.[77] In 1741, Pierre-César de Cadenet liquidated a number of unprofitable domain-farms in his lordship and combined these lands with heretofore uncultivated wastes for a new peasant village at Charleval. Sixty-four families took up tenures in the new village at Charleval whose *finage* covered 190 ha. The foundation charter, modeled on the late medieval *actes d'habitation* and drawn up with the aid of feudal lawyers, included the full range of *droits seigneuriaux*, from *tasques* to *corvées*. Once the lands were in full production, the annual revenues, derived primarily from the proportional *tasques*, came to nearly 6000 *livres,* a sum far greater than the old domain-farms had ever produced. Similar new villages, established by *parlementaires*, appeared at Bandol in 1715, at Lamonon in 1745, and at Sainte-Croix in 1787.

Lords in Provence had always had an abundance of uncultivated lands and marginally productive domain-farms. The expansion of aristocratic and bourgeois farms through clearings and the liquidation of peasant tenures, the dominant pattern in the realm, produced only modest results in Provence. In fact, in many parts of Basse-Provence tenures increased and directly held noble properties shrank. For many lords, the profits from new tenures burdened with heavy renders and fees far exceeded incomes that could be derived from commercial oriented agriculture in existing or new domain-farms. At Rognonas, nobles and bourgeois of Avignon owned 87% of the land in 1645, but only 46% in 1760. During the same period, the number of petty peasant homesteads quadrupled. Lords created tenures and bourgeois carved up their *métairies* or *bastides* into tiny farms and detached fields. Lords used seigneurial tenures while bourgeois employed either short-term leases or perpetual *rentes foncières*, but both lords and bourgeois engaged in exploitative rack-renting.[78] As a rule, lords demanded either the *tasques* or fixed renders in kind for the new tenures of the eighteenth century.[79]

Regardless of the exact pattern of lordship, town and village officials and seigneurial agents worked together under royal supervision in an institutional arrangement in which they shared judicial, police, administrative, and fiscal tasks.[80] This institutional integration of communal governance and lordship did not prevent disputes between the communities and their lords, over the fiscal status of properties, over common lands and uncultivated waste lands, etc. Indeed, there was a flood of litigation between lords and their subjects in the last century of the old regime in Provence, but rarely any violence.[81] The litigation did not cripple the joint governance of the communities, nor did it seriously poison relations between the parties.[82]

For the most part, the lords of Provence had only modest incomes in keeping with the quite limited economic potential of the province. At the end of the seventeenth century, there were about 300 nobles in Provence, but only 180 on the eve of the Revolution. These 180 nobles held 355 lordships, whereas commoners owned 715 petty fiefs.[83] There was only one elevation of a lordship to the rank of a ducal-peerage in Provence in the early modern era.[84] The *parlementaires* of Aix were well-represented in the higher echelons of the Provençal nobility and three-quarters of these magistrates had revenues that were less than 20,000 *livres* a year, half had revenues of between 5,000 and 15,000 *livres*.[85]

The nobles of Provence were relatively poor and in most regions of Provence drew a greater than average share of their incomes from feudal dues. The normal pattern in France as a whole was that nobles derived a quarter or less of their total incomes from feudal dues. In Provence, the *droits seigneuriaux* were nearly as important as non-seigneurial incomes. The high showing of feudal revenues was linked directly to the quite limited potential for commercial development of agriculture in Provence which made the easy profits of exploitative feudalism irresistible. For the *parlementaires* of Aix in the eighteenth century, the average for feudal dues in total noble budgets was 41%.[86] In 1719, roughly 60% of the revenues of the barony of La Tour d'Aigues came from *droits seigneuriaux*.[87] Only lords with substantial holdings in the Rhône valley approached the national norm. Even there, the physical and economic environment of the river valley lent itself only to domain-farms of modest size. Provence had nothing remotely comparable to the vast aristocratic and ecclesiastical domain-farms of the Ile-de-France with their capitalist tenant farmers.[88]

Finally, the church in Provence was very poorly endowed.[89] Only 15% of the roughly 600 communities in Provence had an ecclesiastical lord. Ecclesiastical establishments exercised sole jurisdiction over 115 communities and were joint co-seigneurs, usually with the king, in another 35.[90] The bishoprics at Marseille, Aix, Gap, and Apt had very modest possessions that shrank further in the early modern period. Only a handful of ancient monasteries, most notably the abbeys of Lerins and Saint-Victor of Marseille, had respectable incomes, but even these were modest when compared to the great benefices of the realm. The wealthiest ecclesiastical lord in Provence was the Order of Malta.[91]

The tithe was the mainstay of many ecclesiastical establishments.[92] In the 150 communities where the lord was an ecclesiastical establishment, the tithe and the *tasque* were merged into a single and heavy payment, for example, 1/8 at Ganabobie and Sigonce. The rates of the tithe ran from a high of 1/10 to as low as 1/60, but the most common rates were in the range of 1/12 to 1/16. The tithe rates were consequently significantly lower than the *tasques*, which were often assessed at 1/7 and even 1/5 for vineyards, but the tithe fell on a much wider range of agricultural products, not only the grains, grapes, but flax, lambs, colts, even piglets, garlic, legumes, almonds, walnuts, and onions. In Basse-Provence, tithes on grains were more common than tithes on olives, olive oil, grapes and wine, agricultural commodities that became important only in the early modern centuries. *Abonnements*, fixed annual payments that replaced the proportional tithes, appeared in 349 communities that had a lay lord.

Bordelais and Aquitaine

At the end of the Middle Ages, Bordelais and Aquitaine, the hinterland of Bordeaux north of the Garonne river, were already among the principal wine exporting regions in France. Between 1500 and 1789, the pull of the export market produced quite significant economic changes in southwestern France, but Bordeaux's ancient privileges meant that Bordelais and Aquitaine responded to the stimulus of the export market in different ways.[93] Bordeaux and Bordelais enjoyed exclusive access to the export market for wine until Christmas each year. This privilege, granted initially by the English kings but repeatedly confirmed by later French kings, placed the interior of Aquitaine at a competitive disadvantage in the wine trade since its wines could not be sold for export from Bordeaux until after December 25. Although modified somewhat from time to time and even temporarily suspended by Turgot in 1776, Bordeaux's privilege survived until the end of the old regime.[94]

In Bordelais, the growth of the export market for wine stimulated the planting of vineyards, initially at a relatively modest pace in the sixteenth century and more rapidly in the seventeenth century as the Dutch emerged as the dominant traders in western Europe. Despite royal edits issued during the reign of Louis XV which prohibited further planting of vines, the vineyards continued to expand in the eighteenth century with the burgeoning demand in Europe and in the colonial market in the West Indies.

Little by little as incomes rose in the early modern centuries and tastes became more refined, the vintages and the viticultural zones in Bordelais became more sharply defined. At the end of the Middle Ages, the better wines of the *graves* already stood apart in price and in reputation from the common, low quality claret of the *palus* and other less prestigious viticultural areas.[95] The move towards higher quality, perceptible from the sixteenth century, accelerated rapidly during the reign of Louis XIV. Louis XIV's wars seriously disrupted the wine trade with England. England turned to Portugal and Spain for common wines, and levied high tariffs on French wines. Although the common wines of Bordelais still found markets in the Netherlands and the Baltic areas, the market in England was effectively closed.

In response to the English tariffs, the noble and to a lesser extent bourgeois wine producers in Bordelais in the eighteenth century concentrated on perfecting the production and conservation of luxury wines which alone could now penetrate the English market.[96] In the second half of the eighteenth century, a keg of luxury wine could easily sell for a hundred times the price of a keg of common wine. Around 1750, kegs of wine from Lafite, Latour, Margaux and Haut-Brion sold for between 1200 and 2000 *livres*, while less prestigious wines in the premier viticultural areas of Médoc and the *graves* brought only 200 to 250 *livres*.[97] By the 1770s the wines of the *graves* and Médoc were classified as first, second, and third quality *crus*.[98]

At the end of the old regime, the aristocracy of Bordeaux owned 3200 ha of vineyards that produced nearly 80,000 hl of high quality wine, but these pre-eminent vintages accounted for no more than 10 to 15% of the total volume of wines exported from Bordeaux. As in the past, peasant and bourgeois vineyards from Bordelais and vineyards from the hinterland of Aquitaine supplied the overwhelming majority of the wines exported from Bordeaux.[99]

The changes in the wine market produced concomitant changes in the vineyards. The largely undifferentiated vineyards of the Middle Ages gave way to more clearly delineated viticultural regions distinguished by the quality of their vintages. The *graves,* Médoc and the *palus* of Ambès emerged as the regions most suited to the production of quality wine. By the late seventeenth century, lords and bourgeois had largely replaced peasants as the principal land owners in these viticultural areas. The hierarchy of vineyards clarified further in the eighteenth century. Unquestionably the most prestigious vineyards were Haut-Brion in the *graves*, and Margaux, Lafite and Latour in Médoc. In the eighteenth century, the *seigneurie* of Haut-Brion had a total surface of 264 ha. The seigneurial reserve, the foremost vineyard in Bordelais, accounted for 73 ha of which 38 ha was in vineyards. Common lands took up 85,5 ha and the rest, 104 ha consisted of seigneurial tenures. Nobles owned 34% of the tenures, bourgeois 41%, and members of the lower classes only 19%.[100]

The economic dynamism of Bordeaux and Bordelais in the early modern centuries transformed the social composition of the nobility and affected every seigneurial institution and practice. New families rose from commerce to royal office, filled the *Parlement* of Bordeaux, married into and largely replaced the older noble families.[101] The noble class shrank in number, but rose in wealth. By the end of the seventeenth century, the noble magistrates of Bordeaux were the leading lords of Bordelais and their estates were both larger and much better organized than those of the feudal lords of the late Middle Ages. An astounding 12 new ducal-peerages appeared in the Bordelais region in the early modern centuries, nearly as many as in the Ile-de-France and in Champagne, both of which had 16, and ahead of Normandie, which had 10.[102] At the end of the old regime, there were only 185 nobles in the Bordelais, while the neighboring regions of Périgord and Agenais had 366 and 439 respectively.[103] The noble magistrates of the *Parlement,* who were the principal owners of the quality vineyards, equaled the international merchants of Bordeaux in wealth and far surpassed them in social prestige.[104]

Between 1500 and 1789, the relative importance of seigneurial renders and domain-farms in noble budgets reversed positions. Tho medieval lords in Bordelais owned seigneurial domain-farms, small polycultural estates called *bourdieux*. These domain-farms were broadly similar to the seigneurial *métaires* elsewhere in the Midi, and they produced only modest revenues. Around 1450–1500, both ecclesiastical and noble lords seem to have drawn their principal revenues from seigneurial renders levied on vineyards and grain fields rather than from their domain-farms.[105] By the late seventeenth century and certainly in the eighteenth century, lords drew most of their income from their domain-farms and relatively minor revenues from *droits seigneuriaux*.

The expansion of the seigneurial domain-farms and of bourgeois *métairies* in Bordelais between 1500 and 1789 followed the same chronology and used the same methods of land accumulation and consolidation as in the other regions of France.[106] Part of the new land came from clearing, but much came from long established tenures. The main transfer of properties from peasants to nobles and bourgeois occurred in the sixteenth and seventeenth century, but the movement continued at a brisk pace until the end of the old regime. Indebtedness often paved the way for sales. Lords monitored land sales carefully through their agents and often made use of their rights of pre-emptive purchase, *retrait*, to seize desirable tenures and fiefs that came on the market.[107] The upperclass quality vineyards that were the pride of Bordelais at the time of the Revolution were all carefully constructed during the early modern centuries by the patient accumulation and exchange of fiefs and tenures and by clearing of new lands.[108]

In the eighteenth century, Nicolas Alexandre de Ségur, *président à mortier* in the *Parlement* of Bordeaux, owned Château Lafite and Château Latour, while the *marquis* d'Aulède owned Château Margaux and a good share of Haut-Brion.[109] Although luxury wines were the principal product of these prestige properties, virtually all of the upper-class landed estates were still polycultural farms. Château Margaux covered 171 ha, of which 72.5 ha was in vines and the rest in plow land and pasture.[110]

The economic dynamism of Bordeaux and Bordelais produced changes in the seigneurial institutions and practices which were hardly less spectacular than the transformations of the vineyards themselves. The *seigneurie* of 1750–1789 differed as much from the *seigneurie* of 1450–1500 as the elegant Renaissance and Baroque châteaux of Médoc or the *graves* differed from the medieval castles. Here too the *parlementaires* set the example for the scrupulous management of lordship. Despite the fact that *droits seigneuriaux* in the eighteenth century brought in on average only about 11% of total noble incomes, lords poured vast amounts of energy and money into maintaining and embellishing their lordships.[111] *Seigneuries* and better still titled lordships were indispensable components of the noble lifestyle.[112]

If the lordships of Bordelais were essentially show-piece prestige properties, lords nevertheless brought the same modernizing techniques to the administration of these lordships which they deployed in the creation and management of their vineyards. Montesquieu, undoubtedly the most famous eighteenth century lord of Bordelais, had every *droit seigneurial* collected on his lands even though he resided in Paris.[113] Lords maximized their returns from *droits seigneuriaux* by adjusting the fees and renders of lordship to fit the needs of the market. Noble fiefs and seigneurial tenures, *baux à fief roturiers*, remained the foundation of property ownership until the end of the old regime. Lords continued to use seigneurial tenures with great frequency in the eighteenth century for properties which came back into their hands as well as for lands to be cleared.[114] The *bail à fief* was in practice a very flexible perpetual contract. Lords adjusted the various components depending on the circumstances. When major construction was needed, say for a mill, lords often waived the entrance fee. For lands to be cleared, lords required the construction of a house and the clearing of the lands within three years, but typically waived the first few years of renders. The lord supplied the land, but all of the other costs fell on the shoulders of the tenant.

For established tenures, the entrance fee was often the equivalent of a sale price. In the eighteenth century, entrance fees typically fell in the range of 10 to 100 times and value of the annual *cens*.[115] Sometimes, the rates were even higher. One new tenure in the eighteenth century had a very modest annual *cens* of 20 *sols*, but an entrance fee of 4000 *livres*, payable in the form of perpetual *rente constituée* of 200 *livres* a year.[116] In the 1780s, the Lacotte brothers, architects and home builders in Bordeaux, paid 20,000 *livres* in entrance fees for ancient urban tenures they planned to sell as housing lots.[117] To a certain extent, the entrance fee replaced the antique *esporle* as the sign of seigneurial dependance.[118]

The *esporle* or *acapte* was the transfer tax of a few *deniers* assessed when a a tenure passed by inheritance to a new tenant or when one lord succeeded another.

One of the most striking changes in the seigneurial system of Bordelais was the gradual elimination of the *agrières*. At the end of the Middle Ages, the *agrière*, a proportional annual render assessed at 1/4 or 1/5 on vineyards and 1/7 on grainfields, was the most widespread seigneurial land tax in Bordelais.[119] In the early modern era, the *agrière* fell mainly on the vineyards rather than on grainfields and hayfields. The most common rate found in the *terriers* of the seventeenth and eighteenth century was 1/5.[120] As bourgeois and noble tenants replaced peasants as the legal owners of the land, they sought to eliminate the *agrières* because these proportional renders stood in the way of maximizing incomes from farms. No one wanted to pay a proportional render on a quality vintage. Even vineyards that produced only common wines could not be easily leased on a sharecropping basis if they were subject to *agrières*.

The upper-class land investors, both noble and bourgeois, were willing to pay dearly to be rid of these proportional renders.[121] At the same time, lords lost interest in the *agrières* as a source of marketable wine since they were now essentially concerned with producing and marketing quality wines. Lords demanded and received extortionate payments to commute the *agrières* on established tenures and equally significant payments to agree not to establish them on new tenures. In 1727, Nicolas de Ségur collected 3100 *livres* from three bourgeois tenants in the parish of Bègles for commutations of *agrières* into simple cash *cens*. Similarly in 1727, M. Lecomte, a *conseiller* in the *Parlement*, received 8000 *livres* for commutations of *agrières* in the parish of Talence.[122] By the end of the old regime, *agrières* probably fell on no more than 10% of the tenures. *Agrières* had disappeared entirely from Saint-Morillon by the middle of the eighteenth century.[123] Similarly, fixed *cens* in kind disappeared in favor of fixed *cens* in cash. Consequently, transactions to eliminate the *agrières* and huge entrance fees for new tenures without *agrières* replaced the venerable proportional renders as income producers in seigneurial budgets.

There were scarcely any rights of lordship which could not be turned to account. For a price, lords agreed to eliminate all seigneurial taxes and fees on a tenure and thereby transformed the property into an *allod* subject only to the jurisdiction of the lord's court. For a suitable fee too, lords transformed common tenures into noble fiefs.[124] There was even a lively trade in arrears of seigneurial dues. As long as the correct legal procedures were followed, the obligation of paying the seigneurial renders, *cens* and fees was imprescriptible and constituted a privileged form of debt in the event of judicial seizure and sale of real property. In 1764, Alexandre de Ségur, the most prestigious lord in Bordelais, sold the right to collect the arrears of annual *cens* and renders, *lods et ventes,* and payments in lieu of *corvées* in the lordships of Frans and Saint-Ujean for 500 *livres.* Similarly, the abbey of Faize sold arrears that covered the years 1740 to 1747 for 4862 *livres* 14 sols in 1748.[125] Lords even sold their right of pre-emptive purchase in their *seigneuries* to bourgeois land speculators of Bordeaux.[126] These land developers then monitored the land sales, intervened and seized desirable properties for the price stipulated in the sale contract.

Lords in Bordelais did not liquidate lordship, but exploited its revenue potential to the fullest at a time of rapid economic growth when wealthy bourgeois and nobles had displaced peasants as the most important tenants in many *seigneuries.* Upperclass tenants were particularly anxious to shed *solidarité,* the ancient obligation which held each and every tenant in a given tenure or community fully responsible for any arrears of *cens* owned by any co-tenant. Legally *solidarité* meant that the wealthiest tenants were the most likely targets for court-ordered collections even though they had paid their share of the collective obligation. For a hefty fee, lords agreed to eliminate collective accountability. One bourgeois of Bordeaux paid 2000 *livres* to be freed from joint responsibility.[127]

The rapid rise in land prices and the increased frequency of land sales greatly enhanced the value of the transfer fees for seigneurial tenures and noble fiefs, the *lods et ventes,* assessed at 1/8. By the middle of the eighteenth century, the *lods et ventes* had become the principal revenue producing *droit seigneurial* in many lordships. Between 1762 and 1771, annual revenues from *lods et ventes* for the abbey of Sainte-Croix fluctuated between 1520 and 7530 *livres* while revenue from all other seigneurial *cens* ranged between 14 and 528 *livres.*[128] Similarly, the average annual revenues of the collegial church of Saint-Seurin for the last decade and a half of the old regime were 1479 *livres* for all *agrières* and annual *cens* in cash and kind, 10,632 *livres* from tithes, and 39,272 *livres* for the *lods et ventes*. Total revenues from *lods et ventes* in the last fourteen years of the old regime for Saint-Seurin were an impressive 549,811 *livres*.[129]

Not all seigneurial rights lent themselves equally to lucrative profit-maximizing management. *Corvées* appeared only here and there and lords paid little attention to them. Likewise, *banalités* were in a state of advanced decrepitude.[130] Seigneurial tolls brought in significant revenues to lords lucky enough to own them, but the monarchy in the eighteenth century was hostile to them, subjected them to close royal supervision, and harassed their owners with repeated legal procedures until they agreeing to abandon them for compensation. In the larger Bordelais region of Guyenne, royal officials succeeded in eliminating 206 out of 361 tolls between 1730 and the Revolution.[131]

Seigneurial market taxes were also valuable to lords, but hated by the monarchy. The market fees at Cadillac were leased for 1200 *livres* a year in 1766. One of the most famous cases involved a tax of 1/8 the price of all fish sold in Bordeaux. According to ancient custom in Bordeaux, fish could only be sold at a special walled market called La Clie. This right was part of the *seigneurie* of Puy-Paulin which belonged to the Foix-Candale family. In 1707, the last of the Foix-Candale sold Puy-Paulin to the king, but like so many royal lordships this *seigneurie* passed almost immediately into the hands of royal favorites, the *engagistes*, who acquired perpetual property rights in the lordship. In 1719, the lease of the fish tax yielded 3600 *livres* a year. The Duke of Nevers collected the tax as *engagiste* in the 1720s as did the Duke of Polignac from 1769. The fishermen of Bordeaux filed a lawsuit against this tax in 1781. The intendant lent his considerable support to the fishermen and in 1785 the royal *Conseil* abolished the tax.[132]

There were many ecclesiastical lordships in Bordeaux and Bordelais, but they were not particularly well-endowed. Ecclesiastical lordships consisted essentially of perpetual urban and rural tenures rather than domain-farms. Although a few valuable vineyards belonged to the church, the ecclesiastical lordships did not play a prominent role in the remodeling of the vineyards in Bordelais in the early modern centuries. Rather, the ecclesiastical lordships relied essentially on seigneurial dues and the tithe for the bulk of their incomes.[133] The

ⅿⅽⅽⅺ ⅽⅾⅿⅿⅿⅿ ⅼⅽⅾ for the tithe was 1/13.[134] The predominance of tenures and hence *droits seigneuriaux* over domain farms characterized all of the major ecclesiastical lords of Bordeaux and Bordelais, the archbishopric, the cathedral chapter of Saint-André, the collegial church of Saint-Seurin, as well as the abbeys of La Sauve Majeure and Sainte-Croix. 90% of the chapter of Saint-Emilion's net revenues of about 30,000 *livres* at the end of the old regime came from tithes.[135]

The ecclesiastical lords used the same modern techniques in administering and in modifying the renders and fees on their tenures as the magistrates of the *Parlement*. But measured both by local and national standards, the ecclesiastical lordships of Bordelais were only moderately wealthy. The archbishopric of Bordeaux at the end of the eighteenth century had total revenues of only 65,777 livres, of which a modest 10,790 came from domain lands.[136]

Aquitaine also experienced very dramatic economic changes between 1500 and 1789.[137] The ancient privilege of Bordeaux meant that Aquitaine could not compete on an equal footing with Bordelais in the wine trade. A few areas produced high quality wines: Gaillac, Nérac, Bergerac, and Sainte-Foy. However, most of the Aquitaine hinterland produced an ocean of common wine that went on the market as *eau-de-vie.*[138] Most of this brandy went into the Dutch and northern European export market.

Aquitaine also produced hard winter wheat that was ground, packed and shipped to the West Indies in the eighteenth century. The major wheat producing areas were located along the Moyenne-Garonne, in Agenais, Condomois and Quercy.[139] The rapid growth of the market for wheat in the West Indies had a profound effect on Aquitaine. Aquitaine had long supplied Bordeaux with wheat. Bordeaux's population doubled in the eighteenth century from 55,000 to 110,000, while the population of the French West Indies rose from 100,000 to 700,000. Hence, by the late eigtenth century Aquitaine supplied most of the wheat for a market which was considerably larger then that of Paris.[140]

The expansion of wheat production for export went hand in hand with the rapid spread of maize from the late seventeenth century. Maize soon became a staple of the diet of the lower classes. The typical upper-class *métairie* in the eighteenth century produced wheat as the cash crop and maize for the sharecropper and his family. Aquitaine also exported dried prunes, figs, walnuts and chestnuts. Likewise, there was also a booming market for hemp transformed into ropes and sail cloth.

Did these economic changes produce alterations in the seigneurial institutions of Aquitain comparable to those that occurred in Bordelais? The answer is no. Our best information concerns Agenais, Haut and Bas-Quercy, the present *départements* of Lot-et-Garonne, Lot and Tarn-et-Garonne. The evidence from these areas of Aquitaine strongly suggests that the changes in lordship and in the noble class itself were far less dramatic than those found in Bordelais.

Not surprisingly, nobles expanded their domain-farms in response to the economic pull of the export markets. Nevertheless, revenues from seigneurial dues held up better as a proportion of noble budgets in Aquitaine than they did in Bordelais. Revenues from *lods et ventes* naturally increased as too did incomes from banal grain mills, but the economic changes in Aquitaine seem to have had very little impact on the annually assessed seigneurial renders. Commutation of payments in kind to cash *cens* were far less common than in Bordelais. Often the contracts used for resettlement of the lordships in the late fifteenth and sixteenth century remained in use until the end of the old regime. At Colonges in Agenais in the sixteenth century, each *journal* of agricultural land bore seigneurial dues of 12 *deniers*, 1/2 a measure of wheat, 1/2 a measure of rye, 2 chickens, 2 *corvées*, and a *quarton* of oats for every 20 *journaux* of land.[141] In the duchy of Duras in Agenais in the eighteenth century, the seigneurial dues were still assessed mainly in kind in the form of a proportional render. The duchy encompassed lands in ten parishes and had about 5500 subjects. The lease of the barony in 1782 specified an annual payment of 30,000 *livres*.[142] The domain lands were of modest size and most of the revenues came from *droits seigneuriaux*

Revenues from seigneurial dues brought in a far higher proportion of noble revenues in Quercy than in Bordelais. In 89 *seigneuries* in Bas-Quercy near Moissac and Montauban studied in the eighteenth century, *droits seigneuriax* accounted for 40% of noble incomes, a figure that was nearly four times the average for lordships in Bordelais. Lords in Quercy expanded their domain-farms in the early modern centuries but not nearly on the scale found in lordships in

Dordoloir The royal fiscal records indicate that nobles in this region of Bas-Quercy owned only 15% of the land.[143] Also, most seigneurial dues were still paid in kind rather than in cash. The basic pattern in Bas-Quercy was fixed quantities of wheat, oats, poultry, eggs and chestnuts, with only small sums payable in cash.[144]

In many lordships of Quercy, seigneurial dues outweighed revenues from domain lands as can be seen in the *seigneurie* of Beaucaire near Moissac on the eve of the Revolution.[145] This large lordship, which belonged to the Pechpeyrou family, stretched over 30 parishes and had 2200 tenants. Total revenues at the end of the old regime were 50,416 *livres*. The largest revenue producer by far was a banal grain mill at Moissac that was in existence from at least the twelfth century. Over the centuries, the lords increased the size of the mill in keeping with the expansion of the grain trade. In the twelfth century, the mill had 4 grindstones, 7 in the sixteenth century, and 20 in the late eighteenth century along with a fulling mill. The annual lease of the grain mill on the eve of the Revolution was for 35,000 *livres*. The mill was seized and sold in the Year II to twenty investors for 700,000 *livres*. Even without the grain mill and its banal revenues, the income from other *droits seigneuriaux* still outweighed revenues from the domain lands: 8,096 to 7, 320 *livres*. Renders paid in principally in wheat, rye, and oats, along with annual dues paid in chickens, eggs, chestnuts and small quantities of wine were worth 6,671 *livres*. A seigneurial monopoly right for fishing at Moissac brought in an additional 1425 *livres* which raised the total for *droits seigneuriaux* to 8,096. The lordship had 11 *métairies* that covered 295 ha and which brought in 7,320 *livres*.

The social transformation of the noble class was also far less pronounced in Aquitain than it was in Bordelais.[146] The nobility was more numerous, less wealthy, and older than in Bordelais. There were 200 noble families just in the corner of Bas-Quercy near Moissac and Montauban. Three-quarters of the noble fiefs were relatively small and produced modest incomes of between 2500 and 10,000 *livres*. Between 1589 and 1739, only 20% of lordships or fiefs changed hands through sales. Montauban had a *Cour des Aides* and a *Bureau des finances*, but the robe nobles of Quercy were far less numerous and far less aggressive than their counterparts in Bordelais. In 1689, fully 84% of the fiefs belonged to old noble families. In 1789, old nobles still held 54%, while 35% belonged to ennobled royal office holders.

Gascogne and the Western Pyrénées

Under the old regime, the large area located south and west of the Garonne river was lightly populated and economically underdeveloped.[147] In the Middle Ages, Gascogne produced a multiplicity of petty counts and viscounts who established tiny feudal states such as Béarn, Armagnac, Astarac, Comminges, and Bigorre, but no native prince powerful enough to unify the region. Similarly, neither the kings of England nor the kings of France were ever sufficiently interested in Gascogne during the Middle Ages to pursue a determined policy of political and institutional unification. By the beginning of the sixteenth century, most of the petty princes had disappeared and their territories had passed into the hands of the kings of France. With the accession of Henry IV, the last of the states of any significance in the area, Béarn and Basse-Navarre, became part of the royal domain.

While the kings of France were unquestionably the principal lords in southwestern France under the old regime, the ancient *comtés* and *vicomtés* survived as distinct institutional entities in the royal domain. Consequently, the legal customs that governed lordship remained as fragmented as they had been in the Middle Ages. Nevertheless, there were three easily recognizable patterns of lordship which cut across the boundaries of the ancient principalities. These regional styles of lordship appeared in three quite distinct geographical settings. They were already apparent in the Middle Ages and became more sharply defined between 1500 and 1789.

The first and by far the most widespread pattern of lordship appeared in the lower elevations north of the Pyrénées along the river valleys and in the plains. These areas were the most conducive to population concentration and modest economic development. The principal feature of lordship in Armagnac, Astarac, Commignes, and in lowland regions of Bigorre, Béarn and Basse-Navarre north of the Pyrénées was the predominance of seigneurial renders and dues assessed on individual tenures. These individually assessed *censives* or *fiefs* had three origins. The oldest derived from the simple fragmentation of the ancient *mansi*, large groupings of lands that in ancient times bore single, collective seigneurial taxes. More commonly, the individually assessed tenures derived from the regulations found in the medieval charters associated with the foundation of new villages, *sauvetés, castelnaux,* and *bastides*, and in charters granted to long-established settlements. These charters transformed the old fiscal system of *casaux* into individually assessed holdings.[148] Finally, the rest of the individually assessed holdings came from new tenures cut from the boundless uncultivated lands as population slowly rose in the early modern centuries. In the royal *vicomté* of Sioule, the *capitaines châtelaines* established 174 new tenures that they carved from the vacant lands between 1690 and 1753. The *droits seigneuriaux* were always light, a few sols and a measure of grain.[149] Allods, lands not subject to seigneurial renders and dues, still existed in the seventeenth century, but constant pressure from royal agents reduced their numbers.[150]

Regardless of the exact historical origin of these tenures, the typical renders included fixed payments in cash and kind and almost never proportional renders. These renders and annual fees were extremely modest. Normally, there were only a few tenures in a lordship assessed renders in kind and the rates were always very low.[151]

The second pattern of lordship appeared in the high mountain valleys and in the nearly foothills of the Pyrénées. In those areas, remnants of an ancient seigneurial system of assessment which employed a large and artificial unit of assessment, the *mansus* or *casal,* survived here and there throughout the early modern period. This fiscal system was admirably suited to areas with dispersed settlement and it was very easy to administer. It disappeared in most of southwestern France as medieval population increased and land holdings fragmented, but it survived in parts of the remote and lightly populated regions, in the high mountain valleys of the Pyrénées and in the adjacent foothills of Bigorre, Béarn and Soule. Even here, this ancient fiscal system appeared as a remnant of earlier practice.[152]

The *casal* appeared either as a single assessment for an entire community or more interestingly as a set number of *casaux* that remained unchanged century after century. In the second variant, the heads of households, *capcasaux*, were the descendants of the originally assessed inhabitants of the community. Social and economic practices within the communities reinforced rather than undermined the ancient system of seigneurial assessment. Although the settlements had virtually boundless summer pastures in the high mountains at their disposal, lands in the lower elevations suitable for cultivation near the villages were very limited. Consequently, the physical environment could only support a set number of fully developed farmsteads.

The number of these farmsteads remained unchanged generation after generation and often century after century. Younger children served as unmarried shepherds or remained spinsters in the family house. At most, younger siblings and a few day laborers received small plots of land carved from the original farmsteads of the village notables. The tenants of the small holdings, called *botoyers* or *estalgers*, owed rent to the village notables, the *capcasaux*. Pressures within the community enforced strict social distinctions, maintained the ancient homesteads, and eliminated the need to alter the old system of seigneurial assessment.

The social and economic polarization of peasant villages into major land owners, *capcazaux*, and small holders was certainly far more widespread in the Pyrénées than the survival of the ancient system of seigneurial assessment in which only the major heads of household paid dues and renders.[153] Nevertheless, there were places where the social system reinforced the fiscal structure of lordship. At Bilhères, a village located in the valley of Ossau in Béarn, the ancient fiscal system found in the *censier* of 1385 was still in existence in the seventeenth century. The *censier* listed 56 major houses, *casalères*, that owed cens directly to the lord in grain and cash, and two hereditary fiscal agents called *abbadies*. The *casalères* and *abbadies* were still there in the seventeenth century, but by then there was also an underclass of botoyers that was dependent on the major houses.[154]

The third and final system of seigneurial assessment appeared only in the Landes, the vast stretch of low lying land south of Bordeaux and north of Bayonne that flooded every fall. The harsh physical environment produced a distinctive seigneurial system that appeared in the Middle Ages and remained in force until 1789.[155] In the Landes, the village communities as a whole held lands from their lords on what amounted to collective, perpetual *censive* contracts. The communities as a whole owed their lords certain annual payments, *questes* in cash and/or kind, which they collected from their members. The *queste* was a very modest seigneurial tax. In five parishes in the *seigneurie* of Laboheyre, the rate was 14 *livres* 5 *sols* per parish. The communities administered the lands on collective tenure themselves. Individuals within the community normally had the right, *droit de perprise*, to clear and appropriate properties subject to the rules of the community.[156]

On the periphery of the Landes, the more common system of individual censive tenures reappeared. At Saint-Symphorien, located on the norther-eastern boundary of the Landes, local lords in the eighteenth century cut new tenures from the uncultivated land. Many of these new holdings belonged to upperclass investors who planted their new properties with pine trees.[157]

None of the systems of seigneurial assessment in Gascogne and the Pyrénées produced important revenues for lords. The lightness of *droits seigneuriaux* in southwestern France explains the unusually small volume of litigation over them in the judicial records of the region.[158] The economic burden of the *droits seigneuriaux* was so slight that royal tax officials often neglected to deduct the *cens* when they calculated the net taxable income of properties subject to the royal direct taxes.[159]

Although lords derived only derisory incomes from seigneurial dues and renders, they kept their records in good order. Usually lords or their agents simply kept the seigneurial records up to date by demanding written *reconnaissances* of tenure when properties changed hands through sale or inheritance rather than by undertaking the more spectacular and costly procedure of renewing their *terriers*. However, royal agents and officials working for the *engagistes* of royal lordships frequently renewed the *terriers* in their lands.[160]

The feudal hierarchy underwent considerable modification in the early modern centuries, at least in some of the feudal *pays*.[161] At the end of the Middle Ages, the noble hierarchy in Gascogne was pyramidal in shape. At the top there a few counts and viscounts with extensive landed holdings, a middle range of baronies and small lordships, and a multiplicity of noble fiefs without tenants and rights of justice. In some of the feudal *pays*, the king alone exercised justice and there was no radical change in the feudal hierarchy during the old regime. Such was the case in Béarn. In the eighteenth century, Béarn had 400 petty nobles that drew very modest revenues from seigneurial dues and small *métairies*.[162] Elsewhere, changes between 1500 and 1789 stood the medieval aristocratic pyramid on its head. At the end of the old regime, most of Gascogne had a superfluity of titled lordships, a considerably swollen middle range of baronies, and few petty fiefs.

These changes in the structure of the noble hierarchy were the result of several long term trends: the absorption of lesser fiefs into greater, the concentration of lordships through marriage, the sale of royal lordships, and the elevation by the kings of lesser lordships into titled fiefs. In the eighteenth century, there were 282 noble fiefs in the three royal *prévôtés* of Dax, Saint-Sever and Mont-de-Marsan. Of these, 15 were titled lordships (duchies, marquisats, counties and viscounties), 65 were baronies, 97 were *seigneuries* with rights of full justice, while there were only 40 minor lordships, *caveries,* with tenants and rights to medium and low justice, and 65 noble fiefs with neither tenants nor justice.[163]

At the same time that noble properties grew larger and rose in prestige, there was a considerable upgrading of the quality of seigneurial justice. The professionalization of seigneurial justice was apparent everywhere in France from the sixteenth century, but it was particularly well-documented in Gascogne.[164] The more important lordships maintained very active seigneurial courts which rendered indispensible judicial services at the level of first instance.[165]

Finally, some mention must be made of the ecclesiastical lordships in Gascogne. While the seigneurial system was light in southwestern France, the ecclesiastical tithe was among the heaviest in France.[166] In most of the territory of the archbishopric of Auch, rates for tithes on the major grains were 1/10 or higher. There were also tithes on poultry, sheep and wool.[167] The extraordinarily high rates for the major tithe were based on a royal judicial inquiry carried out in 1563–64 in 522 parishes in the wake of major anti-tithe protests.

While there was much grumbling and a steady stream of litigation over the tithe in the seventeenth and eighteenth century, the longstanding grievances took a dramatic new turn at the end of the old regime.[168] Between the sixteenth and the end of the eighteenth century, noble and bourgeois land investors constructed innumerable new *métairies*. These upperclass proprietors in the eighteenth century were more aggressive and better able to afford the costs of litigation than peasant small holders. In 1777, socially prominent landowners in the village of Mouchès refused to pay tithes at a rate higher than 1/10. The royal *sénéchal* rendered a sentence against the community. The community appealed to the *Parlement* of Toulouse which in 1781 rendered an opinion that rates higher than 1/10 were illegal. Suddenly there were 400 new lawsuits over the tithe.

The church owned little land directly in southwestern France and derived most of its revenues from the tithe.[169] At the end of the old regime, the wealthiest benefice by far in Gascogne was the archbishopric of Auch which had revenues of around 150,000 *livres,* most of which came from the tithe.[170]

CHAPTER SIX

1750–1789

In every age of an exceptionally long history, a multiplicity of historical forces shaped lordship. Between 1750 and 1789, a number of changes in the political climate, in society and in the economy prepared the way for the end of this ancient institution.

Initially around 1750, there were few signs that anything much had changed. Lordship had an absolutely solid foundation in the customary laws of the realm, in the jurisprudence of the sovereign courts, and in the king's council. In the last few decades of the old regime, lordship was as strong as it had ever been, but no stronger. The view that lords in the second half of the eighteenth century carried out a significant strengthening of heretofore weak and even decadent *seigneuries* is part of the mythology of the French Revolution.[1] The notion of a sudden and effective upgrading of lordships, called a feudal or seigneurial reaction, appeared first in the writing of late nineteenth century, pro-republican historians.[2] Adopted and amplified by two generations of Marxist historians, the feudal reaction remained part of the standard historical account of the origins of the Revolution until the 1970s.[3] Yet, those living at the time of the Revolution were unaware that such a feudal reaction had occurred.[4]

In the last forty years or so, a mountain of monographic research on lordship in the early modern centuries, material unavailable to either the early pro-republican historians or the early Marxists, has shown that strict management with regular renewal of the seigneurial land registers, the *terriers*, was standard practice for lords in every province of the realm between 1500 and 1789. Piecemeal upgrading of the seigneurial records, one tenure at a time, was also part of the day to day administration of lordship between the major replacements of the entire *terriers*.[5] The timing of the renewal of *terriers* depended on the vicissitudes of the histories of the realm, the individual provinces, as well as the internal histories of the seigneurial families.

The elegantly written and leather bound *terriers* of the immediate pre-Revolutionary period, fitted out with attractive surveyor's maps of the lordships, were just the last examples of a truly remarkable and unbroken institutional tradition of seigneurial record keeping which was as old as lordship itself. Indeed, the basic legal format of the late eighteenth century *terriers* as well as the judicial procedures which produced them were all based on the legal traditions of the late Roman fiscal administration. Whether they realized it or not, the eighteenth century feudal lawyers who drew up the last *terriers* stood in the shadow of the Merovingian and Carolingian scribes who produced the parchment polyptychs of the early Middle Ages.

More significantly, the eighteenth century *terriers*, while undoubtedly more pleasing to the eye than the medieval and sixteenth century *terriers*, were invariably based on these earlier documents. The eighteenth century renewal of *terriers* was also part of the self-conscious and ostentatious display of lordship in its last century of existence, more a manifestation of the art of the feudal lawyer than a really efficacious instrument of improved seigneurial management.[6] On a more practical level, French handwriting had changed so much in the early modern centuries that by the eighteenth century the late Medieval Latin and sixteenth century French *terriers* and titles could be read only by those trained in paleography.[7]

While it would be too much to say that the Revolution of 1789, the massive peasant uprising, and the decrees of August 4 which solemnly promised to abolish the tithe and lordship were the culmination of a steadily rising movement of opposition, it would be equally inaccurate to say that the end of the tithe and lordship simply fell from the sky unannounced. Certainly, no one in France predicted the dramatic events of 1789, yet there were unmistakable signs that support for the tithe and lordship by the upper classes and acceptance of these same institutions by the lower classes in France were eroding.[8] Changes in the political culture of France, as well as changes in the economy and in society prepared the way for the events of 1789.

Although never loved by its subjects, lordship enjoyed at least the grudging and fatalistic acceptance of the population at large. The unassailable legal position of lordship, supported not only by the entire hierarchy of royal courts but also by royal military force when necessary, produced a sullen but ever watchful circumspection in the behavior of both the property owning peasantry and the bourgeoisie. Violent protests against lordship and the tithe were very rare and invariably swiftly punished by the forces of order. Consequently, most of the opposition took the form of litigation.

In the last few decades of the old regime, there was a new aggressiveness in the litigation over the tithe which drew very significant support from bourgeois property owners and even nobles. In Languedoc, a center of opposition to the tithe for centuries, litigation swelled after 1760.[9] In Quercy, the volume of the anti-tithe litigation rose significantly and its tone became shrill.[10] Tithes were unusually heavy in south-western France and the range of products subject to the tithe unusually wide. Tithes fell not only on the major grains, but on poultry, hogs, and sheep. The spread of maize as a popular crop for the diets of the lower classes led inevitably to disputes. The *Parlement* of Toulouse upheld the ecclesiastical lords in their demands for tithes on maize. Property owning peasants joined hands with bourgeois landowners in these lawsuits. The *cahiers* of the third estate in Quercy contained sharply worded anti-clerical criticisms of the higher clergy. The fruits of their labors were being drained off to support the opulent lifestyles of bishops, abbots and monks while they lived in poverty.

Anti-tithe litigation with firm support from bourgeois and even noble property owners was even more intense in the archbishopric of Auch, capital of the old county of Armagnac in Gascogne.[11] Although lawsuits over tithes on maize occurred here as well as in nearby Quercy, it was a 1781 decision by the *Parlement* of Toulouse, traditionally as resolute a supporter of the ecclesiastical tithe as any sovereign court in the realm, which set off a massive flood of litigation.[12] The tithes in the diocese of Auch were unusually high, well above 1/10, and had been for centuries. The legal foundation for these rates was a formal judicial inquiry carried out between 1561 and 1563. The rates were 1/10 or higher in 480 parishes of the diocese of Auch for which records have survived.

In 29% of the communities the rate was 4/31, in 26% 4/34, and in another 27% communities 4/40 or 1/10.

In a completely uncharacteristic ruling, the *Parlement* of Toulouse in 1781 overturned the decisions of lower royal courts which had upheld the traditional high rates, rejected the findings of the 1561–63 judicial inquiry, and ruled that rates in excess of 1/10 were excessive and illegal. Immediately, hundreds of communities in the diocese of Auch that traditionally had paid the higher rates filed lawsuits for relief. Pending the outcome of their suits, many communities refused to pay at all. The records of the village assembles show clearly that noble and bourgeois property owners joined arms with peasant farmers in a united front.

Similarly, from 1770–1775, bourgeois and aristocratic property owners led the resistance to the tithe in the viticultural areas of Champagne.[13] From the middle of the eighteenth century, resistance to the tithe grew as the wines of Champagne increased in reputation and became more marketable. Bourgeois and nobles owned the bulk of the vineyards. At Epernay, bourgeois and nobles initiated the lawsuits and paid most of the costs of litigation. At Verzenay, the Marquis of Sillery enjoyed widespread support among the peasant *vignerons* because he led the resistance to the tithe collectors, the abbeys. Sillery owned extensive vineyards at Sillery, Puissieulx, Ludes, Verzenay, and Prunay that brought him annual revenues of nearly two million livres in the late eighteenth century.

Village communities with or without support from the upper classes also became more aggressive in lawsuits against their lords in Bourgogne. Villagers filed countless lawsuits against grasping lords and demanded titles, usually in vain. In 1784 for example, the inhabitants of Arc-sur-Tille in the duchy of Saulx-Tavannes refused to pay the seigneurial *taille*, in Bourgogne called the *droit d'indire*, when a member of the Saulx-Tavannes family became a knight of the Holy Spirit. They lost the case initially in the royal *bailliage* and then on appeal to the *Parlement* of Dijon. The *Parlement* in 1787–1788 ordered Arc-sur-Tille to pay the *taille* and the expenses of litigation.[14] In the *seigneurie* of Isle-sur-Montréal in Basse-Bourgogne, aggressive litigation over *tierces*, the proportional render in kind, over mortmain, and over the forest began in the early eighteenth century and continued down to the Revolution. The men who initiated these suits were mainly upperclass landowners such as notaries, legal professionals in the royal *bailliage*, even nobles.[15]

After 1750 and especially in the 1770s and 1780s in Bourgogne, Champagne, Lorraine, Alsace, and Provence, feudal lawyers working for tenants, both upperclass tenants and peasants, set off a battery of litigation against lordship.[16] Tenants were no longer willing to accept immemorial custom as the foundation of lordship. They challenged long-established customs, ancient court sentences, and called into question the legality of arbitrated settlements from the fourteenth through the seventeenth century Lawsuits initiated by villagers were unusually numerous in Bourgogne and in Champagne in part because the rural communities were able to finance their cases with revenues from their common lands, especially their forests.[17] Lumber prices and prices for firewood rose dramatically and the communities had a surplus of wood to sell. The *Parlement* of Bourgogne rejected most of the new arguments and upheld the traditional customs. Consequently, the litigation only exacerbated tensions between subjects and their lords.

While it is undeniable that peasants and bourgeois were often at odds with the lords, it would be misleading to suggest that they were uniformly hostile to lordship. After all, the management of lordships and the collection of seigneurial dues and tithes constituted not only one of the principal economic enterprises in old regime France, but also one of the most lucrative. Peasants and bourgeois collected virtually all of the seigneurial dues and all of the tithes assessed in France. Bourgeois staffed the seigneurial courts, filled high administrative offices in the titled lordships, and served as feudal lawyers. The administration of lordship was a highly profitable business which paved the way for social advance and further accumulation of wealth. As long as lordship survived, peasants and bourgeois did not shy from participating in its administration. And when it eventually disappeared, they adjusted easily.[18]

From a completely different corner, it is clear that changes in the policies of the absolute monarchy prepared the way for the end of lordship. From the middle of the eighteenth century, reformers of various stripes urged both Louis XV and Louis XVI to undertake fundamental reforms. Lordship was certainly not at the top of any reform agenda, but there was a growing body of learned opinion which viewed lordship as an archaic institution which stood in the way of the modernization of the state and the economy.

The physiocrats criticized lordship as a restriction on individual property rights and an impediment to the improvement of agriculture.[19] Reform-minded ministers like Turgot were very impressed by the bold initiative of King Charles-Emmanuel III of Piedmont-Sardinia who with edicts in the 1760s and 1770s set in motion an ambitious project to liquidate lordship in Savoie. The reforms in Savoie and a little later in Baden indicated that there was a substantial body of learned opinion on the continent of Europe in favor of eliminating lordship. The reformers both inside and outside of France did not question the legitimacy of the property rights of the lords to a substantial part of the apparatus of lordship. Lords would have to be given compensation for relinquishing their rights. The reforms in Savoie were particularly impressive because they included a relatively simple, if immensely expensive, system whereby the state acted as the financial guarantor for the indemnification of the lords.[20]

There is no doubt that Turgot included the elimination of lordship in his ill-fated agenda for reforming France in the early 1770s. Turgot secretly supported a minor Enlightenment writer named Boncerf who published an inflammatory pamphlet entitled *Les inconvénients des droits féodaux* which criticized lordship as a barbarous institution left over from the worst days of feudalism. Turgot's purpose seems to have been to test the potential support for the elimination of lordship.[21] The *Parlement* of Paris vehemently denounced the pamphlet and even held a public burning of the offensive publication. Massive riots provoked by Turgot's reform of the grain trade policies drove the reforming minister from power in 1776 and nothing more was heard of his plan to eliminate lordship.

By the 1760s and 1770s, critics other than the physiocrats also attacked lordship. The Marquis d'Argenson's *Considérations sur le gouvernement ancien et présent de la France*, available only from the 1760s, argued the standard thesis that the rights of the lords originated in the violence of feudal anarchy and hence were not legitimate at all. Voltaire denounced lordship and especially mortmain on humanitarian grounds.[22] The criticism of lordship penned by the *philosophes* was characteristically shrill, polemical, and anticlerical, while the writings of the professional jurists who defended the rights of the lords was narrowly legal, pedantic, and uninspired.[23] The two sides argued from different premises. The critics argued from new principals, while the jurists defended legal custom.

Support for mortmain also weakened somewhat in the royal courts and especially in the *Parlement* of Paris. In a number of highly publicized court decisions, the *Parlement* of Paris reversed its long-standing jurisprudence on mortmain by striking down the *droit de suite*.[24] According to this custom, the lord of a *seigneurie* with mortmain could claim the entire estate of a subject of his lordship who died without a legitimate, direct heir. What made this particular custom so monstrous in the eyes of reformers was that the lord could claim not only the property located within his lordship, but all property regardless of where it was located and regardless of where the deceased party had resided, provided that the individual in question had not obtained formal freedom from mortmain.

The first case came before the *Parlement* of Paris in 1760. Pierre Truchot, son of a fugitive serf from Nivernais and a free mother, was born in Paris where he lived his entire life. Pierre died in 1756 without a direct heir living in common with him. He left a modest estate worth 18,000 *livres* to collateral heirs. The Truchot family owned nothing in Nivernais, but Pierre's father had neglected to obtain formal freedom from mortmain before leaving Nivernais for Paris. The Marquis of La Tournelle, lord of the servile *seigneurie* in Nivernais, claimed the estate by right of the *droit de suite*. The case went first to the royal *Châtelet* in Paris which ruled by default in favor of the collateral heirs. The Marquis appealed to the *Parlement* of Paris. Influential lawyers argued the case for the collateral heirs and published broadsides to influence public opinion. They argued that the restrictive laws of mortmain should not apply outside of the territory of Nivernais and at the bare minimum the *droit de suite* certainly expired by prescription after more than forty years of uncontested residence in Paris. Moreover, they argued, Pierre Truchot was a free man, a bourgeois of Paris and hence not subject to the laws of Nivernais. In support of their argument they produced the royal letters patent and edicts issued by Charles V, Louis XI, and Louis XIV that established the rights of the bourgeoisie of Paris.

With little comment, the *Parlement* upheld the decision of the *Châtelet* and reversed its own long-held jurisprudence on the *droit de suite*. Shortly after-wards, another case involving the *droit de suite* came before the *Parlement* of Paris. In this case, Anne Fourgeoit, a widow and a fugitive serf from Cham-pagne, died in Paris in 1763 where she had resided with her husband for half a century. She left her estate, worth around 40,000 *livres*, to a nephew and two nieces. The Marquis of La Hage, lord of the servile *seigneurie* in Champagne which Fourgeoit had left decades earlier, claimed the estate. Once again, the *Châtelet* decided in favor of the collateral heirs, the lord appealed, and once again the *Parlement* of Paris in 1765 decided in favor of the heirs against the lord. In yet another case, the *Parlement* of Paris in 1769 nullified the *droit de suite* and ruled against the Marquis of Ballon in a case that involved the heirs of a serf from Bugey who died at Lyon.

In these remarkable cases, the *Parlement* did not strayed far from traditional legal reasoning. The *Parlement* did not venture onto the shaky ground of natural law or evoke an equally uncertain spirit of humanity. Rather, the court chose between two well-established laws that were in conflict. In essence, the *Parlement* held that the provisions of the *droit de suite* no longer applied to an individual who through decades of uncontested residence had acquired the rights of a bourgeois.

In the 1760s and 1770s, enlightened writers demanded the abolition of mortmain.[25] In 1765, Damours, a lawyer involved in a case over serfdom against the Cathedral Chapter of Verdun, published his *Mémoire pour l'entière abolition de la servitude en France*. The book was immediately suppressed, the author suspended from practice for three months, and his client lost. In the 1770s, Voltaire brought the plight of the serfs of Franche-Comté to the attention of the entire nation with a flood of pamphlets that denounced the practices of the Cathedral Chapter of Saint-Claude. The case of the serfs of Franche-Comté passed through many courts, among them the *Parlement* of Besançon and the royal *Conseil*. The Cathedral Chapter won the case, but Voltaire scored a major public opinion victory.

By the late 1770s, proponents of the abolition of mortmain squared off against high ranking lords in a pamphlet war set off by a flurry of lawsuits before the sovereign courts.[26] The *Parlement* of Paris heard a case brought by the

Marquise du Cheylade in Franche-Comté that claimed the entire estate of a fugitive serf who died at Fontainebleau. Publicists for and against rushed into print. Henrion de Pansey, one of the most famous feudal lawyer in the realm, attacked mortmain while Dom Grappin, a Benedictine monk, published a defense of mortmain in the two Bourgognes which received public commendation by the judges of the *Parlement* of Besançon. At the same time, another well-publicized case came before the royal *Conseil* that involved Bertier de Sauvigny, royal intendant of Paris. Bertier de Sauvigny claimed 140 estates worth an estimated quarter of a million *livres* that he alleged had escheated to him as lord of the servile barony of Isle-sous-Montréal in Franche-Comté.

At court, Necker joined the crusade against mortmain. While Necker was hardly the skilled statesman that Louis XVI and all of France desperately needed at this time, he nevertheless championed at least minor reforms. Necker was a deeply religious man with economic ideas similar to those of the physiocrats. He personally abominated serfdom in all its forms, but shrank from advocating any arbitrary abolition of what he, along with most of his contemporaries, considered the legitimate property rights of the lords.

In 1779, Necker persuaded Louis XVI to issue a reforming edit which set up a mechanism for the liquidation of mortmain in the lordships of the royal domain and which abolished without compensation the *droit de suite* on the lands of the royal domain and everywhere else in France.[27] In a preliminary memorandum and in the preamble to the edict, Necker followed the physiocrats and Voltaire by evoking natural law and economic pragmatism. While he admitted the legitimate property rights of the lords to some of the practices associated with serfdom, he called for the outright abolition of the *droit de suite* without compensation in the name of social justice.

According to the 1779 edict, henceforth any serf could obtain personal freedom for himself and for his property located outside the servile lordship by simply establishing residence in a free area. The lord was entitled to exercise his right of escheat in mortmain only for the properties located in the servile lordship, not for any properties located outside it.

The 1779 royal edict certainly did not end the debate on mortmain.[28] Most of the sovereign courts registered the 1779 edict without trouble. The *Parlement* of Paris enforced the edict with vigor by ruling against the Marquise du Cheylard in 1779, against the Cathedral Chapter of Nevers in 1781, and most tellingly against Bertier de Sauvigny in 1784. But the *Parlement* of Besançon in Franche-Comté refused to register it in 1780. Until 1788 lords in Franche-Comté continued to exercise their traditional rights with the full support of the provincial sovereign court. In 1788, the keeper of the seals Lamoignon de Basville had the 1779 edict forcibly registered *manu militari* along with his ill-fated judicial reform edicts.

Engagistes who had put up good money to buy parts of the royal domain refused to abandon any of their rights. They argued that the royal edit 1779 which abolished the *droit de suite* was an illegal violation of their contractual rights. Similarly, the princes of the blood refused to apply the edict in their apanages.[29] Various royal courts issued contradictory opinions which simply underscored the inability of the absolute monarchy to carry out any reform successfully.

The question of mortmain revealed the deep fissures within the high aristocracy and even within the church.[30] Some lords followed royal example by offering to abolish mortmain entirely. A few, such as the Bendictine Abbey of Saint-Rambert in Bugey, the Cathedral Chapter of Tournus in Mâconnais, the archbishop of Besançon and the Benedictine Abbey of Saint-Amand in Cambrésis abolished mortmain for token annual payments, but usually they demanded very high, even extortionate, payments for the surrender of their rights. The Cathedral Chapter of Saint-Claude, the target of Voltaire's literary campaign against mortmain, exceeded all others in rapacity. Shortly after the promulgation of the 1779 edict, 12,000 tenants of the Cathedral Chapter in Franche-Comté offered 100,000 *livres* plus interest in installments over ten years to be freed from mortmain. Officials of the Cathedral Chapter studied the offer, but rejected it as insufficient. An outpouring of petitions to the king, even efforts by the bishop of Saint-Claude produced no results. At the same time, peers of the realm, such as the Duke of Nevers, and foreign princes, such as the Duke of Württemberg, were characteristically ungenerous.[31]

The failure of reform in the church was particularly important since an estimated two-thirds of all of those affected by mortmain in France were subjects of ecclesiastical lordships.[32] While nothing but hardness of heart held back aristocratic lords from eliminating mortmain on their lands, reform-minded clerics often faced insurmountable opposition from other clerics and the law courts when they attempted to eliminate mortmain. The experience of Loius Aynard de Clermont-Tonnerre, the last commendatory abbot of the Abbey of Luxeuil in Franche-Comté illustrates the point.[33] Clermont-Tonnerre, a member of a prestigious noble family and a progressive, energetic and enlightened man, was untiring in his efforts to eliminate mortmain at Luxeuil, but was frustrated by the legal and bureaucratic complexities of the church, the law courts, and the royal administration.

The abbot was fully aware that he could not simply abolish mortmain. He did not own the abbey, but was merely the administrator of it. To procede, he needed the cooperation of many parties. The monks at Luxeuil were opposed and found a spokesman in Dom Grappin who wrote a famous defense of mortmain. The Cardinal de la Rochemont, general minister of ecclesiastical benefices in France, cited canon law which prohibited the diminution of the value of any benefice for whatever reason. Any reform would also have to have the approval of the King, the guardian of the property of the church. When Necker fell from power, Maurepas blocked reform. Seeing that his plan for a general abolition of mortmain on all the lands of the abbey was going nowhere, the abbot then proceeded to negotiate with individual villages that still had enough forest land to sell to pay something for abolition. Approval of this scheme involved the consent of the royal forest officials of *maitrise des eaux et forêts* and they were opposed. Clermont-Tonnerre was still pressing his case for abolition of mortmain and still running into stone walls when the Revolution began.

In the end, the 1779 royal edict produced only modest results outside the crown properties directly administered by royal officials. Relatively few lords followed royal example. In the great majority of the servile lordships, mortmain survived right down to the Revolution. Elsewhere in Europe, enlightened opinion led many governments to abolish the remnants of serfdom on the eve of the Revolution: the Hapsburgs, the Margrave of Baden, the republic of Geneva, etc.[34] The failure of reform in France simply underscored the extreme weakness of the monarchy in its final days.

There can be little doubt that the stubborn and heartless refusal of very prominent aristocratic and ecclesiastical lords to abolish mortmain as well as the boundless rapacity of the few lords who agreed to abandon their rights soured learned public opinion on lordship as a whole and contributed substantially to the erosion of support among the literate classes for lordship in its entirety.

However, neither the litigation of tenants nor the arguments of the reformers had much immediate effect in weakening the legal position of lordship. What eventually brought the entire edifice of lordship down was the violence opposition of the lower classes. Here the monarchy itself paved the way for the demise of lordship with its hapless agrarian and economic reforms. From the early 1760s, the monarchy initiated a number of reforms inspired by the physiocrats that stirred up hatred for lordship and even for lords as a privileged group in society.[35]

With the encouragement of the physiocrats, Louis XV and Louis XVI issued and number of edicts and letters patent which promoted enclosure and called for the division of the common lands in certain provinces of France.[36] The royal reforms dealing with open pasture, the common lands, and the grain trade came at a time when population growth in many parts of France outstripped economic development and the appearance of new jobs. Prices rose, wages fell in real purchasing power, underemployment and unemployment grew. For many of the rural poor, access to land seemed the only likely solution to their predicament.[37] The reformers serving the King meant well, but their actions in practice exacerbated social and economic tensions rather than assuaged them.

The physiocrats were anxious to promote increased production of grains in France. They considered French agriculture economically backward largely because, in their opinion, a number of communal uses, most notably open pasture, prevented individual owners from modernizing their farming practices. Open pasture was far from universal in eighteenth century France. In many regions of France, enclosure of grainfields, pastures and hayfields had been going on for centuries. Open pasture was unusual in the Midi and in most of western France. Open pasture was widespread in central France and appeared in its purest forms in northeastern France, in Champagne, Bourgogne, and Lorraine. It was precisely in these provinces where population increase outstripped economic development. For the landless poor, pasturing a few head of sheep or a cow on the fallows and hayfields after cutting made the difference between scraping by and going hungry. Access to land was essential for survival.[38]

In these underdeveloped regions, enclosure posed an immediate danger to the economic survival of the landless rural poor. As the economic position of the rural lower classes deteriorated, social tensions mounted. Lords were often the largest property owners in the villages. It mattered not a whit whether the large farms had existed for centuries or were recent creations, or whether enclosures were old or new. The upper classes had adequate lands, while the rural poor went without. By siding with the large property owners against the small on the issue of enclosure, the monarchy unquestionably exacerbated social and economic tensions.

Likewise, the physiocrats' plans for dividing the common lands stirred up social animosities.[39] The physiocrats viewed the commons as unproductive and wasted resources that could be turned to account economically by dividing them for cultivation. In addition to encouraging the division of the common lands, the monarchy embraced a quite astounding new policy of how these communal properties should be parceled out. For centuries, the customary laws in France had limited access and use of the common lands to property owning residents of the communities. The monarchy, anxious to promote both increased production and to provide land for the swelling mass of landless rural inhabitants, required that any division of commons should include allotments for all of the residents of the communities, not just the property owners.

What brought the lords and lordship into these proposed divisions of common lands was the law of *triage.* According to the ordinances of the 1660s issued by Louis XIV, the lord had the right to demand a third of any division of common lands. In virtually every province affected by the new laws on division of the commons there were vehement denunciations of lords. Hence the royal efforts at economic reform not only sharpened divisions within the peasantry by pitting land owners against the landless, but turned everyone against the lords whose heartless cupidity even extended to taking a share of communal property. At the onset of the Revolution, most of the communities in Southern Champagne, half of those in Provence, and many in Bourgogne were engaged in long term la wouite with their lords over common lands.[40]

The ill-advised policies of the monarchy in the matter of the grain trade, in particular the edicts of Bertin in 1763 and of Turgot in 1774 that drew on the free-market ideas of the physiocrat Quesnay, inadvertently stirred up even more hatred of the lords than the policies on enclosures and common lands because they affect the entire realm, not just provinces here and there.[41] The reformers thought they were promoting economic growth, but the grain trade policies led not only to subsistence riots but also to outpourings of hatred and even violence by the lower classes against the lords.

By removing the time-tested practices which allowed provincial governments, the intendants, and municipal authorities to manage the food supply in times of dearth, the monarchy threw the impoverished urban and rural lower classes without defenses onto the market to fend for themselves. Without royal controls on the grain trade, prices skyrocketed during times of shortages. The starving masses could not afford bread at uncontrolled prices. They quickly grew desperate, turned violent and attacked bakeries, grain wagons, and the granaries of the aristocratic and ecclesiastical lords.

The progression from bread riots to attacks on the lords and their agents appeared in full light during the Flour War of 1775. In the grip of panic and hunger, reason disappeared and the logic of the rioters leaped from grain supplies to hateful symbols of economic and social superiority. The Flour War of 1775 is particularly important because it foreshadowed both the events and the revolutionary psychology of the uprisings of 1789.[42] During a two week period between April 27 and May 11, hundreds of violent events occurred in the immense grain supply zone for Paris, a region which stretched across 100 km. Hundreds and even thousands of rural inhabitants moved in waves and converged on the major towns. Rioters attacked bakers in urban centers and descended on the large grain farms which belonged to the church, the lords and the wealthy bourgeois classes.

The scale of the movements during the 1775 Flour War and the better organization distinguished these disorders from earlier market riots. The starving masses articulated demands which drew on a long tradition of Christian egalitarianism. For them food at affordable prices and access to land were fundamental rights of life and those who stood in the way of those goals were enemies. As wealthy landowners and hoarders of grain, the ecclesiastical and aristocratic lords as well as their agents, the capitalist tenant-farmers, attracted much of the hatred and abuse. The royal administration responded by mobilizing military force and by temporarily reinstating the traditional grain trade policies. The forces of order prevented the Flour War from spreading to the rest of the realm, but the immensity of this outpouring of rage undermines any notion that all was calm in France prior to 1789.

Anti-seigneurial acts of violence increased mainly north of the Loire in the 1770s and 1780s. In Bourgogne, insurgents at Molesmes in 1777 burned 40 *arpents* of forest which belonged to the Abbey of Molesme, destroyed a paper mill, broke down the door to the kitchen of the convent and helped themselves to food. At Spoy around the same time, insurgents attacked enclosures and cut down trees. Elsewhere, vandals destroyed the symbols of seigneurial authority such as family crests, pillories, gallows, dovecotes, and banal machinery.[43] Similarly, conflicts in Bourgogne over the communal use of the forests and a steady stream of misdemeanors such as theft of wood and illegal pasturing of animals led up to the much more spectacular violence in the forests in Bourgogne in 1789.[44]

While virtually all of the major episodes of rural violence in the last few decades prior to 1789 occurred north of the Loire, the attitudes expressed in these episodes were the common property of the rural classes everywhere in France.[45] The attitudes and emotions that destroyed lordship in 1789 were not new and they were not narrowly anti-seigneurial. Economic conditions in the last few decades prior to the Revolution sharpened tensions and enlivened old grievances. In a setting where every mouthful of food counted, ancient conflicts between lords and subjects over tithes, forests, seigneurial dues, and common lands took on new urgency and inflamed passions.[46]

At least among the lower classes the opposition to lordship in the last years of the old regime was part of a much larger social and economic animosity against the dominance and wealth of the aristocracy, the high clergy, their agents and tenant-farmers, and occasionally the wealthy bourgeois classes.[47] Often the hatred of the lords was most intense among the landless urban and rural lower classes who paid neither seigneurial renders nor tithes since most of them cultivated only a small garden, if that. The lower classes hated the lords for their haughty social domination and attacked the symbols of this domination, the special pew in the parish church, the exclusive hunting rights. But the lower classes also hated the royal Masters of the Waters and Forests, the royal tax collectors, the tax farmers, and the land engrossers regardless of their class, millers, bakers, and grain merchants.[48]

Hence the anti-feudal sentiments and actions of the French lower classes prior to and during the Revolution revealed a popular antipathy to order, regulation and taxation, to oppressive innovation, to privilege, and to ostentatious wealth.[49] With provocations as diverse as the arrest of a deserter from the militia, a rise in grain prices, or the strenuous enforcement of forest regulations, the undisciplined populace flew into a rage and stuck out violently against authorities of all sorts.

The changed mood of the nation appeared clearly in the *cahiers* and more spectacularly in the rural disorders of the spring and summer of 1789. Not surprisingly, most of the *cahiers* of the nobles maintained a discreet silence on the question of lordship. Only 14% of the noble *cahiers* called for the elimination of the seigneurial dues. By contrast, 64% of the *cahiers* of the third estate called for their abolition.[50] While some of the most eloquent critics of the old regime monarchy and its institutions were nobles, most of the nobles did not follow the lead of the enlightened few. They were socially conservative, anxious to weaken the absolute monarchy and eliminate ministerial despotism, but largely indifferent to a positive reform program beyond the restoration of antique institutions like the Estates General and the provincial assemblies, organized as they always had been into three orders. The nobles were particularly attached to the institutions and laws which set them apart from the rest of humanity. For them, lordship and the hated *droits seigneuriaux* had an inestimable value that far exceeded mere revenues.[51]

There can be no doubt that the effective collapse of the entire institutional apparatus of the absolute monarchy in 1788–1789 in the midst of intense political turmoil and widespread economic crisis emboldened many to lash out against lordship and the tithe. 1788–89 also produced a rapid development of political self-awareness among the urban and rural lower classes, exacerbated animosities, and gave new life to old grievances.[52] For France as a whole in 1789, riots and revolts related to the supply of adequate food were far more common than anti-feudal uprisings. Only 28% of the major uprisings in 1789 had a significant anti-feudal content.[53]

In the late eighteenth century, France was a mosaic of regions that differed in their social structures, their economic systems, their population densities, and their systems of lordship. Many areas, such as Bretagne and Auvergne, did not budge in 1788-1789 from the traditional posture of prudent resignation in matters that touched lordship, while other areas, such as Bourgogne, Mâconnais, and Champagne rose up in violence after decades of public opposition to lordship and the tithe.[54] Elsewhere, as in Alsace, a long history of sullen opposition to lordship that appeared in passive resistance, insolence, slowness in paying dues, demonstrations of ill-will in executing corvées and petty fraud preceded the spectacular violence of 1789.[55] And finally, there were provinces such as Provence where relations between lords and their subjects were generally amicable despite nearly continuous litigation. In Provence, the violent anti-seigneurial incidents came suddenly in 1789 without any warning.[56]

There was no necessary or direct link between the economic burden of the seigneurial dues and the uprisings against them in the summer of 1789.[57] *Droits seigneuriaux* absorbed 7–10% of the taxable net product of agriculture in both Haute-Normandie and in Dauphiné. Haute-Normandie did not rise up against the lords in the summer of 1789, but Dauphiné was one of the major centers of anti-feudal violence. The resentment of the aristocracy and the seigneurial system were essentially social and psychological phenomena rather than merely a question of the economic weight or lordship.[58] But, the material conditions of life undoubtedly shaped attitudes and it is often possible to identify the circumstances which mollified or exacerbated peasant attitudes towards lordship at the end of the old regime.

In Haute-Normandie, upwards of 80% of the farmland belonged to the upper classes and much of this land was subject to seigneurial dues.[59] Hence the lords themselves and the bourgeois property owners paid the bulk of the *droits seigneuriaux* and the tithes, or more accurately their tenant farmers paid them in the names of their employers For the capitalist tenant farmers of Haute-Normandie, the *droits seigneuriaux* and the tithes were just one more cost of doing business.

The rural poor of Haute-Normandie paid only a fraction of the feudal dues. Moreover, land engrossing had effectively dissolved all but remnants of the landowning peasantry. Rural villages were immense, but without the common bond of landownership the sense of community evaporated. The rural poor in Haute-Normandie had at best a tangential relationship with lords and lordship. They were employed in the rural textile industry and in a multiplicity of artisanal or tertiary sector jobs associated with trade on the Seine. The lower classes in Haute-Normandie in 1789 were largely indifferent to lordship but were totally preoccupied with high food prices in a time of unemployment.

Very different conditions prevailed in Dauphiné.[60] Dauphiné was far less economically developed than Normandie, upper class properties far less extensive, and rural employments much less diverse. A majority of rural inhabitants were still peasant farmers who paid feudal dues and tithes themselves. The villages had a very strong sense of communal cohesiveness, equally strong village administrations. Lordship was an ever-present and well-hated institution. Not only did the peasants hate the lords and the higher ecclesiastical authorities for the burdensome feudal dues and tithes, they were at loggerheads with them over communal lands and hunting rights. Not surprisingly, anti-feudal violence was far more evident in Dauphiné in 1789 than in distant Normandie. The troubled areas in Dauphiné saw a good sixty castles pillaged, set on fire and destroyed. The crowds did not lash out just in blind hatred, rather they had a plan. They seized the seigneurial *terriers*, the feudal titles, whether these were stored in the castles or in the offices of the notaries. The crowds burned the seigneurial records so that the *droits* could not be enforced in the future.

The anti-feudal uprisings of 1789 occurred on a scale and with an intensity never seen before in France. Nevertheless, they expressed the same animosities and hopes and often followed the same trajectory from grain riots to violence against the symbols of economic and social domination that had appeared earlier in the century.[61] Although the anti-feudal uprisings were still a minority phenomenon in 1789 they were widespread enough to terrify the delegates in the

National Constituent Assembly to vote to abolish lordship on August 4.

Anti-seigneurial violence did not end in the summer of 1789. Many areas of France that demonstrated little or no public animosity to lordship in the spring and summer 1789, such as Bretagne, Auvergne, and Aquitaine were centers of anti-seigneurial violence a few months later.[62] In the summer of 1789, anti-seigneurial violence occurred in 28–30% of the insurrectionary events, in 87% of uprisings in early 1790, 69% in 1791, and 73% of those in early 1792.[63]

The violence against lordship after the summer of 1789 stemmed from the determination of the lords and the delegates in the Constituent Assembly to force tenants to indemnify lords for the loss of their legitimate property rights. The difficult task of sorting out which parts of lordship constituted legitimate property and which did not fell to the members of the *Comité des droits féodaux* headed by Merlin de Douai. The legal reasoning of the committee members was perfectly standard French jurisprudence and indeed reflected the legal opinion everywhere in western Europe.[64]

The legal experts distinguished between the *droits seigneuriaux* which were tantamount to rentals for a surrender of land and those which flowed from usurped sovereign authority. The first were legitimate property rights; the second were not. Consequently, lords received nothing for surrendering their honorific rights, their patrimonial seigneurial tribunals, their exclusive monopoly rights, but were to receive compensation for the rest. *Droits seigneuriaux* collected in cash were to be capitalized by a multiplier of 20 times their yearly value, while those collected in agricultural products were to be capitalized by a multiplier of 25. Each lord would have to work out the details of the indemnification with his tenants. In the meantime, lords could continue collecting the old dues.

The peasants refused to accept the legal reasoning of the reformers and the lords. With renewed opposition and quite spectacular anti-feudal violence, they contributed substantially to the ongoing social, political and legal revolution which ultimately abolished lordship outright and without compensation in June of 1793.[65]

CONCLUSION

Lordship was always a pre-eminently aristocratic institution. In the Middle Ages when the princes exercised the same governing authority over their lands as the king did over his domain, lordship was the institutional expression of real political authority. When the princes vanished from France at the end of the Middle Ages, lordship as a political institution vanished with them.

Under the old regime, lordship was essentially an aristocratic prestige property. Although the kingdom was alive with dukes, counts, marquis, and barons, these aristocrats were pale reflections of their medieval predecessors. The authority which they exercised over the lands of their lordships was an authority tolerated by the kings, even delegated by the kings if you accept the arguments of the royal jurists. Old regime society was every bit as aristocratic in its values as medieval society, but the aristocrats and the church, itself a profoundly aristocratic institution, operated under the strict control of the absolute monarchy.

As a form of property, lordship was an indispensable component of the aristocratic lifestyle. The honorific rights of lordship symbolized the social superiority of the nobility. While lordship undoubtedly had a value that far exceeded any income which this prestige property produced, the revenues of lordship were far from negligible. The economy of old regime France was still predominantly agrarian, and consequently the nobles were above all else landed aristocrats.

Lordship had always been a composite form of property which combined directly owned domain lands with revenues from tenants or subjects. The domain lands of the aristocracy were far from negligible in the Middle Ages, but there is also no doubt that these aristocratic directly owned properties expanded in the early modern centuries as the economy itself grew. Although there were always differences in the internal composition of the lordships for nobles at different levels of the aristocratic hierarchy, in general the nobles of France derived the bulk of the seigneurial incomes from their domain lands rather than from their *droits seigneuriaux*.

Lordship also performed essential public services under the old regime. The seigneurial courts served nearly everywhere in France as the tribunals of first instance for an array of civil and even minor criminal cases. Likewise, lordship continued to provide the institutional framework for local governance in the smaller towns and villages where the bulk of the French population resided.

Prior to 1750, virtually no one in France could envision a world without lordships and nobles. It certainly never occurred to the old regime kings of France to abolish lordship. Lordship was an ancient institution that was as deeply rooted in the traditions and laws of France as the monarchy itself. Indeed, once the aristocrats had lost their own governing authority, both the privileged aristocracy and lordship depended on the support of the kings for survival.

It is easy enough to imagine a different history of the old regime monarchy in the eighteenth century. The French Revolution was not inevitable. If Louis XV and Louis XVI had been energetic reformers comparable to Maria Theresa of Austria or Duke Leopold of Tuscany they might well have saved the monarchy by modernizing it. D'Argenson, Malesherbes, and Turgot had the detailed reform agendas. It is much more difficult to imagine how any eighteenth century kings of France could have modernized the monarchy without eliminating both the privileged nobility and lordship.

As it turned out, the Revolution quickly swept away the aristocratic society and lordship, overhauled an equally aristocratic church, but attempted, at least initially, to save the monarchy.

Notes

Chapter One. Lordship Under the Old Regime

1. Jean–Marie Constant, "L'évolution de la noblesse de la sénéchaussée de La Flèche de la fin du XVIe siècle à 1789," *Etat et société en France aux XVIIe et XVIIIe siècles. Mélanges offerts à Yves Durand*. Paris: Presses de l'Université de Paris-Sorbonne, 2000, 155–64. J. Russel Major, "The Crown and Aristocracy in Renaissance France," *American Historical Review*, 69, 1963–64, 631–45.

2. James B. Wood, *The Nobility of the Election of Bayeux, 1463–1666. Continuity Through Change*. Princeton: Princeton University Press, 1980, 96–97. Jean-Marie Constant, "L'enquête de noblesse de 1667 et les seigneurs de Beauce," *Revue d'histoire moderne et contemporaine*, 21, 1974, 548–66.

3. Guy Lemarchand, *La fin du féodalisme dans le Pays de Caux*. Paris: Editions du CNRS, 1989, 169–70.

4. Guy Lemarchand, "La France au XVIIIe siècle: élites ou noblesse et bourgeoisie," *Cahiers d'histoire de l'institut de recherches marxistes*, 51, 1993, 105—07. Michel Cassan, "Une approche de la noblesse de Bas-Limousin," *Travaux du centre de recherches sur les origines de l'Europe moderne*, 6, 1986, 4–31. Wood, *The Nobility of the Election of Bayeux*, 23–55.

5. Michel Nassiet, "Le problème des effetifs de la noblesse dans la France du XVIIIe siècle," *Traditions et innovations dans la société française du XVIIIe siècle*. Paris: Presses de l'Université de Paris-Sorbonne, 1995, 97–121.

6. Lemarchand, *La fin du féodalisme*, 317–28. Annie Antoine, *Fiefs et villages du Bas-Maine au XVIIIe siècle. Etude de la seigneurie et de la vie rurale*. Mayenne: Editions régionales de l'Ouest, 1994, 184–87.

7. Christophe Levantal, *Ducs et pairs et duchés-pairies laïques à l'époque moderne*

(1510 1790) Paris: Editions Maisonneuve & La Rose, 1996. Jean–Pierre Labatut, *Les ducs et pairs de France au XVIIe siècle*. Paris: Presses uni. de France 1972.

8. James Lowth Goldsmith, *Lordship in France, 500–1500*. New York: Peter Lang, 2003, 199–211.

9. Goldsmith, *Lordship in France, 500–1500*, 285–93.

10. Guy Chaussinand-Nogaret, *La noblesse au XVIIIe siècle*. Bruxelles: Editions Complexe, 1984, 17.

11. Jean Gallet, "Les transformations de la seigneurie en France entre 1600 et 1789," *Histoire, économie et société*, 18, 1999, 63–81. Guy Lemarchand, "Déclin ou résurrection? La seigneurie rurale dans la France du XVIe siècle et de la première moitié du XVIIe siècle," *Cahiers d'histoire de l'institut de recherches marxistes*, 59, 1995, 5–25.

12. Gallet, "Les transformations de la seigneurie," 64–72.

13. René Filhol, *Le premier président Christofle de Thou et la réformation des coutumes*. Paris: Librairie du Recueil Sirey, 1937. Marcel Garaud, *Histoire générale du droit privé français (de 1789 à 1804)*. Vol. II. *La Révolution et la propriété foncière*. Paris: Recueil Sirey, 1958, 8–174.

14. Martine Grinberg, "La rédaction des coutumes et les droits seigneuriaux. Nommer, classer, exclure," *Annales*. 52, 1997, 1017–38.

15. Régine Robin, "Fief et seigneurie dans le droit et l'idéologie juridique à la fin du XVIIIe siècle," *Annales historiques de la Révolution française*, 43, 1971, 554–602. Annie Antoine, "La seigneurie, la terre et les paysans," *Bulletin de la société d'histoire moderne*, 1999, 15–33.

16. Antoine, *Fiefs et villages*, 255, 273–75. Jean Bastier, *La féodalité au siècle des Lumières dans la région de Toulouse (1730–1790)*. Paris: Bibliothèque nationale, 1975, 56–58, 281–83, 309.

17. Jean Bastier, *La féodalité au siècle des Lumières, dans la région de Toulouse (1730–1790)*. Paris: Bibliothèque national, 1975, 258. Philippe Huppé, *Le gisant de la féodalité dans l'ombre des Lumières. La féodalité dans la baronnie du Pouget et la vicomté de Plaissan au 18e siècle*. Montagnac: Editions Monique Mergoil, 1998, 151.

18. Gérard Aubin, *La seigneurie en Bordelais au XVIIIe siècle d'après la pratique notariale (1715–1789)*. Rouen: Publications de l'Université de Rouen, 1989, 291.

19. Yves Durand, "L'idéal social en Champagne méridionale du XVIe au XVIIIe siècle," *Actes du 92e Congrès national des sociétés savantes. Strasbourg-Colmar, 1967. Section d'histoire moderne et contemporaine*, III, 111–23.

20. Gallet, "Les transformations de la seigneurie," 80.

21. Goldsmith, *Lordship in France, 500–1500*, 285–93.

22. Paul Ourliac & Jean-Louis Gazzaniga, *Histoire du droit privé français de l'An mil au*

Code civil. Paris: Albin Michel, 1985, 205–29.

23. Marcel Garaud, *Histoire générale du droit privé français (de 1789 à 1804).* Paris: Recueil Sirey, 1958, 15–109.

24. Goldsmith, *Lordship in France, 500–1500,* 287–88.

25. Pierre de Saint-Jacob, "Le droit de lods en Bourgogne à la fin de l'Ancien Régime," *Mémoires de la société pour l'histoire du droit et des institutions des anciens pays bourguignons, comtois et romands,* 1952, 161.

26. Pierre de Saint-Jacob, *Les paysans de la Bourgogne du Nord au dernier siècle de l'Ancien Régime.* Paris: Les Belles Lettres, 1960, 43–44.

27. Gérard Aubin, *La seigneurie en Bordelais au XVIIIe siècle d'après la pratique notariale (1715–1789).* Rouen: Publications de l'Université de Rouen, 1989, 199.

28. Octave Meyer, *La régence épiscopale de Saverne.* Strasbourg: Imprimerie alsacienne, 1935, 113–14. Marc Drouot, "Seigneur et seigneurie au XVIe siècle. L'exploitation de la seigneurie de Thann en 1581," *Revue d'Alsace,* 119, 1993, 119–38. Georges Livet, *L'intendance d'Alsace de la Guerre de Trente Ans à la mort de Louis XIV, 1634–1715.* 2e éd. Strasbourg: Presses universitaires de Strasbourg, 1991, 308–20.

29. Jean-Marie Boehler, *Une société rurale en milieu rhénan: la paysannerie de la plaine d'Alsace (1648–1789).* Strasbourg: Presses universitaires de Strasbourg, 1995, 1208–09.

30. Lucien Sittler, "Un siècle de vie paysanne: l'évolution d'une commune de la plaine d'Alsace. Fergersheim-Ohnheim avant et après la Guerre de Trente Ans," *Paysans d'Alsace.* Strasbourg: Le Roux, 1959, 81–98. Boehler, *Une société rurale en milieu rhénan,* 1212–13, 2329–41. Etienne Juillard, *La vie rurale dans la plaine de Basse-Alsace. Essai de géographie sociale.* Strasbourg: Le Roux, 1953, 76–78, 507–08.

31. Abel Mathieu, *La seigneurie de Pont-les-Remirement (St-Amé, Dommartin, St-Etienne) sous l'ancien régime.* Epinal: Editions du Sabin d'Or, 1979, 68. Didier Varlet, "Les revenus de la seigneurie de Bitche à la veille de la guerre de Trente Ans (1621–1632)," *Annales de l'Est,* 40, 1988, 287–88. Georges Bugler, *La fin de l'ancien régime dans le pays de Montbéliard.* Besançon: Annales littéraires de l'Université de Besançon, 1989, 63.

32. Michel Belotte, *La région de Bar-sur-Seine à la fin du Moyen Age, du début du XIIIe siècle au milieu du XVIe siècle.* Lille: Université de Lille, 1973, 260–61.

33. Raymond Monnier, "Antony. Une commune de la banlieu parisienne à la veille de la Révolution," *Annales historiques de la Révolution française,* 52, 1980, 264. Jonathan Dewald, *Pont-St-Pierre 1398–1789. Lordship, Community and Capitalism in Early Modern France.* Berkeley: University of California Press, 1987, 218–22.

34. Gabriel Debien, *En Haut-Poitou. Défricheurs au travail, XVe–XVIIIe siècles.* Paris: Armand Colin, 1952, 37. Jean Gallet, *La seigneurie bretonne (1450–1680).* Paris: Publications de la Sorbonne, 1983, 377–415.

35.   Jacques Bottin, "Le paysan, l'Etat et le seigneur en Normandie, milieu du XVIe–milieu du XVIIe siècle," *Genèse de l'état moderne. Prélèvement et redistribution*. Paris: Editions du Centre national de la recherche scientifique, 1987, 101–10. Jacques Bottin, *Seigneurs et paysans dans l'ouest du Pays de Caux 1540–1650*. Paris: Edition La Sycomore, 1983, 63–66.

36.   Monnier, "Antony. Une commune de la banlieu parisienne," 264. Hiroyuki Ninomiya, "Un cadre de vie rurale au XVIIe et au XVIIIe siècle: la seigneurie de Fleury-en-Bière," *Paris et Il-de-France. Mémoires*, 18–19, 1967–68, 58. Jean-Marc Moriceau, *Les fermiers de l'Île-de-France, XVe–XVIIIe siècle*. Paris: Fayard, 1994, 121.

37.   Hervé Revel, "Evolution des patrimoines fonciers à Tremblay-en-France, de l'ancien régime au lendemain de la Révolution," *Bulletin de la société d'études historiques de Tremblay*, 1990, 2–19.

38.   Pierre Deyon, "Quelques remarques sur l'évolution du régime seigneurial en Picardie, XVIe–XVIIIe siècles," *Revue d'histoire moderne et contemporaine*, 8, 1961, 271–75. Belotte, *La région de Bar-sur-Seine*, 37–39. Jean-Jacques Clère, *Les paysans de la Haute-Marne et la Révolution française*. Paris: Comité des travaux historiques et scientifiques, 1988, 118.

39.   Michel Cart, "La crise économique des communautés rurales ardennaises à la fin de l'ancien régime (1770–1789)," *Revue historique ardennaise*, 25, 1990, 24–25.

40.   Jean Bart, *La Révolution française en Bourgogne*. Clermont-Ferrand: La Française d'Edition et d'Imprimerie, 1996, 42. Patrice Beck, "De la grange au village: Crepey en Bourgogne (XIIe–XVIIe siècle)," *Le village médiéval et son environnement. Etudes offertes à Jean-Marie Pesez*. Paris: Publications de la Sorbonne, 1998, 453–57. Colette Merlin, "Impositions, charges et résistance paysanne dans la petite montagne jurassienne à la veille de la Révolution," in Maurice Gresset, éd. *La Franche-Comté à la veille de la Révolution*. Paris: Les Belles Lettres, 1988, 19.

41.   Debien , *En Haut-Poitou. Défricheurs au travail*, 17–29.

42.   Poitrineau, *La vie rurale en Basse-Auvergne*, 341–51. Michel Leymarie, "Les redevances foncières seigneuriales en Haute-Auvergne," *Annales historiques de la Révolution française*, 1968, 316–31. Robert Darpoux, "La vie rurale vers la fin du XVIIIe siècle dans le Brivadois," *La Révolution française dans le Brivadois*. Brioude: Société de l'almanach de Brioude, 1989, 204–06. Robert Darpoux, "Une seigneurie de montagne à la veille de la Révolution," *Almanach de Brioude et de son arrondissement*, 62, 1982, 175–85. Michel Leymarie, "Rentes seigneuriales et produit des seigneuries dans l'élection de Tulle en Limousin," *Annales historiques de la Révolution française*, 1970, 594–98. Albert Massonie, "La seigneurie de Soudeilles-Lieuteret en 1582," *Lemouzi*, 125, 1993, 87–92.

43.   Emile Appolis, *Un pays languedocien au milieu du XVIIIe siècle. Le diocèse civil de Lodève. Etude administrative et économique*. Albi: Imprimerie coopérative du Sud-

Ouest, 1951, 98–105. Jean Bastier, *La féodalité au siècle des Lumières dans la région de Toulouse (1730–1790)*. Paris: Bibliothèque nationale, 1975, 216–17. Gilbert Larguier, *Le drap et le grain en Languedoc. Narbonne et Narbonnais 1300–1789*. Perpignan: Presses universitaires de Perpignan, 1996, 309–10. Monique Cubells, *La Provence des Lumières. Les parlementaires d'Aix au XVIIIe siècle*. Paris: Maloine, 1984, 147–49.

44. Rino Bandoch, "Les revenus de la noblesse du Bas-Quercy et sa place dans l'économie à la veille de la Révolution," *Montauban et les anciens pays de Tarn-et-Garonne. Actes du XLIe congrès des sociétés académiques et savantes de Languedoc-Pyrénées-Gascogne*, 1986, 346.

45. Aubin, *La seigneurie en Bordelais*, 326–33.

46. Pierre Boulanger, "La crise de l'économie et de la société champenoise dans les dernières années de l'ancien régime," *Mémoires de la société d'agriculture, commerce, sciences et arts du département de la Marne*, 100, 1985, 139–40.

47. Jérôme Decoux, "Fraude et fraudeurs dans le monde de transport au XVIIIe siècle: le cas des droits de la vicomté de l'eau de Rouen," *Les Normands et le fisc*. Elbeuf: Société de l'histoire d'Elbeuf, 1994, 131–38.

48. Claude Michaud, *L'église et l'argent sous l'ancien régime. Les receveurs généraux du clergé de France aux XVIe–XVIIe siècle*. Paris: Fayard, 1991, 542. Henri Marion, *La dîme ecclésiastique en France au XVIIIe siècle et sa suppression*. Bordeaux: Imprimerie de l'Université et des Facultés, 1912, 117.

49. Appolis, *Un pays languedocien*, 106.

50. Bastier, *La féodalité au siècle des Lumières*, 213.

51. Aubin, *La seigneurie en Bordelais*, 346–47.

52. Jean Nagle, "Un aspect de la propriété seigneuriale à Paris aux XVIIe et XVIIIe siècles: les lods et ventes," *Revue d'histoire moderne et contemporaine*, 24, 1977, 571–73.

53. Nagle, "Un aspect de la propriété seigneuriale," 570–81.

54. Antoine, *Fiefs et villages*, 228.

55. Nagle, "Un aspect de la propriété seigneuriale," 577–78.

56. Antoine, *Fiefs et villages*, 229–30.

57. Jean-François Noël, "Seigneurie et propriété urbaine sous l'Ancien Régime. Autour de la maison de Bertrand d'Argentré à Vitré," *Revue d'histoire moderne et contemporaine*, 38, 1991, 193–94.

58. Appolis, *Un pays languedocien*, 107.

59. Michel Broquereau, "Des banalités en Poitou aux XVIIe et XVIIIe siècles," *Bulletin de la société des antiquaires de l'Ouest*, sér. 4, 5, 1959, 215–62.

60. Lemarchand, *La fin du féodalisme*, 32. Jonathan Dewald, *Pont-St-Pierre 1398–1789. Lordship, Community and Capitalism in Early Modern France*. Berkeley: University

of California Press, 1987, 224.

61.   Bastier, *La féodalité au siècle des Lumières*, 173. Huppé, *Le gisant de la féodalité*, 61.

62.   Cubells, *La Provence des Lumières*, 144–45.

63.   Rino Bandoch, "La riche noblesse provinciale à la veille de la Révolution. Les Pechpeyrou de Beaucaire," *Bulletin de la société archéologique de Tarn-et-Garonne*, 109, 1984, 111–27.

64.   Antoine, *Fiefs et villages*, 207–08.

65.   Ourliac, Paul & Jean-Louis Gazzaniga, *Histoire du droit privé français de l'an mil au Code civil*. Paris: Aubin-Michel, 1985, 167. Aubin, *La seigneurie en Bordelais*, 58–63. Gallet, "Les transformations de la seigneurie," 66–67.

66.   Francis Loirette, "Un épisode des résistances locales aux empiètements du pouvoir royal: la défense du franc-alleu agenais au XVIIe siècle," in Francis Loirette, *L'état et la région: L'Aquitaine au XVIIe siècle*. Bordeaux: Presses universitaires de Bordeaux, 1998, 119–42.

67.   Henri Boudrie, "Affranchissement de rentes féodales à Meymac," *Lemouzi*, 1986, 123–26.

68.   Françoise Sabatie, "Stagnation démographique, réaction seigneuriale et mouvements révolutionnaires dans la région de Toulouse. Le cas de Buzet-sur-Tarn," *Annales historiques de la Révolution française*, 43, 1971, 189.

69.   Loirette, "Un épisode des résistances locales," 134–36.

70.   Abel Poitrineau, *La vie rurale en Basse-Auvergne au XVIIIe siècle*. Paris: Presses universitaires de France, 1965, 343. Michel Leymarie, "La faible importance des alleux en Haute-Auvergne révélée par le centième denier," *Annales historiques de la Révolution française*, 49, 1977, 429–35.

71.   Aubin, *La seigneurie en Bordelais*, 49.

72.   Aubin, *La seigneurie en Bordelais*, 62–63.

73.   Clère, Jean-Jacques *Les paysans de la Haute-Marne et la Révolution française*. Paris: CTHS, 1988, 125. Bastier, *La féodalité au siècle des Lumières*, 258–60. Aubin, *La seigneurie en Bordelais*, 286–91.

74.   Anne Zink, *Clochers et troupeaux. Les communautés rurales des Landes et du Sud-Ouest avant la Révolution*. Bordeaux: Presses universitaire de Bordeaux, 1997, 153–60.

75.   Lemarchand, *La fin du féodalisme*, 28. Aubin, *La seigneurie en Bordelais au XVIIIe siècle*, 286.

76.   Bastier, *La féodalité au siècle des Lumières*, 259–60.

77.   Huppé, *Le gisant de la féodalité*, 151.

78.   Cubells, *La Provence des Lumières*, 135.

79.   Leymarie, Michel "Les redevances foncières seigneuriales en Haute-Auvergne, "

Annales historiques de la Révolution française, 1968, 371 76. Leymarie, "Rentes seigneuriales et produit des seigneuries dans l'élection de Tulle en Limusin," *Annales historiques de la Révolution française,* 1970, 594–98. Jean Bastier, "Droits féodaux et revenus agricoles en Rouergue à la veille de la Révolution," *Annales du Midi,* 95, 1983, 282, 285–87.

80. Clère, *Les paysans de la Haute-Marne,* 120–21. Antoine, *Fiefs et villages,* 223–25. Bastier, *La féodalité au siècle des Lumières,* 262–79. Aubin, *La seigneurie en Bordelais au XVIIIe siècle,* 264–73.

81. Philippe Goujard, *L'abolition de la "féodalité" dans le Pays de Bray (1789–1793).* Paris: Bibliothèque nationale, 1979, 30–34.

82. Leymarie, "Les redevances foncières seigneuriales," 330–38.

83. Georges Lefebvre, "Répartition de la propriété et de l'exploitation foncières à la fin de l'ancien régime," in Georges Lefebvre, *Etudes sur la Révolution française.* 2e éd. Paris: Presses universitaires de France, 298–300.

84. Hélène de Tarde, "Contrats de fermage et de métayage en Narbonnais de 1660 à 1789," *Société d'histoire du droit et des institutions des anciens pays de droit écrit. Recueil de mémoires et travaux,* 1983, 133–49. Goujard, *L'abolition de la "féodalité",* 62–68, 162–63.

85. Antoine, *Fiefs et villages,* 245–54.

86. Aubin, *La seigneurie en Bordelais,* 60–62. Loirette, "Un épisode des résistances locales," 119–42. Zink, *Clochers et troupeaux,* 133–37. Nagle, "Un aspect de la propriété seigneuriale," 570–81.

87. Goldsmith, *Lordship in France, 500–1500,* 47.

88. Belotte, Michel *La région de Bar-sur-Seine à la fin du Moyen Age, du début du XIIIe au milieu du XVIe siècle.* Lille: Université de Lille, 1973, 252–64.

89. Jean Denaix, "La châtellenie de Hattonchâtel en 1546. Situation politique, fiscale, sociale," *Annales de l'Est,* 1957, 93–124.

90. René Germain, *Les campagnes bourbonnaises à la fin du Moyen Age (1370–1530).* Clermont-Ferrand: Institut d'Etudes du Massif Central, 1987, 278–86. John W. Shaffer, *Family and Farm. Agrarian Change and Household Organization in the Loire Valley, 1500–1900.* Albany: State University of New York, 1982, 24–33. Romain Baron, "La vie rurale dans la région de Varzy dans la seconde moitié du 17e siècle," *Mémoires de l'académie académique du Nivernais,* 69, 1987, 47. Pierre Charbonnier, *Une autre France. La seigneurie en Basse-Auvergne du XIVe au XVIe siècle.* Clermont-Ferrand: Institut d'Etudes du Massif Central, 1980, 99–114, 637–60.

91. Cubells, *La Provence des Lumières,* 158–59.

92. Antoine, *Fiefs et villages,* 203–09.

93. Jacques Bottin, *Seigneurs et paysans dans l'ouest du Pays de Caux 1540–1650.* Paris: Edition Le Sycomore, 1983, 53. Denise Angers, *Le terrier de la famille d'Orbec à*

Cideville (Haute-Normandie) XIVe–XVIe siècles. Montréal: Les presses de l'Université de Montréal, 1993, 73–77. Catherine Bébéar, "Le temporel de l'abbaye de Montivilliers à la fin du Moyen Age," *Cahiers Léopold Delisle*, 47, 1998 41–59.

94. Lemarchand, *La fin du féodalisme*, 46–49. Leymarie, "Les redevances foncières seigneuriales," 371–76. Leymarie, "Rentes seigneuriales," 594–98. Clère, *Les paysans de la Haute-Marne*, 125. Bastier, *La féodalité au siècle des Lumières*, 258–60. Aubin, *La seigneurie en Bordelais*, 286–91. Zink, *Clochers et troupeaux*, 153–60. Huppé, *Le gisant de la féodalité*, 151. Cubells, *La Provence des Lumières*, 135. Bastier, "Droits féodaux," 282–87.

95. Lefebvre, "La répartition de la propriété," 298–300.

96. Lemarchand, *La fin du féodalisme*, 130–32.

97. Clère, *Les paysans de la Haute-Marne*, 26.

98. Georges Frêche, *Toulouse et la région Midi-Pyrénées au siècle des Lumières, vers 1670–1789*. Paris: Editions Cujas, 1975, 147–53.

99. Charles Girault, "La propriété foncière de la noblesse sarthoise au XVIIIe siècle," *La province du Maine*, 35, 1955, 201–14.

100. Jean Jacquart, *La crise rurale en Ile-de-France, 1550–1670*. Paris: Armand Colin, 1974, 101–17.

101. Jean Jacquart, "Tenure, propriété, exploitation," in Serge Bianchi et al., *La terre et les paysans en France et en Grande-Bretagne du début du XVIIe siècle à la fin du XVIIIe siècle*. Paris: Armand Colin, 1999, 30. Bernard Garnier, "La mise en herbe dans le pays d'Auge aux XVIIe et XVIIIe siècles," *Annales de Normandie*, 25, 1975, 157–80. Bernard Garnier, "Pays herbagers, pays céréaliers et pays "ouverts" en Normandie (XVIe–début XIXe siècle)," *Revue d'histoire économique et sociale*, 53, 1975, 493–525. Frêche, *Toulouse et la région Midi-Pyrénées*, 152–53.

102. Gallet, "Les transformations de la seigneurie," 76.

103. Jean-Marc Moriceau, *Les fermiers de l'Île-de-France, XVe–XVIIIe siècle*. Paris: Fayard, 1994, 79–89. Jacquart, *La crise rurale en Ile-de-France*, 213–47, 623–39, 723–40. René Pijassou, *Un grand vignoble de qualité. Le Médoc*. Paris: Tallandier, 1980, 316–23, 422. Robert Boutruche, dir. *Histoire de Bordeaux. IV. Bordeaux de 1453 à 1715*. Bordeaux: Fédération historique du Sud-Ouest, 1966, 169–79 Jean Gallet, *La seigneurie bretonne (1450–1680)*. Paris: Publications de la Sorbonne, 1983, 311–48. Emmanuel Le Roy Ladurie, "Sur Montpellier et sa campagne aux XVIe et XVIIe siècles," *Annales E.S.C.*, 12, 1957, 223–30. Frêche, *Toulouse et la région Midi-Pyrénées*, 164–69, 208. Pierre de Saint-Jacob, "Mutations économiques et sociales dans les campagnes bourguignonnes à la fin du XVIe siècle," *Etudes rurales*, 1961, 34–49.

104. Gilles Postel-Vinay, *La rente foncière dans le capitalisme agricole. Analyse de la voie "classique" du développement du capitalisme dans l'agriculture à partir de l'exemple*

du Soissonnais. Paris: François Maspero, 1974, 16–89.

105.   Jean-Marc Moriceau, "Fermage et métayage (XIIe–XIXe siècle)," *Histoire et sociétés rurales*, 1, 1994, 155–90.

106.   Gallet, "Les transformations de la seigneurie, " 77, 80.

107.   Robert Forster, *The Nobility of Toulouse in the Eighteenth Century. A Social and Economic Study.* Baltimore: Johns Hopkins, 1960, 32–37.

108.   A. Chéron & G. de Sarret de Coussergues, *Une seigneurie en Bas-Languedoc. Coussergues et les Sarret.* Bruxelles: Hayez, 1963, 203–48. Frêche, *Toulouse et la région Midi-Pyrénées*, 249.

109.   Aubin, *La seigneurie en Bordelais*, 76. François-Georges Pariset, dir. *Histoire de Bordeaux. V. Bordeaux au XVIIIe siècle.* Bordeaux: Fédération historique du Sud-Ouest, 1968, 184.

110.   Jean-Marie Constant, "Gestion et revenus d'un grand domaine aux XVIe et XVIIe siècles d'après les comptes de la baronnie d'Auneau," *Revue d'histoire économique et sociale*, 50, 1972, 165–202. Albert Colombet, *Les parlementaires bourguignons à la fin du XVIIIe siècle.* Dijon: Chez L'Auteur, 1937, 117.

111.   Moriceau, *Les fermiers de l'Île-de-France*, 98–119, 225–27, 234, 613–40. Pierre Brunet, *Structure agraire et économie rurale des plateaux tertiaires entre la Seine et l'Oise.* Caen: Caron et Cie, 1960, 277–90.

112.   Pierre de Saint-Jacob, *Les paysans de la Bourgogne du nord au dernier siècle de l'Ancien Régime.* Paris: Les Belles Lettres, 1960, 45–48. Poitrineau, *La vie rurale en Basse-Auvergne*, 186–208.

113.   Gallet, *La seigneurie bretonne*, 343–45, 547–68. Suzanne Fiette, "Un grand domaine du Lauragais dans la seconde moitié du XVIIIe siècle (1750–1793)," *Bulletin de l'association française des historiens économistes*, 13, 1980, 19–35. Frêche, *Toulouse et la région Midi-Pyrénées*, 222, 246. Pierre Deffontaines, *Les hommes et leurs travaux dans les pays de la moyenne Garonne (Agenais, Bas-Quercy).* Agen: Librairie Quesseveur, 1978 (orig. Lille, 1932), 142.

114.   Serge Dontenwill, "Cadres de vie des paysans et prise en charge de l'espace agraire dans le Centre-Est de la France au temps de Louis XIV," *La terre et les paysans en France et en Grande-Bretagne de 1600 à 1800.* Paris: Editions du Temps, 1998, 169–92. Béatrice de Varine, *Villages de la vallée de l'Ouche aux XVIIe et XVIIIe siècles. La seigneurie de Marigny-sur-Ouche.* Roanne: Editions Horvarth, 1979, 84–85.

115.   G. Antonetti, "Le partage des forêts usagères ou communales entre les seigneurs et les communautés d'habitants," *Revue historique de droit français et étranger*, 41, 1963, 245–48.

116.   Alain Roquelet, *La vie de la forêt normande à la fin du Moyen Age. Le coutumier d'Hector de Chartres.* Rouen: Société de l'histoire de Normandie, 1984. Goldsmith,

Lordship in France, 500–1500, 215–16, 306–07.

117. Michel Devèze, *La vie de la forêt française au XVI e siècle*. Paris: S.E.V.P.E.N, 1961, vol. 1, 77–180.

118. Devèze, *La vie de la forêt*, vol. I, 13–55.

119. Michel Devez, "Le pâturage au XVIe siècle dans la moitié nord de la France d'après les "coutumes"," *Bulletin philologique et historique*, 1967, I, 29–42. André-Marcel Burg, "Le droit de glandée et l'élevage du porc en forêt de Haguenau au début du XVIe siècle," *Bulletin philologique et historique*, 1967, I, 129–36.

120. Michel Devèze "La forêt française: aspects sociaux et économiques aux XVIe et XVIIe siécles," *Bulletin de la société d'histoire moderne*, 52, 1953, 6–10.

121. Marcel Marion, *Dictionnaire des institutions de la France aux XVIIe et XVIIIe siècles*. New York: Burt Franklin, 1968 (orig. Paris, 1923), 525. Devèze, *La vie de la forêt*, vol. 1, 271–317. Roland Mousnier, *Les institutions de la France sous la monarchie absolue*. 2e éd. Paris: Presses universitaires de France, 1974, Tome 1, 286–88.

122. Devèze, *La vie de la forêt*, vol. 1, 57–93, 96–129.

123. Devèze, *La vie de la forêt*, vol. 1, 131–37, 283.

124. Michel Duval, "Recherches sur l'économie forestière des pays de l'ouest dans la seconde moitié du XVIe siècle," *Revue forestière française*, 1957, 883–85.

125. M. Bach, "Les droits d'usage dans l'ancien comté de Dabo," *Revue forestière française*, 1957, 667–99. Jean-Pierre Husson, *Les hommes et la forêt en Lorraine*. Paris: Editions Bonneton, 1991, 83–88.

126. Michel Philippe, "La forêt de Lyons au milieu du XVIe siècle," *Etudes normandes*, 41, 1992, 63–84.

127. Ourliac & Gazzaniga, *Histoire du droit privé français*, 228–29.

128. Michel Denis, "Grandeaur et décadence d'une forêt. Paimont du XVIe au XIXe siècle," *Annales de Bretagne*, 64, 1957, 257–73. Eugène Martres, "Forêts cantaliennes (XVIIIe–XXème siècles). Vicissitudes et exploitation," *Revue de la Haute-Auvergne*, 37, 1961, 433–60.

129. Devèze, *La vie de la forêt*, vol. 1, 131–37, 281–84. Antonetti, "Le partage des forêts," 261–85, 418–42.

130. Devèze. *La vie de la forêt*, vol. 1, 291.

131. Xavier de Massary, "Les "usages" dans le nord-est de l'arrondissement de Château-Thierry. 1ère partie: XVIe–XVIIIe siècle," *Mémoires de la féderation des sociétés d'histoire et d'archéologie de l'Aisne*, 32, 1987, 9–37.

132. Devèze, *La vie de la forêt*, vol. 1, 167–204.

133. Michel Devèze, "Superficie et propriété des forêts du Nord et de l'Est de la France vers la fin du règne de François Ier (1540–1547)," *Annales. Economies. Sociétés. Civilisations*, 15, 1960, 485–92.

134. Michel Devèze, "Forêts communales de la France du Nord-Est et de l'Allemagne rhénane dans la seconde moitié du XVIIe siècle," *Actes du 90e Congrès national des sociétés savantes. Nice, 1965. Section d'histoire moderne et contemporaine*, Tome I, 75. François Vion-Delphine, "Les forêts du nord de la Franche-Comté à la veille de la Révolution (d'après les cahiers de doléances des bailliages d'Amont et de Baume)," in Maurice Gresset, éd. *La Franche-Comté à la veille de la Révolution*. Paris: Les Belles Lettres, 1988, 39–68. Husson, *Les hommes et la forêt*, 67–118. Roland Ganghofer, "Aspects des communautés rurales en Alsace du 13e au 20e siècle," *Les communautés rurales. 4. Europe occidentale. Recueils de la société Jean Bodin pour l'histoire comparative des institutions. 43*. Paris: Dessain et Tolra, 1984, 440–43.

135. Clément Martin, "La forêt de la Serre-basse à Saint-Denis. Cadre juridique, économie et histoire," *Bulletin de la société d'études scientifiques de l'Aude*, 88, 1988, 13–20.

136. Roger Dufraisse, "La forêt de Haguenau sous la Révolution et l'Empire," *Etudes haguenoviennes*, 3, 1958–1961, 148–52.

137. René Georglette, "Abrégé de l'histoire des forêts françaises depuis la promulgation de l'ordonnance de 1669 jusqu'à la veille de la Révolution," *Revue forestière française*, 1957, 403–18.

138. Henri Sée, "Le partage des biens communaux en France à la fin de l'ancien régime," *Revue historique de droit français et étranger*. 1923, 47–49. Camille Trapenard, *Le pâturage communal en Haute-Auvergne (XVIIe–XVIIIe siècles)*. Bar-le-Duc: Imprimerie Contant-Laguerre, 1904, 40–48.

139. Pierre Charbonnier, "L'exploitation de la forêt des Dôme sous l'ancien régime," *Revue d'Auvergne*, 101, 1987, 17–26.

140. Michel Duval, "Economie forestière et féodalité dans l'ouest à la veille de la Révolution," *Annales de Bretagne*, 64, 1957, 347–58. And by the same author: "Gestion et exploitation des bois de mainmorte en Cornouaille aux XVIIe et XVIIe siècles," *Bulletin de la société archéologique du Finistère*, 124, 1995, 393–413; and " Les forêts royales en Cornouaille sous l'Ancien régime: la gruerie de Quimperlé (1545–1790)," *Bulletin de la société archéologique du Finistère*, 115, 1986, 161–94.

141. Antonetti, "Le partage des forêts," 599–612. Arlette Brosselin, *La forêt bourguignonne (1660–1789)*. Dijon: Editions de l'Université de Dijon, 1987, 107–13.

142. Antonetti, "Le partage des forêts," 613–21.

143. Nadine Vivier, *Propriété collective et identité communale. Les biens communaux en France 1750–1914*. Paris: Publications de la Sorbonne, 1998, 42–44.

144. Andrée Corvol, "Forêt et communautés en Basse-Bourgogne au dix-huitième siècle," *Revue historique*, 256, 1976, 31. Maurice Bordes, "La vitalité des communautés provençales au XVIIIe siècle," *Provence historique*, 23, 1973, 22–25.

145. Goujard, *L'abolition de la "féodalité"*, 58–60.

146. Jean Bart, *La liberté ou la terre. La mainmorte en Bourgogne au siècle des Lumières*.

Dijon: Université de Dijon, 1984, 190–92.

147.   Vivier, *Propriété collective*, 40. Dulauni, *Ta région de Bar-sur-Seine*, 293–94. Michel Derlange, *Les communautés d'habitants en Provence au dernier siècle de l'Ancien Régime*. Toulouse: Publications de l'Université Toulouse-Le Mirail, 1987, 53–65, 443–44.

148.   Michel Devèze, "Les forêts françaises à la veille de la Révolution de 1789," *Revue d'histoire moderne et contemporaine*, 1966, 242–44. G. Buttoud, "Les projects forestiers de la Révolution (1789–1798)," *Revue forestière française*, 35, 1983, 9. Buttoud estimates the communal forests at 1,500,000 ha, slightly more than the figure advanced by Devèze. Georges Plaisance, "La répartition des forêts communales en France et ses causes profondes," *Bulletin philologique et historique*, 1963, I, 399–417.

149.   Clère, *Les paysans de la Haute-Marne*, 35.

150.   Lemarchand, *La fin du féodalisme*, 19.

151.   Jean Duma, "Les Bourbon-Penthièvre à Rambouillet. La constitution d'une duché-pairie au XVIIIe siècle," *Revue d'histoire moderne et contemporaine*, 29, 1982, 291–304.

152.   Hiroyuki Ninomiya, "Un cadre de vie rurale au XVIIe et XVIIIe siècle: la seigneurie de Fleury-en-Bière," *Paris et Ile-de-France. Mémoires*, 18–19, 1967–1968, 78–79.

153.   André Plaisse, *La baronnie de Neubourg. Essai d'histoire agraire, économique et sociale*. Paris: Presses universitaires de France, 1961, 502–03.

154.   J. Delaspre, "La naissance d'un paysage rural au XVIIIe siècle sur les hauts plateaux de l'est du Cantal et du nord de la Margeride," *Revue de géographie alpine*, 40, 1952, 493–97. Nicole Lemaître, *Bruyères, communes et mas. Les communaux en Bas-Limousin depuis le XVIe siècle*. Ussel: Musée du pays d'Ussel, 1981. Nicole Lemaître, *Un horizon bloqué. Ussel et la montagne limousine aux XVIIe et XVIIIe siècles*. Ussel: Musée du pays d'Ussel, 1978, 96, 202. Appolis, "La question de la vaine pâture," 97–132. P. Marres, "La garrigue. Son exploitation à travers les âges," *Revue historique et littéraire du Languedoc*, 1944, 178–90, 380–93. Aubin, *La seigneurie en Bordelais*, 214. Robert Elissondo, "La propriété des terres communes en Pays de Soule à la fin de l'ancien régime," *Société des sciences, lettres et arts de Bayonne*, 144, 1988, 145–62. Pierre Féral "Les processus de défrichement de la forêt lectouroise sous l'Ancien Régime," *Gens et choses de Bigorre. Actes du XXIIe Congrès d'études régionales. Fédération des sociétés académiques et savantes de Languedoc-Pyrénées-Gascogne*, 1966, 121–34.

155.   Marie-Pierrette Foursans-Bourdette, "Agriculture et industrie en Béarn au XVIIIe siècle," *Revue juridique et économique du sud-ouest. Série économique*, 13, 1964, 191.

156.   Maurice Bordes, "Les communautés villageoises des provinces méridionales à l'époque moderne," in *Les communautés villageoises en Europe occidentale du Moyen*

Age aux Temps Modernes. Auch: Centre culturel de l'abbaye de Floran, 1984, 143–64. Pierre Tucoo-Chala, "T a mise en place du système ossalois. Permanences et premières mutations," in *Ecologie de la vallée d'Ossau. Recherches pour une synthèse*. Paris: CNRS, 1978, 73–85.

157. Marc Bloch, "La lutte pour l'individualisme agraire dans la France du XVIIIe siècle," *Annales d'histoire économique et sociale*, II, 1930, 329–83, 511–56. Henri Sée, "La question de la vaine pâture en France à la fin de l'Ancien Régime," *Revue d'histoire économique et sociale*, 1914, 3–25. R.-J. Bernard, "Les communautés rurales en Gévaudan sous l'ancien régime," *Revue du Gévaudan, des Causses et des Cévennes*, 17, 1971, 115–47. Derlange, *Les communautés d'habitants*, 460.

158. Sée, "Le partage des biens communaux," 47–81. Vivier, *Propriété collective*, 42–91. Marcel Laurent, "Le partage des communaux à Ennezat," *Revue d'Auvergne*, 82, 1978, 167–95.

159. Jean-Lucien Gay, "Deux enquêtes sur les obligations des mainmortables dans la Franche-Comté méridionale," *Mémoires de la société pour l'histoire du droit et des institutions des anciens pays bourguignons, comtois et romands*, 1961, 75–106.

160. Goldsmith, *Lordship in France, 500–1500*, 139–52, 223–34, 312–23.

161. Anne-Marie Patault, *Hommes et femmes de corps à la fin du Moyen Age*. Nancy: Annales de l'Est, 1978, 129. Thierry Bressan, "La mainmorte dans la France du XVIIIe siècle. Le cas des provinces du Centre," *Histoire et sociétés rurales*, 6, 1996, 54.

162. Jeanne Laurent, *Un monde rural en Bretagne au XVe siècle. La quévaise*. Paris: S.E.V.P.E.N., 1972.

163. Françoise Bériac, "Seigneurs et tenanciers des alentours de Verteuil vers 1490–1500," in *Soulac et les pays médocains. Actes du 41e Congrès de la fédération historique du Sud-Ouest, 1988*. Bordeaux: Fédération historique du Sud-Ouest, 1989, 253–65. Gérard D. Guyon, "L'abbaye bénédictine Sainte-Croix de Bordeaux et la crise du domaine seigneurial aux XVe et XVIe siècles," *Revue Mabillon*, 70, 1998, 177–78.

164. Bressan, "La mainmorte dans la France," 51–76.

165. Belotte, *La région de Bar-sur-Seine*, 252–53, 262, 350.

166. J.-J. Clère, "Servitude et liberté dans le bailliage de Chaumont-en-Bassigny (XVIe–XVIIIe siècles)," *Mémoires de la société pour l'histoire du droit et des institutions des anciens pays bourguignons, comtois et romands*, 1983, 239–69.

167. M. Alexis, "Etude sur la situation économique et sociale de la commune de Givry-en-Argonne aux XVIIe et XVIIIe siècles," *Actes du 78e Congrès national des sociétés savantes*, 1953, 127–29.

168. Jean Imbert, "Quelques aspects juridiques de la mainmorte seigneuriale en Lorraine (XVIe–XVIIIe siècles)," *Mémoires de la société pour l'histoire du droit et des institutions des anciens pays bourguignons, comtois et romands*, 13, 1950–1951,

177 210
169.   Imbert, "Quelques aspects juridiques," 102.
170.   Gallet, "Les transformations de la seigneurie," 73.
171.   Goldsmith, *Lordship in France, 500–1500*, 342–44.
172.   Bart, *La liberté ou la terre*, 11, 33–62, 79, 119–26, 161–68, 175–212.
173.   Bart, *La liberté ou la terre*, 185–205. Varine, *Villages de la vallée de l'Ouche*, 33–34, 121–36.
174.   Jean-Marie Augustin, "La mainmorte dans la terre de Mouthe de la fin du XVIe siècle à la Révolution," *Mémoires de la société d'émulation du Doubs*, 23, 1981, 45–91.
175.   P. Bavoux, "Les particularités de la mainmorte dans la terre de Luxeuil," *Mémoires de la société pour l'histoire du droit et des institutions des anciens pays bourguignons, comtois et romands*, 13, 1950–1951, 61–89.
176.   J. Brelot, "La mainmorte dans la région de Dole," *Mémoires de la société pour l'histoire du droit et des institutions des anciens pays bourguignons, comtois et romands*, 1950–1951, 91–108.
177.   Suzanne Daveau, *Les régions frontalières de la montagne jurassienne. Etude de géographie humaine*. Université de Lyon: Institut d'Etudes rhodaniennes, 1959, 43–55.
178.   Thierry Bressan, "L'idée d'affranchissement général dans la principauté de Monbéliard (seconde moitié du XVIIIe siècle)," *Mémoires de la société pour l'histoire du droit et des institutions des anciens pays bourguignons, comtois et romands*, 54, 1997, 129–30.
179.   Brelot, "La mainmorte," 95–99.
180.   H. Mercier, "Etude sur la mainmorte dans le pays de Montbéliard," *Mémoires de la société pour l'histoire du droit et des institutions des anciens pays bourguignons, comtois et romands*, 1950–1951, 109–24.
181.   Goldsmith, *Lordship in France, 500–1500*, 319–20.
182.   Baron, "La vie rurale dans la région de Varzy, 47. Louis Gueneau, *L'organisation du travail à Nevers aux XVIIe et XVIIIe siècles*, 1660–1790. Paris: Hachette, 1919, 590.
183.   Guy Thuillier, "Les communautés des laboureurs," in Guy Thuillier, *Aspects de l'économie nivernaise au XIXe siècle*. Paris: Armand Colin, 1966, 35–36.
184.   Shaffer, *Family and Farm*, 23–49.
185.   Germain, "Du servage au libertés," 357–79. René Germain, *Les campagnes bourbonnaises à la fin du Moyen Age (1370–1530)*. Clermont-Ferrand: Institut d'Etudes du Massif Central, 1987, 245–84.
186.   Raquel Homet, "Remarques sur le servage en Bourbonnais au XVe siècle," *Journal of Medieval History*, 10, 1984, 195–207.
187.   Christiane Parouty, "Le fief de Lussat à la fin de l'ancien régime," *Mémoires de la société des sciences naturelles et archéologiques de la Creuse*, 47, 1999, 87–91.

188. Thierry Bressan, "Servage et lumières: le rejet du droit de suite par le parlement de Paris (1760–1765)," *Revue historique*, 296, 368. Bart, *La liberté ou la terre*, 161–68.

189. Goldsmith, *Lordship in France, 500–1500*, 216–19, 303–08.

190. Marc Bloch, *Les caractères originaux de l'histoire rurale française*. Paris: Armand Colin, 1988 (orig. 1931), 162–80.

191. Béatrice F. Hyslop, *L'apanage de Philippe-Egalité, duc d'Orléans (1785–1791)*. Paris: Société des Etudes robespierristes, 1965, 127–58.

192. Bottin, *Seigneurs et paysans*, 74. Bébéar, "Le temporel de l'abbaye de Montivilliers," 99.

193. Madeleine Foisil, *Le sire de Gouberville. Un gentilhomme normand au XVIe siècle*. Paris: Aubier-Montagne, 1981.

194. Brigitte Maillard, *Les campagnes de Touraine au XVIIIe siècle. Structures agraires et économie rurale*. Rennes: Presses universitaires de Rennes, 1998, 111.

195. Forster, *The Nobility of Toulouse*, 37, 47–65.

196. Colombet, *Les parlementaires bourguignons*, 117.

197. Aubin, *La seigneurie en Bordelais*, 76–77, 246.

198. Gallet, "Les transformations de la seigneurie," 77. Emile Mireaux, *Une province française au temps du Grand Roi. La Brie*. Paris: Hachette, 1958, 79. Varine, *Villages de la vallée de l'Ouche*, 145–56.

199. Moriceau, *Les fermiers de l'Île-de-France*, 79–129, 225–66, 478–503, 613–615, 773–83.

200. Jacquart, *La crise rurale en Ile-de-France*, 430–44.

201. Michel Vovelle, "Sade, seigneur de village," in Michel Vovelle, *De la cave au grenier*. Québec: Serge Fleury, 1980, 197–98.

202. Gallet, "Les transformations de la seigneurie," 78. Jacques Péret, "Bourgeoisie rurale et seigneurs au XVIIIe siècle: les fermiers généraux du duché de la Meilleraye," *Bulletin de la société des antiquaires de l'Ouest*, sér. 4, 12, 1974, 367–70.

203. Roger Duchêne, "Madame de Sévigné et la gestion de ses biens bourguignons," *Annales de Bourgogne*, 1965, 19–50 & 113–32.

204. Pierre Schilte, "L'agonie d'un domaine seigneurial. Correspondance de Piette Gruson, régisseur du château de la Varenne de 1772 à 1794," *La province du Maine*, 91, 1989, 161–83.

205. Jonathan Dewald, *The Formation of a Provincial Nobility. The Magistrates of the Parlement of Rouen, 1499–1610*. Princeton: Princeton University Press, 1980, 305–07.

206. Nathalie Hinault, "Paysans et seigneurs du marquisat de Lonrai aux XVIIe et XVIIIe siècles," *Bulletin de la société historique et archéologique de l'Orne*, 115, 1996, 163–70.

207. André Paris, "Une justice seigneuriale témoin et acteur dans la lutte pour l'individual-

Isaac agraire. Le bailliage et comté de Pontchartrain (Yvelines) dans la première moitié du XVIIIe siècle," *Actes du 100e Congrès national des sociétés savantes. Section d'histoire moderne et contemporaine. 1975.* Paris: Bibliothèque nationale, 1977, 397–99. Serge Dontenwill, "Un type social dans les campagnes brionnaises au XVIIe siècle: le procureur fiscal, fermier de seigneurie et crédirentier," *Bulletin du centre d'histoire économique et sociale de la région lyonnaise*, 1974, n. 4, 1–41.

208.   Thierry Claerr, "La gestion du comté de Dammartin-en-Goël à la fin du XVe siècle d'après l'étude du compte de 1495–1496," *Paris et Ile-de-France. Mémoires*, 50, 1999, 149–200. Lemarchand, *La fin du féodalisme*, 42–44. Guy Lemarchand, "Le temporel et les revenus de l'abbaye de Fécamp pendant le XVIIe et XVIIIe siècle," *Annales de Normandie*, 15, 1965, 525–49.

209.   Didier Varlet, "Les revenus de la seigneurie de Bitche à la veille de la guerre de Trente Ans (1621–1632)," *Annales de l'Est*, 40, 1988, 285.

210.   Daniel Roche, "Aperçus sur la fortune et les revenus des princes de Condé à l'aube du XVIIIe siècle," *Revue d'histoire moderne et contemporaine*, 14, 1967, 217–43. Sandrine Bula, "L'apanage du comte d'Artois (1773–1790)," *Positions des thèses. Ecole des Chartes*, 1989, 55–63 and the full text: *L'apanage du comte d'Artois (1773–1790)*. Paris: Ecole des Chartes, 1993. Jean Duma, *Les Bourbon-Penthièvre (1678–1793). Une nébuleuse aristocratique au XVIIIe siècle*. Paris: Publications de la Sorbonne, 1995, 92, 345–400. François-Charles Mougel, "La fortune des princes de Bourbon-Conti. Revenus et gestion, 1655–1791," *Revue d'histoire moderne et contemporaine*, 18, 1971, 30–49.

211.   Vincent Maroteaux, "Propriété et seigneurie dans l'Ouest parisien de la fin du Moyen Age au début du XIXe siècle: l'exemple du domaine de Versailles," *Positions des thèses. Ecole des Chartes*, 1984, 108.

212.   Lucille Bourrachot, "L'administration des biens d'une baronnie quercynoise à la fin du XVIIIe siècle: Castelnau-Bretenoux," *Bulletin de la société des études littéraires, scientifiques et artistiques du Lot*, 74, 1953, 147–53.

213.   Robert Forster, *The House of Saulx-Tavanes. Versailles and Burgundy, 1700–1830*. Baltimore: Johns Hopkins, 1971, 61–62, 206.

214.   Romain Baron, "La bourgeoisie de Varzy au XVIIe siècle," *Annales de Bourgogne*, 36, 1964, 161–208.

215.   Raymond Proust, "Petits fermiers de seigneurie au XVIIIe siècle," *Bulletin de la société historique et scientifique des Deux-Sèvres*, 3, 1970, 421–32.

216.   Benoît Garnot, *La justice en France de l'an mil à 1914*. Paris: Nathan, 1993.

217.   Goldsmith, *Lordship in France, 500–1500*, 308–12.

218.   Nicolas Delasselle, "Une justice seigneuriale à Coulanges-la-Vineuse et au Val-de-Mercy au XVIIIe siècle," *Bulletin de la société des sciences historiques et naturelles de l'Yonne*, 128, 142–43. Gallet, "Les transformations de la seigneurie," 69.

219. Jean-Pierre Jessenne, *Pouvoir au village et Révolution. Artois, 1760–1848*. Lille. Presses universitaires de Lille, 1987, 32–45. Zink, *Clochers et troupeaux*, 414. Guy Cabourdin, "Les relations des communautés villagoises de Lorraine avec les seigneurs (XVIe–XVIIIe siècles)," in *Les communautés villagoises en Europe occidentale du Moyen Age aux Temps modernes*. Auch: Centre culturel de l'Abbaye de Flaran, 1984, 259–61. Jean Gallet, *Le bon plaisir du baron de Fénétrange*. Nancy: Presses universitaires de Nancy, 1990, 143–45. Abel Mathieu, *La seigneurie de Pont-les-Remirement (St-Amé, Dommartin, St-Etienne) sous l'ancien régime*. Epinal: Editions du Sapin d'Or, 1979, 45–62. Jean-Michel Boehler, *Une société rurale en milieu rhénan: la paysannerie de la plaine d'Alsace (1648–1789)*. Strasbourg: Presses universitaires de Strasbourg, 1995, 1260, 1285–96, 1472. Georges Livet, *L'intendance d'Alsace de la guerre de Trente Ans à la mort de Louis XIV, 1634–1715*. 2e éd. Strasbourg: Presses universitaires de Strasbourg, 1991, 728.

220. Delasselle, "Une justice seigneuriale," 142. Huppé, *Le gisant de la féodalité*, 25.

221. Delasselle, "Une justice seigneuriale" 152.

222. Delasselle, "Une justice seigneuriale," 152–53.

223. L. Despois, *Histoire de l'autorité royale dans le comté de Nivernais*. Paris: Giard et Brière, 1912, 426.

224. Iain A. Cameron, *Crime and Repression in the Auvergne and in Guyenne 1720–1790*. Cambridge: Cambridge University Press, 1981.

225. Clère, *Les paysans de la Haute-Marne*, 105.

226. Pierre Villard, *Les justices seigneuriales dans la Marche*. Paris: Pichon et Durand-Auzias, 1969 204–11. Marc Pitre & Daniel Hickey, "Rendre justice dans une communauté rurale de l'ancien régime: Grignan et l'affaire Bertholon en 1702," *Cahiers d'histoire*, 44, 1999, 375–97.

227. Delasselle, "Une justice seigneuriale," 157–59. Christelle Clément, "Le règlement des différends dans le Châtillonnais: les audiences civiles des justices seigneuriales du bailliage de la Montagne (18e siècle)," *Annales de Bourgogne*, 70, 1998, 188.

228. Delasselle, "Une justice seigneuriale," 141.

229. Delasselle, "Une justice seigneuriale," 160.

230. Clément, "Le règlement des différends," 180–81.

231. Bernard Bonnin, "Le Dauphiné à la veille de la Révolution: formes de l'économie et structures sociales," in Vital Chomel, éd. *Les débuts de la Révolution française en Dauphiné, 1788–1791*. Grenoble: Presses universitaires de Grenoble, 1988, 14–15.

232. Antoine, *Fiefs et villages*, 259–61. Gallet, *La seigneurie bretonne*, 494–96, 523–24, 539–41.

233. André Giffard, *Les justices seigneuriales en Bretagne aux XVIIe et XVIIIe siècles*. Paris: Arthur Rousseau, 1903, 107–58.

234. Villard, *Les justices seigneuriales*, 81–92. Gallet, *La seigneurie bretonne*, 431.

235 Pierre Deyon, "Quelques remarques sur l'évolution du régime seigneurial en Picardie, XVIe–XVIIIe siècles," *Revue d'histoire moderne et contemporaine*, 8, 1961, 275.

236. Dewald, *Pont-St-Pierre*, 64.

237. Bastier, *La féodalité au siècle des Lumières*, 104. Zink, *Clochers et troupeaux*, 163.

238. Jack Thomas, "L'activité toulousaine de la justice seigneuriale du canal de communication des Deux-Mers en Languedoc," *Le canal du Midi et les voies navigables dans le Midi de la France*. Castelnaudary: Société d'études scientifiques de l'Aude, 1998, 21–29.

239. Sylvain Soleil, "Le mantien des justices seigneuriales à la fin de l'Ancien Régime: faillite des institutions royales ou récuperation? L'exemple angevin," *Revue historique de droit français et étranger*, 74, 1996, 95 and note 50.

240. Despois, *Histoire de l'autorité royale*, 340–67, 372.

241. Duma, *Les Bourbon-Penthièvre*, 82.

242. Cubells *La Provence des Lumières*, 142. Jean Meyer, *La noblesse bretonne au XVIIIe siècle*. Paris: Imprimerie nationale, 1966, 794–801. Aubin, *La seigneurie en Bordelais*, 176.

243. Michel Cassan, "Officiers "moyen", officiers seigneuriaux. Quelques perspectives de recherche," *Cahiers du centre de recherches historiques*, 27, 71–83. Huppé, *Le gisant de la féodalité*, 37.

244. For a recent study that repeats the standard criticisms that were common in the older literature see: Didier Catarina, "Justices et seigneuries en Languedoc à l'époque moderne," *La terre et les pouvoirs en Languedoc et en Roussillon du Moyen Age à nos jours*. Montpellier: Fédération historique du Languedoc méditerranéen et du Roussillon, 1992, 167–72.

245. Cassan, "Officers "moyen", officiers seigneuriaux," 80.

246. Mitchio Hamada, "Une seigneurie et sa justice en Beaujolais aux XVIIe et XVIIIe siècles: Saint-Leger," *Bulletin du centre d'histoire économique et sociale de la région lyonnaise*, 1985, n. 2, 25–27.

247. Soleil, "Le mantien des justices seigneuriales," 89–91.

248. Jean Merley, *La Haute-Loire de la fin de l'ancien régime aux débuts de la Troisième République*. Le Puy: Cahiers de la Haute-Loire, 1974, 74.

249. Francine Rolley, "Une frontière introuvable. Officiers royaux et officiers seigneuriaux dans deux bailliages bourguignons au XVIIe siècle," *Cahiers du centre de recherches historiques*, n. 27, 2001, 87–105.

250. Huppé, *Le gisant de la féodalité*, 24–25.

251. Cassan, "Officiers "moyen", officiers seigneuriaux," 79–80. Clément, "Le règlement des différends," 189. Jean-François Noël, "Une justice seigneuriale en Haute-Bretagne à la fin de l'ancien régime: la châtellenie de la Motte-de-Gennes," *Annales de Bretagne et des pays de l'Ouest*, 83, 1976, 153. Villard, *Les justices seigneuriales*,

223–34.

252. Zink, *Clochers et troupeaux*, 166. Villard, *Les justices seigneuriales*, 234. Huppé, *Le gisant de la féodalité*, 43.

253. Noël, "Une justice seigneuriale," 153.

254. Delasselle, "Une justice seigneuriale," 144.

255. J. Bindet, "Les dernières années de la baronnie de Marcey," *Revue de l'Avranchin et du pays de Granville*, 44, 1967, 225–40. Antoine, *Fiefs et villages*, 249–54.

256. Pierre Lemercier, *Les justices seigneuriales de la région parisienne de 1580 à 1789*. Paris: Domat-Montchrestien, 1933, 141. Villard, *Les justices seigneuriales*, 214–23. Huppé, *Le gisant de la féodalité*, 44–45.

257. Delasselle, "Une justice seigneuriale," 150.

258. Noël, "Une justice seigneuriale," 157. Delasselle, "Une justice seigneuriale," 163–68.

259. Serge Bianchi, "Les communautés villageoises françaises au siècle des Lumières," in Serge Bianchi et al., *La terre et les paysans en France et en Grande-Bretagne du début du XVIIe siècle à la fin du XVIIIe siècle*. Paris: Armand Colin, 1999, 191–212. Bordes, "Les communautés villageoises," 143–64.

260. Bianchi, "Les communautés villageoises," 192. Lemarchand, *La fin du féodalisme*, 55. Antoine Follain, "Les communautés rurales en Normandie sous l'ancien régime. Identité communautaire, institutions du gouvernement local et solidarités," *Revue d'histoire moderne et contemporaine*, 45, 1998, 691–721.

261. Bernard Quilliet, "Les fiefs parisiens et leurs seigneurs laïcs au XVIIIème siècle," *Histoire, économie et société*, 1, 1982, 565.

262. Hilton L. Root, "En Bourgogne: l'état et la communauté rurale, 1661–1789," *Annales E.S.C.*, 37, 1982, 288–302.

263. Jean-Pierre Gutton, *Villages du Lyonnais sous la monarchie (XVIe–XVIIIe siècles)*. Lyon: Presses universitaires de Lyon, 1978, 87–91. Zink, *Clochers et troupeaux*, 218.

264. Janyne Gillot-Voisin, "La communauté des habitants de Givry au XVIIIe siècle," *Cahiers de l'association interuniversitaire de l'Est*, 11, 1966, 21–49. Françoise Vignier, "La justice de Magny-sur-Tille (XVe–XVIIIe siècles)," *Mémoires de la société pour l'histoire du droit et des institutions des anciens pays bourguignons, comtois et romands*, 1962, 278–88. Louis Ligeron, "L'assolement dans la vallée moyenne de la Saône," *Annales de Bourgogne*, 44, 1972, 5–47. Lemarchand, *La fin du féodalisme*, 21–23, 55–58. Antoine, *Fiefs et villages*, 259–73. Noël, "Une justice seigneuriale," 138.

265. Huppé, *Le gisant de la féodalité*, 30–31.

266. Zink, *Clochers et troupeaux*, 204.

267. Zink, *Clochers et troupeaux*, 205–06.

268. Huppé, *Le gisant de la féodalité*, 18–19, 30–31.

269. Delasselle, "Une justice seigneuriale, 148–49, 161. Clère, *Les paysans de la Haute-*

Maria, 107.

Chapter Two: Regional Patterns of Lordship, I

1.   Marion, *Dictionnaire des institutions de la France*, 95–96.
2.   Dominique Dinet, "Une institution méconnue: la commende," *Etat et société en France aux XVIIe et XVIIIe siècles. Mélanges offerts à Yves Durand.* Paris: Presses de l'Université de Paris-Sorbonne, 2000, 195–208. Dominique Dinet, "Les grands domaines des réguliers en France (1560–1790): une relative stabilité?," *Revue Mabillon*, 71, 1999, 257–69.
3.   Michaud, *L'église et l'argent*, 542. Marion, *La dîme ecclésiastique*, 117.
4.   Lemarchand, "Le temporel et les revenus de l'abbaye de Fécamp," 542.
5.   Marion, *La dîme ecclésiastique en France*, 117.
6.   Frêche, *Toulouse et la région Midi-Pyrénées*, 530–31.
7.   Jacques Marcadé, "La dîme au XVIIIe siècle: l'exemple du diocèse de Poitiers," *Bulletin de la société des antiquaires de l'Ouest*, 11, 1997, 65.
8.   Jacques Bouveresse, "Contribution à l'étude de la dîme: la jurisprudence de Lorraine au XVIIIe siècle," *Annales de l'Est*, série 5, 33, 1981, 107.
9.   Pierre Deyon, *Contribution à l'étude des revenus fonciers en Picardie. Les fermages de l'Hôtel-Dieu d'Amiens et leurs variations de 1515 à 1789.* Lille: René Girard, 1967, 3–40. Frêche, *Toulouse et la région Midi-Pyrénées*, 536–45.
10.   Marion, *La dîme ecclésiastique*, 18–19.
11.   Marion, *La dîme ecclésiastique*, 5.
12.   Deyon, *Contribution à l'étude des revenus fonciers*, 41–42. Deyon, "Quelques remarques sur l'évolution du régime seigneurial," 271–74.
13.   Marie-Thérèse Lorcin, "Un musée imaginaire de la ruse paysanne. La fraude des décimables du XIVe au XVIIIe siècle dans la région lyonnaise," *Etudes rurales*, 51, 1973, 112–24.
14.   George Clause, "Le vigneron champenois du XVIIIe au XIXe siècle. De la pauvreté contestataire de 1789 à la Révolution de 1911," *Etudes champenoises*, 6, 1988, 19–20. Pierre L. Féral, "A la veille de la Révolution: les problèmes de la dîme, de la coussure et de la glane," *La France pre-révolutionnaire.* Paris: Editions Publisud, 1991, 27–39. Jean Rives, *Dîme et société dans l'archevêché d'Auch au XVIIIe siècle.* Paris: Commission d'histoire économique et sociale de la Révolution française. Mémoires et Documents, 32, 1976. Jean Rives, "Les refus de dîmes dans le diocèse d'Auch à la veille de la Révolution," *Actes du 96e Congrès national des sociétés savantes. Section d'histoire moderne et contemporaine*, 1971, 237–57.
15.   P. Gagnol, *La dîme ecclésiastique en France au XVIIIe siècle.* Genève: Slatkine-Megariotis Reprints, 1974 (Paris, 1911), 22–31. Marion, *La dîme ecclésiastique*, 5, 94, 105.

16. Marion, *La dîme ecclésiastique,* 38–40.

17. Marion, *La dîme ecclésiastique,* 54–72. Georges Lefebvre, *Les paysans du Nord pendant la Révolution française.* Paris: Armand Colin, 1972 (orig. 1924), 103–12.

18. Marcel Lachiver, *Vin, vigne et vignerons en région parisienne du XVIIe au XVIIIe siècle.* Pontoise: Société historique et archéologique de Pontoise, 1982, 222–29.

19. Goujard, *L'abolition de la "féodalité",* 44.

20. Henri Pellerin, "Herbages et labours en Pays d'Auge. Bonneville-la Louvet," *Le Pays d'Auge,* 18, 1968, 11–16.

21. Emile Appolis, *Un pays languedocien au miliu du XVIIIe siècle. Le diocèse civil de Lodève. Etude administrative et économique.* Albi: Imprimerie coopérative du Sud-Ouest, 1951, 118–25. Gagnol, *La dîme ecclésiastique,* 134–53.

22. Guy Astoul, "La contestation des dîmes en Quercy à la veille de la Révolution," *Histoire et sociétés rurales,* 1997, 147–61. Louis Ligeron, "Notes sur la culture du maïs dans la vallée moyenne de la Saône," *Annales de Bourgogne,* 40, 1968, 197–204.

23. Marc Glotz, "La culture de la pomme de terre dans le Sundgau au XVIIIe siècle," *Annuaire de la société d'histoire sundgauvienne,* 1984, 81–94.

24. Louis Ligeron, "Culture et maraîchage à Vielverge et Soissons (XVIe–XVIIIe siècles)," *Annales de Bourgogne,* 42, 1970, 153–68.

25. Louis Ligeron, "La dîme dans les clos," *Annales de Bourgogne,* 49, 1977, 5–23.

26. Dinet, "Les grands domaines des réguliers en France," 259, 269. Lefebvre, "Répartition de la propriété," 298–306. Philippe Gillossou, "Structures agraires à Wissous au XVIIIe siècle (1709–1789)," *Bulletin de la société historique et archéologique de Corbeil, d'Etampes et du Hurepoix,* 75, 1969, 19. Hervé Revel, "Evolution des patrimoines fonciers à Tremblay-en-France, de l'ancien régime au lendemain de la Révolution," *Bulletin de la société d'études historiques de Tremblay,* 1990, 2–19. Clère, *Les paysans de la Haute-Marne,* 26–29. Maillard, *Les campagnes de Touraine,* 152–53.

27. Aubin, *La seigneurie en Bordelais,* 1989, 72–74. Guyon, "L'abbaye bénédictine Sainte-Croix," 163–79.

28. Philippe Loupès, *Chapitres et chanoines de Guyenne aux XVIIe et XVIIIe siècles.* Paris: Ecole des Hautes Etudes en Sciences Sociales, 1985, 91–118. Philippe Loupès, "Le chapitre de Saint-Emilion sous l'ancien régime," *Saint-Emilion Libourne. Actes du XXIXe Congrès d'études régionales de la Fédération historique du Sud-Ouest,* 1979, 73–95.

29. Maurice Bordes, *D'Etigny et l'administration de l'intendance d'Auch, 1751–1767.* Auch: Frédéric Cocharux Imprimeur, 1957, 24–25.

30. Nagle, "Un aspect de la propriété seigneuriale à Paris, 578.

31. Lemarchand, *La fin du féodalisme,* 28.

32. Ivan Coulas, "Les aliénations du temporel ecclésiastique sous Charles IX et Henri III

(1563–87)," *Revue d'histoire de l'église de France*, 144, 1958, 5–56.

33.   Dinet, "Les grands domaines des réguliers," 204–65.

34.   Moriceau, *Les fermiers de l'Île-de-France*, 85.

35.   Maarten Ultee, *The Abbey of St. Germain des Prés in the Seventeenth Century*. New Haven: Yale, 1981, 65.

36.   Dinet, "Les grands domaines des réguliers," 265–66.

37.   Moriceau, *Les fermiers de l'Ile-de-France*, 85.

38.   Mailliard, *Les campagnes de Touraine*, 92.

39.   Bernard Bodinier, "Les biens des chapitres normands et la Révolution," *Chapitres et cathédrales en Normandie*. Caen: Musée de Normandie, 1997, 29–31.

40.   Dinet, "Les grands domaines des réguliers," 269.

41.   Jean Fournée, "Un aspect de la fiscalité ecclésiastique: réflexions sur les dîmes de l'abbaye de Belle-Etoile," *Les Normands et le fisc. XXIXème Congrès des sociétés historiques et archéologiques de Normandie*. Elbeuf-sur-Seine: Société de l'histoire de l'Elbeuf, 1996, 218.

42.   Pierre Goubert, "Disparités de l'ancien France rurale," *Cahiers d'histoire*, 12, 1967, 55–65.

43.   Raymonde Monnier, "Antony. Une commune de la banlieu parisienne à la veille de la Révolution," *Annales historique de la Révolution française*, 52, 1980, 262–79.

44.   Georges Viard, "Les revenus de l'abbaye de Morimond vers 1760," *Les cahiers haut-marnais*, 1994, 145–48.

45.   Boehler, *Une société rurale en milieu rhénan*, 532–33.

46.   Dinet, "Une institution méconnue: la commende," 195–208.

47.   Lemarchand, "Le temporel et les revenus de l'abbaye de Fécamp," 545.

48.   Lemarchand, "Le temporel et les revenus de l'abbaye de Fécamp," 535.

49.   Guy Lemarchand, "Les monastères de Haute-Normandie au XVIIIe siècle," *Annales historiques de la Révolution française,* 37, 1965, 1–28.

50.   Jean-Marie Le Gall, "Deux communautés bénédictines parisiennes pendant les guerres de religion. Saint-Martin-des-Champs et Saint-Germain-des-Prés," *Paris et Ile-de-France. Mémoires*, 50, 1999, 229–31.

51.   Dinet, "Les grands domaines des réguliers," 261.

52.   Michel Fontenay, "Le revenu des chevaliers de Malte en France d'après les "estimes" de 1533, 1583 et 1776," *La France d'ancien régime. Etudes réunies en l'honneur de Pierre Goubert*. Toulouse: Privat, 1984, I, 262.

53.   Gérard Gangneux, "Une commanderie de l'Ordre de Malte aux XVIIe et XVIIIe siècles: Poët-Laval en Dauphiné," *Cahiers d'histoire*, 9, 1964, 359–61.

54.   Gérard Gangneux, "Une commanderie languedocienne au XVIIIe siècle: Saint-Jean de Pézenas," *Actes du 86e Congrès national des sociétés savantes. Montpellier, 1961. Section d'histoire moderne et contemporaine*. Paris: Imprimerie nationale, 1962,

281–96.

55. Dinet, "Les grands domaines des réguliers," 261.

56. Bébéar, "Le temporel de l'abbaye de Montivilliers," 55–65, 107. Bottin, *Seigneurs et paysans*, 62–67.

57. Jacques Marcadé, "Des petits notables ruraux. les fermiers généraux de l'abbaye de Sainte-Croix," *Sociétés et idéologies des temps modernes. Hommage à Arlette Jouanna*. Montpellier: Université de Montpellier III, 1996, vol. I, 197–210. Jacques Marcadé, "Un grand domaine au XVIIIe siècle: les seigneuries de Vasles, Vasseroux et Saint-Philibert," *Bulletin de la société des antiquaires de l'Ouest*, sér. 4, 18, 1985, 67–78.

58. Marie-Claude Dinet-Lecomte, "Quelques réflexions sur les finances hospitalières en France au XVIIIe siècle," *Etat et société en France aux XVIIe et XVIIIe siècles. Mélanges offerts à Yves Durand*. Paris: Presses de l'Université de Paris-Sorbonne, 2000, 209.

59. Dinet-Lecomte, "Quelques réflexions sur les finances hospitalières," 211–12.

60. Dinet-Lecomte, "Quelques réflexions sur les finances hospitalières," 216.

61. Dinet-Lecomte, "Quelques réflexions sur les finances hospitalières," 218.

62. Georges Durand, *Le patrimoine foncier de l'Hôtel-Dieu de Lyon (1482–1791)*. Lyon: Centre d'histoire économique et sociale de la région lyonnaise 1974.

63. Durand, *Le patrimoine foncier de l'Hôtel-Dieu*, 27,75, 235–39, 387–88.

64. Deyon, *Contribution à l'étude des revenus fonciers*, 6, 65.

65. Dinet, "Une institution méconnue: la commende," 202–04.

66. Dinet, "Les grands domaines des réguliers," 261.

67. Gaston zeller, *Les institutions de la France au XVIe siècle*. Paris: Presses universitaires de France, 1948, 83–92.

68. Jean-François Lassalmonie, "La politique fiscale de Louis XI (1461–1483)," in *L'argent au Moyen Age*. Congrès de la société des historiens médiévalistes de l'enseignement publique supérieur. Paris: Publications de la Sorbonne, 1998, 225–65.

69. Pierre Gresser, "Les conséquences financières pour le domaine comtal de la conquête du comté de Bourgogne par Louis XI," in Jean Kerhervé, éd., *Finances, pouvoirs et mémoire: mélanges offerts à Jean Favier*. Paris: Fayard, 1999, 397–411.

70. Zeller, *Les institutions de la France*, 83–92.

71. B. Combes de Patris, "Un conflit féodal à Salles-Comtaux au XVIIIe siècle," *Revue de Rouergue*, 20, 1966, 5–24. Oddly enough, this obscure article contains a lucid account of the legal procedures for the alienation of crown lands.

72. Zeller, *Les institutions de la France*, 83.

73. Mousnier, *Les institutions de la France*, 425–29.

74. Duma, *Les Bourbon-Penthièvre*, 48.

75. Hyslop, *L'apanage de Philippe-Egalité*, 50-52.

76. Sandrine Bula, "L'apanage du comte d'Artois (1773–1790)," *Positions des thèses. Ecole des Chartes*, 1989, 56.

77. Françoise de Noirfontaine, "Les privilèges de la vicomté de Turenne," in *Etat et société en France aux XVIIe et XVIIIe siècles. Mélanges offerts à Yves Durand.* Presses de l'université de Paris-Sorbonne, 2000, 427.

78. Maroteaux, "Propriété et seigneurie dans l'ouest parisien," 103–13.

79. M. Greengrass, "Property and Politics in Sixteenth-Century France: the Landed Estate of Constable Anne de Montmorency," *French History*, 2, 1988, 371–98.

80. Roche, "Aperçus sur la fortune," 226–29.

81. Christian Renou, "Un compte de la ferme de Chilly au XVIIIe siècle," in Michel Balard, éd., *Paris et ses campagnes sous l'ancien régime. Mélanges offerts à Jean Jacquart.* Paris: Publications de la Sorbonne, 1994, 37.

82. Levanthal, *Ducs et pairs*, 163–166, 1105.

83. Levanthal, *Ducs et pairs*, 194–197.

84. Levanthal, *Ducs et pairs*, 1105–07.

85. Jacques Péret, *Seigneurs et seigneuries en Gâtine poitevine. Le duché de La Meilleraye, XVIIe–XVIIIe siècles.* Poitiers: Société des Antiquaires de l'Ouest, 1976.

86. Péret, *Seigneurs et seigneuries*, 5–25.

87. Péret, *Seigneurs et seigneuries*, 25–47.

88. Péret, *Seigneurs et seigneuries*, 49–156.

89. Duma, *Les Bourbon-Penthièvre*, 24–105, 143–66, 365, 569–70.

90. Duma, "Les Bourbon-Penthièvre à Rambouillet," 301.

91. Duma, *Les Bourbon-Penthièvre*, 571.

92. Duma, " Les Bourbon-Penthièvre," 304.

93. Duma, "Les Bourbon-Penthièvre," 292.

94. Duma, *Les Bourbon-Penthièvre*, 365.

95. Hyslop, *L'apanage de Philippe-Egalité*, 52, 77–80.

96. Roche, "Aperçus sur la fortune et les revenus des princes de Condé," 217–43. Mougel, "La fortune des princes de Bourbon-Conty," 30–49.

97. Bula, "L'apanage du comte d'Artois," 55–63.

98. Michel Mollat, éd., *Histoire de l'Île-de-France et de Paris.* Toulouse: Privat, 1971, 155–69.

99. Mollat, *Histoire de l'Île-de-France*, 160–350.

100. Mollat, *Histoire de l'Île-de-France*, 279–80.

101. Michel Fontenay, "Paysans et marchands ruraux de la vallée de l'Essonnes dans la seconde moitié du XVIIe siècle," *Paris et Ile-de-France. Mémoires*, 9, 1957–1958, 177.

102. Jérôme Blachon, "Des Cisterciens aux seigneurs laïques: histoire de la ferme d'Ithe (XIIe–XVIIIe siècles)," *Paris et Ile-de-France. Mémoires*, 49, 1998, 133–217.

103. There is a massive literature on the construction of the commercial farms in the Ile de France, the tenant farmers, the farming practices, and the like. Along the way, the authors also shed light on lordship, but lordship is rarely their principal concern. Also there is a massive imbalance in the geographical distribution of studies. The most valuable farmlands north of Paris were precisely those areas where the seigneurial records were destroyed during the Revolution, whereas the records for the less valuable land south of Paris survived. See these often-cited works: Brunet, *Structure agraire et économie rurale*. Jacquart, *La crise rurale en Ile-de-France*. Moriceau, *Les fermiers de l'Île-de-France*. Postel-Vinay, *La rente foncière dans le capitalisme agraire*.

104. Jacques Dupâquier, "Paysage et société: le Vexin français au XVIIIe siècle," *Mémoires de la société historique et archéologique de Pontoise et du Vexin*, 67, 1977, 56–58.

105. Jean-Pierre Blazy, "Les campagnes du pays de France au début du XVIIIe siècle d'après l'enquête de 1717," *Bulletin de la société d'histoire et d'archéologie de Gonesse et du pays de France*, 10, 1989, 35–45.

106. Dupâquier, "Paysage et société," 52.

107. Pierre Cousteix, "Fermes seigneuriales à Soisy-sur-Ecole au XVIIIe siècle," *Bulletin de la société historique et archéologique de Corbeil, d'Étampes et du Hurepoix*, 89, 1983, 73.

108. Mollat, *Histoire de l'Île-de-France*, 7–22.

109. Moriceau, *Les fermiers de l'Île-de-France*, 121.

110. Revel, "Evolution des patrimoines fonciers," 2–19.

111. Claerr, "La gestion du comté de Dammartin-en-Goële," 155–76.

112. François Lecoq, "Le fief de La Bussière. Les baux à ferme," *Bulletin d'histoire locale de Souppes-sur-Loing*, 1988, 30–45.

113. Monnier, "Antony. Une commune de la banlieu parisienne," 265–66.

114. Valérie Noël, "Le terroir de Sucy au XVe siècle: étude du censier de 1412," *Paris et Ile-de-France. Mémoires*, 50 1999, 53–54, 64–65, 133.

115. Ninomiya, "Un cadre de vie rurale," 58–60.

116. Lachiver, *Vin, vigne et vignerons*, 224–30.

117. Maroteaux, "Propriété et seigneurie," 109.

118. Jacquart, *La crise rurale en Ile-de-France*, 77.

119. Nagle, "Un aspect de la propriété seigneuriale à Paris, " 570–81.

120. Nagle, "Un aspect de la propriété seigneuriale," 578–79.

121. Nagle, "Un aspect de la propriété seigneuriale," 574.

122. Jacquart, *La crise rurale en Ile-de-France*, 436.

123. Hervé Brussier, "Le mouvement des mutations foncières d'après le fonds des ensaisinements du chapitre cathédral de Notre-Dame de Paris, 1518–1609," *Paris et*

Ile-de-France. Mémoires, 37, 1986, 153–84.

124.   Paris, "Une justice seigneuriale, 398–402.

125.   Claerr "La gestion du comté de Dammartin-en-Goële," 149–200. Duma, *Les Bourbon-Penthièvre*, 345–400. Bula, "L'apanage du comte d'Artois," 58–63.

126.   Louis Trénard, éd. *Histoire des Pays-Bas français*. Toulouse: Privat, 1972. 111–15, 200–07, 235–43, 304–20.

127.   René Robinet, "Sainghin-en-Mélantois, de Charles-Quint à la Révolution française, " *Bulletin de la commission historique du département du Nord*, 42, 1980–84, 11–36.

128.   S. Gruzinski, "Changement et continuité dans deux seigneuries des Pays-Bas méridionaux: l'abbaye d'Anchin et la baronnie de Cysoing, fin du XVe-début du XVIIe siècle," *Revue du Nord*, 55, 1973, 305–15. Christiane Marmande, "La propriété et l'exploitation de la terre en Cambrésis à la veille de la Révolution," *Jadis en Cambrésis*, 43, 1989, 6–12. Georges Lefebvre, *Les paysans du Nord pendant la Révolution française*. Paris: Armand Colin, 1972 (orig. 1924), 11–12.

129.   Alain Derville, *Les villes de Flandre et d'Artois (900–1500)*. Villeneuve d'Ascq: Presses universitaires du Septentrion, 2002.

130.   Alain Derville, "Les communautés villageoises de la Flandre wallonne d'après l'enquête de 1449," *Les communautés villageoises en Europe occidentale du Moyen Age aux temps modernes*. Auch: Centre culturel de l'abbaye de Flaran, 1984, 221–27.

131.   Jean-Pierre Jessenne, "Le pouvoir des fermiers dans les villages d'Artois (1770–1848)," *Annales E.S.C.*, 38, 1983, 702–34. Jessenne, *Pouvoir au village*, 17–47.

132.   Trénard, *Histoire des Pays-bas français,*237. Hugues Neveux, *Vie et déclin d'une structure économique. Les grains du Cambrésis, fin du XIVe-début du XVIIe siècle*. Paris: Mouton, 1980, 7–20.

133.   Dominique Rosselle, "Terre et économie. La mise en valeur de la terre dans la France du Nord (XVIe-XVIIIe siècle). Réflexion à partir d'un modèle artésien," *La terre à l'époque moderne*. Paris: Association des historiens modernistes des universités, 1983, 55–80.

134.   Serge Gruzinski, "Recherches sur le monde rural dans les Pays-bas méridionaux (1480–1630)," *Ecole nationale des chartes. Positions des thèses*, 1973, 116. François Wartelle, "Les communautés rurales du Pas-de-Calais et le système féodal en 1789–1790," *Cahiers d'histoire de l'institut de recherches marxistes*, 32, 1988, 100–21. Lefebvre, *Les paysans du Nord*, 140, 163.

135.   Hermann Van Der Wee & Eddy Van Cauwenberghe, "Histoire agraire et finances publiques en Flandre du XIVe au XVIIe siècle," *Annales E.S.C.*, 28, 1973, 1051–65.

136.   Gérard Sivery, *Structures agraires et vie rurale dans le Hainaut à la fin du Moyen Age*. Lille: Publications de l'Université de Lille, 1977–80, II, 456–71, 567–71.

137.   Trénard, *Histoire des Pays-bas français*, 308

138.   Lefebvre, *Les paysans du Nord*, 5.

139. Lefebvre, *Les paysans du Nord*, 104–12.

Chapter Three. Regional Patterns of Lordship, II

1.   Belotte, *La région de Bar-sur-Seine*, 107–12, 134–36.
2.   Belotte, *La région de Bar-sur-Seine*, 129–31. Clère, "Servitude et liberté," 258.
3.   Belotte, *La région de Bar-sur-Seine*, 124–31, 350–54.
4.   Clère "Servitude et liberté," 239–69.
5.   Belotte, *La région de Bar-sur-Seine*, 350.
6.   Belotte, *La région de Bar-sur-Seine*, 39, 136, 214–15, 252, 260–64. Clère, *Les paysans de la Haute-Marne*, 112–13.
7.   Michel Cart, "La crise économique des communautés rurales ardennaises à la fin de l'ancien régime (1770–1789)," *Revue historique ardennaise*, 25, 1990, 3–35.
8.   Belotte, *La région de Bar-sur-Seine*, 268–70. Clause, " Le vigneron champenois," 13–19.
9.   Pierre Boulanger, "La crise de l'économie et de la société champenoise dans les dernières années de l'ancien régime," *Mémoires de la société d'agriculture, commerce, sciences et arts du département de la Marne*, 100, 1985, 139–40.
10. Belotte, *La région de Bar-sur-Seine*, 98–116, 268–71. Cart, "La crise économique," 24–25. Clause, "Le vigneron champenois," 18–19. Clère, *Les paysans de la Haute-Marne*, 115–116. Marcel Maillot, "Le vignoble à Saint-Amand-sur-Fion (XVIe aux XVIIIe siècles)," *Mémoires de la société d'agriculture, commerce, sciences et arts du département de la Marne*, 95, 1980, 103–20.
11. Clère, *Les paysans de la Haute-Marne*, 123–126.
12. Clère, *Les paysans de la Haute-Marne*, 36–38.
13. Massary, "Les "usages"," 9–37.
14. Laurent Bourquin, "La noblesse de Champagne dans son espace régional vers le milieu du XVIIe siècle," *Sociétés et idéologies des temps modernes*. Montpellier: Université de Montpellier III, 1996, vol. I, 59–77. Belotte, *La région de Bar-sur-Seine*, 88–94, 175–208, 238–40, 321–32.
15. Laurent Bourquin, "Les seigneuries de la noblesse champenoise pendant les guerres de religion: crise ou prosperité?," in Michel Balard, éd., *Paris et ses campagnes sous l'ancien régime. Mélanges offerts à Jean Jacquart*. Paris: Publications de la Sorbonne, 1994, 99–108.
16. Clère, *Les paysans de la Haute-Marne*, 35.
17. Clère, *Les paysans de la Haute-Marne*, 26.
18. Belotte, *La région de Bar-sur-Seine*, 284–95.
19. Alexis, "Etude sur la situation économique et sociale," 128–29.
20. Clause, "Le vigneron champenois," 19.
21. Clère, *Les paysans de la Haute-Marne*, 117.

22 Sténhane Douillot, "La baronnie eccésiastique de Luzy au XVIIIe siècle," *Les cahiers haut-marnais*, 1993, 49–54. Viard, "Les revenus de l'abbaye de Morimond," 142 60.

23. Belotte, *La région de Bar-sur-Seine*, 253.

24. Belotte, *La région de Bar-sur-Seine*, 54–59.

25. Jean Richard, *éd.*, *Histoire de la Bourgogne*. Toulouse: Privat, 1978, 286–95.

26. Gaston Roupnel, *La ville et la campagne au XVIIe siècle. Etude sur les populations du pays dijonnais*. Paris: S.E.V.P.E.N., 1955, 167–249. Pierre Ponsot, "Le patrimoine d'un parlementaire dijonnais en Bresse sous le règne de Louis XIV," *Actes du 50e Congrès de l'association bourguignonne des sociétés savantes*, 1979, II, 217–23.

27. Colombet, *Les parlementaires bourguignons*, 65–76, 98–144, 153–87.

28. Richard, *Histoire de la Bourgogne*, 207–68.

29. Brosselin, *La forêt bourguignonne*, 95–96.

30. Roland Gadille, *Le vignoble et la côte bourguignonne. Fondements physiques et humains d'une viticulture de haute qualité*. Paris: Les Belles Lettres, 1967.

31. Laurent Champier, "Les fondements humains du vignoble mâconnais," *Annales de l'Académie de Mâcon*, 44, 1958–1959, 65–75.

32. Dontenwill, "Un type social," 11–21.

33. Forster, *The House of Saulx-Tavannes*, 56–60, 70–78, 91–155.

34. Régine Robin, *La société française en 1789: Semur-en-Auxois*. Paris: Plon, 1970, 130–33.

35. Varine, *Villages de la vallée de l'Ouche*, table 24.

36. Levantal, *Ducs et pairs*, 1105.

37. Michel Devèze, "Le bailliage de Mâcon en 1666," *Actes du 89e Congrès national des sociétés savantes. Section d'histoire moderne et contemporaine*, 1964, t. 2, v. 2, 833–59.

38. Jean Bart, *La Révolution française en Bourgogne*. Clermont-Ferrand: La Française d'Edition et d'Imprimerie, 1996, 42–44. Georges Chevrier, "Le droit d'indire d'après la coutume officielle du duché de Bourgogne (XVIe–XVIIIe siècles)," *Mémoires de la société pour l'histoire du droit et des institutions des anciens pays bourguignons, comtois et romands*, 1952, 8–34.

39. Bart, *La Révolution française en Bourgogne*, 48.

40. Bart, *La Révolution française en Bourgogne*, 49.

41. Jean Chiffre, "Granges et villages nouveaux en Bourgogne aux XVIe et XVIIe siècles. Le rôle des abbayes dans la transformation du paysage rural," *Revue géographique de l'Est*, 22, 1982, 183–97.

42. Patrice Beck, "De la grange au village: Crepey en Bourgogne (XIIe–XVIIe siècle)," in *Le Village médiéval et son environnement. Etudes offertes à Jean-Marie Pesez*. Paris: Publications de la Sorbonne, 1998, 447–59.

43. Louis Ligeron, "Les ventes de communaux après les guerres religieuses (1595–1610),"

Annales de Bourgogne, 54, 1982, 5–16.

44. Rouphel, *La ville et la campagne*, 250–79.

45. Pierre de Saint-Jacob, "Le droit de lods en Bourgogne à la fin de l'Ancien Régime," *Mémoires de la société pour l'histoire du droit et des institutions des anciens pays bourguignons, comtois et romands*, 1952, 161–62.

46. Saint-Jacob, *Les paysans de la Bourgogne*, 43–44, 90, 136.

47. Clément, "Le règlement des différends," 179–90.

48. Varine, *Villages de la vallée de l'Ouche*, 140–45. Vignier, "La justice de Magny-sur-Tille," 278–88.

49. J.-P. Moreau, *La vie rurale dans le sud-est du bassin parisien entre les vallées de l'Armaçon et de la Loire. Etude de géographie humaine.* Paris: Les Belles Lettres, 1958.

50. Bart, *La Révolution française en Bourgogne*, 44.

51. Bart, *La liberté ou la terre*, 180–85.

52. Bart, *La liberté ou la terre*, 202, 190.

53. Bart, *La liberté ou la terre*, 191–93.

54. Robin, *La société française en 1789*, 120.

55. Serge Dontenwill, *Une seigneurie sous l'ancien régime: l'Étoile en Brionnais du XVIe au XVIIIe siècle (1575–1778).* Roanne: Editions Horvath, 1973, 87–89, 132. Varine, *Villages de la vallée de l'Ouche*, 131–32.

56. René Durr, "Persistance et âpreté de l'esprit de privilège: les "échoites" de mainmorte dans la seigneurie de l'Isle-sur-Serein à la fin de l'ancien régime," *Bulletin de la société des sciences historiques et naturelles de l'Yonne*, 111, 1979, 107–26.

57. Guy Cabourdin, *Encyclopédie illustrée de la Lorraine. Histoire de la Lorraine. Les temps modernes. 1. De la Renaissance à la Guerre de Trente Ans.* Nancy: Editions Serpenoises, 1990, Vol. 3–1, 10, 99–100, 139–41.

58. Cabourdin, *Encyclopédie illustrée de la Lorraine*, Vol. 3–1, 61, 99–100, 149, 162, 212.

59. Bouveresse, "Contribution à l'étude de la dîme," 99–150. Jean Kieffer, "Le plat-pays thionvillois à la veille de la Révolution," *Les cahiers lorrains*, 1989, 135–40.

60. Cabourdin, "Les relations des communautés villageoises," 259–61.

61. Jean Gallet, "La seigneurie de Sarreguemines au XVIIIe siècle, 1660–1750," *Les cahiers lorrains*, 1986, 48–49.

62. Jean Peltre, "Du XVIe au XVIIIe siècle: une génération de nouveaux villages en Lorraine," *Revue géographique de l'Est*, 1966, 3–27. Guy Cabourdin, *Encyclopédie illustrée de la Lorraine. Histoire de la Lorraine. Les temps modernes. 2. De la paix de Westphalie à la fin de l'ancien régime.* Nancy: Editions Serpenoises, 1990, vol. 3–2, 26–35, 95–103. Guy Cabourdin, "L'exploitation de la terre de 1500 à la guerre de Trente Ans," *Mémoires de l'académie de Stanislas*, 7e série, VIII, 1979–80,

115–74

63. François Roth, *Encyclopédie illustrée de la Lorraine. Histoire de Lorraine. L'époque contemporaine. De la Révolution à la Grande Guerre.* Nancy: Editions Serpenoises, 1992, vol. 4–1, 6.

64. François-Yves Lemoigne, "Le commerce des provinces étrangères (Alsace-Evêchés-Lorraine) dans la deuxième moitié du XVIIIe siècle," in Pierre Léon, éd., *Aires et structures du commerce français au XVIIIe siècle.* Lyon: Centre d'histoire économique et sociale de la région lyonnaise, 1975, 173–200.

65. Guy Cabourdin, "Routes et grand commerce en Lorraine du milieu du XVIe siècle à la guerre de Trente Ans," *Transports et voies de communication.* Paris: Les Belles Lettres, 1977, 81–96. Cabourdin, *Terre et hommes en Lorraine, 1550–1635. Toulois et comté de Vaudémont.* Nancy: Université de Nancy II/Annales de l'Est, 1977, vol. 1, 78–87.

66. Denis Schneider, "Production, conjoncture et gestion seigneuriale, dans le bailliage d'Allemagne du duché de Lorraine, vers 1600," *Revue d'histoire moderne et contemporaine,* 45, 1998, 723–45.

67. Cabourdin, *Terres et hommes en Lorraine,* vol. 1, 229–37.

68. Fernand Braudel, *Civilisation matérielle, economie et capitalisme, XVe–XVIIIe siècle.* 3 vols. Paris: Armand Colin, 1979 and a shorter but still book-length summary by Braudel, *Afterthoughts on Material Civilization and Capitalism.* Baltimore: The Johns Hopkins University Press, 1977.

69. Jean Peltre, "Le laboureur et sa terre dans la Lorraine du XVIIIe siècle" *Mémoires de l'académie de Stanislas,* 7, 1979–80, 83–94.

70. Jacques Perot, "Recherches sur la vie rurale d'un village du pays messin. Ogy du XVIe au XVIIIe siècle," *Ecole nationale des chartes. Positions des thèses,* 1970, 179–84.

71. Jean Peltre, "Les remembrements en Lorraine à l'époque moderne (XVIIe–XVIIIe siècles)," *Annales de l'Est,* 28, 1976, 197–246.

72. Cabourdin, *Encyclopédie illustrée de la Lorraine,* Vol. 3–2, 35, 95, 101.

73. Jean Peltre, "L'évolution des méthodes d'arpentage en Lorraine du XVIe au XVIIIe siècle et ses conséquences sur la structure agraire," *Beiträge zur Genese der Siedlungs-und Agrarlandschaft in Europa.* Franz Steiner Verlag: Wiesbaden, 1968, 138–44. François Reitel, "A propos de l'openfield lorraine," *Revue géographique de l'Est,* 1966, 29–51.

74. Cabourdin, *Terre et hommes en Lorraine,* vol. 1, 241–48. Cabourdin, "Les relations des communautés villageoises," 259–61.

75. Imbert, "Quelques aspects juridiques de la mainmorte," 177–210. Cabourdin, *Terre et hommes en Lorraine,* vol. 2, 622–24.

76. Imbert, "Quelques aspects juridiques de la mainmorte," 177–210.

77. Imbert, "Quelques aspects juridiques de la mainmorte," 198–207.

78. Cabourdin, *Encyclopédie illustrée de la Lorraine*, vol. 3-2, 112-14

79. Cabourdin, *Terre et hommes en Lorraine*, 248-51.

80. Denaix, "La châtellenie de Hattonchâtel," 93-124.

81. François Reitel, "Quelques aspects de la campagne lorraine de la fin du XVIe siècle au début du XVIIIe siècle," *Bulletin de la société lorraine des études locales dans l'enseignement public*, 25, 1964, 9-18.

82. Jean Gallet, "Deux seigneuries du Salunois à la veille de la Révolution: Arraye et Vergaville," *Annales de l'Est*, 42, 1990, 3-34.

83. Denaix, "La châtellenie de Hattonchâtel," 114. Mathieu, *La seigneurie de Pont-les-Remirement*, 68-73.

84. Varlet, "Les revenus de la seigneurie de Bitche," 281-302.

85. Gallet, "La seigneurie de Sarreguemines," 37-57. Cabourdin, *Terre et hommes en Lorraine*, 260-62.

86. Gallet, "Deux seigneuries," 21-22.

87. Philippe Dollinger, éd. *Histoire d'Alsace*. Toulouse: Privat, 1984, 277-97.

88. Livet, *L'intendance d'Alsace*, 308-17. Erich Pelzer, "La noblesse alsacienne sous la monarchie française," *Revue d'Alsace*, 113, 1987, 305-20.

89. Dollinger, *Histoire d'Alsace*, 133-37. Monique Fave-Schwartz "Les Rathsamhausen, une famille de la noblesse rurale alsacienne, 1250-1450," *Revue d'Alsace*, 109, 1980, 31-48.

90. Livet, *L'intendance d'Alsace*, 22, 306.

91. Jean-Claude Gass, "Les forêts de Strasbourg et les conditions de leur appropriation," *Saisons d'Alsace*, 32, 1988, 34-50. Christine Geissert, "Les rentes constituées de l'oeuvre Saint-Georges Haguenau (XIVe-XVIIe siècle)," *Revue de l'Église d'Alsace*, 41-42, 1982-1983, 1-42, esp. 28-30 for the *Rechtspflege*. Jean-Paul Grasser, "Population et société à Haguenau au XVIIIe siècle: démographie, structures et couches sociales, assistance," *Etudes haguenoviennes*, 8, 1982, 107.

92. Georges Bischoff, "L'abbaye de Murbach et ses paysans à la fin du Moyen Age," *Histoire de l'Alsace rurale*. Strasbourg: Librairie Istra, 1983, 133-18. Henri Dubled, "L'administration de la seigneurie rurale en Alsace du XIIIe au XVe siècle," *Vierteljahrschrift für Sozial-und Wirtschaftsgeschichte*, 52, 1965, 433-84. Dubled, "Les grandes tendances de l'exploitation au sein de la seigneurie rurale en Alsace du XIIIe au XVe siècle," *Vierteljahrschrift für Sozial-und Wirtschaftsgeschichte*, 49, 1962, 41-121. Dubled, "Les paysans d'Alsace au Moyen Age (VIIIe-XVe siècle). Grands traits de leur histoire," *Paysans d'Alsace*. Strasbourg: Le Roux, 1959, 21-50. Francis Rapp, "Du domaine à l'état: les avatars de la seigneurie rurale," *Histoire de l'Alsace rurale*. Strasbourg: Librairie Istra, 1983, 83-99.

93. Henri Dubled, "Etudes sur la fortune foncière du monastère de Felbach (Haut-Rhin), depuis sa fondation jusqu'à la fin du XVe siècle," *Annuaire de la société d'histoire*

sundgauvienne, 1958, 17–52.

94.   Christian Wilsdorf, "Un domaine dans la première moité du XIIIe siècle. le "cour du comte" à Woffenheim d'après son coutumière," *Histoire de l'Alsace rurale*. Strasbourg: Librairie Istra, 1983, 101–12.

95.   Georges Bischoff, *Gouvernés et gouvernants en Haute-Alsace à l'époque autrichienne. Les Etats et pays antérieurs des origines au milieu du XVIe siècle*. Strasbourg: Librairie Istra, 1982, 19. Gerard Munch, "La prisée de la terre ou seigneurie d'Altkirch en 1390 d'après un texte inédit tiré des archives de la chambre des comptes de Dijon," *Annuaire de la société d'histoire sundgauvienne*, 1991, 103–41.

96.   Bischoff, *Gouvernés et gouvernants en Haute-Alsace*, 15–31. Dollinger, *Histoire d'Alsace*, 223. Livet, *L'intendance d'Alsace*, 179–80.

97.   Volker Press, "Vorderösterreich in der habsburgishen Reichspolitik des spätcn Mittelalters und der frühen Neuzeit," in Hans Maier, Volker Press, & Dieter Stievermann, *Vorderösterreich in der frühen Neuzeit*. Sigmaringen: Jan Thorbeck Verlag, 1989, 1–41.

98.   Octave Meyer, *La régence épiscopale de Saverne*. Strasbourg: Imprimerie alsacienne, 1935, 113–14.

99.   Boehler, *Une société rurale en milieu rhénan*, 1208–09.

100.   Livet, *L'intendance d'Alsace*, 550–51.

101.   Marc Drouot, "Seigneur et seigneurie au XVIe siècle. L'exploitation de la seigneurie de Thann en 1581," *Revue d'Alsace*, 119, 1993, 119–38.

102.   Livet, *L'intendance d'Alsace*, 824–40.

103.   Dollinger, *Histoire d'Alsace*, 287–88. Odile Kammerer, "Les Colmariens dans leur campagne: à propos du terroir d'Ursule Marx von Eckwersheim, née von Westhusen, 1535," *Annuaire de la société d'histoire et d'archéologie de Colmar*, 31, 1983, 37–45.

104.   Bischoff, "L'abbaye de Murbach," 116–17. Etienne Juillard, *La vie rurale dans la plaine de Basse-Alsace. Essai de géographie sociale*. Strasbourg: Le Roux, 1953, 76–78, 507–08.

105.   Dollinger, *Histoire d'Alsace*, 172–78.

106.   Tom Scott, *Freiburg and the Breisgau. Town-Country Relations in the Age of Reformation and Peasants' War*. Oxford: Clarendon Press, 1986.

107.   Dollinger, *Histoire d'Alsace*, 180–81, 210–13.

108.   Georges Bischoff, "Les paysans de Haute-Alsace en 1525," *Histoire de l'Alsace rurale*, 129–36. Jean Rott, "La Guerre des Paysans et ses suites en Basse-Alsace: le cas du Hattgau," *Histoire de l'Alsace rurale*, 119–28.

109.   Lucien Sittler, "Un siècle de vie paysanne: l'évolution d'une commune de la plaine d'Alsace. Fergersheim-Ohnheim avant et après la Guerre de Trente Ans," *Paysans d'Alsace*, 81–98.

110.   Boehler, *Une société rurale*, 1212–13, 2329–41.

111. Boehler, *Une société rurale*, 264–65.

112. Livet, *L'intendance d'Alsace*, 827–29.

113. Boehler, *Une société rurale*, 1212–22.

114. Guy Cabourdin, "La population de Strasbourg sous l'ancien régime," *Annales de démographie historique*, 1967, 267–73.

115. Robert Mischlich, "Le régime international de la navigation du Rhin," *Saisons d'Alsace*, 10, 1965, 367–87. Janie Salvi-Jacob, "Evolution du courant d'échange rhénan: Strasbourg face à ses rivales aux XVIIe et XVIIIe siècles," *Transports et voies de communication*. Paris: Les Belles Lettres, 1977, 117–29.

116. Jean-Marie Boehler, "Economie agraire et société rurale dans la plaine d'Alsace aux XVIIe et XVIIIe siècles: l'amorce des mutations," *Histoire de l'Alsace rurale*, 213–18. Boehler, *Une société rurale*, 506–08. Roland Marx, *La Révolution et les classes sociales en Basse-Alsace. Structures agraires et vente des biens nationaux*. Paris: Bibliothèque nationale, 1974, 50, 62–65. Erich Pelzer, "Nobles, paysans et la fin de la féodalité en Alsace," *La Révolution française et le monde rural*. Paris: Editions du C.T.H.S., 1989, 41–54.

117. Boehler, "Economie agraire et société rurale," 177–226. Jean-Michel Boehler, "De la reconstruction agraire à la mise en vente des biens nationaux: possession de la terre, conjoncture agraire et rapports sociaux dans la plaine d'Alsace (XVIIe–XVIIIe siècles)," *Histoire, économie et société*, 18, 1999, 43–62. Boehler, *Une société rurale*, 511–32.

118. Ganghofer, "Aspects des communautés rurales en Alsace," 433–57.

119. Boehler, "Economie agraire et société rurale," 184.

120. Jean Vogt, "A propos de la propriété bourgeoise en Alsace (XVIe–XVIIIe siècles)," *Revue d'Alsace*, 100, 1961, 48–66. Vogt, "Un mécanisme foncier et social insoupçonné. Le rôle de la vente de terres paysannes confiées aussitôt aux vendeurs en Basse-Alsace (XVIe–XVIIIe siècles)," *Francia*, 24, 1997, 1–28.

121. Jean Vogt, "Patrimoine rural et politique foncière d'un bourgeois de Strasbourg au milieu du XVIIe siècle: Ruprecht Reichart, économe de la Toussaint," *Pays d'Alsace*, 61–62, 1968, 31–34. Vogt, "Les problèmes des tenure," *Histoire de l'Alsace rurale*, 245–53. Vogt, "Notes agraires rhénanes: problèmes de tenure au coeur de la Basse-Alsace au milieu du XVIIIe siècle," *Cahiers de l'association interuniversitaire de l'Est*, 5, 1963, 32–41.

122. Robert Zimmerman, "Un exemple de rente monastique: Oelenberg au XVIe siècle," *Histoire de l'Alsace rurale*, 139–48.

123. Boehler, *Une société rurale*, 543–73.

124. Marcel Thomann, "Le droit rural à la Faculté de Droit de Strasbourg," *Histoire de l'Alsace rurale*, 271–79.

125. Jean Vogt, "Aspects de la vente des biens nationaux dans la région de Wissembourg,"

Revue d'Alsace 99, 1960, 90–103. Vogt, "Propriété et tenure: les biens nationaux à la lumière des pratiques antérieures et postérieures," *Revue d'Alsace*, 116, 1989–1990, 145–71.

126.   Ganghofer, "Aspects des communautés rurales en Alsace," 433–57. Boehler, *Une société rurale*, 1260–96. Dubled, "Etudes sur la fortune foncière," 32. Dubled, "La communauté de village en Alsace au XIIIe siècle," *Revue d'histoire économique et sociale*, 41, 1963, 5–33. Dubled, "La justice de la seigneurie foncière en Alsace aux XIVe et XVe siècles," *Schweizerische Zeitschrift für Geschichte*, 10, 1960, 337–75.

127.   Marie-Thérèse Lorcin, *Les campagnes de la région lyonnaise aux XIVe et XVe siècles.* Lyon: Imprimerie Bosc Frères, 1974.

128.   Lorcin, *Les campagnes de la région lyonnaise*, 90–105, 254–78. René Fédou, *Le terrier de Jean Jossard, co-seigneur de Châtillon-Azergues, 1430–1463.* Paris: Bibliothèque nationale, 1966, 36–38.

129.   Lorcin, *Les campagnes de la région lyonnaise*, 294–300.

130.   Marie Thérèse Lorcin, "Décimateurs et décimables en Lyonnais aux XIVe et XVe siècles," *Economies et sociétés au Moyen Age. Mélanges offerts à Edouard Perroy.* Paris: Publications de la Sorbonne, 1973, 350–54.

131.   Lorcin, "Un musée imaginaire de la ruse paysanne," 112–24.

132.   Gutton, *Villages du Lyonnais*, 87–97.

133.   Hamada, "Une seigneurie et sa justice," 19–31. Christiane Lombard-Déaux, "Les seigneuries ecclésiastiques du Lyonnais et du Beaujolais (XVIIe et XVIIIe siècles)," *Cahiers d'histoire*, 39, 1994, 19–35.

134.   Maurice Garden, "La région Rhône-Alpes: une construction de l'histoire encore incertaine," *Lyon et l'Europe. Hommes et sociétés. Mélanges offerts à Richard Gascon.* Lyon: Presses universitaires de Lyon, 1980, I, 267–80. Gilbert Garrier, "La formation d'un complexe écono-social de type "rhodanien": Chaponost (1730–1822)," in Pierre Léon, éd., *Structures économiques et problèmes sociaux du monde rural dans la France du Sud-Est.* Paris: Les Belles Lettres, 1966, 315–69.

135.   Richard Gascon, *Grand commerce et vie urbaine au XVIe siècle. Lyon et ses marchands (environs de 1520—environs de 1580).* Paris: S.E.V.P.E.N., 1971.

136.   André Latreille, éd., *Histoire de Lyon et du Lyonnais.* Toulouse: Privat, 1975, 212–15, 234–36, 249–51.

137.   Georges Durand, *Vin, vigne et vignerons en Lyonnais et Beaujolais (XVIe–XVIIIe siècles).* Lyon: Presses universitaires de Lyon, 1979, 111–28, 134–37, 216–34.

138.   Latreille, éd., *Histoire de Lyon et du Lyonnais,* 1975, 168–70.

139.   René Fédou, *Les hommes de loi lyonnais à la fin du Moyen Age.* Paris: Les Belles Lettres, 1964, 211–29, 362–73. Gilbert Garrier, "Premières lignes d'une recherche collective: l'appropriation foncière citadine dans la région Rhône-Alpes du XIVe au XXe siècle," *Bulletin du centre d'histoire économique et sociale de la région*

lyonnaise, no.2, 1975, 43–59.

140. Latreille, éd., *Histoire de Lyon et du Lyonnais*, 162. Françoise Bayard, "Ville et campagnes dans la fortune de Pierre Perrachon, noble lyonnais de 1642 à 1688," *Villes et campagnes, XVe–XXe siècle*. Lyon: Presses universitaires de Lyon, 1977, 105–31.

141. Laurent Champier, "Lyon et sa région agricole (fin du XVIIIe siècle et première moitié du XIXe siècle)," *Actes du 89e Congrès national des sociétés savantes. Séction de géographie*. Paris: Bibliothèque nationale, 1965, 33–46.

142. Durand, *Le patrimoine foncier de l'Hôtel-Dieu*, 15–19, 235–39, 388.

143. Edouard Gruter, *La naissance d'un grand vignoble. Les seigneuries de Pizay et Tanay en Beaujolais au XVIe et XVIIe siècles*. Lyon: Presses universitaires de Lyon, 1977, 47–121.

144. Levantal, *Ducs et pairs et duchés-pairies*, 1105.

145. Maurice Garden, *Lyon et les Lyonnais aux XVIIIe siècle*. Paris: Les Belles-Lettres, 1970, 362, 380–98.

146. Christiane Grosseau, "Les officiers de justice à Lyon (1740–1790). Etude d'un groupe socio-professionnel," *Bulletin du centre d'histoire économique et sociale de la région lyonnaise*, n. 3, 1972, 71–75.

147. André Allix, "Le trafic en Dauphiné à la fin du Moyen Age. Esquisse rétrospective de géographie économique," *Revue de géographie alpine*, 9, 1923, 373–420. Philippe Arbos, *La vie pastorale dans les Alpes françaises. Etude de géographie humaine*. Paris: Armand Colin, 1923.

148. Vital Chomel, "De la principauté à la province, 1349–1456," in Bernard Bligny, éd., *Histoire du Dauphiné*. Toulouse: Privat, 1973, 172–173. Chomel, "L'héritage médiévale et les schismes de l'âge moderne," in Bligny, *Histoire du Dauphiné*, 193–94. Bernard Bonnin, "Les deux derniers siècles de la monarchie absolue, 1634–1790," in Bligny, *Histoire du Dauphiné*, 249–53.

149. Laurent Champier, " Le défrichement de la forêt de Bièvre (Bas-Dauphiné). Essai d' interprétation d' un type de terroir méridional," *Revue de géographie de Lyon*, 29, 1952, 436–50. Pierre Vaillant," La société delphinoise, 1029–1349," in Bligny, *Histoire du Dauphiné*, 142–143.

150. Vital Chomel, "Un censier dauphinois inédit. Méthode et portée de l'édition du Probus," *Bulletin philologique et historique*, 1964, 319–409. Henri Falque-Vert, *Les hommes et la montagne en Dauphiné au XIIIe siècle*. Grenoble: Presses universitaires de Grenoble, 1997, 168–96.

151. Falque-Vert, *Les hommes et la montagne*, 175, 190–92.

152. Chomel, "De la principauté à la province," 172–73. Falque-Vert, *Les hommes et la montagne*, 206–17.

153. Falque-Vert, *Les hommes et la montagne*, 225–44.

154.   Vital Chomel, "Francs et rustiques dans la seigneurie dauphinoise au temps des affranchissements," *Bulletin philologique et historique*, 1965, 285–308.

155.   Vital Chomel, "Ressources domaniales et subsides en Dauphiné (1355–1364)," *Provence historique*, 25, 1975, 179–92.

156.   Marcel Baudon, "Les communautés rurales d'une haute vallée de Tarentaise au XVe siècle à la lumière des registres terriers de Saint-Martin-de-Belleville," *Actes du 108e Congrès national des sociétés savantes. Section de philologie et d'histoire*, 1983, 141–60.

157.   Georges de Manteyer, *Le livre-journal tenu par Fazy de Rame en langage enbrunais (6 juin 1471–10 juillet 1507)*. Gap, 1932, vol. 1, 38.

158.   Pierre Vaillant, *Les libertés des communautés dauphinoise (Des origines au 5 janvier 1355)*, Paris: Recueil Sirey, 1951.

159.   Falque-Vert, *Les hommes et la montagne*, 168–73.

160.   Harriet G. Rosenberg, *A Negotiated World: Three Centuries of Change in a French Alpine Community*. Toronto: University of Toronto Press, 1988.

161.   Bernard Bonnin, "L'endettement des communautés rurales en Dauphiné au XVIIe siècle," *Bulletin du centre d'histoire économique et sociale de la région lyonnaise*, n. 3, 1971, 1–9. Jean Egret, *Le Parlement de Dauphiné et les affaires publiques dans la deuxième moitié du XVIIIe siècle*. Roanne: Editions Horvath, 1988 (orig. 1942), vol. II, 52–61.

162.   Levantal, *Ducs et pairs et duchés-pairies*, 1105.

163.   Bonnin, "Le Dauphiné à la veille de la Révolution, 14–15.

164.   Falque-Vert, *Les hommes et la montagne*, 158–59, 203, 211, 217, 369–80.

165.   Bonnin, " Les deux derniers siècles de la monarchie absolue," 249.

166.   Jean Nicolas, *La Révolution française dans les Alpes. Dauphiné et Savoie 1789–1799*. Toulouse: Privat, 1989, 12.

167.   Gérard Chianéa, *La condition juridique des terres en Dauphiné au 18e siècle (1700–1789)* Paris: Mouton, 1969. Fr. Burckard, "Les rapports des seigneurs et des habitants de la Motte-Chalançon du XIVe au XVIIIe siècle," *Bulletin d'archéologie et de statistique de la Drôme*, 74, 1958, 16–20. Vital Chomel, "Esquisse d'une histoire du Grésivaudan," *Evocations. Bulletin mensuel du groupe d'études historiques et géographiques du Bas-Dauphiné*, 1986, 85–102. Gangneux, "Une commanderie de l'Ordre de Malte," 355–83.

168.   Bonnin, "Les deux derniers siècles de la monarchie absolue," 252. Pitre & Hickey, "Rendre justice dans une communauté rurale," 375–97. Jean Sauvageon, "Les cadres de la société rurale dans la Drôme à la fin de l'ancien régime: survivances communautaires, survivances féodales et régime seigneurial," in Robert Chagny, éd., *Aux origines provinciales de la Révolution*. Grenoble: Presses universitaires de Grenoble, 1990, 35–44.

169. Bonnin, "Le Dauphiné à la veille de la Révolution," 14–15. Bonnin, "Un aspect de la société rurale. Les milieux dominants en Dauphiné au XVIIe siècle," in *Lyon et l'Europe. Mélanges d'histoire offerts à Richard Gascon*. Lyon: Presses universitaires de Lyon, 1980, I, 47–66.

170. Bernard Bonnin, "Qui détenait les pouvoirs dans les communautés rurales? L'exemple dauphinois au XVIIe siècle," *Communautés rurales et pouvoirs dans les pays méditerranéens (XVIe–XXe siècles)*. Nice: Centre de la Méditerranée moderne et contemporaine, 1978, 19–45.

171. Vital Chomel, "L'économie seigneuriale et rente féodale en Grésivaudan d'après la comptabilité du marquis Pierre de Marcieu, lieutenant général en Dauphiné (1760–1793)," *Actes des 115e et 116e Congrès national des sociétés savantes*, 1990–1991, I, 17–30.

172. Egret, *Le Parlement de Dauphiné*, II, 62–63.

Chapter Four. Regional Patterns of Lordship, III

1. Michel de Boüard, éd. *Histoire de la Normandie*. Toulouse: Privat, 1970, 255–346.

2. Garnier, "La mise en herbe," 157–80. Garnier, "Pays herbagers, pays céréaliers," 493–525.

3. Guy Lemarchand, "L'abolition de la féodalité," *A travers la Normandie en Révolution, 1789–1800*. Rouen: Comité régional d'histoire de la Révolution française, 1992, 184.

4. M. Bouloiseau, "Aspects sociaux de la crise cotonnière dans les campagnes rouennaises en 1788–1789," *Actes du 81e Congrès national des sociétés savantes. Section d'histoire moderne et contemporaine*, 1956, 411. Guy Lemarchand, "Structure sociale d'après les rôles fiscaux et conjoncture économique dans le Pays de Caux: 1690–1789," *Bulletin de la société d'histoire moderne*, 68, 1969, 7–11.

5. Goujard, *L'abolition de la "féodalité"*, 51–69.

6. Angers, *Le terrier de la famille d'Orbec*, 73–77. Yannick Lecherbonnier, "L'abbaye de Belle-Etoile. Le temporel. Des origines à la fin de la guerre de Cents Ans," *Le pays bas-normand*, 73, 1980, 662–63. Yves Poncelet, "Le temporel de l'abbaye de Saint-Wandrille aux XIVe et XVe siècles," *Annales de Normandie*, 29, 1979, 310–13. Bébéar, "Le temporel de l'abbaye de Montivilliers," 41–59. Bottin, *Seigneurs et paysans*, 52.

7. Angers, *Le terrier de la famille d'Orbec*, 78–79. Lecherbonnier, "L'abbaye de Belle-Etoile," 668.

8. Bernard Bodinier, "Ce que nous apprennent registres et plans terriers: l'exemple d'un quarantaine de seigneuries de l'Eure à la veille de la Révolution," *Le monde rural en Normandie*. Caen: Musée de Normandie, 1998, 185. Lemarchand, *La fin du féodalisme*, 31–32.

9. Bindet, "Les dernières années de la baronnie de Marcey," 225–40.

10   Max Campserveux, "La condition économique et sociale de la noblesse du Cotentin à la fin du Moyen Âge," *Revue de l'Avranchin et du Pays de Granville*, 60, 1983, 255–71, 309–25, 339–49.

11.   For a particularly ingenious, but unconvincing, statement of the old Marxist crisis of feudalism interpretation see: Guy Bois, *Crise du féodalisme. Economie rurale et démographie en Normandie orientale du début du XIVe siècle au milieu du XVIe siècle.* Paris: Ecole des hautes Etudes en Sciences sociales, 1976, 195–35.

12.   Angers, *Le terrier de la famille d'Orbec*, 81–83.

13.   J. Bottin, "Le paysan, l'état et le seigneur en Normandie, milieu du XVIe-milieu du XVIIe siècle," *Genèse de l'état moderne. Prélèvement et redistribution.* Paris: Editions du CNRS, 1987, 101–110.

14.   J. Bottin, "Le paysan, l'état et le seigneur en Normandie, milieu du XVIe-milieu du XVIIe siècle," *Genèse de l'état moderne. Prélèvement et redistribution.* Paris: Editions du CNRS, 1987, 101–110.

15.   Pellerin, "Herbages et labours en Pays d'Auge," 11–16.

16.   Decoux, "Fraude et fraudeurs," 131–38.

17.   Lemarchand, *La fin du féodalisme*, 33–34.

18.   Dewald, *Pont-St-Pierre*, 104.

19.   Lemarchand, *La fin du féodalisme*, 26–28, 46–50.

20.   Fournée, "Un aspect de la fiscalité ecclésiastique," 215–19. Goujard, *L'abolition de la "féodalité"*, 48.

21.   Lemarchand, *La fin du féodalisme*, 34.

22.   Bottin, *Seigneurs et paysans*, 56–62, 174–77, 225–39.

23.   M. Boudin, "Du laboureur aisé au gentilhomme compagnard. Les Perrote de Cairon, de Bretteville-l'Orgueilleuse (1380–1480)," *Annales de Normandie*, 13, 1963, 237–68. Despite the title, the author follows the story into the late seventeenth century.

24.   Lemarchand, *La fin du féodalisme*, 18.

25.   Plaisse, *La baronnie de Neubourg*, 1961, 499–522, 612–21. Dewald, *Pont-St-Pierre*, 218–32.

26.   Goldsmith, *Lordship in France, 500–1500*, 179–84.

27.   Jean Yver, "Notes sur la justice seigneuriale en Normandie au XIIIe siècle," *Revue historique de droit français et étranger*, 37, 1959, 272–73.

28.   Boüard, *Histoire de la Normandie*, 176.

29.   Angers, *Le terrier de la famille d'Orbec*, 22.

30.   Lemarchand, *La fin du féodalisme*, 17.

31.   Angers, *Le terrier de la famille d'Orbec*, 58–65.

32.   Boüard, *Histoire de la Normandie*, 248–49. Dewald, *Pont-St-Pierre*, 90–104, 160–79. Lemarchand, *La fin du féodalisme*, 327–28.

33.   Lemarchand, *La fin du féodalisme*, 40.

34. Dewald, *The Formation of a Provincial Nobility*, 167–70.

35. Levantal, *Ducs et pairs*, 1105.

36. Hinault, "Paysans et seigneurs," 158–84.

37. Lemarchand, *La fin du féodalisme*, 41.

38. Lemarchand, *La fin du féodalisme*, 42.

39. Madeleine Foisil, *Le sire de Gouberville. Un gentilhomme normand au XVIe siècle.* Paris: Aubier Montaigne, 1981.

40. Campserveux, "La condition économique et sociale de la noblesse," 389–441. Wood, *The Nobility of the Election of Bayeux*, 81–97, 120–45.

41. Dewald, *The Formation of a Provincial Nobility*, 164.

42. Lemarchand, *La fin du féodalisme*, 21–25.

43. Angers, *Le terrier de la famille d'Orbec*, 54–55. Dewald, *Pont-St-Pierre*, 170.

44. Follain, "Les communautés rurales en Normandie," 691–721. Lemarchand, *La fin du féodalisme*, 55–58.

45. Bodinier, "Les biens des chapitres normands," 27–40. Poncelet, "Le temporel de l'abbaye de Saint-Wandrille," 301–30. Georges Bottin-Louvet, "Le chapitre d'Avrances à la fin de l'ancien régime," *Chapitres et cathédrales de Normandie.* Caen: Musée de Normandie, 1997, 13–26.

46. Bodiner, "Les biens des chapitres normands," 30–31.

47. Lecherbonnier, "L'abbaye de Belle-Etoilc," 587–678.

48. Lemarchand, "Les monastères de Haute-Normandie," 1–28.

49. Lemarchand, "Le temporel et les revenus de l'abbaye de Fécamp," 525–49.

50. Lemarchand, *La fin du féodalisme*, 42.

51. Jean-Pierre Leguay & Hervé Martin, *Fastes et malheurs de la Bretagne ducale, 1213–1532.* Rennes: Ouest-France, 1982, 183–86. Gallet, *La seigneurie bretonne*, 108, 167–99, 186–87.

52. Catherine Bertho-Leclerc, "La presqu'île de Rhuys au XVIIIe siècle. La terre, la mer et les hommes en Basse Bretagne à la fin de l'ancien régime (1680–1790)," *Positions des thèses. Ecole nationale des chartes*, 1976, 17–26.

53. Leguay & Martin, *Fastes et malheurs*, 270–71. Monique Chauvin-Lechaptois, *Les comptes de la châtellenie de Lamballe (1387–1482).* Rennes: Université de Haute-Bretagne, 1977, 64–109.

54. Philippe-Jean Hesse, "Le bail à complant: une notion juridique dans l'histoire mouvementée du vignoble nantais," *Bulletin de la société archéologique et historique de Nantes et de Loire-Atlantique*, 120, 1984, 185–215.

55. Leguay & Martin, *Fastes et malheurs*, 272–78.

56. André Chédeville & Noël-Yves Tonnerre, *La Bretagne féodale, XIe–XIIIe siècles.* Rennes: Ouest-France, 1987, 213–18, 323–24. Gallet, *La seigneurie bretonne*, 99–109, 184–88.

57   Jean Kerhervé, "Le domaine ducal de Guingamp-Minibriac au XVe siècle," *Mémoires de la société d'histoire et d'archéologie de Bretagne*, 1918, 130.

58.   Jean Delumeau, éd., *Histoire de la Bretagne*. Toulouse: Privat, 1969, 272. Yann Brékilien, *Les paysans bretons au XIXe siècle*. Paris: Hachette, 1994, 35–37.

59.   Leguay & Martin, *Fastes et malheurs*, 272–74.

60.   Brékilien, *Les paysans bretons*, 35–37.

61.   Gallet, *La seigneurie bretonne*, 187, 211–23.

62.   Vincent Le Floc'h, "Le régime foncier et son application dans le cadre de la paroisse de Plonivel au XVIIIe siècle," *Bulletin de la société archéologique du Finistère*, 92, 1966, 117–205.

63.   Gallet, *La seigneurie bretonne*, 349–64.

64.   Léon Dubreuil, *Les vicissitudes du domaine congéable en Basse-Bretagne à l'époque de la Révolution*. Rennes, Imprimerie Oberthur, 1915, I, 7–15. Michel Duval, "Domaine congéable et dépopulation forestière en Basse-Bretagne à la fin du XVIIIe siècle," *Association bretonne et union régionaliste bretonne. Archéologie-histoire-agriculture. Comptes rendus, procès-verbaux, mémoires*, 2e sér., 65, 1956, 95–106.

65.   Jean Gallet, "Le congément des domaniers en Cornouaille au XVIIIe siècle," *Annales de Bretagne*, 90, 1983, 452.

66.   Pierre Goubert, "Recherches d'histoire rurale dans la France de l'Ouest (XVIIe–XVIIIe siècles)," *Bulletin de la société d'histoire moderne*, sér. 13, n. 2, 1965, 4. T. J. A. Le Goff, *Vannes and Its Region*. Oxford: Clarendon Press, 1981, 161–99.

67.   Jean Gallet, "Le congément des domaniers dans le Trégor au XVIIIe siècle," *Mémoires de la société d'histoire et d'archéologie de Bretagne*, 60, 1983, 143–60; and Gallet, "Le congément des domaniers en Cornouaille, 451–66; and Gallet, "Le congément des domaniers en Bretagne: nouvelles perspectives de recherches," *Enquêtes et documents du centre de recherches sur l'histoire de la France atlantique*, 5, 1980, 31–53.

68.   Gallet, *La seigneurie bretonne*, 364–65.

69.   Leguay & Martin, *Fastes et malheurs*, 210–14.

70.   Leguay & Martin, *Fastes et malheurs*, 212–13.

71.   Gallet, *La seigneurie bretonne*, 79–115, 126–41, 242.

72.   Jean Kerhervé, *L'état breton aux 14e et 15e siècles. Les ducs, l'argent et les hommes*. Paris: Maloine, 1987, 77.

73.   Kerhervé, *L'état breton,* 77–121.

74.   Kerhervé, *L'état breton*, 861–910.

75.   Dominique Le Page, "Noblesse et pouvoir royal en Bretagne (1480–1540)," in Jean Kerhervé, éd., *Noblesse de Bretagne du Moyen Age à nos jours*. Rennes: Presses universitaires de Rennes, 1999, 129–49.

76.   Delumeau, *Histoire de la Bretagne*, 303–04. Duval, "Economie forestière et

féodalité," 347–58. Duval, "Les forêts royales en Cornouaille," 115, 1986, 161–94. Meyer, *La noblesse bretonne*, 780–85.

77. Le Goff, *Vannes and its Region*, 166–68. Alain Croix, *La Bretagne aux 16e et 17e siècles*. Paris: Maloine, 1981, 39–43.

78. Gallet, *La seigneurie bretonne*, 377–415. Denis, "Grandeur et décadence d'une forêt," 257–73.

79. Gallet, *La seigneurie bretonne*, 113–17, 311–48, 377–415.

80. Gallet, *La seigneurie bretonne*, 547–566.

81. Duma, *Les Bourbon-Penthièvre*, 159.

82. Gallet, *La seigneurie bretonne*, 412–15, 484–505..

83. Michel Nassiet, *Noblesse et pauvreté. La petite noblesse en Bretagne, XVe–XVIIIe siècle*. Rennes: Société d'histoire et d'archéologie de Bretagne, 1997, 375–80.

84. Meyer, *La noblesse bretonne*, 1254.

85. François Lebrun, éd., *Histoire des Pays de la Loire. Orléanais, Touraine, Anjou, Maine*. Toulouse: Privat, 1972, 5–6.

86. Lebrun, *Histoire des Pays de la Loire*, 247–57.

87. Lebrun, *Histoire des Pays de la Loire*, 243–44.

88. Levantal, *Ducs et pairs*, 1105.

89. Maillard, *Les campagnes de Touraine*, 73.

90. Maillard, *Les campagnes de Touraine*, 92.

91. Michel Le Mené, *Les campagnes angevines à la fin du Moyen Age (vers 1350–vers 1530). Etude économique*. Nantes: Editions Cid, 1982, 491–92.

92. André Pioger, "Le Fertois aux XVIIe et XVIIIe siècles. Histoire économique et sociale," *Bulletin de la société d'agriculture, sciences et arts de la Sarthe*, 71, 1967–1968, 332–33.

93. Antoine, *Fiefs et villages*, 255–59.

94. Antoine, *Fiefs et villages*, 184–88.

95. Maillard, *Les campagnes de Touraine*, 75–78.

96. Maillard, *Les campagnes de Touraine*, 93.

97. Le Mené, *Les campagnes angevines*, 125–92.

98. Maillard, *Les campagnes de Touraine*, 101. Le Mené, *Les campagnes angevines*, 443. Antoine, *Fiefs et villages*, 203.

99. Bernard Chevalier, "Bailleurs et preneurs en Touraine après la Guerre de Cent Ans. Les défricheurs de la métairie de la Cicogne aux prises avec le chapitre de Saint-Martin," *Etudes rurales*, 16, 1965, 117–24.

100. Maillard, *Les campagnes de Touraine*, 125.

101. Antoine, *Fiefs et villages*, 133.

102. Maillard, *Les campagnes de Touraine*, 103.

103. Claude Chéreau, "Recherches d'histoire agraire angevine dans les vallées de la Sarthe

et du Loir," *Actes du 97e Congrès national des sociétés savantes. Section de géographie*, 1972, 121–34. D. Viaud, "Sur un domaine rural du Vendômois. La Blotinière à la fin du XVIIIe siècle," *Annales historiques de la Révolution française*, 50, 1978, 30–33. Bernard Garnier, "Structure et conjoncture de la rente foncière dans le Haut-Maine aux XVII et XVIIIe siècles," *Problèmes agraires et société rurale. Normandie et Europe du Nord-Ouest*. Caen: Cahier des annales de Normandie, n. 11, 1979, 101–26.

104.	Antoine, *Fiefs et villages*, 207. Jean de La Monneraye, *Le régime féodal et les classes rurales dans le Maine au XVIIIe siècle*. Paris: Receuil Sirey, 1922, 67.

105.	Antoine, *Fiefs et villages*, 207–09.

106.	Le Mené, *Les campagnes angevines*, 471–74, 489–99. Antoine, *Fiefs et villages*, 282–87.

107.	Jean-Louis Ormières, "Le régime seigneurial dans l'Ouest," *La Révolution française et le monde rural*. Paris: Editions du CTHS, 1989, 31–40.

108.	Antoine, *Fiefs et villages*, 222.

109.	Antoine, *Fiefs et villages*, 179–84, 458.

110.	Marcel Mémin, "La campagne mancelle de 1780 vue par les notaires du Mans," *La province du Maine*, 64, 1962, 243–44. Antoine, *Fiefs et villages*, 237.

111.	Antoine, *Fiefs et villages*, 231–34.

112.	Antoine, *Fiefs et villages*, 239–54.

113.	Antoine, *Fiefs et villages*, 249–54.

114.	Constant, "L'enquête de noblesse de 1667," 548–66.

115.	Maillard, *Les campagnes de Touraine*, 89–92.

116.	Robert Tinthoin, "Vie rurale dans le sud de la plaine de Niort au XVIIIe siècle," *Bulletin. Section de géographie. Comité des travaux historiques et scientifiques*, 78, 1965, 1–67.

117.	A. Dernier, "Les freresches de la seigneurie de Vouillé," *Bulletin de la société des antiquaires de l'Ouest*, 7, 1963–1964, 215–37.

118.	Jean Tricard, "Crise et renaissance rurale en Poitou: la seigneurie de Vaussais et Montjean au XVe siècle," *Annales de Bretagne*, 82, 1975, 269–90.

119.	Louis Merle, *La métairie et l'évolution agraire de la Gâtine poitevine*. Paris: SEVPEN, 1958, 49–95. Louis Merle, "Une explication: origines et évolution d'un bocage, l'exemple de la Gâtine poitevine," *Annales E.S.C.*, 12, 1957, 613–18. Gabriel Debien, *En Haut-Poitou. Défricheurs au travail, XVe–XVIIIe siècles*. Paris: Armand Colin, 1952, 2–39. G. Debien, "Defrichements et reprises de fermes par la noblesse et par le clergé en Poitou à la fin du XVIIIe siècle," *Annales historiques de la Révolution française*, 40, 1968, 381–400. Merle stressed depopulating enclosure, but Debien demonstrated that much of the land in *borderies* and *métairies* came from new clearings.

120. Robert Favreau, "Seigneurs et bourgeois en Poitou aux XIVe-XVe siècles: autour du fief de l'Armenteresse ou du Fou," *Bulletin de la société des antiquaires de l'Ouest,* 17, 1984, 179–92.

121. Péret, *Seigneurs et seigneuries,* 5–25.

122. Jacques Péret, "Paysans de Gâtine poitevinc au XVIIIe siècle," *La France d'ancien régime. Etudes réunies en l'honneur de Pierre Goubert.* Toulouse: Privat, 1984, tome II, 532–33.

123. Péret, "Paysans de Gâtine poitevine," 533. Marcel Garaud, "Le régime agraire et les paysans de Gâtine au XVIIIe siècle," *Bulletin de la société des antiquaires de l'Ouest,* 2, 1954, 43–82.

124. Marcadé, "Des petits notables ruraux," 197–210. Péret, "Bourgeoisie rurale et seigneurs," 357–77. Proust, "Petits fermiers de seigneuries," 421–32.

125. Patrick Léon, "Mutations des paysages agraires et de l'habitat: les campagnes du Saint-Amandois du milieu du XVIe au XIXe siècle," *Cahiers d'archéologie et d'histoire du Berry,* 77, 1984, 41 note 28.

126. Françoise Michaud-Fréjaville, "Communautés rurales et seigneurs à la fin du Moyen Age: un exemple berrichon," *Etudes rurales,* 68, 1977, 141–51.

127. Guy Devailly, éd. *Histoire du Berry.* Toulouse: Privat, 1980, 166. Pierre d'Ambly, "Un propriétaire terrien en Berry au XVIIIe siècle," *Cahiers d'archéologie et d'histoire du Berry,* 81, 1985, 61–76. François-P. Gay, *La champagne du Berry. Essai sur la formation d'un paysage agraire et l'évolution d'une société rurale.* Bourges: Editions Tardy, 1967, 66–67, 118–25, 152, 208–09, 255–78, 285.

128. Christian Poitou, "La propriété foncière à Vouzon de la fin de la Guerre de Cent Ans à la veille de la Révolution," *Bulletin de la société archéologique et historique de l'Orléanais,* 3, 1964, 141–52.

129. Marie-Andrée Guyot-Ledoux, "Aspects économiques et sociaux de la vie rurale en Nivernais: la paroisse de Saint-Parize-le-Châtel au milieu du XVIIIe siècle," *Positions des thèses. Ecole national des chartes,* 1972, 57–59.

130. Françoise Michaud-Fréjaville, "Un exemple de seigneurie foncière au XVe siècle. Le prieuré de Gravier," *Cahiers d'archéologie et d'histoire du Berry,* 50–51, 1977, 7–25.

131. Shaffer, *Family and Farm,* 24–33. Baron, "La vie rurale dans la région de Varzy," 47.

132. Shaffer, *Family and Farm,* 29.

133. Romain Baron, "Une paroisse disparue: Saint-Martin-des-Vaux," *Bulletin de la société scientifique et artistique de Clamecy,* 92, 1968, 83–90.

134. Nicole Gotteri-Grambert, "Chassy-en-Morvan. La seigneurie et le domaine," *Mémoires de la société académique du Nivernais,* 55, 1969, 29–54; 56, 1970, 28–38; 57, 1971, 43–66.

135. Shaffer, *Family and Farm,* 50. Guy Thuillier, "Les communautés des laboureurs," in Guy Thuillier, *Aspects de l'économie nivernaise au XIXe siècle.* Paris: Armand Colin,

1966, 33–45. Commandant Du Broc de Segange, "Les anciens communautés de cultivateurs dans le centre de la France," *Bulletin de la société d'émulation du Bourbonnais*, 6, 1898, 211–20, 253–80.

136. Charles Prieuret, "Une association agricole en Nivernais. Histoire de la grosse communauté des Jault, 1580–1847," *Bulletin de la société nivernaise des lettres, sciences et arts*, 1929, 333–83.

137. Shaffer. *Family and Farm*, 49.

138. Nancy Fitch, "The Demographic and Economic Effects of Seventeenth Century Wars: the Case of the Bourbonnais, France," *Review*, 2, 1978, 181–206.

139. Shaffer, *Family and Farm*, 31–33.

140. Jean Chiffre, "Le rôle des communautés familiales dans le peuplement et l'organisation de l'espace rural bourbonnaise," *Etudes bourbonnaises*, 250, 1989, 232–34. Serge du Cray, "Amodiation ou location perpétuelle d'un domaine en Combraille, en 1438, avec affranchissement des locataires," *Bulletin de la société d'émulation du Bourbonnais*, 64, 1989, 393–97. René Germain, "Seigneurie et noblesse en Bourbonnais d'après un dénombrement du ban en 1503," *Seigneurs et seigneuries au Moyen Age*. Paris: CTHS, 1993, 369–80. Germain, *Les campagnes bourbonnaises*, 245–327.

141. Germain, *Les campagnes bourgonnaises*, 299–304.

142. Gueneau, *L'organisation du travail à Nevers*, 332–69. J. Boichard, "Quelques éléments de la vie rurale entre Loire et Allier. Propriété et exploitation du sol," *Revue de géographie de Lyon*, 37, 1962, 250–71.

143. Chiffre, "Le rôle des communautés familiales," 229–36.

144. Léon, "Mutations des paysages," 25.

145. Baron, "La bourgeoisie de Varzy," 170–71.

146. Despois, *Histoire de l'autorité royale*, 211–17, 340–73, 424–27.

147. Bertrand Gille, "Note sur la population de Clermont au XVIIIe siècle," *Revue d'Auvergne*, 83, 1969, 123–34.

148. Poitrineau, *La vie rurale en Basse-Auvergne*, 186–92, 210–15.

149. Charbonnier, *Une autre France*, 962–71.

150. James Lowth Goldsmith, *Les Salers et les d'Escorailles. Seigneurs de Haute Auvergne, 1500–1789*. Clermont-Ferrand: Institut d'Etudes du Massif Central, 1984, 227–30.

151. Charbonnier, *Une autre France*, 679, 958–61. Christian Roche, "Le seigneur du Broc et ses biens (1761–1830)," *Revue d'Auvergne*, 79, 1965, 53.

152. Michel Leymarie, "La propriété et l'exploitation foncière au XVIIe siècle dans la Planèze de Saint-Flour," *Revue de la Haute-Auvergne*, 1965, 482–86. Leymarie, "Les redevances foncières seigneuriales," 361. Danièle Chaumet, "L'évolution de la vie rurale dans trois communes du sud de la Limagne: Plauzat, La Sauvetat et Authezat,"

Revue d'Auvergne, 82, 1968, 157–61. Robert Darpoux, "La vie rurale vers la fin du XVIIIe siècle dans le Brivadois," *La Révolution française dans le Brivadois*. Brioude: Société de l'Almanach de Brioude, 1989, 203–32. Lucien Gachon, "La vie rurale sous le règne de Louis XVI dans une paroisse des Monts du Livradois: Brousse-Montbossier," *104e Congrès national des sociétés savantes. Section de géographie*, 1979, 111–15. Abel Poitrineau, "Propriété et société en Haute-Auvergne à la fin du règne de Louis XV: le cas de Vic," *Cahiers d'histoire*, 6, 1961, 445–49. Poitrineau, *La vie rurale*, 147–60, 186–95, 210–15.

153. Poitrineau, *La vie rurale*, 630–34.

154. Leymarie, "Les redevances foncières seigneuriales," 361–62, 377.

155. Charbonnier, *Une autre France*, 516–43.

156. Marcel Juillard, "Thynière et ses seigneurs," *Revue de la Haute-Auvergne*, 1957, 126–56. Charbonnier, *Une autre France*, 1148. A. Achard, *Une ancienne justice seigneuriale en Auvergne. Sugères et ses habitants*. Clermont-Ferrand: Imprimerie générale, 1929, 146–191. Elisabeth Traissac, "Une propriété rurale de Haute-Auvergne au XVIIIe siècle," *Revue de la Haute-Auvergne*, 40, 1967, 469–89; 41, 1968, 240–62.

157. Daniel Lavaud, "Le village de Gerzat au XVe siècle," *Revue d'Auvergne*, 1976, 201–47. Claude Grimmer, *Vivre à Aurillac au XVIIIe siècle*. Paris: Presses universitaires de France, 1983, 57–80.

158. Goldsmith, *Les Salers et les d'Escorailles*, 54, 107–32.

159. Darpoux, "La vie rurale," 205. Robert Darpoux, "Une seigneurie de montagne à la veille de la Révolution," *Almanach de Brioude et de son arrondissement*, 62, 1982, 175–85. Charbonnier, *Une autre France*, 675–711, 752. Francisque Mège, "Charges et contributions des habitants d'Auvergne à la fin de l'ancien régime. Deuxième partie. Les droits seigneuriaux," *Revue d'Auvergne*, 1898, 130–239. Poitrineau, *La vie rurale*, 341–51.

160. Charles Felgères, *Histoire de la baronnie de Chaudesaigues (depuis ses origines jusqu'à 1789)*. Paris, 1904, 351–53. Charbonnier, *Une autre France*, 675–711. Anne Lemerle-Baudot, "Une petite seigneurie rurale en Auvergne au milieu du XVe siècle d'après le terrier de Clavelier," *Bulletin philologique et historique*, 1965, 329–43. Charles Micolon de Guérines, "Le terrier de 1521 de la seigneurie du Chier, près d'Ambert," *Chroniques historiques d'Ambert et de son arrondissement*, 15, 1993, 27–39.

161. Leymarie, "Les redevances foncières seigneuriales, 316. Juillard, "Thynière et ses seigneurs," 153–56. E. Martres, "Les paysans et leur terroir dans une haute vallée cantalienne. Albepierre du XIIIe au XIXe siècle," *Revue de la Haute-Auvergne*, 1956–57, 168.

162. Goldsmith, *Les Salers et les d'Escorailles*, 191–93.

163   Charbonnier, *Une autre France*, 99–114, 637–60.

164.   Leymarie, "Les redevances foncières seigneuriales, " 301, 316–18. Charbonnier, *Une autre France*, 938–44.

165.   Pierre-François Fournier & Antoine Vergnette, "Les droits seigneuriaux à Aubière. Recueil des documents concernant les contestations dont ils furent l'objet (1422–1789)," *Revue d'Auvergne*, 42, 1928, 1–59.

166.   Michèle Sauvadet, "La seigneurie d'Ambert à la in du Moyen Age," *Revue d'Auvergne*, 100, 1986, 159–82.

167.   J. Semonsous, "Chartes de coutumes et franchises d'entre Cher et Sioule au pays de combraille du XIIIe au XVIIIe siècle," *Revue d'Auvergne*, 70, 1956, 161–200.

168.   Charbonnier, *Une autre France*, 704–05.

169.   Goldsmith, *Les Salers et les d'Escorailles*, 223–26.

170.   Goldsmith, *Les Salers et les d'Escorailles*, 190–93.

171.   Michel Leymarie, "Les mouvements popularies à Maurs et aux environs en 1789 et 1790," *Revue de la Haute-Auvergne*, 1970, 126–32. Leymarie, "Les redevances foncières seigneuriales," 327.

172.   Charbonnier, *Une autre France*, 932–35.

173.   Goldsmith, *Les Salers et les d'Escorailles*, 153–57.

174.   Goldsmith, *Les Salers et les d'Escorailles*, 158–69.

175.   Goldsmith, *Les Salers et les d'Escorailles*, 169–180.

176.   Goldsmith, *Les Salers et les d'Escorailles*, 190.

177.   Jonathan R. Dalby, *Les paysans cantaliens et la Révolution française (1789–1794)*. Clermont-Ferrand: Institut d'Etudes du Massif Central, 1989, 10, 27–44.

178.   Pierre Villard, *Les justices seigneuriales dans la Marche*. Paris: Librairie générale de droit et de jurisprudence, 1969.

179.   Michel Aubrun, "Seigneurs et paysans au temps de Louis XIII d'après le terrier du Plaix-Joliet de 1633," *Mémoires de la société des sciences naturelles et archéologiques de la Creuse*, 43, 1989, 513–21. H. Hemmer, "La seigneurie de La Celette et ses revenus an XVIIe siècle," *Mémoires de la société des sciences naturelles et archéologiques de la Creuse*, 36, 1966, 153–61.

180.   Maurice Sourioux, "La seigneurie de Crocq au XVIIe siècle," *Mémoires de la société des sciences naturelles et archéologiques de la Creuse*, 43, 1989, 633–41.

181.   Nicole Lemaître, *Un horizon bloqué. Ussel et la montagne limousine aux XVIIe et XVIIIe siècles*. Ussel: Musée du pays d'Ussel, 1978.

182.   Nicole Lemaître, *Bruyères, communes et mas. Les communaux en Bas-Limousin depuis le XVIe siècle*. Ussel: Musée du Pays d'Ussel, 1981.

183.   Jean Tricard, "La tenure en Limousin et Marche à la fin du XVe siècle. Etude des structures agraires et foncières," *Annales du Midi*, 88, 1976, 23–39. Julien Denis, "Registre terrier de la prévôté de Verneuil (1503)," *Bulletin de la société archéolo-*

gique et historique du Limousin, 128, 2000, 169–86.

184. Géraud Lavergne, "Le vignoble du prieuré d'Aureil en Bas-Limousin," *Bulletin de la société des lettres, sciences et arts de la Corrèze*, 70, 1966, 7–20.

185. Robert Joudoux, "Du tènement des Vigeries d'Objat aux dîmes de la châtellenie de Voutezac," *Limouzi*, 115, 1990, 17–27.

186. Jean Tricard, "Les limites d'une reconstruction rurale en pays pauvre à la fin du Moyen Age: le cas du Limousin," *Etudes rurales*, 60, 1975, 5–40.

187. Jean Tricard, "Comparsonniers et reconstruction rurale dans le sud du Limousin au XVe siècle," *Actes du 104e Congrès national des sociétés savantes. Section de philologie et d'histoire jusqu'à 1610*, 1979, I, 51–62.

188. A. Petit, "La métairie perpétuelle en Limousin au XVe siècle," *Revue historique de droit français et étranger*, 1919, 365–403. Edmond Barbier & Jean-Paul Laurent, "Bail à métairie perpétuelle, du XVe siècle concernant le village de Lachaud, commune de Champagnac, dans l'ancienne vicomté de Rouchechouart," *Bulletin de la société archéologique et historique du Limousin*, 112, 1957, 500–09.

189. Jean Tricard, "Le métayage en Limousin à la fin du Moyen Age," *Bulletin de l'association des historiens économistes*, 13, 1980, 7–18.

190. Jean Boutier, "Défricher en Bas-Limousin au XVIIIe siècle: immobilisme économique et conflits agraires," *Bulletin de la société des lettres, sciences et arts de la Corrèze*, 82, 1979, 23–44. Yvon Chalard, "Une collectivité rurale au XVIIIe siècle: Saint-Pantaléon-de-Larche," *Bulletin de la société des lettres, sciences et arts de la Corrèze*, 91, 1969, 173–200; 92, 1970, 131–50. Maryse Delbut, "Une paroisse rurale au XVIIIe siècle: Darnets, 1748–1789," *Bulletin de la société scientifique, historique et archéologique de la Corrèze*, 94, 1972, 157–72; 95, 1973, 189–205; & 96, 1974, 105–12.

191. Leymarie, "Rentes seigneuriales, 594–98.

192. Albert Massonie, "La seigneurie de Soudeilles-Lieuteret en 1582," *Limouzi*, 125, 1993, 87–92. Despite its title, this study examines inventories from the sixteenth, seventeenth and eighteenth century.

193. André Delmas, "Les châtellenies de Larche et Tarrasson sous la domination des Noailles, 1583–1789," *Bulletin de la société scientifique, historique et archéologique de la Corrèze*, 85, 1963, 134–73.

194. Louis-Daniel Denoix, "La vicomté de Turenne aux XIVe et XVe siècles," *Bulletin de la société scientifique, historique et archéologique de la Corrèze*, 89, 1967, 127–52; 90, 1968, 43–65. Danielle Oppetit-Perné, "La vicomté de Turenne à la fin du XVe siècle. Essai d'histoire économique," *Ecole national des chartes. Positions des thèses*, 1973, 137–42.

195. Lemaître, *Un horizon bloqué*, 175.

196. Bastier, "Droits féodaux et revenus agricoles, 261–87 For an individual case study:

Marc Vaissière," La seigneurie du Roucous en 1785," *Revue du Rouergue*, 65, 2001, 87–97.

197. Pierre Goubert, "En Rouergue: structures agraires et cadastres au XVIIIe siècle," *Annales. Economies. Sociétés. Civilisations*, 9, 1954, 385.

198. Charles Parain, "Fondements d'une ethnologie historique de l'Aubrac," *L'Aubrac. Etude ethnologique, linguistique, agronomique et économique d'un établissement humain.* Paris: CNRS, 1970–9, vol. 6, tome 2, 25–52.

Chapter Five. Regional Patterns of Lordship, IV

1. Souriac, "Les communautés et leurs terroirs," 193–217.

2. Jean Coppolani, "Une communauté rurale à la veille de la Révolution: Frouzins (Haute-Garonne) d'après le cadastre de 1784," *Revue géographique des Pyrénées et du Sud-Ouest*, 60, 1989, 385–401.

3. Henri Dubled, "Seigneurs et paysans en Languedoc au Moyen Age et sous l'ancien régime. Le cas particulier du village de Gajan (Gard)," *Recueil de mémoires et travaux publié par la société d'histoire du droit et des institutions des anciens pays de droit écrit*, 1958, 1–39. Marcel Guy, "Tournefeuille à la fin de l'ancien régime," *Annales du Midi*, 97, 1985, 53–73.

4. Appolis, *Un pays languedocien*, 38. For a negative assessment of seigneurial justices see: Catarina, "Justices et seigneuries en Languedoc," 167–72.

5. Bastier, *La féodalité au siècle des Lumières*, 104.

6. Thomas, "L'activité toulousaine de la justice seigneuriale," 21–29.

7. Huppé, *Le gisant de la féodalité*, 14–47.

8. Huppé, *Le gisant de la féodalité*, 166–67, 139.

9. Jean Ramière de Fortanier, *Les droits seigneuriaux dans la sénéchaussée et comté de Lauragais (1553–1789)*. Toulouse: Librairie Marqueste, 1932. Old, somewhat dated, but still useful.

10. Tarde, "Contrats de fermage et de métayage," 138.

11. Jean Reboul, *Tavel sur la côte du Rhône (XVIIe-XVIIIe-Révolution)*. Nimes: C. Lacour, 1990, 7.

12. Appolis, *Un pays languedocien*, 98–105.

13. Bastier, *La féodalité*, 216–17.

14. Huppé, *Le gisant de la féodalité*, 183.

15. Larguier, *Le drap et le grain*, 306–12.

16. Bastier, *La féodalité*, 215.

17. Bastier, *La féodalité*, 216. Huppé, *Le gisant de la féodalité*, 132.

18. Appolis, *Un pays languedocien*, 106.

19. Bastier, *La féodalité*, 213.

20. Appolis, *Un pays languedocien*, 105.

21. Bastier, *La féodalité*, 262–79.

22. Huppé, *Le gisant de la féodalité*, 58–61.

23. Appolis, *Un pays languedocien*, 182.

24. Bastier, *La féodalité*, 170.

25. Frêche, *Toulouse et la région Midi-Pyrénées*, 459–75.

26. Gabriel Bernet, "L'économie d'un village du Lauragais au XVIIe siècle: le consulat de Pugnères de 1593 à 1715," *Annales du Midi*, 78, 1966, 481–512.

27. Chéron & Sarret de Coussergues, *Une seigneurie en Bas-Languedoc*, 129–305.

28. Huppé, *Le gisant de la féodalité*, 140–141.

29. Le Roy Ladurie, "Sur Montpellier et sa campagne," 223–30. Albert Soboul, *Les campagnes montpelliéraines à la fin de l'ancien régime. Propriété et cultures d'après les compoix*. Paris: Presses universitaires de France, 1958, 23.

30. Fiette, "Un grand domaine du Lauragais," 19–35.

31. Forster, *The Nobility of Toulouse*, 33.

32. Bastier, *La féodalité*, 225–28.

33. Larguier, *Le drap et le grain*, 679–82, 695–727.

34. Jean-Claude Paulhet, "Les parlementaires toulousains à la fin du dix-septième siècle," *Annales du Midi*, 76, 1964, 189–204.

35. Bastier, *La féodalité*, 258–59.

36. Huppé, *Le gisant de la féodalité*, 151.

37. Bastier, *La féodalité*, 56–58.

38. Forster, *The Nobility of Toulouse*, 154.

39. Frêche, *Toulouse et la région Midi-Pyrénées*, 519–51.

40. Frêche, *Toulouse et la région Midi-Pyrénées*, 531.

41. Reboul, *Tavel sur la côte du Rhône*, 67.

42. Frêche, *Toulouse et la région Midi-Pyrénées*, 536–45.

43. Appolis, *Un pays languedocien*, 119–24.

44. Marcel Saby, "Le XIIIe siècle paysan dans la baronnie d'Allègre et ses annexes de Chomelix et de Saint-Just-près-Chomelix," *Almanach de Brioude et de son arrondissement*, 63, 1983, 169–244. Jean-Claude Hélas, "Gap-Francès: la seigneurie et les revenus de la terre," *Provence historique*, 45, 1995, 143–56 with *terriers* from the fifteenth through the eighteenth century. Jean-Claude Hélas, "Le manse en Gévaudan au milieu du XVe siècle," *Annales du Midi*, 102, 1990, 173–78. A. Pantel & E. Servière, "Seigneuries cévennoles," *Revue du Gévaudan, des Causses et des Cévennes*, 1966, 13–55.

45. Merley, *La Haute-Loire de la fin de l'ancien régime*, 164. Gérard Sabatier, "Seigneurie et exploitation paysanne en Velay aux XVIIe et XVIIIe siècles, d'après les terriers," *Bulletin du centre d'histoire économique et sociale de la région lyonnaise*, n. 2, 1973, 28.

46. Gérard Sabatier, "Seigneurie et exploitation paysanne en Velay aux XVIIe et XVIIe siècles, d'après les terriers," *Bulletin du centre d'histoire économique et sociale de la région lyonnaise*, n. 2, 1973,15–32.

47. Maxime de La Rochette de Rochegonde, "Les redevances féodales dans l'ancienne seigneurie de Saint-Ilpize," *Almanach de Brioude et de son arrondissement*, 42, 1962, 215–22.

48. Bernard Rivet, *Une ville au XVIe siècle: Le Puy en Velay*. Le Puy-en-Velay: Cahiers de la Haute-Loire, 1988, 237

49. Rivet, *Une ville*, 236. Bernard Rivet, "La seigneurie du Puy au XVIe siècle: remarques complémentaires," *Cahiers de la Haute-Loire*, 1990, 156–60.

50. Michel Carlat, "La Chartreuse de Bonnefoy, ses granges et les communautés paysannes du Gerbier-Mézenac de 1500 à 1788: jalons pour une histoire économique et sociale," *Cahiers de la Haute-Loire*, 1986, 103–45.

51. Gérard Sabatier, "L'espace économique d'un grand domaine vellave au XVIIIe siècle," *Bulletin historique, scientifique, littéraire, artistique et agricole de la société académique du Puy et de la Haute-Loire*, 56, 1980, 179–87.

52. Merley, *La Haute-Loire*, 166.

53. François Crouzet, "Une communauté d'habitants dans la seconde moitié du XVIIIe siècle: Tence en Velay," *Cahiers de la Haute-Loire*, 1987, 111–36.

54. Merley, *La Haute-Loire*, 74, 159.

55. Edouard Baratier, éd. *Histoire de la Provence*. Toulouse: Privat, 1976, 266–393. Derlange, *Les communautés d'habitants*, 15–22. François-Xavier Emmanuelli, "La vie urbaine dans le Midi de la France et particulièrement en Provence aux XVIIe et XVIIIe siècles," *Recherches régionales*, 24, 1983, 59–87.

56. Derlange, *Les communautés d'habitants*, 81–136, 144–58.

57. Derlange, *Les communautés d'habitants*, 86.

58. Goldsmith, *Lordship in France, 500–1500*, 272–73.

59. Derlange, *Les communautés d'habitants*, 147.

60. Gabriel Audisio, "Une grande migration alpine en Provence (1460–1560)," *Bollettino storico-bibliografico subalpino*, 87, 1989, 111–16.

61. Derlange, *Les communautés d'habitants*, 147.

62. Derlange, *Les communautés d'habitants*, 147.

63. Cubells, *La Provence des Lumières*, 147–49.

64. Thomas F. Sheppard, *Lourmarin in the Eighteenth Century. A Study of a French Village*. Baltimore: The Johns Hopkins Press, 1971, 137–38.

65. Derlange, *Les communautés d'habitants*, 148–50.

66. Derlange, *Les communautés d'habitants*, 110.

67. Derlange, *Les communautés d'habitants*, 148–49.

68. Joseph Billioud, "Une baronnie de grands négociants marseillais: La Tour d'Aigues, "

Provence historique, 19, 1969, 119–20.

69. Derlange, *Les communautés d'habitants*, 86–87.

70. F. Farnarier, "La seigneurie de Lançon. Période française (1481–1564)," *Provence historique*, 10, 1960, 225–31.

71. Chanoine Corriol, "Acquisition de biens et droits seigneuriaux par la communauté de Bayons," *Bulletin de la société scientifique et littéraire des Alpes-de-Haute-Provence*, 33, 1955, 244–52.

72. Derlange, *Les communautés d'habitants*, 53–65.

73. Derlange, *Les communautés d'habitants*, 150–54.

74. Cubells, *La Provence des Lumières*, 150–56.

75. Cubells, *La Provence des Lumières*, 150.

76. Cubells, *La Provence des Lumières*, 156.

77. Cubells, *La Provence des Lumières*, 158–60.

78. Edouard Maur, "Rognonas de 1582 à 1789. Contribution à l'histoire agraire de la Basse-Provence," *Cahiers du centre d'études des sociétés méditerranéennes*, 1968, 193–233.

79. Roger Livet & Augustin Roux, *Eléments d'histoire agraire du terroir provençal. Saint-Saturnin-lès-Apt*. Aix-en-Provence: La Pensée universitaire, 1957, 71–81.

80. Maurice Bordes, "L'administration des communautés d'habitants en Provence et dans le comté de Nice à la fin de l'ancien régime. Traits communs et diversité," *Annales du Midi*, 84, 1972, 369–96. And by the same author: "La vitalité des communautés provençales," 12–32; and: "Les communautés villageoises," 143–64. Derlange, *Les communautés d'habitants*, 119–21.

81. René Pillorget, *Les mouvements insurrectionnels de Provence entre 1596 et 1715*. Paris: Editions A. Pedone, 1975, 243–64.

82. Cubells, *La Provence des Lumières*, 197–208 Derlange, *Les communautés d'habitants*, 123–25. Thomas F. Sheppard, *Lourmarin in the Eighteenth Century. A Study of A French Village*. Baltimore: The Johns Hopkins Press, 1971, 185–208.

83. Derlange, *Les communautés d'habitants*, 85.

84. Levantal, *Ducs et pairs*, 1105.

85. Cubells, *La Provence des Lumières*, 112.

86. Cubells, *La Provence des Lumières*, 135.

87. Billioud, "Une baronnie de grands nécociants marseillais," 119.

88. Cubells, *La Provence des Lumières*, 161–95.

89. Derlange, *Les communautés d'habitants*, 87–88.

90. Derlange, *Les communautés d'habitants*, 87, 141.

91. Gérard Gangneux, "Economie et société rurales d'après les archives de l'ordre de Malte, *Cahiers d'histoire*, 17, 1972, 53–60; and by the same author, *L'ordre de Malte en Camargue du 17e au 18e siècle*. Grenoble. Presses universitaires de Grenoble,

1979, 11, 14–44, 144.

92.   Derlange, *Les communautés d'habitants*, 137–41.

93.   Robert Boutruche, dir. *Histoire de Bordeaux. IV. Bordeaux de 1453 à 1715.* Bordeaux: Fédération historique du Sud-Ouest, 1966. Pariset, dir. *Histoire de Bordeaux. V*, 143–205.

94.   P. J. J. Franc de Ferrière, "Le pays de nouvelle conqueste. Origine et privilèges," *Saint-Emilion Libourne. Actes du XXIXe Congrès d'études régionales.* Libourne: Fédération historique du Sud-Ouest, 1979, 65–72.

95.   Boutruche, *Histoire de Bordeaux IV*, 100–103.

96.   Henri Enjalbert, "La naissance des grands vins et la formation du vignoble moderne de Bordeaux: 1647–1767," in A. Huetz de Lemps, dir., *Géographie historique des vignobles*, Paris: CNRS, 1978, I, 59–88.

97.   Aubin, *La seigneurie en Bordelais*, 389.

98.   Pariset, *Histoire de Bordeaux, V*, 155–74.

99.   Aubin, *La seigneurie en Bordelais*, 390.

100.   Pijassou, *Un grand vignoble de qualité*, I, 333.

101.   Boutruche, *Histoire de Bordeaux, IV*, 84, 172–83, 486–92.

102.   Levantal, *Ducs et pairs*, 1105.

103.   Pariset, *Histoire de Bordeaux, V*, 355–56.

104.   Robert Forster, "The Noble Wine Producers of the Bordelais in the Eighteenth Century," *Economic History Review*, 14, 1961, 18–33.

105.   Robert Boutruche, *La crise d'une société. Seigneurs et paysans du Bordelais pendant la Guerre de Cent Ans.* Paris: Les Belles Lettres, 1947, 249–69, 295–315, 333–39.

106.   Bourtruche, *Histoire de Bordeaux, IV*, 171. Jean Cavignac, "La vigne en Haut-Médoc au XVIe siècle," *Vignobles et vins d'Aquitaine. Actes du XXe Congrès d'études régionales.* Bordeaux: Fédération historique du Sud-Ouest, 1970, 79–92. J.-P. Rajchenbach, "L'emprise foncière d'un bourg garonnais sous l'ancien régime: Langon," *Les cahiers du Bazadais*, 23, 1983, 3–39.

107.   Aubin, *La seigneurie en Bordelais*, 1989, 375–80.

108.   Charles Higounet, dir. *La seigneurie et le vignoble de Château Latour. Histoire d'un grand cru du Médoc (XIV–XXe siècle).* Bordeaux: Fédération historique du Sud-Ouest, 1974, 2 vols. René Pijassou, "La viticulture bordelaise dans la deuxième moitié du XVIIe siècle," *Vignobles et vins d'Aquitaine. Actes du XXe Congrès d'études régionales.* Bordeaux: Fédération historique du Sud-Ouest, 1970, 237–60. Pijassou, *Un grand vignoble de qualité.*

109.   Paul Butel, "Grands propriétaires et production des vins du Médoc au XVIIIe siècle," *Revue historique de Bordeaux et du département de la Gironde*, 12, 1963, 129–41.

110.   Pariset, *Histoire de Bordeaux, V*, 174–76.

111.   Aubin, *La seigneurie en Bordelais*, 287–88.

112. Aubin, *La seigneurie en Bordelais*, 411.

113. Joseph Boyreau, "Saint-Morillon au XVIIIe siècle. Essai sur la vitalité de la féodalité dans une commune rurale au temps de Montesquieu," *Revue archéologique de Bordeaux*, 85, 1994, 190.

114. Paul Massé, "Le dessèchement des marais du Bas-Médoc," *Revue historique de Bordeaux et du département de la Gironde*, 6, 1957, 25–68. Aubin, *La seigneurie en Bordelais*, 100–02.

115. Aubin, *La seigneurie en Bordelais*, 346–47.

116. Aubin, *La seigneurie en Bordelais*, 102–04.

117. Aubin, *La seigneurie en Bordelais*, 337.

118. Aubin, *La seigneurie en Bordelais*, 346.

119. Françoise Bériac, "Seigneurs et tenanciers des alentours de Verteuil vers 1490–1500," *Soulac et les pays médocains. Actes du 41e Congrès de la fédération historique du Sud-Ouest. 1988*. Bordeaux: Fédération historique du Sud-Ouest, 1989, 259–60. Nathalie Mouthon-Sepau, "Etude d'une seigneurie foncière dans le dernier tiers du XVe siècle: la seigneurie de Condat et Barbane, " *Revue historique et archéologique du Libournais et de la vallée de la Dordogne*, 1995, 93–102.

120. Aubin, *La seigneurie en Bordelais*, 276–77.

121. Aubin, *La seigneurie en Bordelais*, 278–81, 326–32.

122. Aubin, *La seigneurie en Bordelais*, 332.

123. Boyreau, "Saint-Morillon au XVIIIe siècle, 188.

124. Aubin, *La seigneurie en Bordelais*, 334.

125. Aubin, *La seigneurie en Bordelais*, 308.

126. Aubin, *La seigneurie en Bordelais*, 345.

127. Aubin, *La seigneurie en Bordelais*, 335.

128. Aubin, *La seigneurie en Bordelais*, 303.

129. Aubin, *La seigneurie en Bordelais*, 580.

130. Aubin, *La seigneurie en Bordelais*, 188–93.

131. Aubin, *La seigneurie en Bordelais*, 199–200.

132. Aubin, *La seigneurie en Bordelais*, 204–205.

133. Guyon, "L'abbaye bénédictine Sainte-Croix, 163–79. Loupès, *Chapitres et chanoines de Guyenne*, 91–120.

134. Aubin, *La seigneurie en Bordelais*, 116–18.

135. Loupès, "Le chapitre de Saint-Emilion, 74.

136. Aubin, *La seigneurie en Bordelais*, 72–74.

137. Charles Higounet, dir. *Histoire de l'Aquitaine*. Toulouse: Privat, 1971, 301–58. Christian Desplat, "Economie et société rurales en Aquitaine aux XVIIe et XVIIIe siècles," *Histoire Economie et Société*, 18, 1999, 133–55. Jean-Pierre Poussou, "Agriculture et commerce au 18e siècle: l'exemple du Sud-Ouest de la France,"

Irlande et France, XVIIe–XXe siècles. Paris: Ecole des Hautes Etudes en Sciences Sociales, 1980, 99–115. Deffontaines, *Les hommes et leurs travaux.*

138. Boutruche, *Histoire de Bordeaux, IV*, 466. Henri Enjalbert, "Le commerce de Bordeaux et la vie économique dans le bassin aquitain au XVIIe siècle," *Annales du Midi,* 62, 1950, 21–35.

139. Pariset, *Histoire de Bordeaux,V,* 209.

140. Pariset, *Histoire de Bordeaux,* V, 224–27.

141. Lucile Bourrachot, "Tenanciers et seigneur à Colonges au XVIe siècle d'après un procès en matière féodale," *Revue de l'Agenais,* 120, 1993, 297–322.

142. Pierre Ferrari, "La seigneurie de Duras au XVIIIe siècle," *Revue de l'Agenais,* 122, 1995, 243–65.

143. Rino Bandoch, "Les revenus de la noblesse du Bas-Quercy et sa place dans l'économie à la veille de la Révolution," *Montauban et les anciens pays de Tarn-et-Garonne. Actes du XLIe Congrès des sociétés académiques et savantes de Languedoc-Pyrénées-Gascogne,* 1986, 346–49.

144. Rino Bandoch, "Une source méconnue: les atlas seigneuriaux. L'exemple de Montpezat-de-Quercy," *Bulletin de la société archéologique de Tarn-et-Garonne,* 1993, 207–11. Philippe Calmon, "Deux notes sur les droits seigneuriaux dans la région de Figeac au XVIIIe siècle," *Bulletin de la société des études littéraires, scientifiques et artistique du Lot,* 107, 1986, 75–82. Jean Lartigaut, "Un ménage cadurcien au XVIIe siècle. Arnaud de Basombes et Anne de Molières d'après leurs livres de raison," *Bulletin de la société des études littéraires, scientifiques et artistiques du Lot,* 84, 1983, 18–26.

145. Rino Bandoch, "La riche noblesse provinciale à la veille de la Révolution. Les Pechpeyrou de Beaucaire," *Bulletin de la société archéologique de Tarn-et-Garonne,* 109, 1984, 111–27.

146. Bandoch, "Les revenus de la noblesse du Bas-Quercy," 345–51, 354–55.

147. Bordes, *D'Etigny et l'administration de l'intendance d'Auch.* Pierre Féral, "L'évolution de l'agriculture lectouroise du XVIe au XIXe siècle," *Histoire de Lectour.* Auch: Imprimerie Bouquet, 1972, 213–75. Christian Desplat, "Crise et projects économiques à Bayonne et en Labourd à la fin du XVIIIe siècle," *Bayonne et sa région. Actes du XXXIIIe Congrès d'études régionales. Bayonne, 1981.* Fédération historique du Sud-Ouest, 1983, 263–77. Christian Desplat, "Institutions et réalités pastorales dans les Pyrénées occidentales françaises à l'époque moderne," *L'élevage et la vie pastorale dans les montagnes de l'Europe au moyen âge et à l'époque moderne.* Clermont-Ferrand: Institut d'Etudes du Massif Central, 305–24.

148. Benoît Cursent, *Des maisons et des hommes. La Gascogne médiévale (XIe–XVe siècle).* Toulouse: Presses universitaires du Mirail, 1998, 201–34.

149. Elissondo, "La propriété des terres communes," 147.

150. Jean-Jacques Meliet & Philippe Rouche, "Structures agraires et économie rurale en Dallongue au XVIIème siecle (1661–1690)," *Du Couserans au Gave de Pau. Tradition et renouveau. Actes du XIe Congrès d'études régionales. Fédération des sociétés académiques et savantes de Languedoc-Pyrénées-Gascogne,* 1985, 129–65. Anne Zink, *Clochers et troupeaux. Les communautés rurales des Landes et du Sud-Ouest avant la Révolution.* Bordeaux: Presses universitaires de Bordeaux, 1997, 135.

151. Zink, *Clochers et troupeaux,* 153.

152. Cursent, *Des maisons et des hommes,* 298–307, 326–409.

153. Zink, *Clochers et troupeaux,* 63–66.

154. G. de Monsembernard, "Un village pyrénéen du XIVe au XVIIe siècle. Bilhères en Ossau," *Bulletin de la société archéologique et historique du Gers,* 93, 1992, 18–42.

155. Pierre-Amand Claverie, "La transformation des Landes de Gascogne," *Bulletin de la société de Borda,* 82, 1958, 203–12; and "Les Landes de Gascogne autrefois. L'ère agro-sylvo-pastorale," *Bulletin de la société de Borda,* 81, 1957, 325–37. Jean-Jacques Taillentou, "Conflits entre les ducs d'Albret et les barons du Marensin," *Bulletin de la société de Borda,* 119, 1994, 331–40.

156. Zink, *Clochers et troupeaux,* 145.

157. René Pijassou, "Structures foncières, société rurale et occupation du sol à Saint-Symphorien du XVIIIe au milieu du XIXe siècle," *La Grande Lande. Histoire naturelle et géographie historique.* Paris: CNRS, 1985, 269–86.

158. Zink, *Clochers et troupeaux,* 90–91.

159. Zink, *Clochers et troupeaux,* 147.

160. Zink, *clochers et troupeaux,* 133–37.

161. Bordes, *D'Étigny et l'administration,* 26–32.

162. Foursans-Bourdette, "Agriculture et industrie en Béarn," 187–258. And by the same author, *Economie et finances en Béarn au XVIIIe siècle.* Bordeaux: Editions Bière, 1963, viii, 26–27, 49.

163. Zink, *Clochers et troupeaux,* 260.

164. Zink, *Clochers et troupeaux,* 163–87.

165. Zink, *Clochers et troupeaux,* 204–49.

166. Féral, "A la veille de la Révolution," 27–39. Rives, *Dîme et société.*

167. A. de Galéjac, "Contribution à l'étude des dîmes dans une paroisse du Comminges comtal. Poucharramet," *Revue de Comminges,* 82, 1967, 111–18.

168. Rives, *Dîme et société,* 145–62. Rives, "Les refus de dîmes," 237–57.

169. Bordes, *D'Étigny et l'administration,* 24–25.

170. Bordes, *D'Étigny et l'administration,* 24–25.

Chapter Six. 1750–1789

1.   William Doyle, "Was There an Aristocratic Reaction in Pre-Revolutionary France,?"
     Past and Present, 57, 1972, 97–122. Jean Gallet, "Réflexion sur la réaction
     seigneuriale et féodale en France au XVIIIe siècle," in *Etat et société en France aux
     XVIIe et XVIIIe siècles. Mélanges offerts à Yves Durand*. Paris: Presses de
     l'Université de Paris-Sorbonne, 2000, 241–57. Olwen Hufton, "The Seigneur and the
     Rural Community in Eighteenth Century France," *Transactions of the Royal
     Historical Society*, ser. 5, 29, 1979, 21–40. Annie Antoine, "La réaction féodale: une
     notion mal adaptée au Bas-Maine," *La Mayenne: archéologie, histoire*, 12, 1989,
     49–77. Antoine, *Fiefs et villages*, 243–54.

2.   Aimé Cherest, *La chute de l'ancien régime*. Paris: Hachette, 1884, vol. I, 48–56.
     Philippe Sagnac, *Quomodo jura dominii aucta fuerint regnante Ludovico sexto
     decimo*. Le Puy: R. Marchessou, 1898. Alfonse Aulard, *La Révolution et le régime
     féodal*. Paris: Librairie Félix Alcan, 1919, 35–69. Aulard doubted that any significant
     intensification of lordship had occurred.

3.   Albert Soboul, "De la pratique des terriers à la veille de la Révolution," *Annales.
     Economies. Sociétés. Civilisations*, 19, 1964, 1049–65. Albert Soboul, *La Civilisation
     et la Révolution française. I. La crise de l'ancien régime*. Paris: Arthaud, 1970,
     88–91.

4.   Gallet, "Réflexion sur la réaction seigneuriale," 256.

5.   Marcel Garaud, "Le régime féodal en France à la veille de son abolition," in
     L'abolition de la "féodalité" dans le monde occidental. Paris: CNRS, 1971, vol. I,
     109–14. P. Léon et al., "Régime seigneurial et régime féodal dans la France du Sud-
     Est: déclin ou permanence? (XVIIe–XVIIIe siècles)," in *L'abolition de la féodalité*,
     166.

6.   Bianchi, "Les commmunautés villageoises françaises," 198.

7.   Gallet, "Réflexion sur la réaction seigneuriale," 251.

8.   Serge Bianchi, "Contestations et révoltes paysannes," in Serge Bianchi et al., *La terre
     et les paysans en France et en Grande-Bretagne du début du XVIIe siècle à la fin du
     XVIIIe siècle*. Paris: Armand Colin, 1999, 216–32.

9.   Frêche, *Toulouse et la région Midi-Pyrénées*, 536–45.

10. Astoul, "La contestation des dîmes en Quercy," 147–61.

11. Rives, "Les refus des dîmes," 238–39.

12. Rives, *Dîme et société*, 145–62. Rives, "Les refus des dîmes," 237–57. Féral, "A la
     veille de la Révolution," 27–34.

13. Clause, "Le vigneron champenois," 17–19.

14. Bart, *La Révolution française en Bourgogne*, 48–53.

15. Mary Anne Quinn, "Pratiques et théories de la coutume. Allodialité et conflits de
     droits dans la seigneurie de l'Isle-sous-Montréal au XVIIIe siècle," *Etudes rurales*,

nos. 103–04, 71–104.

16 Jean Richard, "Une redevance foncière bourguignonne du XIIe au XVIIIe siècle," *Mémoires de la société pour l'histoire du droit et des institutions des anciens pays bourguignons, comtois et romands*, 1962, 255–68. Cabourdin, "Les relations des communautés," 259–61. Gallet, "Deux seigneuries," 3–34. G. Gangneux, "Communauté rurale et seigneurie de l'ordre de Malte: Saint-Pierre-Avex aux temps modernes," *Provence historique*, 21, 1970, 351–60.

17. Hilton Root, "Seigneuries et communautés villageoises: les litiges à la veille de la Révolution française," *Mémoires de la société pour l'histoire du droit et des institutions des anciens pays bourguignons, comtois et romands*, 1986, 187–212.

18. Proust, "Petits fermiers de seigneuries," 421–32. Bastier, *La féodalité au siècle des Lumières*, 63–65. Billioud, "Une baronnie de grands négociants," 118–32.

19. J. Q. C. Mackrell, *The Attack on Feudalism in Eighteenth-Century France*. London: Routledge & Kegan Paul, 1973, 133–62.

20. Jean Nicolas, "La fin du régime seigneurial en Savoie (1771–1792)," in *L'abolition de la "féodalité" dans le monde occidental*. Paris: CNRS, 1971, vol. I, 515–25.

21. Mackrell, *The Attack on Feudalism*, 160–65.

22. Mackrell, *The Attack on Feudalism*, 17–47, 104–62.

23. Mackrell, *The Attack on Feudalism*, 48–76. J. H. M. Salmon, "Renaissance Jurists and Enlightened Magistrates: Perspectives on Feudalism in Eighteenth Century France," *French History*, 8, 1994, 387–402.

24. Bressan, "Servage et lumières," 365–81.

25. Thierry Bressan, "Un episode important et méconnu du procès du régime seigneurial en France: l'édit d'août 1779 contre les survivances serviles," *Histoire économie et société*, 15, 1996, 573–74. Thierry Bressan, "La critique de la condition mainmortable en France à la veille de la Révolution (1779–1789)," *Annales historiques de la Révolution française*, 1997, 75–91.

26. Bressan, "Un episode important," 575–76.

27. Gallet, "Les transformations de la seigneurie," 74. Bressan, "Un episode important," 576–577.

28. Bressan, "Un episode important," 578–95.

29. Bressan, "Un episode important," 580, 588–89.

30. Bressan, "Un episode important," 581–93.

31. Bressan, "L'idée d'affranchissement," 129–52.

32. Bressan, "Un episode important," 590.

33. Jules Finot, "La mainmorte dans la terre de l'abbaye de Luxeuil. Projet d'affranchissement des mainmortables par l'abbé de Clermont-Ferrand (1775–1789)," *Revue historique de droit français et étranger*, 1880, 217–89.

34. Bressan, "Un episode important," 590–95.

35.	Clère, *Les paysans de la Haute-Marne*, 145.
36.	Bloch, "La lutte pour l'individualisme agraire," 330 93, 511–556 860 "La question de la vaine pâture," 3–25.
37.	Bianchi, "Contestations et révoltes paysannes," 216–21.
38.	Florence Gauthier, *La voie paysanne dans la Révolution française. L'exemple picard.* Paris: François Maspero, 1977.
39.	Vivier, *Propriété collective*, 46–91. Sée, "Le partage des biens communaux," 47–81.
40.	Bianchi, "Contestations et révoltes paysannes," 222.
41.	Bianchi, "Contestations et révoltes paysannes," 224–25.
42.	Bianchi, "Contestations et révoltes paysannes," 224–26, 229–32. Georges Lefebvre, "Les foules révolutionnaires," in Georges Lefebvre, *La Grande Peur de 1789*. Paris: Armand Colin, 1988, 241–64. Lefebvre, *Les paysans du Nord*, 347–65.
43.	Bart, *La Révolution française en Bourgogne*, 54–55.
44.	Brosselin, *La forêt bourguignonne*, 169–83, 249–54.
45.	H. Bourderon, "La lutte contre la vie chère dans la généralité de Languedoc au XVIIIe siècle," *Annales du Midi*, 66, 1954, 155–70.
46.	Cart, "La crise économique des communautés rurales ardennaises," 3–35.
47.	Florence Gauthier & Guy-Robert Ikni, "Le mouvement paysan en Picardie: meneurs, pratiques, maturation et signification historique d'un programme (1775–1794)," *Mouvements populaires et conscience sociale, XVIe–XIXe siècles*. Paris: Maloine, 1985, 435–48.
48.	Bianchi, "Les communautés villageoises françaises," 208–11.
49.	Andrée Corvol, "La coercion en milieu forestier," *Mouvements popularies et conscience sociale, XVIe–XIXe siècles*. Paris: Maloine, 1985, 199–207. And in the same collection: Anne Marie Cocula-Vaillières, "La contestation des privilèges seigneuriaux dans le fonds des Eaux et Forêts. L'exemple aquitain dans la seconde moitié du XVIIIe siècle," 209–15. Abel Poitrineau, "Le détonateur économico-fiscal et la charge des rancoeurs catégorielles profondes lors des explosions de la colère populaire en Auvergne, au XVIIIe siècle," 361–69. Jacques Frayssenge & Nicole Lemaître, "Les émotions populaires en Rouergue au XVIIIe siècle," 371–81.
50.	Chaussinand-Nogaret, *La noblesse au XVIIIe siècle*, 225.
51.	Lemarchand, "La France au XVIIIe siècle," 115–20.
52.	Bianchi, "Les communautés villageoises françaises," 211. Wartelle, "Les communautés rurales du Pas-de-Calais," 100–21. Michel Vovelle, "Les troubles sociaux en Provence (1750–1789)," *Actes du 93e Congrès national des sociétés savantes. Tours 1968. Section d'histoire moderne et contemporaine*. Paris: Bibliothèque nationale, 1971, II, 325–72.
53.	John Markoff, "Violence, Emancipation, and Democracy: The Countryside and the French Revolution," *American Historical Review*, 100, 1995, 373.
54.	Emmanuel Le Roy Ladurie, "Révoltes et contestations rurales en France de 1675 à

1788," *Annales. Economies. Sociétés. Civilisations,* 29, 1974, 6–22. Clère, *Les paysans de la Haute-Marne,* 131–50. Fernand Evrard, "Les paysans du Mâconnais et les brigandages de Juillet 1789," *Annales de Bourgogne,* 19, 1947, 7–39, 97–121. Poitrineau, *La vie rurale en Basse-Auvergne,* 738.

55. Boehler, *Une société rurale,* 1303–44.

56. François-Xavier Emmanuelli, "Une relecture de la pré-révolution provençale," in *La France pré-révolutionnaire.* Paris: Editions du Publisud, 1991, 97–110. Cubells, *La Provence des Lumières,* 197–210.

57. Gérard Aubin, "La crise du prélèvement seigneurial à la fin de l'ancien régime," in Robert Chagny, *Aux origines provinciales de la Révolution.* Grenoble: Presses universitaires de Grenoble, 1990, 24. Michel Briard, "Campagnes françaises en révolution," in Serge Bianchi et al., *La terre et les paysans en France et en Grande-Bretagne du début du XVIIe siècle à la fin du XVIIIe siècle.* Paris: Armand Colin, 1999, 248.

58. Pelzer, "Nobles, payans et la fin de la féodalité," 41–54.

59. Goujard, *L'abolition de la "féodalité",* 8–73, 161–63. Lemarchand, *La fin du féodalisme,* 3–53, 130, 425. Lemarchand, "Les campagnes de Haute-Normandie à la veille de la Révolution," *Bulletin de la société d'histoire moderne et contemporaine,* 89, 1990, 6–10.

60. Vital Chomel, "La Grande Peur et la révolution des paysans dauphinois," in Vital Chomel, éd., *Les débuts de la Révolution française en Dauphiné, 1788–1791.* Grenoble: Presses universitaires de Grenoble, 1988, 175–99. Egret, *Le parlement de Dauphiné,* II, 51–71. Nicolas, *La Révolution française dans les Alpes,* 11–89. Jean Nicolas, "Le paysan et son seigneur en Dauphiné à la veille de la révolution," in *La France d'ancien régime. Etudes réunies en l'honneur de Pierre Goubert.* Toulouse: Privat, 1984, II, 497–507.

61. Briard, "Campagnes françaises en révolution," 243–66.

62. Briard, "Campagnes françaises en révoltuion," 255–66. Dalby, *Les paysans cantaliens et la Révolution française.* Leymarie, "Les mouvements populaires à Maurs," 126–32. Jean Boutier, "Jacqueries en pays croquant. Les révoltes paysannes en Aquitaine (décembre 1789–Mars 1790)," *Annales E.S.C.,* 34, 1979, 760–86.

63. Markoff, "Violence, Emancciptation, and Democracy," 373.

64. Philippe Sagnac & P. Caron, *Les comités des droits féodaux et de législation et l'abolition du régime seigneurial (1789–1793).* Paris: Imprimerie nationale, 1907. Garaud, *Histoire générale du droit privé.II. La Révolution et la propriété foncière.*

65. Briard, "Campagnes françaises en révolution," 254–66.

BIBLIOGRAPHY

Achard, A. *Une ancienne justice seigneuriale en Auvergne. Sugères et ses habitants.* Clermont-Ferrand: Imprimerie générale, 1929.

Alexis, M. "Etude sur la situation économique et sociale de la commune de Givry-en-Argonne aux XVIIe et XVIIIe siècles," *Actes du 78e Congrès national des sociétés savantes,* 1953, 125–34.

Allix, André "Le trafic en Dauphiné à la fin du Moyen Age. Esquisse rétrospective de géographie économique," *Revue de géographie alpine,* 9, 1923, 373–420.

Ambly, Pierre d' "Un propriétaire terrien en Berry au XVIIIe siècle," *Cahiers d'archéologie et d'histoire du Berry,* 81, 1985, 61–76.

Angers, Denise *Le terrier de la famille d'Orbec à Cideville (Haute-Normandie) XIVe–XVIe siècles.* Montréal: Les presses de l'Université de Montréal, 1993.

Antoine, Annie *Fiefs et villages du Bas-Maine au XVIIIe siècle. Etude de la seigneurie et de la vie rurale.* Mayenne: Editions régionales de l'Ouest, 1994.

———, "La réaction féodale: une notion mal adaptée au Bas-Maine," *La Mayenne: archéologie, histoire,* 12, 1989, 49–77.

———, "La seigneurie, la terre et les paysans," *Bulletin de la société d'histoire moderne,* 1999, 15–33.

Antonetti, G. "Le partage des forêts usagères ou communales entre les seigneurs et les communautés d'habitants," *Revue historique de droit français et étranger,* 41, 1963, 238–86, 418–42, 592–634.

Appolis, Emile "La question de la vaine pâture en Languedoc au XVIIIe siècle," *Annales historiques de la Révolution française,* 15, 1938, 97–132.

———, *Un pays languedocien au miliu du XVIIIe siècle. Le diocèse civil de Lodève. Etude administrative et économique.* Albi: Imprimerie coopérative du Sud-Ouest, 1951.

Arbos, Philippe *La vie pastorale dans les Alpes françaises. Etude de géographie humaine.* Paris: Armand Colin, 1923.

Astoul, Guy "La contestation des dîmes en Quercy à la veille de la Révolution," *Histoire et sociétés rurales,* 1997, 147–61.

Aubin, Gérard "La crise du prélèvement seigneurial à la fin de l'ancien régime," in Robert

Chagny, *Aux origines provinciales de la Révolution*. Grenoble: Presses universitaires de Grenoble, 1990, 23–33.

————, *La seigneurie en Bordelais au XVIIIe siècle d'après la pratique notariale (1715–1789)*. Rouen: Publications de l'Université de Rouen, 1989.

Aubrun, Michel "Seigneurs et paysans au temps de Louis XIII d'après le terrier du Plaix-Joliet de 1633," *Mémoires de la société des sciences naturelles et archéologiques de la Creuse*, 43, 1989, 513–21.

Audisio, Gabriel "Une grande migration alpine en Provence (1460–1560)," *Bollettino storico-bibliografico subalpino*, 87, 1989, 65–140, 511–59.

Augustin, Jean-Marie "La mainmorte dans la terre de Mouthe de la fin du XVIe siècle à la Révolution," *Mémoires de la société d'émulation du Doubs*, 23, 1981, 45–91.

Aulard, Alfonse *La Révolution et la régime féodal*. Paris: Librairie Félix Alcan, 1919.

Bach, M. "Les droits d'usage dans l'ancien comté de Dabo," *Revue forestière française*, 1957, 667–99.

Bandoch, Rino "La riche noblesse provinciale à la veille de la Révolution. Les Pechpeyrou de Beaucaire," *Bulletin de la société archéologique de Tarn-et-Garonne*, 109, 1984, 111–27.

————, "Les revenus de la noblesse du Bas-Quercy et sa place dans l'économie à la veille de la Révolution," *Montauban et les anciens pays de Tarn-et-Garonne. Actes du XLIe congrès des sociétés académiques et savantes de Languedoc-Pyrénées-Gascogne*, 1986, 345–58.

————, "Une source méconnue: les atlas seigneuriaux. L'exemple de Montpezat-de-Quercy," *Bulletin de la société archéologique de Tarn-et-Garonne*, 1993, 207–11.

Baratier, Edouard éd. *Histoire de la Provence*. Toulouse: Privat, 1976.

Barbier, Edmond & Jean-Paul Laurent, "Bail à métairie perpétuelle, du XVe siècle concernant le village de Lachaud, commune de Champagnac, dans l'ancienne vicomté de Rouchechouart," *Bulletin de la société archéologique et historique du Limousin*, 112, 1957, 500–09.

Baron, Romain "La bourgeoisie de Varzy au XVIIe siècle," *Annales de Bourgogne*, 36, 1964, 161–208.

————, "La vie rurale dans la région de Varzy dans la seconde moitié du 17e siècle," *Mémoires de l'académie académique du Nivernais*, 69, 1987, 35–61.

————, "Une paroisse disparue: Saint-Martin-des-Vaux," *Bulletin de la société scientifique et artistique de Clamecy*, 92, 1968, 83–90.

Bart, Jean *La liberté ou la terre. La mainmorte en Bourgogne au siècle des Lumières*. Dijon: Université de Dijon, 1984.

————, *La Révolution française en Bourgogne*. Clermont-Ferrand: La Française d'Edition et d'Imprimerie, 1996.

Bastier, Jean "Droits féodaux et revenus agricoles en Rouergue à la veille de la Révolution,"

Annales du Midi, 95, 1983, 261–87.

——, *La féodalité au siècle des Lumières dans la région de Toulouse (1730–1790)*. Paris: Bibliothèque national, 1975.

Baudon, Marcel "Les communautés rurales d'une haute vallée de Tarentaise au XVe siècle à la lumière des registres terriers de Saint-Martin-de-Belleville," *Actes du 108e Congrès national des sociétés savantes. Section de philologie et d'histoire*, 1983, 141–60.

Bavoux, P. "Les particuliarités de la mainmorte dans la terre de Luxeuil," *Mémoires de la société pour l'histoire du droit et des institutions des anciens pays bourguignons, comtois et romands*, 13, 1950–1951, 61–89.

Bayard, Françoise "Ville et campagnes dans la fortune de Pierre Perrachon, noble lyonnais de 1642 à 1688," *Villes et campagnes, XVe–XXe siècle*. Lyon: Presses universitaires de Lyon, 1977, 105–31.

Bébéar, Catherine "Le temporel de l'abbaye de Montivilliers à la fin du Moyen Age," *Cahiers Léopold Deslisle*, 47, 1998, 3–76; 48, 1999, 77–181.

Beck, Patrice "De la grange au village: Crepey en Bourgogne (XIIe–XVIIe siècle)," in *Le Village médiéval et son environnement. Etudes offertes à Jean-Marie Pesez*. Paris: Publications de la Sorbonne, 1998, 447–59.

Belotte, Michel *La région de Bar-sur-Seine à la fin du Moyen Age, du début du XIIIe au milieu du XVIe siècle*. Lille: Université de Lille, 1973.

Bériac, Françoise "Seigneurs et tenanciers des alentours de Verteuil vers 1490–1500," in *Soulac et les pays médocains. Actes du 41e Congrès de la fédération historique du Sud-Ouest, 1988*. Bordeaux: Fédération historique du Sud-Ouest, 1989, 253–65.

Bernard, R.-J. "Les communautés rurales en Gévaudan sous l'ancien régime," *Revue du Gévaudan, des Causses et des Cévennes*, 17, 1971, 110–65.

Bernet, Gabriel "L'économie d'un village du Lauragais au XVIIe siècle: le consulat de Pugnères de 1593 à 1715," *Annales du Midi*, 78, 1966, 481–512.

Bertho-Leclerc, Catherine "La presqu'île de Rhuys au XVIIIe siècle. La terre, la mer et les hommes en Basse Bretagne à la fin de l'ancien régime (1680–1790)," *Positions des thèses. Ecole nationale des chartes*, 1976, 17–26.

Bianchi, Serge "Contestations et révoltes paysannes," in Serge Bianchi et al., *La terre et les paysans en France et en Grande-Bretagne du début du XVIIe siècle à la fin du XVIIIe siècle*. Paris: Armand Colin, 1999, 216–32.

———, "Les communautés villageoises françaises au siècle des Lumières," in Serge Bianchi et al., *La terre et les paysans en France et en Grande-Bretagne du début du XVIIe siècle à la fin du XVIIIe siècle*. Paris: Armand Colin, 1999, 191–212.

Billioud, Joseph "Une baronnie de grands négociants marseillais: La Tour d'Aigues," *Provence historique*, 19, 1969, 118–32.

Bindet, J. "Les dernières années de la baronnie de Marcey," *Revue de l'Avranchin et du pays de Granville,* 44, 1967, 225–40.

Bischoff, Georges *Gouvernes et gouvernants en Haute Alsace à l'époque autrichienne. Les Etats et pays antérieurs des origines au milieu du XVIe siècle.* Strasbourg: Librairie Istra, 1982.

———, "L'abbaye de Murbach et ses paysans à la fin du Moyen Age," *Histoire de l'Alsace rurale.* Strasbourg: Librairie Istra, 1983, 113–18.

———, "Les paysans de Haute-Alsace en 1525," *Histoire de l'Alsace rurale.* Strasbourg: Librairie Istra, 1983, 129–36.

Blachon, Jérôme "Des Cisterciens aux seigneurs laïques: histoire de la ferme d'Ithe (XIIe–XVIIIe siècles)," *Paris et Ile-de-France. Mémoires,* 49, 1998, 133–217.

Blazy, Jean-Pierre "Les campagnes du pays de France au début du XVIIIe siècle d'après l'enquête de 1717," *Bulletin de la société d'histoire et d'archéologie de Gonesse et du pays de France,* 10, 1989, 35–45.

Bloch, Marc "La lutte pour l'individualisme agraire dans la France du XVIIIe siècle," *Annales d'histoire économique et sociale,* II, 1930, 329–83, 511–56.

———, *Les caractères originaux de l'histoire rurale française.* Paris: Armand Colin, 1988.

Bodinier, Bernard "Ce que nous apprennent registres et plans terriers: l'exemple d'un quarantaine de seigneuries de l'Eure à la veille de la Révolution," *Le monde rural en Normandie.* Caen: Musée de Normandie, 1998, 181–94.

———, "Les biens des chapitres normands et la Révolution," *Chapitres et cathédrales en Normandie.* Caen: Musée de Normandie, 1997, 27–40.

Boehler, Jean-Michel "De la reconstruction agraire à la mise en vente des biens nationaux: possession de la terre, conjoncture agraire et rapports sociaux dans la plaine d'Alsace (XVIIe–XVIIIe siècles)," *Histoire, économie et société,* 18, 1999, 43–62.

———, "Economie agrairie et société rurale dans la plaine d'Alsace aux XVIIe et XVIIIe siècles: l'amorce des mutations," *Histoire de l'Alsace rurale.* Strasbourg: Librairie Istra, 1983, 213–18.

———, *Une société rurale en milieu rhénan: la paysannerie de la plaine d'Alsace (1648–1789).* Strasbourg: Presses universitaires de Strasbourg, 1995.

Boichard, J. "Quelques éléments de la vie rurale entre Loire et Allier. Propriété et exploitation du sol," *Revue de géographie de Lyon,* 37, 1962, 250–71.

Bois, Guy *Crise du féodalisme. Economie rurale et démographie en Normandie orientale du début du XIVe siècle au milieu du XVIe siècle.* Paris: Ecole des hautes Etudes en Sciences sociales, 1976.

Bonnin, Bernard "Le Dauphiné à la veille de la Révolution: formes de l'économie et structures sociales," in Vital Chomel, éd. *Les débuts de la Révolution française en Dauphiné, 1788–1791.* Grenoble: Presses universitaires de Grenoble, 1988, 9–31.

———, "L'endettement des communautés rurales en Dauphiné au XVIIe siècle," *Bulletin du centre d'histoire économique et sociale de la région lyonnaise,* n. 3, 1971, 1–9.

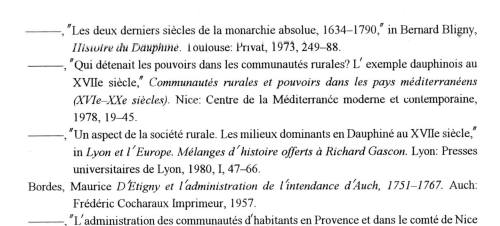

———, "Les deux derniers siècles de la monarchie absolue, 1634–1790," in Bernard Bligny, *Histoire du Dauphiné*. Toulouse: Privat, 1973, 249–88.

———, "Qui détenait les pouvoirs dans les communautés rurales? L'exemple dauphinois au XVIIe siècle," *Communautés rurales et pouvoirs dans les pays méditerranéens (XVIe–XXe siècles)*. Nice: Centre de la Méditerranée moderne et contemporaine, 1978, 19–45.

———, "Un aspect de la société rurale. Les milieux dominants en Dauphiné au XVIIe siècle," in *Lyon et l'Europe. Mélanges d'histoire offerts à Richard Gascon*. Lyon: Presses universitaires de Lyon, 1980, I, 47–66.

Bordes, Maurice *D'Étigny et l'administration de l'intendance d'Auch, 1751–1767*. Auch: Frédéric Cocharaux Imprimeur, 1957.

———, "L'administration des communautés d'habitants en Provence et dans le comté de Nice à la fin de l'ancien régime. Traits communs et diversité," *Annales du Midi*, 84, 1972, 369–96.

———, "La vitalité des communautés provençales au XVIIIe siècle," *Provence historique*, 23, 1973, 22–32.

———, "Les communautés villageoises des provinces méridionales à l'époque moderne," in *Les communautés villageoises en Europe occidentale du Moyen Age aux Temps modernes*. Auch: Centre culturel de l'Abbaye de Flaran, 1984, 143–64.

Bottin, Jacques "Le paysan, l'Etat et le seigneur en Normandie, milieu du XVIe–milieu du XVIIe siècle," *Genèse de l'état moderne. Prélèvement et redistribution*. Paris: Editions du Centre national de la recherche scientifique, 1987, 101–10.

———, *Seigneurs et paysans dans l'ouest du Pays de Caux, 1540–1650*. Paris: Le Sycomore, 1983.

Bottin-Louvet, Georges "Le chapitre d'Avrances à la fin de l'ancien régime," *Chapitres et cathédrales de Normandie*. Caen: Musée de Normandie, 1997, 13–26.

Boüard, Michel de éd. *Histoire de la Normandie*. Toulouse: Privat, 1970.

Boudin, M. "Du laboureur aisé au gentilhomme compagnard. Les Perrote de Cairon, de Bretteville-l'Orgueilleuse (1380–1480)," *Annales de Normandie*, 13, 1963, 237–68.

Boudrie, Henri "Affranchissement de rentes féodales à Meymac," *Lemouzi*, 1986, 123–26.

Boulanger, Pierre "La crise de l'économie et de la société champenoise dans les dernières années de l'ancien régime," *Mémoires de la société d'agriculture, commerce, sciences et arts du département de la Marne*, 100, 1985, 97–158.

Bouloiseau, M. "Aspects sociaux de la crise cotonnière dans les campagnes rouennaises en 1788–1789," *Actes du 81e Congrès national des sociétés savantes. Section d'histoire moderne et contemporaine*, 1956, 403–28.

Bourderon, H. "La lutte contre la vie chère dans la généralité de Languedoc au XVIIIe siècle," *Annales du Midi*, 66, 1954, 155–70.

Bourquin, Laurent "La noblesse de Champagne dans son espace régional vers le milieu du

XVIIe siècle," *Sociétés et idéologies des temps modernes. Hommage à Arlette Jouanna*. Montpellier: Université de Montpellier III, 1996,vol. I, 39–77.

———, "Les seigneuries de la noblesse champenoise pendant les guerres de religion: crise ou prosperité?," in Michel Balard, éd., *Paris et ses campagnes sous l'ancien régime. Mélanges offerts à Jean Jacquart*. Paris: Publications de la Sorbonne, 1994, 99–108.

Bourrachot, Lucille "L'administration des biens d'une baronnie quercynoise à la fin du XVIIIe siècle: Castelnau-Bretenoux," *Bulletin de la société des études littéraires, scientifiques et artistiques du Lot*, 74, 1953, 147–53.

———, "Tenanciers et seigneur à Colonges au XVIe siècle d'après un procès en matière féodale," *Revue de l'Agenais*, 120, 1993, 297–322.

Boutier, Jean "Défricher en Bas-Limousin au XVIIIe siècle: immobilisme économique et conflits agraires," *Bulletin de la société des lettres, sciences et arts de la Corrèze*, 82, 1979, 23–44.

———, "Jacqueries en pays croquant. Les révoltes paysannes en Aquitaine (décembre 1789–Mars 1790)," *Annales E.S.C.*, 34, 1979, 760–86.

Boutruche, Robert dir. *Histoire de Bordeaux. IV. Bordeaux de 1453 à 1715*. Bordeaux: Fédération historique du Sud-Ouest, 1966.

———, *La crise d'une société. Seigneurs et paysans du Bordelais pendant la Guerre de Cent Ans*. Paris: Les Belles Lettres, 1947

Bouveresse, Jacques "Contribution à l'étude de la dîme: la jurisprudence de Lorraine au XVIIIe siècle," *Annales de l'Est*, série 5, 33, 1981, 99–150.

Boyreau, Joseph "Saint-Morillon au XVIIIe siècle. Essai sur la vitalité de la féodalité dans une commune rurale au temps de Montesquieu," *Revue archéologique de Bordeaux*, 85, 1994, 183–207.

Braudel, Fernand *Afterthoughts on Material Civilization and Capitalism*. Baltimore: The Johns Hopkins University Press, 1977.

———, *Civilisation matérielle, economie et capitalisme, XVe–XVIIIe siècle*. 3 vols. Paris: Armand Colin, 1979

Brékilien, Yann *Les paysans bretons au XIXe siècle*. Paris: Hachette, 1994.

Brelot, J. "La mainmorte dans la région de Dole," *Mémoires de la société pour l'histoire du droit et des institutions des anciens pays bourguignons, comtois et romands*, 1950–1951, 91–108.

Bressan, Thierry "La critique de la condition mainmortable en France à la veille de la Révolution (1779–1789)," *Annales historiques de la Révolution française*, 1997, 75–91.

———, "La mainmorte dans la France du XVIIIe siècle. Le cas des provinces du Centre," *Histoire et sociétés rurales*, 6, 1996, 51–76.

———, "L'idée d'affranchissement général dans la principauté de Monbéliard (seconde moitié du XVIIIe siècle)," *Mémoires de la société pour l'histoire du droit et des institutions des anciens pays bourguignons, comtois et romands,* 54, 1997, 129–52.

———, "Servage et lumieres: le rejet du droit de suite par le parlement de Paris (1760–1765)," *Revue historique,* 296, 365–81.

———, "Un episode important et méconnu du procès du régime seigneurial en France: l'édit d'août 1779 contre les survivances serviles," *Histoire économie et société,* 15, 1996, 571–99.

Briard, Michel "Campagnes françaises en révolution," in Serge Bianchi et al., *La terre et les paysans en France et en Grande-Bretagne du début du XVIIe siècle à la fin du XVIIIe siècle.* Paris: Armand Colin, 1999, 243–66.

Broquereau, Michel "Des banalités en Poitou aux XVIIe et XVIIIe siècles," *Bulletin de la société des antiquaires de l'Ouest,* sér. 4, 5, 1959, 215–62.

Brosselin, Arlette *La forêt bourguignonne (1660–1789).* Dijon: Editions universitaires de Dijon, 1987.

Brunet, Pierre *Structure agraire et économie rurale des plateaux tertiaires entre la Seine et l'Oise.* Caen: Caron et Cie, 1960.

Brussier, Hervé "Le mouvement des mutations foncières d'après le fonds des ensaisinements du chapitre cathédral de Notre-Dame de Paris, 1518–1609," *Mémoires de Paris et Ile-de-France,* 37, 1986, 153–84.

Bugler, Georges *La fin de l'ancien régime dans le pays de Montbéliard.* Besançon: Annales littéraires de l'Université de Besançon, 1989.

Bula, Sandrine *L'apanage du comte d'Artois (1773–1790).* Paris: Ecole des Chartes, 1993.

———, "L'apanage du comte d'Artois (1773–1790)," *Positions des thèses. Ecole des Chartes,* 1989, 55–63.

Burckard, Fr. "Les rapports des seigneurs et des habitants de la Motte-Chalançon du XIVe au XVIIIe siècle," *Bulletin d'archéologie et de statistique de la Drôme,* 74, 1958, 16–20.

Burg, André-Marcel "Le droit de glandée et l'élevage du porc en forêt de Haguenau au début du XVIe siècle," *Bulletin philologique et historique,* 1967, I, 129–36.

Butel, Paul "Grands propriétaires et production des vins du Médoc au XVIIIe siècle," *Revue historique de Bordeaux et du département de la Gironde,* 12, 1963, 129–41.

Buttoud, G. "Les projects forestiers de la Révolution (1789–1798)," *Revue forestière française,* 35, 1983, 9–20.

Cabourdin, Guy *Encyclopédie illustrée de la Lorraine. Histoire de la Lorraine. Les temps modernes. 1. De la Renaissance à la Guerre de Trente Ans.* Nancy: Editions Serpenoise, vol. 3-1, 1990.

———, *Encyclopédie illustrée de la Lorraine. Histoire de la Lorraine. Les temps modernes. 2. De la paix de Westphalie à la fin de l'ancien régime.* Nancy: Editions Serpenoise, vol 3-2, 1990.

———, "La population de Strasbourg sous l'ancien régime," *Annales de démographie historique,* 1967, 267–73.

———, "Les relations des communautés villageoises de Lorraine avec les seigneurs (XVIe–XVIIIe siècles)," *Les communautes villageoises en Europe occidentale du Moyen Age aux Temps modernes*. Auch: Centre culturel de l'abbaye de Flaran, 1984, 259–61.

———, "L'exploitation de la terre de 1500 à la guerre de Trente Ans," *Mémoires de l'Académie de Stanislas*, 7e série, VIIII, 1979–80, 115–24.

———, "Routes et grand commerce en Lorraine du milieu du XVIe siècle à la guerre de Trente Ans," *Transports et voies de communication*. Paris: Les Belles Lettres, 1977, 81–96.

———, *Terre et hommes en Lorraine, 1550–1635. Toulois et comté de Vaudémont*. Nancy: Université de Nancy II, Annales de l'Est, 1977, 2vols.

Calmon, Philippe "Deux notes sur les droits seigneuriaux dans la région de Figeac au XVIIIe siècle," *Bulletin de la société des études littéraires, scientifiques et artistique du Lot*, 107, 1986, 75–82.

Cameron, Iain A. *Crime and Repression in the Auvergne and in Guyenne 1720–1790*. Cambridge: Cambridge University Press, 1981.

Campserveux, Max "La condition économique et sociale de la noblesse du Cotentin à la fin du Moyen Age," *Revue de l'Avranchin et du Pays de Granville*, 59, 1982, 255–71, 309–25, 339–49.

Carlat, Michel "La Chartreuse de Bonnefoy, ses granges et les communautés paysannes du Gerbier-Mézenac de 1500 à 1788: jalons pour une histoire économique et sociale," *Cahiers de la Haute-Loire*, 1986, 103–45.

Cart, Michel "La crise économique des communautés rurales ardennaises à la fin de l'ancien régime (1770–1789)," *Revue historique ardennaise*, 25, 1990, 3–35.

Cassan, Michel "Officiers "moyen", officiers seigneuriaux. Quelques perspectives de recherche," *Cahiers du centre de recherches historiques*, 27, 71–83.

———, "Une approche de la noblesse de Bas-Limousin," *Travaux du centre de recherches sur les origines de l'Europe moderne*, 6, 1986, 4–31.

Catarina, Didier "Justices et seigneuries en Languedoc à l'époque moderne," *La terre et les pouvoirs en Languedoc et en Roussillon du Moyen Age à nos jours*. Montpellier: Fédération historique du Languedoc méditerranéen et du Roussillon, 1992, 167–72.

Cavignac, Jean "La vigne en Haut-Médoc au XVIe siècle," *Vignobles et vins d'Aquitaine. Actes du XXe Congrès d'études régionales*. Bordeaux: Fédération historique du Sud-Ouest, 1970, 79–92.

Chalard, Yvon "Une collectivité rurale au XVIIIe siècle: Saint-Pantaléon-de-Larche," *Bulletin de la société des lettres, sciences et arts de la Corrèze*, 91, 1969, 173–200; 92, 1970, 131–50.

Champier, Laurent "Le défrichement de la forêt de Bièvre (Bas-Dauphiné). Essai d'interprétation d'un type de terroir méridional," *Revue de géographie de Lyon*, 29, 1952, 436–50.

———, "Les fondements humains du vignoble mâconnais," *Annales de l'Académie de Mâcon*,

44, 1958–1959, 65–75.

———, "Lyon et sa région agricole (fin du XVIIIe siècle et première moitié du XIXe siècle)," *Actes du 89e Congrès national des sociétés savantes. Séction de géographie*. Paris: Bibliothèque nationale, 1965, 33–46.

Charbonnier, Pierre "L'exploitation de la forêt des Dôme sous l'ancien régime," *Revue d'Auvergne*, 101, 1987, 17–26.

———, *Une autre France. La seigneurie en Basse-Auvergne du XIVe au XVIe siècle*. Clermont-Ferrand: Institut d'Etudes du Massif Central, 1980.

Chaumet, Danièle "L'évolution de la vie rurale dans trois communes du sud de la Limagne: Plauzat, La Sauvetat et Authezat," *Revue d'Auvergne*, 82, 1968, 157–87.

Chaussinand-Nogaret, Guy *La noblesse au XVIIIe siècle*. Bruxelles: Editions Complexe, 1984.

Chauvin-Lechaptois, Monique *Les comptes de la châtellenie de Lamballe (1387–1482)*. Rennes: Université de Haute-Bretagne, 1977, 64–109.

Chédeville André & Noël-Yves Tonnerre, *La Bretagne féodale, XIe–XIIIe siècles*. Rennes: Ouest-France, 1987.

Chéreau, Claude "Recherches d'histoire agraire angevine dans les vallées de la Sarthe et du Loir," *Actes du 97e Congrès national des sociétés savantes. Section de géographie*, 1972, 121–34.

Cherest, Aimé *La chute de l'ancien régime*. Paris: Hachette, 1884, 3 vols.

Chéron, A. & G. de Sarret de Coussergues, *Une seigneurie en Bas-Languedoc. Coussergues et les Sarret*. Bruxelles: Hayez, 1963.

Chevalier, Bernard "Bailleurs et preneurs en Touraine après la Guerre de Cent Ans. Les défricheurs de la métairie de la Cicogne aux prises avec le chapitre de Saint-Martin," *Etudes rurales*, 16, 1965, 117–24.

Chevrier, Georges "Le droit d'indire d'après la coutume officielle du duché de Bourgogne (XVIe–XVIIIe siècles)," *Mémoires de la société pour l'histoire du droit et des institutions des anciens pays bourguignons, comtois et romands*, 1952, 8–34.

Chianéa, Gérard *La condition juridique des terres en Dauphiné au 18e siècle (1700–1789)* Paris: Mouton, 1969.

Chiffre, Jean "Granges et villages nouveaux en Bourgogne aux XVIe et XVIIe siècles. Le rôle des abbayes dans la transformation du paysage rural," *Revue géographique de l'Est*, 22, 1982, 183–97.

———, "Le rôle des communautés familiales dans le peuplement et l'organisation de l'espace rural bourbonnais," *Etudes bourbonnaises*, 250, 1989, 229–36.

Chomel, Vital "De la principauté à la province, 1349–1456," in Bernard Bligny, éd., *Histoire du Dauphiné*. Toulouse: Privat, 1973, 161–90.

———, "Esquisse d'une histoire du Grésivaudan," *Evocations. Bulletin mensuel du groupe d' études historiques et géographiques du Bas-Dauphiné*, 1986, 85–102.

———, "Francs et rustiques dans la seigneurie dauphinoise au temps des affranchissements,"

Bulletin philologique et historique, 1965, 285–308.

————, "La Grande Peur et la révolution des paysans dauphinois," in Vital Chomel, éd., *Les débuts de la Révolution française en Dauphiné, 1788–1791*. Grenoble: Presses universitaires de Grenoble, 1988, 175–99.

————, "L'économie seigneuriale et rente féodale en Grésivaudan d'après la comptabilité du marquis Pierre de Marcieu, lieutenant général en Dauphiné (1760–1793)," *Actes des 115e et 116e Congrès national des sociétés savantes*, 1990–1991, I, 17–30.

————, "L'héritage médiévale et les schismes de l'âge moderne," in Bligny, *Histoire du Dauphiné*. Toulouse: Privat, 1973, 191–218.

————, "Ressources domaniales et subsides en Dauphiné (1355–1364)," *Provence historique*, 25, 1975, 179–92.

————, "Un censier dauphinois inédit. Méthode et portée de l'édition du Probus," *Bulletin philologique et historique*, 1964, 319–409.

Claerr, Thierry "La gestion du comté de Dammartin-en-Goële à la fin du XVe siècle d'après l'étude du compte de 1495–1496," *Paris et Ile-de-France. Mémoires*, 50, 1999, 149–200.

Clause, Georges "Le vigneron champenois du XVIIIe au XIXe siècle. De la pauvreté contestataire de 1789 à la Révolution de 1911," *Etudes champenoises*, 6, 1988, 13–36.

Claverie, Pierre-Amand "La transformation des Landes de Gascogne," *Bulletin de la société de Borda*, 82, 1958, 203–12;

————, "Les Landes de Gascogne autrefois. L'ère agro-sylvo-pastorale," *Bulletin de la société de Borda*, 81, 1957, 325–37.

Clément, Cristelle "Le règlement des différends dans le Châtillonnais: les audiences civiles des justices seigneuriales du bailliage de la Montagne (18e siècle)," *Annales de Bourgogne*, 70 1998, 179–90.

Clère, Jean-Jacques *Les paysans de la Haute-Marne et la Révolution française*. Paris: Comité des travaux historiques et scientifiques, 1988.

————, "Servitude et liberté dans le bailliage de Chaumont en Bassigny," *Mémoires de la société pour l'histoire du droit et des institutions des anciens pays bourguignons, comtois et romands*, 40, 1983, 239–69.

Cocula-Vaillières, Anne Marie "La contestation des privilèges seigneuriaux dans le fonds des Eaux et Forêts. L'exemple aquitain dans la seconde moitié du XVIIIe siècle," *Mouvements populaires et conscience sociale, XVIe–XIXe siècles*. Paris: Maloine, 1985, 209–15.

Colombet, Albert *Les parlementaires bourguignons à la fin du XVIIIe siècle*. Dijon: Chez l'Auteur, 1937.

Combes de Patris, B. "Un conflit féodal à Salles-Comtaux au XVIIIe siècle," *Revue de Rouergue*, 20, 1966, 5–24.

Constant, Jean-Marie "Gestion et revenus d'un grand domaine aux XVIe et XVIIe siècles d'après les comptes de la baronnie d'Auneau," *Revue d'histoire économique et sociale*, 50, 1972, 165–202.

———, "L'enquête de noblesse de 1667 et les seigneurs de Beauce," *Revue d'histoire moderne et contemporaine*, 21, 1974, 548–66.

———, "L'évolution de la noblesse de la sénéchaussée de La Flèche de la fin du XVIe siècle à 1789," *Etat et société en France aux XVIIe et XVIIIe siècles. Mélanges offerts à Yves Durand.* Paris: Presses de l'Université de Paris-Sorbonne, 2000, 155–64.

Coppolani, Jean "Une communauté rurale à la veille de la Révolution: Frouzins (Haute-Garonne) d'après le cadastre de 1784," *Revue géographique des Pyrénées et du Sud-Ouest*, 60, 1989, 385–401.

Corriol, Chanoine "Acquisition de biens et droits seigneuriaux par la communauté de Bayons," *Bulletin de la société scientifique et littéraire des Alpes-de-Haute-Provence*, 33, 1955, 244–52.

Corvol, Andrée "Forêt et communautés en Basse-Bourgogne au dix-huitième siècle," *Revue historique*, 256, 1976, 15–36

———, "La coercion en milieu forestier," *Mouvements popularies et conscience sociale, XVIe–XIXe siècles.* Paris: Maloine, 1985, 199–207.

Coulas, Ivan "Les aliénations du temporel ecclésiastique sous Charles IX et Henri III (1563–87)," *Revue d'histoire de l'église de France*, 144, 1958, 5–56.

Cousteix, Pierre "Fermes seigneuriales à Soisy-sur-Ecole au XVIIIe siècle," *Bulletin de la société historique et archéologique de Corbeil, d'Étampes et du Hurepoix*, 89, 1983, 65–78.

Cray, Serge du "Amodiation ou location perpétuelle d'un domaine en Combraille, en 1438, avec affranchissement des locataires," *Bulletin de la société d'émulation du Bourbonnais*, 64, 1989, 393–97.

Croix, Alain *La Bretagne aux 16e et 17e siècles.* Paris: Maloine, 1981.

Crouzet, François "Une communauté d'habitants dans la seconde moitié du XVIIIe siècle: Tence en Velay," *Cahiers de la Haute-Loire*, 1987, 111–36.

Cubells, Monique *La Provence des Lumières. Les parlementaires d'Aix au XVIIIe siècle.* Paris: Maloine, 1984.

Cursent, Benoît *Des maisons et des hommes. La Gascogne médiévale (XIe–XVe siècle).* Toulouse: Presses universitaires du Mirail, 1999.

Dalby, Jonathan R. *Les paysans cantaliens et la Révolution française (1789–1794).* Clermont-Ferrand: Publications de l'Institut du Massif Central, 1989.

Darpoux, Robert "La vie rurale vers la fin du XVIIIe siècle dans le Brivadois," *La Révolution française dans le Brivadois.* Brioude: Société de l'almanach de Brioude, 1989, 203–32.

———, "Une seigneurie de montagne à la veille de la Révolution," *Almanach de Brioude et de son arrondissement*, 62, 1982, 175–85.

Daveau, Suzanne *Les régions frontalières de la montagne jurassienne. Etude de géographie humaine.* Université de Lyon: Institut d'Etudes rhodaniennes, 1959.

Debien, Gabriel "Defrichements et reprises de fermes par la noblesse et par le clergé en Poitou à la fin du XVIIIe siècle," *Annales historiques de la Révolution française,* 40, 1968, 381–400.

——, *En Haut-Poitou. Défricheurs au travail, XVe–XVIIIe siècles.* Paris: Armand Colin, 1952.

Decoux, Jérôme "Fraude et fraudeurs dans le monde de transport au XVIIIe siècle: le cas des droits de la vicomté de l'eau de Rouen," *Les Normands et le fisc.* Elbeuf: Société de l'histoire d'Elbeuf, 1994, 131–38.

Deffontaines, Pierre *Les hommes et leurs travaux dans les pays de la moyenne Garonne (Agenais, Bas-Quercy).* Agen: Librairie Quesseveur, 1978 (orig. Lille, 1932).

Delaspre, J. "La naissance d'un paysage rural au XVIIIe siècle sur les hauts plateaux de l'est du Cantal et du nord de la Margeride," *Revue de géographie alpine,* 40, 1952, 493–97.

Delasselle, Nicolas "Une justice seigneuriale à Coulanges-la-Vineuse et au Val-de-Mercy au XVIIIe siècle," *Bulletin de la société des sciences historiques et naturelles de l'Yonne,* 128, 1996, 141–68.

Delbut, Maryse "Une paroisse rurale au XVIIIe siècle: Darnets, 1748–1789," *Bulletin de la société scientifique, historique et archéologique de la Corrèze,* 94, 1972, 157–72; 95, 1973, 189–205; & 96, 1974, 105–12.

Delmas, André "Les châtellenies de Larche et Tarrasson sous la domination des Noailles, 1583–1789," *Bulletin de la société scientifique, historique et archéologique de la Corrèze,* 85, 1963, 134–73.

Delumeau, Jean éd. *Histoire de la Bretagne.* Toulouse: Privat, 1969.

Denaix, Jean "La châtellenie de Hattonchâtel en 1546. Situation politique, fiscale, sociale," *Annales de l'Est,* 1957, 93–124.

Denis, Julien "Registre terrier de la prévôté de Verneuil (1503)," *Bulletin de la société archéologique et historique du Limousin,* 128, 2000, 169–86.

Denis, Michel "Grandeaur et décadence d'une forêt. Paimont du XVIe au XIXe siècle," *Annales de Bretagne,* 64, 1957, 257–73.

Denoix, Louis-Daniel "La vicomté de Turenne aux XIVe et XVe siècles," *Bulletin de la société scientifique, historique et archéologique de la Corrèze,* 89, 1967, 127–52; 90, 1968, 43–65.

Derlange, Michel *Les communautés d'habitants en Provence au dernier siècle de l'ancien régime.* Toulouse: Université Toulouse-Le Mirail, 1987.

Dernier, A. "Les freresches de la seigneurie de Vouillé," *Bulletin de la société des antiquaires de l'Ouest,* 7, 1963–1964, 215–37.

Derville, Alain "Les communautés villageoises de la Flandre wallonne d'après l'enquête de

1449," *Les communautés villageoises en Europe occidentale du Moyen Age aux temps modernes*. Auch: Centre culturel de l'abbaye de Flaran, 1984, 221–27.

———, *Les villes de Flandre et d'Artois (900–1500)*. Villeneuve d'Ascq: Presses universitaires du Septentrion, 2002.

Desplat, Christian "Crise et projects économiques à Bayonne et en Labourd à la fin du XVIIIe siècle," *Bayonne et sa région. Actes du XXXIIIe Congrès d'études régionales. Bayonne, 1981*. Fédération historique du Sud-Ouest, 1983, 263–77.

———, "Economie et société rurales en Aquitaine aux XVIIe et XVIIIe siècles," *Histoire Economie et Société*, 18, 1999, 133–55.

———, "Institutions et réalités pastorales dans les Pyrénées occidentales françaises à l'époque moderne," *L'élevage et la vie pastorale dans les montagnes de l'Europe au moyen âge et à l'époque moderne*. Clermont-Ferrand: Institut d'Etudes du Massif Central, 305–24.

Despois, L. *Histoire de l'autorité royale dans le comté de Nivernais*. Paris: Giard & Brière, 1912.

Devailly, Guy éd. *Histoire du Berry*. Toulouse: Privat, 1980.

Devèze, Michel "Forêts communales de la France du Nord-Est et de l'Allemagne rhénane dans la seconde moitié du XVIIe siècle," *Actes du 90e Congrès national des sociétés savantes. Nice, 1965. Section d'histoire moderne et contemporaine*, Tome I, 75.

———, "La forêt française: aspects sociaux et économiques aux XVIe et XVIIe siécles," *Bulletin de la société d'histoire moderne*, 52, 1953, 6–10.

———, *La vie de la forêt française au XVIe siècle*. Paris: S.E.V.P.E.N, 1961. 2 vols.

———, "Le bailliage de Mâcon en 1666," *Actes du 89e Congrès national des sociétés savantes. Section d'histoire moderne et contemporaine*, 1964, t. 2, v. 2, 833–59.

———, "Le pâturage au XVIe siècle dans la moitié nord de la France d'après les "coutumes"," *Bulletin philologique et historique*, 1967, I, 29–42.

———, "Les forêts françaises à la veille de la Révolution de 1789," *Revue d'histoire moderne et contemporaine*, 1966, 241–72.

———, "Superficie et propriété des forêts du Nord et de l'Est de la France vers la fin du règne de François Ier (1540–1547)," *Annales. Economies. Sociétés. Civilisations*, 15, 1960, 485–92.

Dewald, Jonathan *Pont-St-Pierre 1398–1789. Lordship, Community and Capitalism in Early Modern France*. Berkeley: University of California Press, 1987.

———, *The Formation of a Provincial Nobility. The Magistrates of the Parlement of Rouen, 1499–1610*. Princeton: Princeton University Press, 1980.

Deyon, Pierre *Contribution à l'étude des revenus fonciers en Picardie. Les fermages de l'Hôtel-Dieu d'Amiens et leurs variations de 1515 à 1789*. Lille: René Girard, 1967.

———, "Quelques remarques sur l'évolution du régime seigneurial en Picardie, XVIe–XVIIIe siècles," *Revue d'histoire moderne et contemporaine*, 8 1961, 271–80.

Dinet, Dominique "Les grands domaines des réguliers en France (1560–1790): une relative stabilité!," *Revue Mabillon*, 71, 1999, 257–60.

———, " Une institution méconnue: la commende," *Etat et société en France aux XVIIe et XVIIIe siècles. Mélanges offerts à Yves Durand*. Paris: Presses de l'Université de Paris-Sorbonne, 2000, 195–208.

Dinet-Lecomte, Marie-Claude "Quelques réflexions sur les finances hospitalières en France au XVIIIe siècle," *Etat et société en France aux XVIIe et XVIIIe siècles. Mélanges offerts à Yves Durand*. Paris: Presses de l'Université de Paris-Sorbonne, 2000, 209–22.

Dollinger, Philippe éd. *Histoire d'Alsace*. Toulouse: Privat, 1984.

Dontenwill, Serge "Cadres de vie des paysans et prise en charge de l'espace agraire dans le Centre-Est de la France au temps de Louis XIV," *La terre et les paysans en France et en Grande-Bretagne de 1600 à 1800*. Paris: Editions du Temps, 1998, 169–92.

———, *Une seigneurie sous l'ancien régime: l'Etoile en Brionnais du XVIe au XVIIIe siècle (1575–1778)*. Roanne: Editions Horvath, 1973.

———, "Un type social dans les campagnes brionnaises au XVIIe siècle: le procureur fiscal, fermier de seigneurie et crédirentier," *Bulletin du centre d'histoire économique et sociale de la région lyonnaise*, 1974, n. 4, 1–41.

Douillot, Stéphane "La baronnie eccésiastique de Luzy au XVIIIe siècle," *Les cahiers haut-marnais*, 1993, 49–54.

Doyle, William "Was There an Aristocratic Reaction in Pre-Revolutionary France,?" *Past and Present*, 57, 1972, 97–122.

Drouot, Marc "Seigneur et seigneurie au XVIe siècle. L'exploitation de la seigneurie de Thann en 1581," *Revue d'Alsace*, 119, 1993, 119–38.

Dubled, Henri "Etudes sur la fortune foncière du monastère de Felbach (Haut-Rhin), depuis sa foundation jusqu' à la fin du XVe siècle," *Annuaire de la société d' histoire sundgauvienne*, 1958, 17–52.

———, "La communauté de village en Alsace au XIIIe siècle," *Revue d'histoire économique et sociale*, 41, 1963, 5–33.

———, "L'administration de la seigneurie rurale en Alsace du XIIIe au XVe siècle," *Vierteljahrschrift für Sozial-und Wirtschaftsgeschichte*, 52, 1965, 433–84.

———, "La justice de la seigneurie foncière en Alsace aux XIVe et XVe siècles," *Schweizerische Zeitschrift für Geschichte*, 10, 1960, 337–75.

———, "Les grandes tendances de l' exploitation au sein de la seigneurie rurale en Alsace du XIIIe au XVe siècle," *Vierteljahrschrift für Sozial-und Wirtschaftsgeschichte*, 49, 1962, 41–121.

———, "Les paysans d'Alsace au Moyen Age (VIIIe–XVe siècle). Grands traits de leur histoire," *Paysans d'Alsace*. Strasbourg: Le Roux, 1959, 21–50.

———, "Seigneurs et paysans en Languedoc au Moyen Age et sous l'ancien régime. Le cas particulier du village de Gajan (Gard)," *Recueil de mémoires et travaux publié par la société d'histoire du droit et des institutions des anciens pays de droit écrit*, 1958, 1–39.

Dubreuil, Léon *Les vicissitudes du domaine congéable en Basse-Bretagne à l'époque de la Révolution*. Rennes, Imprimerie Oberthur, 1915.

Du Broc de Segange, Commandant "Les anciens communautés de cultivateurs dans le centre de la France," *Bulletin de la société d'émulation du Bourbonnais*, 6, 1898, 211–20, 253–80.

Duchêne, Roger "Madame de Sévigné et la gestion de ses biens bourguignons," *Annales de Bourgogne*, 1965, 19–50 & 113–32.

Dufraisse, Roger "La forêt de Haguenau sous la Révolution et l'Empire," *Etudes haguenoviennes*, 3, 1958–1961, 148–52.

Duma, Jean *Les Bourbon-Penthièvre (1678–1793). Une nebuleuse aristocratique au XVIIIe siècle*. Paris: Publications de la Sorbonne, 1995.

———, "Les Bourbon-Penthièvre à Rambouillet. La constitution d'une duché-pairie au XVIIIe siècle," *Revue d'histoire moderne et contemporaine*, 29, 1982, 291–304.

Dupâquier, Jacques "Paysage et société: le Vexin français au XVIIIe siècle," *Mémoires de la société historique et archéologique de Pontoise et du Vexin*, 67, 1977, 47–58.

Durand, Georges *Le patrimoine foncier de l'Hôtel-Dieu de Lyon (1482–1791)*. Lyon: Centre d'histoire économique et sociale de la région lyonnaise 1974.

———, *Vin, vigne et vignerons en Lyonnais et Beaujolais (XVIe–XVIIIe siècles)*. Lyon: Presses universitaires de Lyon, 1979, 111–28, 134–37, 216–34.

Durand, Yves "L'idéal social en Champagne méridionale du XVIe au XVIIIe siècle," *Actes du 92e Congrès national des sociétés savantes. Strasbourg-Colmar, 1967. Section d'histoire moderne et contemporaine*, III, 111–23.

Durr, René "Persistance et âpreté de l'esprit de privilège: les "échoites" de mainmorte dans la seigneurie de l'Isle-sur-Serein à la fin de l'ancien régime," *Bulletin de la société des sciences historiques et naturelles de l'Yonne*, 111, 1979, 107–26.

Duval, Michel "Domaine congéable et dépopulation forestière en Basse-Bretagne à la fin du XVIIIe siècle," *Association bretonne et union régionaliste bretonne. Archéologie-histoire-agriculture. Comptes rendus, procès-verbaux, mémoires*, 2e sér., 65, 1956, 95–106.

———, "Economie forestière et féodalité dans l'ouest à la veille de la Révolution," *Annales de Bretagne*, 64, 1957, 347–58.

———, "Gestion et exploitation des bois de mainmorte en Cornouaille aux XVIIe et XVIIe siècles," *Bulletin de la société archéologique du Finistère*, 124, 1995, 393–413;

———, " Les forêts royales en Cornouaille sous l'Ancien régime: la gruerie de Quimperlé (1545–1790)," *Bulletin de la société archéologique du Finistère*, 115, 1986, 161–94.

———, "Recherches sur l'économie forestière des pays de l'ouest dans la seconde moitié du XVIe siècle," *Revue forestière française*, 1957, 880–86.

Egret, Jean *Le parlement de Dauphiné et les affaires publiques dans la deuxième moitié du XVIIIe siècle*. Roanne: Editions Horvath, 1988.

Elissondo, Robert "La propriété des terres communes en Pays de Sioule à la fin de l'ancien régime," *Société des sciences, lettres et arts de Bayonne*, 144, 1988, 145–62.

Emmanuelli, François-Xavier "La vie urbaine dans le Midi de la France et particulièrement en Provence aux XVIIe et XVIIIe siècles," *Recherches régionales*, 24, 1983, 59–87.

————, "Une relecture de la pré-révolution provençale," in *La France pré-révolutionnaire*. Paris: Editions du Publisud, 1991, 97–110.

Enjalbert, Henri "La naissance des grands vins et la formation du vignoble moderne de Bordeaux: 1647–1767," in A. Huetz de Lemps, dir., *Géographie historique des vignobles*, Paris: CNRS, 1978, I, 59–88.

————, "Le commerce de Bordeaux et la vie économique dans le bassin aquitain au XVIIe siècle," *Annales du Midi*, 62, 1950, 21–35.

Evrard, Fernand "Les paysans du Mâconnais et les brigandages de Juillet 1789," *Annales de Bourgogne*, 19, 1947, 7–39, 97–121.

Falque-Vert, Henri *Les hommes et la montagne en Dauphiné au XIIIe siècle*. Grenoble: Presses universitaires de Grenoble, 1997.

Farnarier, F. "La seigneurie de Lançon. Période française (1481–1564)," *Provence historique*, 10, 1960, 222–38.

Fave-Schwartz, Monique "Les Rathsamhausen, une famille de la noblesse rurale alsacienne, 1250–1450," *Revue d'Alsace*, 109, 1980, 31–48.

Favreau, Robert "Seigneurs et bourgeois en Poitou aux XIVe–XVe siècles: autour du fief de l'Armenteresse ou du Fou," *Bulletin de la société des antiquaires de l'Ouest*, 17, 1984, 179–92.

Fédou, René *Les hommes de loi lyonnais à la fin du Moyen Age*. Paris: Les Belles Lettres, 1964.

————, *Le terrier de Jean Jossard, co-seigneur de Châtillon-Azergues, 1430–1463*. Paris: Bibliothèque nationale, 1966.

Felgères, Charles *Histoire de la baronnie de Chaudesaigues (depuis ses origines jusqu'à 1789)*. Paris, 1904.

Féral, Pierre L. "A la veille de la Révolution: les problèmes de la dîme, de la coussure et de la glâne," in *La France pré-révolutionnaire*. Paris: Editions Publisud, 1991, 27–39.

————, "Les processus de défrichement de la forêt lectouroise sous l'Ancien Régime," *Gens et choses de Bigorre. Actes du XXIIe Congrès d'études régionales. Fédération des sociétés académiques et savantes de Languedoc-Pyrénées-Gascogne*, 1966, 121–34.

————, "L'évolution de l'agriculture lectouroise du XVIe au XIXe siècle," *Histoire de Lectour*. Auch: Imprimerie Bouquet, 1972, 213–75.

Ferrari, Pierre "La seigneurie de Duras au XVIIIe siècle," *Revue de l'Agenais*, 122, 1995, 243–65.

Fiette, Suzanne "Un grand domaine du Lauragais dans la seconde moitié du XVIIIe siècle (1750–1793)," *Bulletin de l'association française des historiens économistes*, 13, 1980, 19–35.

Filhol, René *Le premier président Christofle de Thou et la réformation des coutumes*. Paris: Librairie du Recueil Sirey, 1937.

Finot, Jules "La mainmorte dans la terre de l'abbaye de Luxeuil. Projet d'affranchissement des mainmortables par l'abbé de Clermont-Ferrand (1775–1789)," *Revue historique de droit français et étranger*, 1880, 217–89.

Fitch, Nancy "The Demographic and Economic Effects of Seventeenth Century Wars: the Case of the Bourbonnais, France," *Review*, 2, 1978, 181–206.

Foisil, Madeleine *Le sire de Gouberville. Un gentilhomme normand au XVIe siècle*. Paris: Aubier-Montagne, 1981.

Follain, Antoine "Les communautés rurales en Normandie sous l'ancien régime. Identité communautaire, institutions du gouvernement local et solidarités," *Revue d'histoire moderne et contemporaine*, 45, 1998, 691–721.

Fontenay, Michel "Le revenu des chevaliers de Malte en France d'après les "estimes" de 1533, 1583 et 1776," *La France d'ancien régime. Etudes réunies en l'honneur de Pierre Goubert*. Toulouse: Privat, 1984, I, 25971.

———, "Paysans et marchands ruraux de la vallée de l' Essonnes dans la seconde moitié du XVIIe siècle," *Paris et Ile-de-France. Mémoires*, 9, 1957–1958, 157–282.

Forster, Robert *The House of Saulx-Tavannes. Versailles and Burgundy, 1700–1830*. Baltimore: Johns Hopkins, 1971.

———, *The Nobility of Toulouse in the Eighteenth Century. A Social and Economic Study*. Baltimore: Johns Hopkins, 1960.

———, "The Noble Wine Producers of the Bordelais in the Eighteenth Century," *Economic History Review*, 14, 1961, 18–33.

Fournée, Jean "Un aspect de la fiscalité ecclésiastique: réflexions sur les dîmes de l'abbaye de Belle-Etoile," *Les Normands et le fisc. XXIXème Congrès des sociétés historiques et archéologiques de Normandie*. Elbeuf-sur-Seine: Société de l'histoire de l'Elbeuf, 1996, 215–19.

Fournier, Pierre-François & Antoine Vergnette, "Les droits seigneuriaux à Aubière. Recueil des documents concernant les contestations dont ils furent l'objet (1422– 1789)," *Revue d'Auvergne*, 42, 1928, 1–59.

Foursans-Bourdette, Marie "Agriculture et industrie en Béarn au XVIIIe siècle," *Revue juridique et économique du Sud-Ouest. Série économique*, 13, 1964, 187–258.

———, *Economie et finances en Béarn au XVIIIe siècle*. Bordeaux: Editions Bière, 1963.

Franc de Ferrière, P. J. J. "Le pays de nouvelle conqueste. Origine et privilèges," *Saint-Emilion Libourne. Actes du XXIXe Congrès d'études régionales*. Libourne: Fédération historique du Sud-Ouest, 1979, 65–72.

Frayssenge, Jacques & Nicole Lemaître, "Les émotions populaires en Rouergue au XVIIIe siècle," *Mouvements sociales et conscience sociale, XVIe–XIXe siècles.* Paris: Maloine, 1985, 371–81.

Frêche, Georges *Toulouse et la région Midi-Pyrénées au siècle des Lumières, vers 1670–1789.* Paris: Cujas, 1975.

Gachon, Lucien "La vie rurale sous le règne de Louis XVI dans une paroisse des Monts du Livradois: Brousse-Montbossier," *104e Congrès national des sociétés savantes. Section de géographie*, 1979, 111–15.

Gadille, Roland *Le vignoble et la côte bourguignonne. Fondements physiques et humains d'une viticulture de haute qualité.* Paris: Les Belles Lettres, 1967.

Gagnol, P. *La dîme ecclésiastique en France au XVIIIe siècle.* Genève: Slatkine-Megariotis Reprints, 1974 (Paris, 1911).

Galéjac, A. de "Contribution à l'étude des dîmes dans une paroisse du Comminges comtal. Poucharramet," *Revue de Comminges*, 82, 1967, 111–18.

Gallet, Jean "Deux seigneuries du Salunois à la veille de la Révolution: Arraye et Vergaville" *Annales de l'Est*, 42, 1990, 3–34.

———, *La seigneurie bretonne (1450–1680).* Paris: Publications de la Sorbonne. 1983.

———, "La seigneurie de Sarreguemines au XVIIIe siècle, 1660–1750," *Les cahiers lorrains,* 1986, 37–57.

———, *Le bon plaisir du baron de Fénétrange.* Nancy: Presses universitaires de Nancy, 1990.

———, "Le congément des domainiers dans le Trégor au XVIIIe siècle," *Mémoires de la société d'histoire et d'archéologie de Bretagne*, 60, 1983, 143–60.

———, "Le congément des domainiers en Bretagne: nouvelles perspectives de recherches," *Enquêtes et documents du centre de recherches sur l'histoire de la France atlantique*, 5, 1980, 31–53.

———, "Le congément des domainiers en Cornouaille au XVIIIe siècle," *Annales de Bretagne*, 90, 1983, 451–66.

———, "Les transformations de la seigneurie en France entre 1600 et 1789," *Histoire, économie et société*, 18, 1999, 63–81.

———, "Réflexion sur la réaction seigneuriale et féodale en France au XVIIIe siècle," in *Etat et société en France aux XVIIe et XVIIIe siècles. Mélanges offerts à Yves Durand.* Paris: Presses de l'Université de Paris-Sorbonne, 2000, 241–57.

Ganghofer, Roland "Aspects des communautés rurales en Alsace du 12e au 20e siècle," *Les communautés rurales. 4. Europe occidentale.* Recueils de la société Jean Bodin pour l'histoire comparative des institutions. 43. Paris: Dessain et Tolra, 1984, 433–57.

Gangneux, Gérard "Communauté rurale et seigneurie de l'ordre de Malte: Saint-Pierre-Avex aux temps modernes," *Provence historique*, 21, 1970, 351–60.

———, "Economie et société rurales d'après les archives de l'ordre de Malte, *Cahiers d'histoire*, 17, 1972, 53–60.

————, *L'ordre de Malte en Camargue du 17e au 18e siècle*. Grenoble: Presses universitaires de Grenoble, 1979.

————, "Une commanderie de l'Ordre de Malte aux XVIIe et XVIIIe siècles: Poët-Laval en Dauphiné," *Cahiers d'histoire*, 9, 1964, 355–83.

————, "Une commanderie languedocienne au XVIIIe siècle: Saint-Jean de Pézenas," *Actes du 86e Congrès national des sociétés savantes. Montpellier, 1961. Section d'histoire moderne et contemporaine*. Paris: Imprimerie nationale, 1962, 281–96.

Garaud, Marcel *Histoire générale du droit privé français (de 1789 à 1804). Vol. II. La Révolution et la propriété foncière*. Paris: Recueil Sirey, 1958.

————, "Le régime agraire et les paysans de Gâtine au XVIIIe siècle," *Bulletin de la société des antiquaires de l'Ouest*, 2, 1954, 43–82.

————, "Le régime féodal en France à la veille de son abolition," in *L'abolition de la "féodalité" dans le monde occidental*. Paris: CNRS, 1971, vol. I, 109–14.

Garden, Maurice "La région Rhône-Alpes: une construction de l'histoire encore incertaine," *Lyon et l'Europe. Hommes et sociétés. Mélanges offerts à Richard Gascon*. Lyon: Presses universitaires de Lyon, 1980, I, 267–80.

————, *Lyon et les Lyonnais au XVIIIe siècle*. Paris: Les Belles-Lettres, 1970.

Garnier, Bernard "La mise en herbe dans le pays d'Auge aux XVIIe et XVIIIe siècles," *Annales de Normandie*, 25, 1975, 157–80.

————, "Pays herbagers, pays céréaliers et pays "ouverts" en Normandie (XVIe–début XIXe siècle)," *Revue d'histoire économique et sociale*, 53, 1975, 493–525.

————, "Structure et conjoncture de la rente foncière dans le Haut-Maine aux XVII et XVIIIe siècles," *Problèmes agraires et société rurale. Normandie et Europe du Nord-Ouest*. Caen: Cahier des annales de Normandie, n. 11, 1979, 101–26.

Garnot, Benoît *La justice en France de l'an mil à 1914*. Paris: Nathan, 1993.

Garrier, Gilbert "La formation d'un complexe écono-social de type "rhodanien": Chaponost (1730–1822)," in Pierre Léon, éd., *Structures économiques et problèmes sociaux du monde rural dans la France du Sud-Est*. Paris: Les Belles Lettres, 1966, 315–69.

————, "Premières lignes d'une recherche collective: l'appropriation foncière citadine dans la région Rhône-Alpes du XIVe au XXe siècle," *Bulletin du centre d'histoire économique et sociale de la région lyonnaise*, no.2, 1975, 43–59.

Gascon, Richard *Grand commerce et vie urbaine au XVIe siècle. Lyon et ses marchands (environs de 1520—environs de 1580)*. Paris: S.E.V.P.E.N., 1971.

Gass, Jean-Claude, "Les forêts de Strasbourg et les conditions de leur appropriation," *Saisons d'Alsace*, 32, 1988, 34–50.

Gauléjac, A. de "Contribution à l'étude des dîmes dans une paroisse de Comminges comtal. Poucharramet," *Revue de Comminges*, 82, 1967, 111–18.

Gauthier, Florence *La voie paysanne dans la Révolution française. L'exemple picard*. Paris: François Maspero, 1977.

———— & Guy-Robert Ikni, "Le mouvement paysan en Picardie: meneurs, pratiques, maturation et signification historique d'un programme (1775–1794)," *Mouvements populaires et conscience sociale, XVIe–XIXe siècles*. Paris: Maloine, 1985, 435–48.

Gay, François-P. *La champagne du Berry. Essai sur la formation d'un paysage agraire et l'évolution d'une société rurale*. Bourges: Editions Tardy, 1967.

Gay, Jean-Lucien "Deux enquêtes sur les obligations des mainmortables dans la Franche-Comté méridionale," *Mémoires de la société pour l'histoire du droit et des institutions des anciens pays bourguignons, comtois et romands*, 1961, 75–106.

Geissert, Christine "Les rentes constituées de l'oeuvre Saint-Georges Hagenau (XIVe–XVIIe siècle," *Revue de l'église d'Alsace*, 41–42, 1982, 1–42.

Georglette, René "Abrégé de l'histoire des forêts françaises depuis la promulgation de l'ordonnance de 1669 jusqu'à la veille de la Révolution," *Revue forestière française*, 1957, 403–18.

Germain, René "Du servage au libertés à la fin du Moyen Age en Bourbonnais," in *Les libertés au Moyen Age*. Montbrison: Les presses de l'imprimerie de la Plaine, 1987, 357–79.

————, *Les campagnes bourbonnaises à la fin du Moyen Age (1370–1530)*. Clermont-Ferrand: Institut d'Etudes du Massif Central, 1987.

————, "Seigneurie et noblesse en Bourbonnais d'après un dénombrement du ban en 1503," *Seigneurs et seigneuries au Moyen Age*. Paris: CTHS, 1993, 369–80.

Giffard, André *Les justices seigneuriales en Bretagne aux XVIIe et XVIIIe siècles*. Paris: Arthur Rousseau, 1903.

Gille, Bertrand "Note sur la population de Clermont au XVIIIe siècle," *Revue d'Auvergne*, 83, 1969, 123–34.

Gillossou, Philippe "Structures agraires à Wissous au XVIIIe siècle (1709–1789)," *Bulletin de la société historique et archéologique de Corbeil, d'Étampes et du Hurepoix*, 74, 1968, 17–54 & 75, 1969, 7–58.

Gillot-Voisin, Janyne "La communauté des habitants de Givry au XVIIIe siècle," *Cahiers de l'association interuniversitaire de l'Est*, 11, 1966, 21–83.

Girault, Charles "La propriété foncière de la noblesse sarthoise au XVIIIe siècle," *La province du Maine*, 35, 1955, 201–14.

Glotz, Marc "La culture de la pomme de terre dans le Sundgau au XVIIIe siècle," *Annuaire de la société d'histoire sundgauvienne*, 1984, 81–94.

Goldsmith, James Lowth *Les Salers et les d'Escorailles. Seigneurs de Haute Auvergne, 1500–1789*. Clermont-Ferrand: Institut d'Etudes du Massif Central, 1984.

————, *Lordship in France, 500–1500*. New York: Peter Lang, 2003.

Gotteri-Grambert, Nicole "Chassy-en-Morvan. La seigneurie et le domaine," *Mémoires de la société académique du Nivernais*, 55, 1969, 29–54; 56, 1970, 28–38; 57, 1971, 43–66.

Goubert, Pierre "Disparités de l'ancien France rurale," *Cahiers d'histoire*, 12, 1967, 55–65.

————, "En Rouergue: structures agraires et cadastres au XVIIIe siècle," *Annales. Economies. Soeiétés. Civilisations*, 9, 1954, 382–86..

————, "Recherches d'histoire rurale dans la France de l'Ouest (XVIIe–XVIIIe siècles)," *Bulletin de la société d'histoire moderne*, sér. 13, n. 2, 1965, 2–8.

Goujard, Philippe *L'abolition de la "féodalité" dans le Pays de Bray (1789–1793)*. Paris: Bibliothèque nationale, 1979.

Grasser, Jean-Paul "Population et société à Hagenau au XVIIIe siècle: démographie, structures et couches sociales, assistance," *Etudes haguenoviennes*, 8, 1982, 93–144.

Greengrass, M. "Property and Politics in Sixteenth-Century France: the Landed Fortune of Constable Anne de Montmorency," *French History*, 2, 1988, 371–98.

Gresser, Pierre "Les conséquences financières pour le domaine comtal de la conquête du comté de Bourgogne par Louis XI," in Jean Kerhervé, éd., *Finances, pouvoirs et mémoire: mélanges offerts à Jean Favier*. Paris: Fayard, 1999, 397–411.

Grimmer, Claude *Vivre à Aurillac au XVIIIe siècle*. Paris: Presses universitaires de France, 1983.

Grinberg, Martine "La rédaction des coutumes et les droits seigneuriaux. Nommer, classer, exclure," *Annales*. 52, 1997, 1017–38

Grosseau, Christiane "Les officiers de justice à Lyon (1740–1790). Etude d'un groupe socio-professionnel," *Bulletin du centre d'histoire économique et sociale de la région lyonnaise*, n. 3, 1972, 71–75.

Gruter, Edouard *La naissance d'un grand vignoble. Les seigneuries de Pizay et Tanay en Beaujolais au XVIe et XVIIe siècles*. Lyon: Presses universitaires de Lyon, 1977.

Gruzinski, Serge "Changement et continuité dans deux seigneuries des Pays-Bas méridionaux: l'abbaye d'Anchin et la baronnie de Cysoing, fin du XVe-début du XVIIe siècle," *Revue du Nord*, 55, 1973, 305–15.

————, "Recherches sur le monde rural dans les Pays-Bas méridionaux (1480–1630)," *Ecole nationale des chartes. Positions des thèses*, 1973, 113–18.

Gueneau, Louis *L'organisation du travail à Nevers aux XVIIe et XVIIIe siècles, 1660–1790*. Paris: Hachette, 1919, 590.

Gutton, Jean-Pierre *Villages du Lyonnais sous la monarchie (XVIe–XVIIIe siècles)*. Lyon: Presses universitaires de Lyon, 1978.

Guy, Marcel "Tournefeuille à la fin de l'ancien régime," *Annales du Midi*, 97, 1985, 53–73.

Guyon, Gérard D. "L'abbaye bénédictine Sainte-Croix de Bordeaux et la crise du domaine seigneurial aux XVe et XVIe siècles," *Revue Mabillon*, 70, 1998, 163–79.

Guyot-Ledoux, Marie-Andrée "Aspects économiques et sociaux de la vie rurale en Nivernais: la paroisse de Saint-Parize-le-Châtel au milieu du XVIIIe siècle," *Positions des thèses. Ecole national des chartes*, 1972, 55–63.

Hamada, Mitchio "Une seigneurie et sa justice en Beaujolais aux XVIIe et XVIIIe siècles: Saint-Leger," *Bulletin du centre d'histoire économique et sociale de la région lyonnaise*, 1985, n. 2, 19–31.

Helas, Jean-Claude "Oup l'ruutsai la aiguouelo ol lou remunus de la terre " *Provence historique*, 45, 1995, 143–56.

———, "Le manse en Gévaudan au milieu du XVe siècle," *Annales du Midi*, 102, 1990, 173–78.

Hemmer, H. "La seigneurie de La Celette et ses revenus an XVIIe siècle," *Mémoires de la société des sciences naturelles et archéologiques de la Creuse*, 36, 1966, 153–61.

Hesse, Philippe-Jean "Le bail à complant: une notion juridique dans l'histoire mouvementée du vignoble nantais," *Bulletin de la société archéologique et historique de Nantes et de Loire-Atlantique*, 120, 1984, 185–215.

Higounet, Charles dir. *Histoire de Bordeaux*. Toulouse: Privat, 1980.

———, dir. *Histoire de l'Aquitaine*. Toulouse: Privat, 1971.

———, dir. *La seigneurie et le vignoble de Château Latour. Histoire d'un grand cru du Médoc (XIV–XXe siècle)*. Bordeaux: Fédération historique du Sud-Ouest, 1974, 2 vols.

Hinault, Nathalie "Paysans et seigneurs du marquisat de Lonrai aux XVIIe et XVIIIe siècles," *Bulletin de la société historique et archéologique de l'Orne*, 115, 1996, 158–84.

Homet, Raquel "Remarques sur le servage en Bourbonnais au XVe siècle," *Journal of Medieval History*, 10, 1984, 195–207.

Hufton, Olwen "The Seigneur and the Rural Community in Eighteenth Century France," *Transactions of the Royal Historical Society*, ser. 5, 29, 1979, 21–40.

Huppé, Philippe *Le gisant de la féodalité dans l'ombre des Lumières. La féodalité dans la baronnie du Pouget et la vicomté de Plaissan au 18e siècle*. Montagnac: Editions Monique Mergoil, 1998.

Husson, Jean-Pierre *Les hommes et la forêt en Lorraine*. Paris: Editions Bonneton, 1991.

Hyslop, Béatrice F. *L'apanage de Philippe-Egalité duc d'Orléans (1775–1791)*. Paris: Société des Etudes robespierristes, 1965, 127–58.

Imbert, Jean "Quelques aspects juridiques de la mainmorte seigneuriale en Lorraine (XVIe–XVIIIe siècles)," *Mémoires de la société pour l'histoire du droit et des institutions des anciens pays bourguignons, comtois et romands*, 13, 1950–51, 177–210.

Jacquart, Jean *La crise rurale en Ile-de-France, 1550–1670*. Paris: Armand Colin, 1974.

———, "Tenure, propriété, exploitation," in Serge Bianchi et al., *La terre et les paysans en France et en Grande-Bretagne du début du XVIIe siècle à la fin du XVIIIe siècle*. Paris: Armand Colin, 1999, 28–37.

Jessenne, Jean-Pierre "Le pouvoir des fermiers dans les villages d'Artois (1770–1848)," *Annales E.S.C.*, 38, 702–34.

———, *Pouvoir au village et Révolution. Artois 1760–1848*. Lille: Presses universitaires de Lille, 1987.

Joudoux, Robert "Du tènement des Vigeries d'Objat aux dîmes de la châtellenie de Voutezac,"

Limouzi, 115, 1990, 17–27.

Juillard, Etienne *La vie rurale dans la plaine de Basse-Alsace. Essai de géographie sociale.* Strasbourd: Le Roux, 1953.

Juillard, Marcel "Thynière et ses seigneurs," *Revue de la Haute-Auvergne*, 1957, 126–56.

Kammerer, Odile "Les Colmariens dans leur campagne: à propos du terroir d' Ursule Marx von Eckwersheim, née von Westhusen, 1535," *Annuaire de la société d' histoire et d' archéologie de Colmar*, 31, 1983, 37–45.

Kerhervé, Jean *L'état breton aux 14e et 15e siècles. Les ducs, l'argent et les hommes.* Paris: Maloine, 1987.

———, "Le domaine ducal de Guingamp-Minibriac au XVe siècle," *Mémoires de la société d'histoire et d'archéologie de Bretagne*, 1978, 123–84.

Kieffer, Jean "Le plat-pays thionvillois à la veille de la Révolution," *Les cahiers lorrains*, 1989, 135–40.

Labatut, Jean–Pierre *Les ducs et pairs de France au XVIIe siècle.* Paris: Presses universitaires de France, 1972.

Lachiver, Marcel *Vin, vigne et vignerons en région parisienne du XVIIe au XVIIIe siècle.* Pontoise: Société historique et archéologique de Pontoise, 1982.

La Monneraye, Jean de *Le régime féodal et les classes rurales dans le Maine au XVIIIe siècle.* Paris: Receuil Sirey, 1922.

Larguier, Gilbert *Le drap et le grain en Languedoc. Narbonne et Narbonnais 1300–1789.* Perpignan: Presses universitaires de Perpignan, 1996.

La Rochette de Rochegonde, Maxime de "Les redevances féodales dans l'ancienne seigneurie de Saint-Ilpize," *Almanach de Brioude et de son arrondissement*, 42, 1962, 215–22.

Lartigaut, Jean "Un ménage cadurcien au XVIIe siècle. Arnaud de Basombes et Anne de Molières d'après leurs livres de raison," *Bulletin de la société des études littéraires, scientifiques et artistiques du Lot*, 84, 1983, 18–26.

Lassalmonie, Jean-François "La politique fiscale de Louis XI (1461–1483)," in *L'argent au Moyen Age.* Congrès de la société des historiens médiévalistes de l'enseignement publique supérieur. Paris: Publications de la Sorbonne, 1998, 225–65.

Latreille, André éd. *Histoire de Lyon et du Lyonnais.* Toulouse: Privat, 1975.

Laurent, Jeanne *Un monde rural en Bretagne au XVe siècle. La quévaise.* Paris: S.E.V.P.E.N., 1972.

Laurent, Marcel "Le partage des communaux à Ennezat," *Revue d'Auvergne*, 82, 1978, 167–95.

Lavaud, Daniel "Le village de Gerzat au Xve siècle," *Revue d'Auvergne*, 1976, 201–47.

Lavergne, Gérard "Le vignoble du prieuré d'Aureil en Bas-Limousin," *Bulletin de la société des lettres, sciences et arts de la Corrèze*, 70, 1966, 7–20.

Lebrun, éd., François *Histoire des Pays de la Loire. Orléanais, Touraine, Anjou, Maine.* Toulouse: Privat, 1972.

Lecherbonnier, Yannick "L'abbaye de Belle-Etoile. Le temporel. Des origines à la fin de la guerre de Cents Ans," *Le pays bas-normand*, 73, 1980, 587–678.

Lecoq, François "Le fief de La Bussière. Les baux à ferme," *Bulletin d'histoire locale de Souppes-sur-Loing*, 1988, 30–45.

Lefebvre, Georges "Les foules révolutionnaires," in Georges Lefebvre, *La Grande Peur de 1789*. Paris: Armand Colin, 1988, 241–64.

——, *Les paysans du Nord pendant la Révolution française*. Paris: Armand Colin, 1972 (orig. 1924).

——, "Répartition de la propriété foncière et de l' exploitation foncières à la fin de l' ancien régime," in Georges Lefebvre, *Etudes sur la Révolution française*. Paris: Presses universitaires de France, 2e éd., 1963, 279–306.

Le Floc'h, Vincent "Le régime foncier et son application dans le cadre de la paroisse de Plonivel au XVIIIe siècle," *Bulletin de la société archéologique du Finistère*, 92, 1966, 117–205.

Le Gall, Jean-Marie "Deux communautés bénédictines parisiennes pendant les guerres de religion. Saint-Martin-des-Champs et Saint-Germain-des-Prés," *Paris et Ile-de-France. Mémoires*, 50, 1999, 201–41.

Le Goff, T. J. A. *Vannes and Its Region*. Oxford: Clarendon Press, 1981.

Leguay Jean-Pierre & Hervé Martin, *Fastes et malheurs de la Bretagne ducale, 1213–1532*. Rennes: Ouest-France, 1982.

Lemaître, Nicole *Bruyères, communes et mas. Les communaux en Bas-Limousin depuis le XVIe siècle*. Ussel: Musée du pays d'Ussel, 1981.

——, *Un horizon bloqué. Ussel et la montagne limousine aux XVIIe et XVIIIe siècles*. Ussel: Musée du pays d'Ussel, 1978.

Lemarchand, Guy "Déclin ou résurrection? La seigneurie rurale dans la France du XVIe siècle et de la première moitié du XVIIe siècle," *Cahiers d'histoire de l'institut de recherches marxistes*, 59, 1995, 5–25.

——, "L'abolition de la féodalité," *A travers la Normandie en Révolution, 1789–1800*. Rouen: Comité régional d'histoire de la Révolution française, 1992, 183–90.

——, *La fin du féodalisme dans le Pays de Caux*. Paris: Editions du CNRS, 1989.

——, "La France au XVIIIe siècle: élites ou noblesse et bourgeosie," *Cahiers d'histoire de l'institut de recherches marxistes*, 51, 1993, 105—23.

——, "Les campagnes de Haute-Normandie à la veille de la Révolution," *Bulletin de la société d'histoire moderne et contemporaine*, 89, 1990, 6–10.

——, "Les monastères de Haute-Normandie au XVIIIe siècle," *Annales historiques de la Révolution française*, 37, 1965, 1–28.

——, "Le temporel et les revenus de l'abbaye de Fécamp pendant le XVIIe et XVIIIe siècle," *Annales de Normandie*, 15, 1965, 525–49.

——, "Structure sociale d'après les rôles fiscaux et conjoncture économique dans le Pays de Caux: 1690–1789," *Bulletin de la société d'histoire moderne*, 68, 1969, 7–11.

Le Mené, Michel *Les campagnes angevines à la fin du Moyen Age (vers 1350–vers 1530). Etude économique.* Nantes. Editions Cid, 1982.

Lemercier, Pierre *Les justices seigneuriales de la région parisienne de 1580 à 1789.* Paris: Domat-Montchrestien, 1933.

Lemerle-Baudot, Anne "Une petite seigneurie rurale en Auvergne au milieu du XVe siècle d'après le terrier de Clavelier," *Bulletin philologique et historique,* 1965, 329–43.

Lemoigne, François-Yves "Le commerce des provinces étrangères (Alsace-Evêchés-Lorraine) dans la deuxième moitié du XVIIIe siècle," in Pierre Léon, éd., *Aires et structures du commerce français au XVIIIe siècle.* Lyon: Centre d'histoire économique et sociale de la région lyonnaise, 1975, 173–200.

Lavaud, Daniel "Le village de Gerzat au XVe siècle," *Revue d'Auvergne,* 1976, 201–47.

Léon, Patrick "Mutations des paysages agraires et de l'habitat: les campagnes du Saint-Amandois du milieu du XVIe au XIXe siècle," *Cahiers d'archéologie et d'histoire du Berry,* 77, 1984, 3–44.

Léon, Pierre et al., "Régime seigneurial et régime féodal dans la France du Sud-Est: déclin ou permanence? (XVIIe–XVIIIe siècles)," in *L'abolition de la féodalité dans le monde occidental.* Paris: CNRS, 1971, 147–68.

Le Page, Dominique "Noblesse et pouvoir royal en Bretagne (1480–1540)," in Jean Kerhervé, éd., *Noblesse de Bretagne du Moyen Age à nos jours.* Rennes: Presses universitaires de Rennes, 1999, 129–49.

Le Roy Ladurie, Emmanuel "Révoltes et contestations rurales en France de 1675 à 1788," *Annales. Economies. Sociétés. Civilisations,* 29, 1974, 6–22.

———, "Sur Montpellier et sa campagne aux XVIe et XVIIe siècles," *Annales E.S.C.,* 12, 1957, 223–30.

Levantal, Christophe *Ducs et pairs et duchés-pairies laïques à l'époque moderne (1519–1790).* Paris: Editions Maisonneuve et Larose, 1996.

Leymarie, Michel "La faible importance des alleux en Haute-Auvergne révélée par le centième denier," *Annales historiques de la Révolution française,* 49, 1977, 429–35.

———, "La propriété et l'exploitation foncière au XVIIe siècle dans la Planèze de Saint-Flour," *Revue de la Haute-Auvergne,* 1965, 482–86.

———, "Les mouvements populaires à Maurs et aux environs en 1789 et 1790," *Revue de la Haute-Auvergne,* 1970, 126–32.

———, "Les redevances foncières seigneuriales en Haute-Auvergne," *Annales historiques de la Révolution française,* 1968, 299–380.

———, "Rentes seigneuriales et produit des seigneuries dans l'élection de Tulle en Limousin," *Annales historiques de la Révolution française,* 1970, 594–98.

Ligeron, Louis "Culture et maraîchage à Vielverge et Soissons (XVIe–XVIIIe siècles)," *Annales de Bourgogne,* 42, 1970, 153–68.

———, "La dîme dans les clos," *Annales de Bourgogne,* 49, 1977, 5–23.

————,"L'assolement dans la vallée moyenne de la Saône," *Annales de Bourgogne*, 44, 1972, 5–41.

————, "Les ventes de communaux après les guerres religieuses (1595–1610)," *Annales de Bourgogne*, 54, 1982, 5–16.

————, "Notes sur la culture du maïs dans la vallée moyenne de la Saône," *Annales de Bourgogne*, 40, 1968, 197–204.

Livet, Georges *L'intendance d'Alsace de la Guerre de Trente Ans à la mort de Louis XIV, 1634–1715*. 2e éd. Strasbourg: Presses universitaires de Strasbourg, 1991.

Livet, Roger & Augustin Roux, *Eléments d'histoire agraire du terroir provençal. Saint-Saturnin-lès-Apt*. Aix-en-Provence: La Pensée universitaire, 1957.

Loirette, Francis "Un épisode des résistances locales aux empiètements du pouvoir royal: la défense du franc-alleu agenais au XVIIe siècle," in Francis Loirette, *L'état et la région: L'Aquitaine au XVIIe siècle*. Bordeaux: Presses universitaires de Bordeaux, 1998, 119–42.

Lombard-Déaux, Christiane "Les seigneuries ecclésiastiques du Lyonnais et du Beaujolais (XVIIe et XVIIIe siècles)," *Cahiers d'histoire*, 39, 1994, 19–35.

Lorcin, Marie-Thérèse "Décimateurs et décimables en Lyonnais aux XIVe et XVe siècles," *Economies et sociétés au Moyen Age. Mélanges offerts à Edouard Perroy*. Paris: Publications de la Sorbonne, 1973, 350–54.

————, *Les campagnes de la région lyonnaise aux XIVe et XVe siècles*. Lyon: Imprimerie Bosc Frères, 1974.

————"Un musée imaginaire de la ruse paysanne. La fraude des décimables du XIVe au XVIIIe siècle dans la région lyonnaise," *Etudes rurales*, 51, 1973, 112–24.

Loupès, Philippe *Chapitres et chanoines de Guyenne aux XVIIe et XVIIIe siècle*. Paris: Ecole des Hautes Etudes en Sciences Sociales, 1985.

————, "Le chapitre de Saint-Emilion sous l'ancien régime," *Saint-Emilion Libourne. Actes du XXIXe Congrès d'études régionales de la Fédération historique du Sud-Ouest*. Libourne, 1979, 73–95.

Maillard, Brigitte *Les campagnes de Touraine au XVIIIe siècle. Structures agraires et économie rurale*. Rennes: Presses universitaires de Rennes, 1998.

Mackrell, J. Q. C. *The Attack on Feudalism in Eighteenth-Century France*. London: Routledge et Kegan Paul, 1973.

Maillot, Marcel "Le vignoble à Saint-Amand-sur-Fion (XVIe aux XVIIIe siècles)," *Mémoires de la société d'agriculture, commerce, sciences et arts du département de la Marne*, 95, 1980, 103–20.

Major, J. Russell "The Crown and Aristocracy in Renaissance France," *American Historical Review*, 69, 1963–64, 631–45.

Manteyer, Georges de *Le livre-journal tenu par Fazy de Rame en langage enbrunais (6 juin 1471–10 juillet 1507)*. Gap, 1932.

Marcadé, Jacques "Des petits notables ruraux: les fermiers généraux de l'abbaye Sainte-Croix," *Sociétés et idéologies des temps modernes. Hommage à Arlette Jouanna.* Montpellier: Université de Montpellier, III, 1996, vol I, 197–210..

———, "La dîme au XVIIIe siècle: l'exemple du diocèse de Poitiers," *Bulletin de la société des antiquaires de l'Ouest*, 11, 1997, 197–210.

———, "Un grand domaine au XVIIIe siècle: les seigneuries de Vasles, Vasseroux et Saint-Philibert," *Bulletin de la société des antiquaires de l'Ouest*, sér. 4, 18, 1985, 67–78.

Marion, Henri *La dîme ecclésiastique en France au XVIIIe siècle et sa suppression.* Bordeaux: Imprimerie de l'Université et des Facultés, 1912.

Marion, Marcel *Dictionnaire des institutions de la France aux XVIIe et XVIIIe siècles.* New York: Burt Franklin, 1968 (orig. Paris, 1923).

———, "Etat des classes rurales au XVIIIe siècle dans la généralité de Bordeaux," *Revue des études historiques*, 68, 1902, 97–139, 209–35, 335–61, 451–78.

Markoff, John "Violence, Emancipation, and Democracy: The Countryside and the French Revolution," *American Historical Review*, 100, 1995, 360–86.

Marmande, Christiane "La propriété et l'exploitation de la terre en Cambrésis à la veille de la Révolution," *Jadis en Cambrésis*, 43, 1989, 6–12.

Maroteaux, Vincent "Propriété et seigneurie dans l'ouest parisien de la fin du Moyen Age au début du XIXe siècle: l'exemple du domaine de Versailles," *Positions des thèses.* Ecole des Chartes, 1984, 103–13.

Marres, P. "La garrigue. Son exploitation à travers les âges," *Revue historique et littéraire du Languedoc*, 1944, 178–90, 380–93.

Martin, Clément "La forêt de la Serre-basse à Saint-Denis. Cadre juridique, économie et histoire," *Bulletin de la société d'études scientifiques de l'Aude*, 88, 1988, 13–20.

Martres, Eugène "Forêts cantaliennes (XVIIIe–XXème siècles). Vicissitudes et exploitation," *Revue de la Haute-Auvergne*, 37, 1961, 433–60.

———, "Les paysans et leur terroir dans une haute vallée cantalienne. Albepierre du XIIIe au XIXe siècle," *Revue de la Haute-Auvergne*, 1956–57, 157–84.

Marx, Roland *La Révolution et les classes sociales en Basse-Alsace. Structures agrairies et vente des biens nationaux.* Paris: Bibliothèque nationale, 1974.

Massary, Xavier de "Les "usages" dans le nord-est de l'arrondissement de Château-Thierry," *Mémoires de la fédération des sociétés d'histoire et d'archéologie de l'Aisne*, 32, 1987, 9–37.

Massé, Paul "Le dessèchement des marais du Bas-Médoc," *Revue historique de Bordeaux et du département de la Gironde*, 6, 1957, 25–68.

Massonie, Albert "La seigneurie de Soudeilles-Lieuteret en 1582," *Lemouzi*, 125, 1993, 87–92.

Mathieu, Abel *La seigneurie de Pont-les-Remirement sous l'ancien régime.* Epinal: Editions du Sapin d'or, 1979.

Maur, Edouard "Rognonas de 1582 à 1789. Contribution à l'histoire agraire de la Basse-

Provence," *Cahiers du centre d'études des sociétés méditerranéennes*, 1968, 193–233.

Mège, Francisque "Charges et contributions des habitants d'Auvergne à la fin de l'ancien régime. Deuxième partie. Les droits seigneuriaux," *Revue d'Auvergne*, 1898, 130–239.

Meliet, Jean-Jacques & Philippe Rouche, "Structures agraires et économie rurale en Ballongue au XVIIème siècle (1661–1690)," *Du Couserans au Gave de Pau. Tradition et renouveau. Actes du XIe Congrès d'études régionales. Fédération des sociétés académiques et savantes de Languedoc-Pyrénées-Gascogne*, 1985, 129–65.

Mémin, Marcel "La campagne mancelle de 1780 vue par les notaires du Mans," *La province du Maine*, 64, 1962, 64, 168–77, 237–46; 66, 1964, 18–39.

Mercier, H. "Etude sur la mainmorte dans le pays de Montbéliard," *Mémoires de la société pour l'histoire du droit et des institutions des anciens pays bourguignons, comtois et romands*, 1950–1951, 109–24.

Merle, Louis *La métairie et l'évolution agraire de la Gâtine poitevine*. Paris: SEVPEN, 1958.

———, "Une explication: origines et évolution d'un bocage, l'exemple de la Gâtine poitevine," *Annales E.S.C.*, 12, 1957, 613–18.

Merley, Jean *La Haute-Loire de la fin de l'ancien régime aux débuts de la Troisième République*. Le Puy: Cahiers de la Haute-Loire, 1974.

Merlin, Colette "Impositions, charges et résistance paysanne dans la petite montagne jurassienne à la veille de la Révolution," in Maurice Gresset, éd. *La Franche-Comté à la veille de la Révolution*. Paris: Les Belles Lettres, 1988, 13–27.

Meyer, Jean *La noblesse bretonne au XVIIIe siècle*. Paris: Imprimerie nationale, 1966.

Meyer, Octave *La régence épiscopale de Saverne*. Strasbourg: Imprimerie alsacienne, 1935.

Michaud, Claude *L'église et l'argent sous l'ancien régime. Les receveurs généraux du clergé de France aux XVIe–XVIIe siècles*. Paris: Fayard., 1991.

Michaud-Fréjaville, Françoise "Communautés rurales et seigneurs à la fin du Moyen Age: un exemple berrichon," *Etudes rurales*, 68, 1977, 141–51.

———, "Un exemple de seigneurie foncière au XVe siècle. Le prieuré de Gravier," *Cahiers d'archéologie et d'histoire du Berry*, 50–51, 1977, 7–25.

Micolon de Guérines, Charles "Le terrier de 1521 de la seigneurie du Chier, près d'Ambert," *Chroniques historiques d'Ambert et de son arrondissement*, 15, 1993, 27–39.

Mireaux, Emile *Une province française au temps du Grand Roi. La Brie*. Paris: Hachette, 1958.

Mischlich, Robert "Le régime international de la navigation du Rhin," *Saisons d'Alsace*, 10, 1965, 367–87.

Mollat, Michel éd., *Histoire de l'Île-de-France et de Paris*. Toulouse: Privat, 1971.

Monnier, Raymonde "Antony. Une commune de la banlieu parisienne à la veille de la Révolution," *Annales historiques de la Révolution française*, 52, 1980, 262–79.

Monsembernard, G. de "Un village pyrénéen du XIVe au XVIIe siècle. Bilhères en Ossau," *Bulletin de la société archéologique et historique du Gers*, 93, 1992, 18–42

Moreau, J.-P. *La vie rurale dans le sud-est du bassin parisien entre les vallées de l'Armaçon et de la Loire. Etude de géographie humaine.* Paris: Les Belles Lettres, 1958.

Moriceau, Jean-Marc "Fermage et métayage (XIIe–XIXe siècle)," *Histoire et sociétés rurales,* 1, 1994, 155–90.

———, *Les fermiers de l'Île-de-France, XVe-XVIIIe siècle.* Paris: Fayard, 1994.

Mougel, François-Charles "La fortune des princes de Bourbon-Conty. Revenus et gestion, 1665–1791," *Revue d'histoire moderne et contemporaine,* 18, 1971, 30–49.

Mousnier, Roland *Les institutions de la France sous la monarchie absolue.* Paris: Presses universitaires de France, 1974. 2 vols.

Mouthon-Sepau, Nathalie "Etude d'une seigneurie foncière dans le dernier tiers du XVe siècle: la seigneurie de Condat et Barbane, " *Revue historique et archéologique du Libournais et de la vallée de la Dordogne,* 1995, 93–102.

Munch, Gerard "La prisée de la terre ou seigneurie d' Altkirch en 1390 d' après un texte inédit tiré des archives de la chambre des comptes de Dijon," *Annuaire de la société d' histoire sundgauvienne,* 1990, 103–41.

Nagle, Jean "Un aspect de la propriété seigneuriale à Paris aux XVIIe et XVIIIe siècles, les lods et ventes, "*Revue d'histoire moderne et contemporaine,* 24, 1977, 570–81.

Nassiet, Michel *Noblesse et pauvreté. La petite noblesse en Bretagne, XVe–XVIIIe siècle.* Rennes: Société d'histoire et d'archéologie de Bretagne, 1997.

———, "Le problème des effetifs de la noblesse dans la France du XVIIIe siècle," *Traditions et innovations dans la société française du XVIIIe siècle.* Paris: Presses de l'Université de Paris-Sorbonne, 1995, 97–121.

Neveux, Hugues *Vie et déclin d'une structure économique. Les grains du Cambrésis, fin du XIVe-début du XVIIe siècle.* Paris: Mouton, 1980, 7–20.

Nicolas, Jean "La fin du régime seigneurial en Savoie (1771–1792)," in *L'abolition de la "féodalité" dans le monde occidental.* Paris: CNRS, 1971, vol. I, 515–25.

———, *La Révolution française dans les Alpes. Dauphiné et Savoie 1789–1799.* Toulouse: Privat, 1989.

———, "Le paysan et son seigneur en Dauphiné à la veille de la révolution," in *La France d'ancien régime. Etudes réunies en l'honneur de Pierre Goubert.* Toulouse: Privat, 1984, II, 497–507.

Ninomiya, Hiroyuki "Un cadre de vie rurale au XVIIe et XVIIIe siècle: la seigneurie de Fleury-en-Bière," *Mémoires. Paris et Ile-de-France,* 18–19, 1967–1968, 37–97 & 20, 1969, 65–126.

Noël, Jean-François "Seigneurie et propriété urbaine sous l'Ancien Régime. Autour de la maison de Bertrand d'Argentré à Vitré," *Revue d'histoire moderne et contemporaine,* 38, 1991, 177–204.

———, "Une justice seigneuriale en Haute-Bretagne à la fin de l'ancien régime: la châtellenie de la Motte-de-Gennes," *Annales de Bretagne et des pays de l'Ouest,* 83, 1976, 127–66.

Noël, Valérie "Le terroir de Sucy au XVe siècle: étude du censier de 1412," *Mémoires. Paris et Ile-de-France*, 50 1999, 33–148.

Noirfontaine, Françoise de "Les privilèges de la vicomté de Turenne," in *Etat et société en France aux XVIIe et XVIIIe siècles. Mélanges offerts à Yves Durand.* Paris: Presses de l'Université de Paris-Sorbonne, 2000, 421–35.

Nortier, Michel "Un exemple intéressant de réduction définitive de redevances au XVIe siècle," *Cahiers Léopold Delisle,* 1962, 48–52.

Oppetit-Perné, Danielle "La vicomté de Turenne à la fin du XVe siècle. Essai d'histoire économique," *Ecole national des chartes. Positions des thèses,* 1973, 137–42.

Ormières, Jean-Louis "Le régime seigneurial dans l'ouest," *La Révolution française et le monde rural.* Paris: Editions du CTHS, 1989, 31–40.

Ourliac, Paul & Jean-Louis Gazzaniga, *Histoire du droit privé français de l'An mil au Code civil.* Paris: Albin Michel, 1985.

Pantel, A. & E. Servière, "Seigneuries cévennoles," *Revue du Gévaudan, des Causses et des Cévennes,* 1966, 13–55.

Parain, Charles "Fondements d'une ethnologie historique de l'Aubrac," *L'Aubrac. Etude ethnologique, linguistique, agronomique et économique d'un établissement humain.* Paris: CNRS, 1970–9, vol. 6, tome 2, 25–52.

Paris, André "Une justice seigneuriale témoin et acteur dans la lutte pour l'individualism agraire. Le bailliage at comté de Pontchartrain dans la première moitié du XVIIIe siècle," *Actes du 100e Congrès national des sociétés savantes. Section d'histoire moderne et contemporaine,* 1975, 393–410.

Pariset, François-Georges dir. *Histoire de Bordeaux. V. Bordeaux au XVIIIe siècle.* Bordeaux: Fédération historique du Sud-Ouest, 1968.

Parouty, Christiane "Le fief de Lussat à la fin de l' ancien régime," *Mémoires de la société des sciences naturelles et archéologiques de la Creuse,* 47, 1999, 87–91.

Patault, Anne-Marie *Hommes et femmes de corps à la fin du Moyen Age.* Nancy: Annales de l'Est, 1978.

Paulhet, Jean-Claude "Les parlementaires toulousains à la fin du dix-septième siècle," *Annales du Midi,* 76, 1964, 189–204.

Pellerin, Henri "Herbages et labours en Pays d'Auge. Bonneville-la Louvet," *Le Pays d'Auge,* 1968, 18, 11–16.

Peltre, Jean "Du XVIe au XVIIIe siècle: une génération de nouveaux villages en Lorraine," *Revue géographique de l'Est,* 1966, 3–27.

——, "Le laboureur et sa terre dans la Lorraine du XVIIIe siècle" *Mémoires de l'académie de Stanislas,* 7, 1979–80, 83–94.

——, "Les remembrements en Lorraine à l'époque moderne (XVIIe–XVIIIe siècles)," *Annales de l'Est,* 28, 1976, 197–246.

——, "L'évolution des méthodes d'arpentage en Lorraine du XVIe au XVIIIe siècle et ses conséquences sur la structure agraire," *Beiträge zur Genese der Siedlungs-und Agrarlandschaft in Europa.* Franz Steiner Verlag: Wiesbaden, 1968, 138–44.

Pelzer, Erich "La noblesse alsacienne sous la monarchie française," *Revue d'Alsace*, 113, 1987, 305–20.

———, "Nobles, payans et la fin de la féodalité en Alsace," *La Révolution française et le monde rural.* Paris: Editions du CTHS, 1989, 41–54.

Péret, Jacques "Bourgeoisie rurale et seigneurs au XVIIIe siècle: les fermiers généraux du duché de la Meilleraye," *Bulletin de la société des antiquaires de l'Ouest*, sér. 4, 12, 1974, 357–77.

———, "Paysans de Gâtine poitevine au XVIIIe siècle," *La France d'ancien régime. Etudes réunies en l'honneur de Pierre Goubert.* Toulouse: Privat, 1984, tome II, 53–42.

———, *Seigneurs et seigneuries en Gâtine poitevine. Le duché de La Meilleraye, XVIIe–XVIIIe siècles.* Poitiers: Société des Antiquaires de l'Ouest, 1976.

Perot, Jacques "Recherches sur la vie rurale d'un village du pays messin. Ogy du XVIe au XVIIIe siècle," *Ecole nationale des chartes. Positions des thèses*, 1970, 179–84.

Petit, A. "La métairie perpétuelle en Limousin au XVe siècle," *Revue historique de droit français et étranger*, 1919, 365–403.

Philippe, Michel "La forêt de Lyons au milieu du XVIe siècle," *Etudes normandes*, 41, 1992, 63–84.

Pijassou, René "La viticulture bordelaise dans la deuxième moitié du XVIIe siècle," *Vignobles et vins d'Aquitaine. Actes du XXe Congrès d'études régionales.* Bordeaux: Fédération historique du Sud-Ouest, 1970, 237–60.

———, "Structures foncières, société rurales et occupation du sol à Saint-Symphorien du XVIIIe au milieu du XIXe siècle," *La Grande Lande. Histoire naturelle et géographie historique.* Paris: CNRS, 1985, 269–86.

———, *Un grand vignoble de qualité. Le Médoc.* Paris: Tallandier, 1980.

Pillorget, René *Les mouvements insurrectionnels de Provence entre 1596 et 1715.* Paris: Editions A. Pedone, 1975.

Pioger, André "Le Fertois aux XVIIe et XVIIIe siècles. Histoire économique et sociale," *Bulletin de la société d'agriculture, sciences et arts de la Sarthe*, 71, 1967–1968, 332–446; 72, 1970, 307–62; 73, 1971–1972, 46–124.

Pitre, Marc & Daniel Hickey, "Rendre justice dans une communauté rurale de l'ancien régime: Grignan et l'affaire Bertholon en 1702," *Cahiers d'histoire*, 44, 1999, 375–97.

Plaisance, Georges "La répartition des forêts communales en France et ses causes profondes," *Bulletin philologique et historique*, 1963, I, 399–417.

Plaisse, André *La baronnie de Neubourg. Essai d'histoire agraire, économique et sociale.* Paris: Presses universitaires de France, 1961

Poitou, Christian "La propriété foncière à Vouzon de la fin de la Guerre de Cent Ans à la veille de la Révolution," *Bulletin de la société archéologique et historique de l'Orléanais*,

3, 1964, 141–52.

Poitrineau, Abel *La vie rurale en Basse-Auvergne au XVIIIe siècle*. Paris: Presses universitaires de France, 1965.

———, "Le détonateur économico-fiscal et la charge des rancoeurs catégorielles profondes lors des exploisions de la colère populaire en Auvergne, au XVIIIe siècle," *Mouvements populaires et conscience sociale, XVIe–XIXe siècles*. Paris: Maloine, 1985.361–69.

———, "Propriété et société en Haute-Auvergne à la fin du règne de Louis XV: le cas de Vic," *Cahiers d'histoire*, 6, 1961, 425–55.

Poncelet, Yves "Le temporel de l'abbaye de Saint-Wandrille aux XIVe et XVe siècles," *Annales de Normandie*, 29, 1979, 301–30.

Ponsot, Pierre "Le patrimoine d'un parlementaire dijonnais en Bresse sous le règne de Louis XIV," *Actes du 50e Congrès de l'association bourguignonne des sociétés savantes*, 1979, II, 217–23.

Postel-Vinay, Gilles *La rente foncière dans le capitalisme agraire. Analyse de la voie "classique" du développement du capitalisme dans l'agriculture à partir de l'exemple du Soissonnais*. Paris:François Maspero, 1974.

Poussou, Jean-Pierre "Agriculture et commerce au 18e siècle: l'exemple du Sud-Ouest de la France," *Irlande et France, XVIIe–XXe siècles*. Paris: Ecole des Hautes Etudes en Sciences Sociales, 1980, 99–115.

Press, Volker "Vorderösterreich in der habsburgishen Reichspolitik des späten Mittelalters und der frühen Neuzeit," in Hans Maier, Volker Press, & Dieter Stievermann, *Vorder-österreich in der frühen Neuzeit*. Sigmaringen: Jan Throbeck Verlag, 1989, 1–41.

Prieuret, Charles "Une association agricole en Nivernais. Histoire de la grosse communauté des Jault, 1580–1847," *Bulletin de la société nivernaise des lettres, sciences et arts*, 1929, 333–83.

Proust, Raymond "Petits fermiers de seigneurie au XVIIIe siècle," *Bulletin de la société historique et scientifique des Deux-Sèvres*, 3, 1970, 421–32.

Quilliet, Bernard "Les fiefs parisiens et leurs seigneurs laïcs au XVIIIème siècle," *Histoire, économie et société*, 1, 1982, 565–80.

Quinn, Mary Anne "Pratiques et théories de la coutume. Allodialité et conflicts de droits dans la seigneurie de l'Isle-sous-Montréal au XVIIIe siècle," *Etudes rurales*, nos. 103–04, 71–104.

Rajchenbach, J.-P. "L'emprise foncière d'un bourg garonnais sous l'ancien régime: Langon," *Les cahiers du Bazadais*, 23, 1983, 3–39.

Ramière de Fortanier, Jean *Les droits seigneuriaux dans la sénéchaussée et comté de Lauragais (1553–1789)*. Toulouse: Librairie Marqueste, 1932.

Rapp, Francis "Du domaine à l' état: les avatars de la seigneurie rurale," *Histoire de l'Alsace rurale*. Strasbourg: Istra, 1983, 83–99.

Reboul, Jean *Tavel sur la côte du Rhône (XVIIe-XVIIIe-Révolution)*. Nimes: C. Lacour, 1990.

Reitel, François "A propos de l'openfield lorraine," *Revue géographique de l'Est*, 1966, 29–51.

———, "Quelques aspects de la campagne lorraine de la fin du XVIe siècle au début du XVIIIe siècle," *Bulletin de la société lorraine des études locales dans l'enseignement public*, 25, 1964, 9–18.

Renou, Christian "Un compte de la ferme de Chilly au XVIIIe siècle," in Michel Balard, éd., *Paris et ses campagnes sous l'ancien régime. Mélanges offerts à Jean Jacquart*. Paris: Publications de la Sorbonne, 1994,

Revel, Hervé "Evolution des patrimoines fonciers à Tremblay-en-France, de l'ancien régime au lendemain de la Révolution," *Bulletin de la société d'études historiques de Tremblay*, 1990, 2–19.

Richard, Jean éd. *Histoire de la Bourgogne*. Toulouse: Privat, 1978.

———, "Une redevance foncière bourguignonne du XIIe au XVIIIe siècle," *Mémoires de la société pour l'histoire du droit et des institutions des anciens pays bourguignons, comtois et romands*, 1962, 255–68.

Rives, Jean *Dîme et société dans l'archevêché d'Auch au XVIIIe siècle*. Paris: Commission d'histoire économique et sociale de la Révolution française. Mémoires et documents, 32, 1976.

———, "Les refus de dîmes dans le diocèse d'Auch à la veille de la Révolution," *Actes du 96e Congrès national des sociétés savantes. Section d'histoire moderne et contemporaine*, 1971, II, 237–57.

Rivet, Bernard "La seigneurie du Puy au XVIe siècle: remarques complémentaires," *Cahiers de la Haute-Loire*, 1990, 153–64.

———, *Une ville au XVIe siècle: Le Puy en Velay*. Le Puy-en-Velay: Cahiers de la Haute-Loire, 1988.

Robin, Régine "Fief et seigneurie dans le droit et l'idéologie juridique à la fin du XVIIIe siècle," *Annales historiques de la Révolution française*, 43, 1971, 554–602.

———, *La société française en 1789: Semur-en-Auxois*. Paris: Plon, 1970.

Robinet, René "Sainghin-en-Mélantois, de Charles-Quint à la Révolution française, "*Bulletin de la commission historique du département du Nord*, 42, 1980–84, 11–36.

Roche, Christian "Le seigneur du Broc et ses biens (1761–1830)," *Revue d'Auvergne*, 79, 1965, 49–64.

Roche, Daniel "Aperçus sur la fortune et les revenus des princes de Condé à l'aube du XVIIIe siècle," *Revue d'histoire moderne et contemporaine*, 14, 1967, 217–43.

Rolley, Francine "Une frontière introuvable. Officiers royaux et officiers seigneuriaux dans deux bailliages bourguignons au XVIIe siècle," *Cahiers du centre de recherches historiques*, n. 27, 2001, 87–105.

Root, Hilton L. "En Bourgogne: l'état et la communauté rurale, 1661–1789," *Annales E.S.C.*, 37, 1982, 288–302.

———, "Seigneuries et communautés villageoises: les litiges à la veille de la Révolution française," *Mémoires de la société pour l'histoire du droit et des institutions des anciens pays bourguignons, comtois et romands,* 1986, 187–212.

Roquelet, Alain *La vie de la forêt normande à la fin du Moyen Age. Le coutumier d'Hector de Chartres.* Rouen: Société de l'histoire de Normandie, 1984.

Rosenberg, Harriet G. *A Negotiated World: Three Centuries of Change in a French Alpine Community.* Toronto: University of Toronto Press, 1988.

Rosselle, Dominique "Terre et économie. La mise en valeur de la terre dans la France du Nord (XVIe-XVIIIe siècle). Réflexion à partir d'un modèle artésien," *La terre à l'époque moderne.* Paris: Association des historiens modernistes des universités, 1983, 55–80.

Roth, François *Encyclopédie illustrée de la Lorraine. Histoire de Lorraine. L'époque contemporaine. De la Révolution à la Grande Guerre.* Nancy: Editions Serpenoise, 1992,

Rott, Jean "La Guerre des Paysans et ses suites en Basse-Alsace: le cas du Hattgau," *Histoire de l'Alsace rurale.* Strasbourg: Librairie Istra, 1983, 119–28.

Roupnel, Gaston *La ville et la campagne au XVIIe siècle. Etude sur les populations du pays dijonnais.* Paris: S.E.V.P.E.N., 1955.

Sabatie, Françoise "Stagnation démographique, réaction seigneuriale et mouvements révolutionnaires dans la région de Toulouse. Le cas de Buzet-sur-Tarn," *Annales historiques de la Révolution française,* 43, 1971, 176–96.

Sabatier, Gérard "L'espace économique d'un grand domaine vellave au XVIIIe siècle," *Bulletin historique, scientifique, littéraire, artistique et agricole de la société académique du Puy et de la Haute-Loire,* 56, 1980, 179–87.

———, "Seigneurie et exploitation paysanne en Velay aux XVIIe et XVIIIe siècles, d'après les terriers," *Bulletin du centre d'histoire économique et sociale de la région lyonnaise,* n. 2, 1973, 9–48.

Saby, Marcel "Le XIIIe siècle paysan dans la baronnie d'Allègre et ses annexes de Chomelix et de Saint-Just-près-Chomelix," *Almanach de Brioude et de son arrondissement,* 63, 1983, 169–244.

Sagnac, Philippe & P. Caron, *Les comités des droits féodaux et de législation et l'abolition du régime seigneurial (1789–1793).* Paris: Imprimerie nationale, 1907.

———, *Quomodo jura dominii aucta fuerint regnante Ludovico sexto decimo.* Le Puy: R. Marchessou, 1898.

Saint-Jacob, Pierre de "Le droit de lods en Bourgogne à la fin de l'Ancien Régime," *Mémoires de la société pour l'histoire du droit et des institutions des anciens pays bourguignons, comtois et romands,* 1952, 161–62.

———, *Les paysans de la Bourgogne du nord au dernier siècle de l'Ancien Régime.* Paris: Les Belles Lettres, 1960.

———, "Mutations économiques et sociales dans les campagnes bourguignonnes à la fin du XVIe siècle," *Etudes rurales,* 1961, 34–49.

Salmon, J. H. M. "Renaissance Jurists and Enlightened Magistrates: Perspectives on Feudalism in Fighteenth Century France," *French History*, 8, 1994, 387–402.

Salvi-Jacob, Janie "Evolution du courant d'échange rhénan: Strasbourg face à ses rivales aux XVIIe et XVIIIe siècles," *Transports et voies de communication*. Paris: Les Belles Lettres, 1977, 117–29.

Sauvadet, Michèle "La seigneurie d'Ambert à la in du Moyen Age," *Revue d'Auvergne*, 100, 1986, 159–82.

Sauvageon, Jean "Les cadres de la société rurale dans la Drôme à la fin de l'ancien régime: survivances communautaires, survivances féodales et régime seigneurial," in Robert Chagny, éd., *Aux origines provinciales de la Révolution*. Grenoble: Presses universitaires de Grenoble, 1990, 35–44.

Schilte, Pierre "L'agonie d'un domaine seigneurial. Correspondance de Piette Gruson, régisseur du château de la Varenne de 1772 à 1794," *La province du Maine*, 91, 1989, 161–83.

Schneider, Denis "Production, conjoncture et gestion seigneuriale, dans le bailliage d'Allemagne du duché de Lorraine, vers 1600," *Revue d'histoire moderne et contemporaine*, 45, 1998, 723–45.

Scott, Tom *Freiburg and the Breisgau. Towm-Country Relations in the Age of Reformation and Peasants' War*. Oxford: Clarendon Press, 1986.

Sée, Henri "La question de la vaine pâture en France à la fin de l'ancien régime," *Revue d'histoire économique et sociale*, 1914, 3–25.

———, "Le partage des biens communaux en France à la fin de l'ancien régime," *Revue historique de droit français et étranger*, 1923, 47–81.

Semonsous, J. "Chartes de coutumes et franchises d'entre Cher et Sioule au pays de combraille du XIIIe au XVIIIe siècle," *Revue d'Auvergne*, 70, 1956, 161–200.

Shaffer, John W. *Family and Farm. Agrarian Change and Household Organization in the Loire Valley, 1500–1900*. Albany: State University of New York, 1982.

Sheppard, Thomas F. *Lourmarin in the Eighteenth Century. A Study of a French Village*. Baltimore: The Johns Hopkins Press, 1971.

Sittler, Lucien "Un siècle de vie paysanne: l'évolution d'une commune de la plaine d'Alsace. Fergersheim-Ohnheim avant et après la Guerre de Trente Ans," *Paysans d'Alsace*. Strasbourg: Le Roux, 1959, 81–98.

Sivery, Gérard *Structures agraires et vie rurale dans le Hainaut à la fin du Moyen Age*. 2 vols. Lille: Publications de l'Université de Lille, 1977–80.

Soboul, Albert "De la pratique des terriers à la veille de la Révolution," *Annales. Economies. Sociétés. Civilisations*, 19, 1964, 1049–65.

———, *La Civilisation et la Révolution française. I. La crise de l'ancien régime*. Paris: Arthaud, 1970.

———, *Les campagnes montpelliéraines à la fin de l'ancien régime. Propriété et cultures d'après les compoix*. Paris: Presses universitaires de France, 1958.

Soleil, Sylvain "Le mantien des justices seigneuriales à la fin de l'Ancien Régime: faillite des institutions royales ou récuperation? L'exemple angevin," *Revue historique de droit français et étranger*, 74, 1996, 83–100.

Souriac, René "Les communautés et leurs terroirs en France méridionale aux XVIIe et XVIIIe siècles," *La terre et les paysans en France et en Grande-Bretagne de 1600 à 1800*. Paris: Editions du temps, 1998, 193–217.

Sourioux, Maurice "La seigneurie de Crocq au XVIIe siècle," *Mémoires de la société des sciences naturelles et archéologiques de la Creuse*, 43, 1989, 633–41.

Taillentou, Jean-Jacques "Conflits entre les ducs d'Albret et les barons du Marensin," *Bulletin de la société de Borda*, 119, 1994, 331–40.

Tarde, Hélène de "Contrats de fermage et de métayage en Narbonnais de 1660 à 1789," *Société d'histoire du droit et des institutions des anciens pays de droit écrit. Recueil de mémoires et travaux*, 1983, 133–49.

Thomas, Jack "L'activité toulousaine de la justice seigneuriale du canal de communication des Deux-Mers en Languedoc," *Le canal du Midi et les voies navigables dans le Midi de la France*. Castelnaudary: Société d'études scientifiques de l'Aude, 1998, 21–29.

Thomann, Marcel "Le droit rural à la Faculté de Droit de Strasbourg," *Histoire de l'Alsace rurale*. Strasbourg: Librairie Istra, 1983, 271–79.

Thuillier, Guy "Les communautés des laboureurs," in Guy Thuillier, *Aspects de l'économie nivernaise au XIXe siècle*. Paris: Armand Colin, 1966, 33–45.

Tinthoin, Robert "Vie rurale dans le sud de la plaine de Niort au XVIIIe siècle," *Bulletin. Section de géographie. Comité des travaux historiques et scientifiques*, 78, 1965, 1–67.

Traissac, Elisabeth "Une propriété rurale de Haute-Auvergne au XVIIIe siècle," *Revue de la Haute-Auvergne*, 40, 1967, 469–89; 41, 1968, 240–62.

Trapenard, Camille *Le pâturage communal en Haute-Auvergne (XVIIe–XVIIIe siècles)*. Bar-le-Duc: Imprimerie Contant-Laguerre, 1904.

Trénard, Louis éd., *Histoire des Pays-Bas français*. Toulouse: Privat, 1972.

Tricard, Jean "Comparsonniers et reconstruction rurale dans le sud du Limousin au XVe siècle," *Actes du 104e Congrès national des sociétés savantes. Section de philologie et d'histoire jusqu'à 1610*, 1979, I, 51–62.

———, "Crise et renaissance rurale en Poitou: la seigneurie de Vaussais et Montjean au XVe siècle," *Annales de Bretagne*, 82, 1975, 269–90.

———, "La tenure en Limousin et Marche à la fin du XVe siècle. Etude des structures agraires et foncières," *Annales du Midi*, 88, 1976, 23–39.

———, "Le métayage en Limousin à la fin du Moyen Age," *Bulletin de l'association des historiens économistes*, 13, 1980, 7–18.

———, "Les limites d'une reconstruction rurale en pays pauvre à la fin du Moyen Age: le cas du Limousin," *Etudes rurales*, 60, 1975, 5–40.

Tucoo-Chala, Pierre "La mise en place du système ossalois. Permanences et premières mutations," in *Ecologie de la vallée d'Ossau. Recherches pour une synthèse*. Paris. CNRS, 1978, 73–85.

Ultee, Maarten *The Abbey of St. Germain des Prés in the Seventeenth Century*. New Haven: Yale, 1981.

Vaillant, Pierre "La société delphinoise, 1029–1349," in Bernard Bligny, éd. *Histoire du Dauphiné*. Toulouse: Privat, 1973, 139–60.

———, *Les libertés des communautés dauphinoise (Des origines au 5 janvier 1355)*, Paris: Recueil Sirey, 1951.

Vaissière, Marc "La seigneurie du Roucous en 1785," *Revue du Rouergue*, 65, 2001, 87–97.

Van Der Wee, Hermann& Eddy Van Cauwenberghe, "Histoire agraire et finances publiques en Flandre du XIVe au XVIIe siècle," *Annales E.S.C.*, 28, 1973, 1051–65.

Varine, Béatrice de *Villages de la vallée de l'Ouche aux XVIIe et XVIIIe siècles. La seigneurie de Marigny-sur-Ouche*. Roanne: Editions Horvath, 1979.

Varlet, Didier "Les revenus de la seigneurie de Bitche à la veille de la guerre de Trente Ans (1621–1632)," *Annales de l'Est*, 40, 1988, 281–302.

Viard, Georges "Les revenus de l'abbaye de Morimond vers 1760," *Les cahiers haut-marnais*, 1994, 142–60.

Viaud, D. "Sur un domaine rural du Vendômois. La Blotinière à la fin du XVIIIe siècle," *Annales historiques de la Révolution française*, 50, 1978, 30–33.

Vignier, Françoise "La justice de Magny-sur-Tille (XVe–XVIIIe siècles)," *Mémoires de la société pour l'histoire du droit et des institutions des anciens pays bourguignons, comtois et romands*, 1962, 278–88.

Villard, Pierre *Les justices seigneuriales dans la Marche*. Paris: Pichon et Durand-Auzias,1969.

Vion-Delphine, François "Les forêts du nord de la Franche-Comté à la veille de la Révolution (d'après les cahiers de doléances des bailliages d'Amont et de Baume)," in Maurice Gresset, éd. *La Franche-Comté à la veille de la Révolution*. Paris: Les Belles Lettres, 1988, 39–68.

Vivier, Nadine *Propriété collective et identité communale. Les biens communaux en France 1750–1914*. Paris: Publications de la Sorbonne, 1998.

Vogt, Jean "A propos de la propriété bourgeoisie en Alsace (XVIe–XVIIIe siècles)," *Revue d'Alsace*, 100, 1961, 48–66.

———, "Aspects de la vente des biens nationaux dans la région de Wissembourg," *Revue d'Alsace*, 99, 1960, 90–103.

———, "Les problèmes de tenure," *Histoire de l'Alsace rurale*. Strasbourg: Librairie Istra, 1983, 245–53.

———, "Notes agraires rhénanes: problèmes de tenure au coeur de la Basse-Alsace au milieu du XVIIIe siècle," *Cahiers de l'association interuniversitaire de l'Est*, 5, 1963, 32–41.

———, "Patrimoine rural et politique foncière d'un bourgeois de Strasbourg au milieu du

XVIIe siècle: Ruprecht Reichart, économe de la Toussaint," *Pays d'Alsace*, 61–62, 1908, 31–34.

———, "Propriété et tenure: les biens nationaux à la lumière des pratiques antérieures et postérieures," *Revue d'Alsace*, 116, 1989–1990, 145–71.

———, "Un mécanisme foncier et social insoupçonné. Le rôle de la vente de terres paysannes confiées aussitôt aux vendeurs en Basse-Alsace (XVIe–XVIIIe siècles)," *Francia*, 24, 1997, 1–24.

Vovelle, Michel "Les troubles sociaux en Provence (1750–1789)," *Actes du 93e Congrès national des sociétés savantes. Tours 1968. Section d'histoire moderne et contemporaine.* Paris: Bibliothèque nationale, 1971, II, 325–72.

———, "Sade, seigneur de village," in Michel Vovelle, *De la cave au grenier.* Québec: Serge Fleury, 1980, 187–208.

Wartelle, François "Les communautés rurales du Pas-de-Calais et le système féodal en 1789–1790," *Cahiers d'histoire de l'institut de recherches marxistes*, 32, 1988, 100–21.

Wilsdorf, Christian "Un domaine dans la première moitié du XIIIe siècle: le "cour du comte" à Wolffenheim d' après son coutumière," *Histoire de l' Alsace rurale.* Strasbourg: Librairie Istra, 1983, 101–12.

Wood, James B. *The Nobility of the Election of Bayeux, 1463–1666. Continuity Through Change.* Princeton: Princeton University Press, 1980.

Yver, Jean "Notes sur la justice seigneuriale en Normandie au XIIIe siècle," *Revue historique de droit français et étranger*, 37, 1959, 272–73.

Zeller, Gaston*Les institutions de la France au XVIe siècle.* Paris: Presses universitaires de France, 1948.

Zimmerman, Robert "Un exemple de rente monastique: Oelenberg au XVIe siècle," *Histoire de l'Alsace rurale.* Strasbourg: Librairie Istra, 1983, 139–48.

Zink, Anne *Clochers et troupeaux. Les communautés rurales des Landes et du Sud-Ouest avant la Révolution.* Bordeaux: Presses universitaires de Bordeaux, 1997.

INDEX